LIBRARY OF HEBREW BIBLE/ OLD TESTAMENT STUDIES

687

Formerly Journal for the Study of the Old Testament Supplement Series

Editors
Claudia V. Camp, Texas Christian University, USA
Andrew Mein, Durham University, UK

Founding Editors
David J. A. Clines, Philip R. Davies and David M. Gunn

Editorial Board
Alan Cooper, Susan Gillingham, John Goldingay,
Norman K. Gottwald, James E. Harding, John Jarick, Carol Meyers,
Daniel L. Smith-Christopher, Francesca Stavrakopoulou,
James W. Watts

PROPHETIC OTHERNESS

Constructions of Otherness in Prophetic Literature

Edited by

Steed Vernyl Davidson and Daniel C. Timmer

LONDON • NEW YORK • OXFORD • NEW DELHI • SYDNEY

T&T CLARK
Bloomsbury Publishing Plc
50 Bedford Square, London, WC1B 3DP, UK
1385 Broadway, New York, NY 10018, USA
29 Earlsfort Terrace, Dublin 2, Ireland

BLOOMSBURY, T&T CLARK and the T&T Clark logo
are trademarks of Bloomsbury Publishing Plc

First published in Great Britain 2021
This paperback edition published 2023

Copyright © Steed Vernyl Davidson, Daniel C. Timmer, and contributors 2021

Steed Vernyl Davidson and Daniel C. Timmer have asserted their right under the Copyright, Designs and Patents Act, 1988, to be identified as Editors of this work.

For legal purposes the Acknowledgements on p. vii constitute an extension of this copyright page.

All rights reserved. No part of this publication may be reproduced or transmitted in any form or by any means, electronic or mechanical, including photocopying, recording, or any information storage or retrieval system, without prior permission in writing from the publishers.

Bloomsbury Publishing Plc does not have any control over, or responsibility for, any third-party websites referred to or in this book. All internet addresses given in this book were correct at the time of going to press. The author and publisher regret any inconvenience caused if addresses have changed or sites have ceased to exist, but can accept no responsibility for any such changes.

A catalogue record for this book is available from the British Library.
Library of Congress Control Number: 2019956638.

ISBN: HB: 978-0-5676-8782-1
PB: 978-0-5677-0061-2
ePDF: 978-0-5676-8783-8

Series: Library of Hebrew Bible/Old Testament Studies, volume 687
ISSN 2513-8758

Typeset by: Trans.form.ed SAS

To find out more about our authors and books visit www.bloomsbury.com and sign up for our newsletters.

Contents

List of Contributors	vii
Abbreviations	ix

Chapter 1
INTRODUCTION
    Steed Vernyl Davidson and Daniel C. Timmer   1

Chapter 2
THINKING WITH OTHERNESS TO READ PROPHETIC TEXTS
    Steed Vernyl Davidson   22

Chapter 3
EDOM, THE PROXIMATE "OTHER":
A SOCIAL IDENTITY READING OF ISAIAH 63:1-6
    Dominic S. Irudayaraj   62

Chapter 4
WHERE IS CLYTEMNESTRA WHEN YOU NEED HER?
GENDER, ALTERITY, AND THE MASCULINE ECONOMY OF PROPHECY
IN ISAIAH 56–66
    Rhiannon Graybill   80

Chapter 5
LANGUAGE AND SILENCE IN ISAIAH'S ORACLES AGAINST THE NATIONS
    Francis Landy   105

Chapter 6
A DRAGON, A REED STAFF, AND A TOWERING CEDAR IN EDEN:
EGYPT IN EZEKIEL 29–32
    Brittany Kim   126

Chapter 7
UNSTABLE CONSTRUCTIONS OF IDENTITY:
OTHERNESS AND AMBIVALENT SUBJECTIVITIES IN EZEKIEL 23
    Diandra Chretain Erickson   151

Chapter 8
THE CONSTRUCTION AND DECONSTRUCTION OF ETHNIC/NATIONAL
OTHERING IN THE BOOK OF THE TWELVE
    Daniel C. Timmer   173

Chapter 9
GEOGRAPHIES OF OTHERNESS:
OTHERNESS IN TERRITORIAL ORGANIZATION IN THE ORACLES AGAINST
THE NATIONS
    Steed Vernyl Davidson   192

Bibliography   208
Index of References   227
Index of Authors   233

LIST OF CONTRIBUTORS

Steed Vernyl Davidson is Professor of Hebrew Bible/Old Testament at McCormick Theological Seminary in Chicago, USA. He is the author of *Empire and Exile: Postcolonial Readings of the Book of Jeremiah* (Bloomsbury, 2011).

Diandra Chretain Erickson received her Ph.D. from the Graduate Theological Union in 2018. She is currently the Director of Digital Learning and Lecturer at the Graduate Theological Union, Berkeley CA, USA.

Rhiannon Graybill is W. J. Millard Professor of Religion and Associate Professor of Religious Studies at Rhodes College in Memphis, USA. She is the author of *Are We Not Men? Unstable Masculinity in the Hebrew Prophets* (Oxford University Press, 2016).

Dominic S. Irudayaraj is Senior Lecturer at Hekima College, Nairobi; Visiting Professor at Biblicum, Rome; and Research Associate at University of Pretoria, South Africa. He is the author of *Violence, Otherness and Identity in Isaiah 63:1-6: The Trampling One Coming from Edom*, LHBOTS 633 (Bloomsbury T&T Clark, 2017).

Brittany Kim is an Adjunct Professor at Northeastern Seminary in Rochester, NY, USA. She is the author of *"Lengthen Your Tent-Cords": The Metaphorical World of Israel's Household in the Book of Isaiah* (Eisenbrauns, 2018).

Francis Landy is Professor Emeritus of Religious Studies at the University of Alberta, Edmonton, Alberta, Canada. He is the author of *Beauty and the Enigma and Other Essays on the Hebrew Bible* (Sheffield Academic Press, 2001), *Hosea* (2nd ed., Sheffield Phoenix Press, 2012), and *Paradoxes of Paradise: Identity and Difference in the Song of Songs* (2nd ed., Sheffield Phoenix Press, 2012).

Daniel C. Timmer is Professor of Biblical Studies for the doctoral program at Puritan Reformed Theological Seminary in Grand Rapids, USA, and Professeur d'Ancien Testament at the Faculté de théologie évangélique in Montreal, Canada. He is the author of *The Non-Israelite Nations in the Book of the Twelve* (Brill, 2015).

ABBREVIATIONS

AASOR	Annual of the American Schools of Oriental Research
AB	Anchor Bible
ABG	Arbeiten zur Bibel und ihrer Geschichte
ABS	Archaeology and Biblical Studies
AIL	Ancient Israel and Its Literature
AOTC	Abingdon Old Testament Commentaries
ApOTC	Apollos Old Testament Commentary
ArBib	Aramaic Bible
ATD	Das Alte Testament Deutsch
BCAW	Blackwell Companions to the Ancient World
BETL	Bibliotheca Ephemeridum Theologicarum Lovaniensium
Bib	*Biblica*
BibInt	Biblical Interpretation Series
BibOr	Biblica et Orientalia
BibSem	The Biblical Seminar
BMW	Bible in the Modern World
BWA(N)T	Beiträge zur Wissenschaft vom Alten (und Neuen) Testament
BZAW	Beihefte zur Zeitschrift für die alttestamentliche Wissenschaft
CAT	Commentaire de l'Ancien Testament
CBQ	*Catholic Biblical Quarterly*
CBR	*Currents in Biblical Research*
ConBOT	Coniectanea Biblica Old Testament Series
CT	*Cuneiform Texts from Babylonian Tablets in the British Museum*
DDD	*Dictionary of Deities and Demons in the Bible.* Edited by Karel van der Toorn, Bob Becking, and Pieter W. van der Horst. Leiden: Brill, 1995. 2nd rev. ed. Grand Rapids: Eerdmans, 1999.
EASA	European Association of Social Anthropologists
ECC	Eerdmans Critical Commentary
FAT	Forschungen zum Alten Testament
FB	Forschung zur Bibel
FOTL	Forms of the Old Testament Literature
FRLANT	Forschungen zur Religion und Literatur des Alten und Neuen Testaments
HAR	*Hebrew Annual Review*
HBAI	*Hebrew Bible and Ancient Israel*
HBM	Hebrew Bible Monographs
HBT	*Horizons in Biblical Theology*

HCOT	Historical Commentary on the Old Testament
HThKAT	Herders Theologischer Kommentar zum Alten Testament
IEJ	*Israel Exploration Journal*
Int	*Interpretation*
JAOS	*Journal of the American Oriental Society*
JBL	*Journal of Biblical Literature*
JNES	*Journal of Near Eastern Studies*
JSOT	*Journal for the Study of the Old Testament*
JSOTSup	Journal for the Study of Old Testament: Supplement Series
KTU	*KTU: The Cuneiform Alphabetic Texts from Ugarit, Ras Ibn Hani, and Other Places*. Edited by Manfried Dietrich, Oswald Loretz, and Joaquin Sanmartín. Münster: Ugarit-Verlag, 1995.
LHBOTS	Library of Hebrew Bible/Old Testament Studies
NAC	New American Commentary
NCB	New Century Bible
NCBC	New Century Bible Commentary
NIBC	New International Bible Commentary
NICOT	New International Commentary on the Old Testament
OBO	Orbis Biblicus et Orientalis
OBT	Overtures to Biblical Theology
OTL	Old Testament Library
OtSt	*Oudtestamentische Studiën*
PMLA	Proceedings of the Modern Language Association
PRSt	*Perspectives in Religious Studies*
RANE	Records of the Ancient Near East
RevExp	*Review and Expositor*
SBL	Society of Biblical Literature
ScrHier	Scripta Hierosolymitana
SemeiaSt	Semeia Studies
SHBC	Smyth & Helwys Bible Commentary
STDJ	Studies on the Texts of the Desert of Judah
TB	Theologische Bücherei: Neudrucke und Berichte aus dem 20. Jahrhundert
TDOT	*Theological Dictionary of the Old Testament*. Edited by G. Johannes Botterweck and Helmer Ringgren. Translated by John T. Willis et al. 16 vols. Grand Rapids: Eerdmans, 1974–2018.
TLOT	*Theological Lexicon of the Old Testament*. Edited by Ernst Jenni, with assistance from Claus Westermann. Translated by Mark E. Biddle. 3 vols. Peabody, MA: Hendrickson, 1997.
VT	*Vetus Testamentum*
VTSup	Supplements to Vetus Testamentum
WBC	Word Biblical Commentary
WMANT	Wissenschaftliche Monographien zum Alten und Neuen Testament
ZAH	*Zeitschrift für Althebräistik*
ZECOT	Zondervan Exegetical Commentary on the Old Testament

Chapter 1

INTRODUCTION

Steed Vernyl Davidson and Daniel C. Timmer

The distinction between the one and the many, or between universals and particulars, is fundamental to interpreting reality. Whether one makes this distinction (as much Western philosophy has) or not (as in the case of Baruch Spinoza), that decision is fraught with value judgments and epistemological commitments.[1] The rise of postcolonial studies roughly half a century ago gave new relevance to this philosophical question by drawing attention to the imperialist "discourse of knowledge" that was part of the colonial project.[2] This discourse involves, in the words of Homi K. Bhabha, "those nationalist or 'nativist' pedagogies that set up the relation of Third World and First World in a binary structure of opposition."[3] Put more simply, the West told the rest of the world what it was (not "us"), what was good for it ("our" good), and that Western ideals and goals were self-evidently superior. At the heart of this discourse is a sharply polarized and binary Self/Other dichotomy.

1. See Richard Bodéüs, "Aristotle," in *The Columbia History of Western Philosophy*, ed. Richard H. Popkin (New York: Columbia University Press, 1999), 56, and on Spinoza's monadic view, see Don Garrett, "Introduction," in *The Cambridge Companion to Spinoza*, ed. Don Garrett (Cambridge: Cambridge University Press, 1996), 1–12 (esp. 2–8). On the linguistic expression of this difference, see M. Davies, "Philosophy of Language," in *The Blackwell Companion to Philosophy*, ed. N. Bunnin and E. P. Tsui-James (Oxford: Blackwell, 2003), 90–146.
2. Leo G. Perdue, *Reconstructing Old Testament Theology: After the Collapse of History*, OBT (Minneapolis, MN: Fortress, 2005), 289.
3. Homi K. Bhabha, *The Location of Culture* (London: Routledge, 1994), 173.

This volume is about difference. We are primarily interested in the constructions of difference but also in the meanings and subsequently the forms of power associated with the differences that demarcate the Self from the Other. Difference as an ontological category conjures up the distinction between divinity and humanity, a concept that is largely intelligible in the domain of systematic theology. However, the assigned differences of human ontology continue to challenge not only intellectual conception but full human striving. In addition, in the Anthropocene period, human ontology as distinct from animal ontology and the consequent implications for the survival of the earth present major challenges. Far from setting out to offer clear-cut solutions to intractable problems such as racism, sexism, and climate change, this volume exposes readers to ways of thinking about and confronting the reality of differences as posed by the construction of the Self and Other.

The Western intellectual tradition can be defined by the preoccupation with the subject and subjectivity. As individual identity is extracted from the communal character and as European culture sees itself as more distinct than other cultures, that is, superior to them, various theoretical analyses emerge to explain what at first are thought to be naturally coded differences. The existentialism of Søren Kierkegaard and Fredrich Nietzsche as well as earlier forays by René Descartes demonstrate the centrality of the question of the subject in Western thought. The ground continued to swell on this question into the twentieth century through the work of thinkers such as Jean-Paul Sartre. The twentieth century marks a shift in thinking from the conception of difference as primarily inherent to one that is social and cultural. The postmodern intervention features thinkers such as Emmanuel Levinas who responds to the ethical challenges presented by otherness,[4] Simone de Beauvoir who confronts the presumption that the category "woman" is naturally occurring as part of a binary of man/woman,[5] and Frantz Fanon whose work helps lay the foundation for postcolonial analysis of purported colonial difference and of racial differences. Fanon positions his work in what he calls a "zone of nonbeing," the space created by an anti-Black world aimed at the suppression of Black life, that he thinks ironically proves essential for the actualization of the "black man."[6]

---

4. Emmanuel Lévinas, *Totality and Infinity: An Essay on Exteriority*, trans. Alphonso Lingis (The Hague: Martinus Nijhoff, 1979), 43.

5. Simone de Beauvoir, *The Second Sex*, trans. Constance Borde and Sheila Malovany-Chevallier (New York: Vintage, 2011), 6.

6. Frantz Fanon, *Black Skins White Masks* (New York: Grove, 2008), xii.

The Western philosophical tradition in its early articulations tends to center upon the self as the starting point of consciousness and ultimately of subjectivity. Relying upon the notion that the thinking person represents being, the self serves as the staging ground from which to know the world in all of its variety. Therefore, the self projects outwards to others and through the observations of difference finds not so much common ground but the basis for hostilities and forms of dominance. This relationship can be explained through various academic fields such as anthropology, phenomenology, psychology, and others that we touch upon below and in Chapter 2. While this antagonist binary marks most theories of otherness, Emmanuel Lévinas takes a different approach and uses the notion of "the face of the Other" as his starting point.[7] Lévinas takes the position that religious traditions (mostly Jewish and Christian) encourage a disposition towards rather than against others. He, therefore, thinks that intersubjectivity serves as a suitable basis for understanding of the self.[8] Yet his different starting point does not intrinsically make for a binary free from any tension, since the distinctions of difference, however conceived, seem to have the potential to generate antagonism. Binaries are not neutral, regardless of how they are formed and what they express.

The history of the theoretical engagement on the topic of otherness reveals a contesting of the centering of the white male subject. Postmodern thought has questioned the ways in which cultures have constructed and represented those regarded as falling outside of Western idealized norms. Not only have social conventions identified certain groups as "other," these groups have been racialized, gendered, and represented as possessing particular "natural" traits. However, this tendency within Western thought to naturalize things under the rubric of "science" is such that, as Michel Foucault indicates with regards to a history of Western scientific knowledge, "one would then be writing only a history of opinions, that is, of the choices operated according to individuals, environments, social groups."[9] Rather than fixed categories or rational data, otherness is a constructed reality based upon artificial categories. In this regard, the non-Western male has served as an object of fascination and as the means for the Western male to understand himself. Theories of otherness are as much about the mechanisms of representations and their discourses as they are about discovering the nature of things.

---

7. Lévinas, *Totality and Infinity*, 24.
8. Ibid., 50.
9. Michel Foucault, *The Order of Things: An Archaeology of the Human Sciences* (London: Routledge, 1989), 82–3.

The rise in theories of otherness during the age of expanded exploration by Western European nations reflects, in part, the necessity to make sense of Europe's expanded knowledge of humanity. To be clear, Europeans as far back as Antiquity were aware of differences in humanity, whether based upon skin color, geographical location, or other physical features. As such, limited awareness of what we now regard as Asians and Africans always formed part of Europe's knowledge. The colonial era simply accelerated what already existed in the ways Europeans thought of themselves in relation to others. Transatlantic explorations and Europe's exposure to the people, flora, and fauna of the Americas upset previously settled knowledge.[10] In fact, the ecological and other diversities of the Americas contributed to a rethinking of presumptions about nature and, in the process, created the need to fill that knowledge gap through science.

Despite the limitations of science, the power of science and other discourses enables the world to be viewed in a Manichean split: the West and the rest. This structuring facilitated Europe's relationship with the rest of the world in what John Jervis views as "a mission, necessarily intolerant of otherness."[11] European colonialism, Christian evangelism, economic globalization, and similar homogenizing movements in the past and present represent different attempts to universalize the world under a single umbrella. This process, on the surface, seeks to eradicate difference, yet it is more an expression of an allergy to otherness. Jervis suggests that universality has the effect of further entrenching otherness through two processes. First, by emphasizing distance in order to make the other as clearly different as possible. Second, by incorporating the other—colonizing, assimilating—in order to deny the other any independent subjectivity.[12] Bhabha points out that this move, though, does not eliminate otherness but instead produces "a reformed, recognizable Other, *as a subject of difference that is almost the same, but not quite.*"[13]

The breadth of theories of otherness stands on a long history of human atrocities. These theories, therefore, represent the best attempt to explain and respond to the failed efforts of human integration. G. W. F. Hegel sets out his dialectic of "lordship and bondage"[14] during the period of

---

10. Alfred W. Cosby, *The Columbian Exchange: Biological and Cultural Consequences of 1492*, 30th Anniversary Edition (Westport, CT: Praeger, 2003), 10.

11. John Jervis, *Transgressing the Modern: Explorations in the Western Experience of Otherness* (Oxford: Blackwell, 1999), 6.

12. Ibid., 7.

13. Bhabha, *Location of Culture*, 122 (emphasis in the original).

14. G. W. F. Hegel, *Hegel: The Phenomenology of Spirit*, trans. Michael Inwood (Oxford: Oxford University Press, 2018), 76.

Europe's robust trafficking of enslaved Africans and more particularly when the Haitian Revolution brought one of the most forceful challenges to the philosophical foundations on which Europe built its economic, political, and cultural structures.[15] Lévinas thinks through the issues of otherness as a Jew in the context and aftermath of the Jewish Holocaust. His work is as much situated within the Jewish intellectual traditions as it is within the maelstrom created by the Nazi attempt to eradicate Jewishness and other forms of otherness. Fanon brings the lived experiences of racial colonialism and racism to bear upon his theorizing of the binaries of black/white and colonizer/colonized at the heart of the violent Algerian struggle for independence from France. Despite the abstraction of these theoretical interventions, they are formed out of the real-life experiences of human atrocities predicated on notions of the supremacy of a particular group over the rest. In turn, the theories or the discourses do not remain abstract since, in many instances, they empower beliefs and direct practices. Abdul JanMohamed believes that the stereotypes created by various systems of otherness are not as troublesome as the fact that they provide "affective benefits" with a sense of "moral difference"[16] that ensures their reproduction.

Along with the diversity of theories that shape our thinking in this chapter and the ones to come, there are different articulations of the term "other." The field of phenomenology largely sets the theoretical ground for understanding otherness. For phenomenologists, the other is distinct from the self and required as a means for the consciousness of the self. In the German tradition, the notion of the self as a constitutive element akin to a thing is written in the conventional capitalized form, *Das Selbst*. This leads to English translations of German works that also use a capitalized form, the Self. As the other part of the binary, "other" can be similarly capitalized in order to indicate that the other is not merely a reflection of the self but a completely constituted being. In most instances, few persons follow a standard convention that reflects a theoretical difference between the capitalized and uncapitalized forms. Different options are used in this volume. Each iteration reflects stated and unstated reasons for the chosen writing style. There are times, however, when theorists make

---

15. For a discussion on the impact of the Haitian Revolution on Hegel's thought, see Susan Buck-Morss, *Hegel, Haiti, and Universal History* (Pittsburgh, PA: University of Pittsburgh Press, 2009).

16. Abdul R. JanMohamed, "The Economy of Manichean Allegory," in *The Postcolonial Studies Reader*, ed. Bill Ashcroft, Gareth Griffiths, and Helen Tiffin (London: Routledge, 1995), 19–23 (20).

a distinction between the different forms, and the capitalization or not in English indicates something beyond the grammatical requirements of German words. Lacan, for instance, uses capital O (in his case since he is writing in French, capital A for *Autre*) when he invests the other with authority and power almost to the point of being transcendent. He uses the lower-case o for what he regards as the projection of the self that is subject to misrecognition. Other French theorists like Jacques Derrida make a similar distinction. Derrida, though, uses *autrui* for the personal other or self projection and *autre* for that which differs in being. This distinction can be lost in English translations that use the capitalization of the English term to represent the different French words.[17] These fine theoretical distinctions matter since they indicate perceptions of otherness as wholly other, participating in nonbeing, projections of the self, or other ways of conceiving otherness. Of course, English language works can make diligent translations that indicate these distinctions, though sometimes they are not as adept as fulfilling this potential. The astute reader needs to consult primary sources to capture these differences. Original English works provide greater transparency around their use of the term.

Otherness in the Social Sciences and in Biblical Studies

These theoretical complexities and the historical realities they engage are directly relevant to biblical interpretation, for the Bible was part of the warp and woof of the Western imperial program.[18] The history of European exploration outside the bounded landmass that connects Europe to parts of Asia and Africa and the imperialism that began in earnest with Columbus bear sober testimony to the terrible effects that this use of the Bible, synthesized with the elements of financial gain and personal and national glory, had on colonized populations.[19] However, occasionally in earlier centuries and increasingly as the colonial era drew to a close, the lamentable results of this imperial reception of the Bible gave rise to critical examination of biblical perspectives on identity, empire, power,

---

17. See for example the translator's note to render *autrui* as "Other" and *autre* as "other," a practice common to other translators of Derrida. Jacques Derrida, *Writing and Difference*, trans. Alan Bass (London: Routledge, 1978), 137 n. 6. See also Lévinas, *Totality and Infinity*, 24 (translator's footnote).

18. R. S. Sugirtharajah, *Exploring Postcolonial Biblical Criticism: History, Method, Practice* (Chichester: Wiley-Blackwell, 2012).

19. Charles C. Mann, *1493: Uncovering the New World Columbus Invented* (New York: Knopf, 2011).

and justice, and such efforts continue apace at present.[20] But historical-linguistic interpretation of the Bible has its own reasons for giving careful attention to the "development, maintenance, and negotiation" of the identities of its characters and indeed of its readers.[21] Whatever epistemological weight one gives its claims, careful analysis of its authors' worldviews, evident in how they define, distinguish, and evaluate individuals, groups, nations, and indeed humanity as a whole, is incumbent upon the reader.

Current interest among interpreters of the Hebrew Bible/Old Testament (and similarly the New Testament[22]) in social identity, and particularly in the Self/Other, is the product of varied influences. In this section, we limit ourselves to sketching the broad lines of several of the most prominent avenues of influence, leaving closer analysis of particular philosophical and theoretical issues for the following chapter.[23] Rather than constructing a diachronic history of ideas or *Wirkungsgeschichte* for these concepts, we touch upon a few select points that are nonetheless connected with one another in myriad ways.[24]

---

20. Wes Howard-Brook, *"Come Out, My People!" God's Call out of Empire in the Bible and Beyond* (Maryknoll, NY: Orbis, 2010); Mark G. Brett, *Decolonizing God: The Bible in the Tides of Empire*, BMW 16 (Sheffield: Sheffield Phoenix, 2009); Hemchand Gossai (ed.), *Postcolonial Commentary and the Old Testament* (London: T&T Clark, 2019).

21. Ronald L. Jackson II, "Introduction," in *Encyclopedia of Identity*, ed. Ronald L. Jackson II (Thousand Oaks, CA: SAGE, 2010), xxvi.

22. See, e.g., David G. Horrell (ed.), *Social-Scientific Approaches to New Testament Interpretation* (Edinburgh: T. & T. Clark, 1999).

23. See further E. Ramsey, "Philosophical History of Identity," in Jackson (ed.), *Encyclopedia of Identity*, 556–60. Charles E. Carter, "A Discipline in Transition: The Contributions of the Social Sciences to the Study of the Hebrew Bible," in *Community and Ideology: Social Science Approaches to the Hebrew Bible*, SBTS 6 (Winona Lake, IN: Eisenbrauns, 1996), 3–36 (5), draws attention to the importance of John Locke's *Essay concerning Human Understanding* for illuminating the relationship between individual experience and perception and thus for the development of the social sciences and their comparative methodological foundation.

24. A genealogical approach to the reception of othering in Biblical Studies is particularly implausible since the explosion of interest in the issue in the 1970s; see Mia R. Genoni, "Otherness, History of," in Jackson (ed.), *Encyclopedia of Identity*, 526–30 (528). The same is true of the influences singled out below, including sociology, as shown by Anselm Hagedorn, "Institutions and Social Life in Ancient Israel: Sociological Aspects," in *Hebrew Bible/Old Testament: The History of Its Interpretation*, vol. 3.2, *The Twentieth Century: From Modernism to Post-Modernism*, ed. M. Sæbø (Göttingen: Vandenhoeck & Ruprecht, 2015), 58–95.

The Sociological Legacy and Otherness

Sociology (occasionally overlapping with anthropology) has been especially proximate to the interests of many biblical interpreters due to the centrality of Israel as a people group and nation in the HB/OT.[25] Prominent among earlier models of societies and their development were the conflict models of Karl Marx (1818–1883) and Max Weber (1864–1920), according to which "society is a mode of organization of individuals" and their "understandable and purpose actions."[26] For our purposes, it is interesting to note Weber's attention to "status groups" and their relation to (or separation from) the larger society in which they appear as well as his belief that religion brought meaning to experience.[27] Hagedorn contends that Weber's "focus on the subjective meanings that individuals attach to their actions" and his attention to social group dynamics have long stimulated research on the history of Israel and the interpretation of its scriptures, and continue to do so.[28]

D. E. Durkheim (1858–1917) developed a different approach to understanding the dynamic significance of human society. His functionalist model proposed what Mayes views as the idea that "society is the prior reality which determines the individual, materially, mentally, and physically."[29] On this view, social processes drive historical change, and the purposes of individual human actors are comparatively unimportant. Following W. Robertson Smith, Durkheim also interpreted religion as a social process that imposed itself upon its practitioners. Yet Durkheim held that religious beliefs are so important for a social group that "they make its unity."[30] This insight anticipates the prominent role that many

---

25. See Hagedorn, "Institutions and Social Life." For a focus on more recent interpreters, see David Pleins, *The Social Visions of the Hebrew Bible: A Theological Introduction* (Louisville, KY: Westminster John Knox, 2001).

26. Andrew D. H. Mayes, "Sociology of the Old Testament," in *The World of Ancient Israel: Sociological, Anthropological and Political Perspectives*, ed. R. E. Clements (Cambridge: Cambridge University Press, 1989), 39–63 (39). Mayes, "Idealism and Materialism in Weber and Gottwald," *Proceedings of the Irish Biblical Association* 11 (1988): 44–8 (44), notes that Weber's work on ancient Judaism was first published as a series of essays in *Archiv für Sozialwissenschaft und Sozialforschung* 44 (1917): 52–138, 349–443, 601–26; 46 (1918): 40–113, 311–66, 541–604.

27. As argued in Mayes, "Sociology of the Old Testament," 40.

28. Hagedorn, "Institutions and Social Life," 74.

29. Mayes, "Sociology of the Old Testament," 41.

30. Emile Durkheim, *The Elementary Forms of the Religious Life*, trans. J. W. Swain (New York: The Free Press, 1915), 59.

contemporary interpreters accord to ideology in the process of group formation, identification, and practice within biblical sources.[31]

The Inheritance of Otherness in Biblical Studies

The unmediated integration of sociological insights in biblical interpretation began as early as Julius Wellhausen (1844–1918) and W. Robertson Smith (1846–1894).[32] The application of conflict models to the question of the evolution of Israelite society is evident as early as the work of Louis Wallis (1876–ca. 1950)[33] and many historians of ancient Israel after him.[34] Functionalist models became prominent thanks to the work of Mary Douglas,[35] Norman Gottwald,[36] and others.[37] Sociological models in general have gained further prominence in the last few decades as Enlightenment-based historical accounts of Israel's past lost their allure.[38] At the same time, sociological discussion has given increased attention to the Other, whether as an impediment to bestowing "unwarranted substance on collectives and identities"[39] or as a motivation to recognize how personal identity and one's relationship to groups are dependent on

---

31. See, e.g., Ehud Ben Zvi and Diana V. Edelman (eds), *Imagining the Other and Constructing Israelite Identity in the Early Second Temple Period*, LHBOTS 456 (London: Bloomsbury, 2014).

32. Carter, "A Discipline in Transition," 13; Hagedorn, "Institutions and Social Life," 64–74.

33. Carter, "A Discipline in Transition," 14; note Wallis's *Sociological Study of the Bible* (Chicago: University of Chicago Press, 1912).

34. George Mendenhall, "The Hebrew Conquest of Palestine," *BibArch* 25 (1962): 66–87.

35. James V. Spickard, "A Revised Functionalism in the Sociology of Religion: Mary Douglas's Recent Work," *Religion* 21 (1991): 141–64. See, for example, Douglas's *In the Wilderness: The Doctrine of Defilement in the Book of Numbers* (Sheffield: Sheffield Academic, 1993).

36. Mayes, "Sociology of the Old Testament," 49–52.

37. Ibid., 52–8 offers a survey through to the late 1980s. Pleins, *The Social Visions of the Hebrew Bible*, covers the subsequent decade as well.

38. John Bimson, "Old Testament History and Sociology," in *Interpreting the Old Testament: A Guide for Exegesis*, ed. C. C. Broyles (Grand Rapids, MI: Baker Academic, 2001), 125–55, esp. 126–7. For a brief overview of these critiques, see Leo G. Perdue, *Reconstructing Old Testament Theology: After the Collapse of History*, OBT (Minneapolis, MN: Fortress, 2005), 8–14.

39. Richard Jenkins, "Society and Social Identity," in Jackson (ed.), *Encyclopedia of Identity*, 766–72 (767).

the other.⁴⁰ These discussions, theories, and perspectives have in turn been integrated into biblical interpretation in myriad ways.⁴¹

The Inheritance of Otherness in the Study of Second Temple Judaism

Sociology overlaps a second field of study that has contributed to the increased awareness of the Other in Biblical Studies, that of sectarianism or religious diversity in Second Temple Judaism. Indeed, "the term 'sect' is associated with the sociological work" of Weber.⁴² Yet as shown by Shemaryahu Talmon's critical appropriation of some of Weber's insights in a landmark essay several decades ago and by similar publications since then, examination of group identity and Othering in early Judaism is a fully fledged area of research in its own right.⁴³ Since sociological models have already received some attention,⁴⁴ here we focus on the interpretation of the dynamics that these models bring to light. A foundational dictum is that "the identification of a sect always deals in some way or other with its counterpart."⁴⁵ Explicit ideological statements along these lines are rare in the biblical material of the early post-exilic period,⁴⁶ and only in the

40. Michael A. Hogg, "Social Identity Theory," in Jackson (ed.), *Encyclopedia of Identity*, 749–52.

41. See Jeremiah W. Cataldo, "The Other: Sociological Perspectives in a Postcolonial Age," in Ben Zvi and Edelman (eds) *Imagining the Other*, 1–19. Examples include Rodney S. Sadler Jr., *Can a Cushite Change His Skin? An Examination of Race, Ethnicity, and Othering in the Hebrew Bible*, LHBOTS 425 (London: T&T Clark, 2005); Laurie Brink, "In Search of the Biblical Foundations of Prophetic Dialogue: Engaging a Hermeneutic of Otherness," *Missiology* 41 (2013): 9–21; Carolyn J. Sharp, "The Formation of Godly Community: Old Testament Hermeneutics in the Presence of the Other," *AThR* 86 (2004): 623–36.

42. Jutta Jokiranta, "Sectarianism," in *The Eerdmans Dictionary of Early Judaism*, ed. J. J. Collins and D. C. Harlow (Grand Rapids, MI: Eerdmans, 2010), 1209–11 (1209).

43. Shemaryahu Talmon, "The Emergence of Jewish Sectarianism in the Early Second Temple Period," in *Ancient Israelite Religion: Essays in Honor of Frank Moore Cross*, ed. P. D. Miller, P. D. Hanson, and S. D. McBride (Minneapolis, MN: Fortress, 1987), 587–616.

44. Bryan Wilson, *The Social Dimensions of Sectarianism: Sects and New Religious Movements in Contemporary Society* (Oxford: Clarendon, 1990), and Jutta Jokiranta, *Social Identity and Sectarianism in the Qumran Movement*, STDJ 105 (Leiden: Brill, 2013) offer representative discussions of their use in this field.

45. Jokiranta, "Sectarianism," 1210.

46. For the beginning of this trajectory, see Joseph Blenkinsopp, *Judaism: The First Phase: The Place of Ezra–Nehemiah in the Origins of Judaism* (Grand Rapids, MI: Eerdmans, 2009).

Hasmonean period did clear factions arise in Palestinian Judaism. These were defined especially by their differing attitudes toward the Jerusalem Temple but also by dynamics related to "urbanization, increased literacy, and millenarian hopes."[47]

As an example, the "Animal Apocalypse" of *1 Enoch*, dated to the mid-second century BCE, represents the ideology of a faction in Judaism that considered the sacrifices offered at the rebuilt Jerusalem Temple to be polluted and therefore ineffective: "they started to place a table [altar] before the tower [temple], with all the food which is upon it being polluted and impure" (89:73).[48] This critique of the dominant religious system went hand in hand with their critique of those who supported it, even though the latter group was also Jewish.[49] In a complex allegory involving various animals, the author recounts the history of humanity with a focus on Israel. Near the end of the account he separates Jews into sheep who hear and see as they should (a minority presented as the in-group) and sheep who see and hear poorly or not at all (the rest of Judaism): "Regarding all these matters, the eyes of the sheep became so dim-sighted that they could not see" (89:74). The author attempted to correct his compatriots' grave errors by conveying his message to them as "words of the Lord of the sheep," but the deafness and blindness of the other sheep continued (90:7). The conflict between the author's group and other Jews is finally resolved when the latter are "cast into this fiery abyss, and they were burned" (90:21) and the former enter a new temple or city that God erects in place of the previous temple (90:29).[50] The inversion of in-group and out-group, and the connection of each with a radically different ultimate status and condition, make *1 Enoch* a powerful ideological tool for inverting the existing social-religious order in Second Temple Judaism.

The sectarian compositions from Qumran offer further examples of religiously determined group identity in Second Temple Judaism. These texts present in various ways the development of ideological and theological grounds for inclusion from and inclusion in the Qumran sect. In a notable case, the Community Rule (1QS) reuses the Priestly Blessing of Num. 6:24-26 both to bless the Qumran community and to curse those outside it (whether Jews or not; 1QS 2:1b-7). The former are chosen by

---

47. Jokiranta, "Sectarianism," 1210.

48. E. Isaac (trans.), "1 (Ethiopic Apocalypse of) Enoch," *OTP* 1:69 (later citations are from idem, 70–1).

49. George W. E. Nickelsburg and James C. VanderKam, *First Enoch* (Minneapolis, MN: Fortress, 2004), 10.

50. See further Patrick A. Tiller, *A Commentary on the Animal Apocalypse* (Atlanta, GA: Scholars Press, 1993), 350.

God and walk in God's ways while the latter belong to Belial and are forever condemnable because of their "wicked, blameworthy deeds" and "faults." This curse effectively excludes all Jews who are not members of the Qumran sect from God's covenants with Israel.[51] Similarly, one finds in 4Q415–418 the narrowing of the referent of the "eternal planting," a title that harks back to historical Israel (e.g., Isa. 5), to the Qumran community itself.[52] In both these cases, the faction adopts the most significant titles of the group that it left, and simultaneously denies to all others membership in their newly defined group.[53] The chronological, textual, and disciplinary proximity of Second Temple Judaism to the Hebrew Bible, and the former's focused attention on the formation and interaction of competing religious groups, have illuminated the interpretation of the latter almost since the publication of the scrolls began.[54]

The Inheritance of Otherness in Postcolonial Studies

As the quotation of Bhabha at the beginning of this chapter implies, postcolonial studies also contribute significantly to the integration of Biblical Studies and the dynamics of group identity that constitute othering.[55] In this context, perhaps the most salient contributions of postcolonial readings to study of the HB/OT are their ability to problematize the concept of identity (especially its binary use)[56] and to underline

---

51. Daniel C. Timmer, "Sectarianism and Soteriology: The Priestly Blessing (Numbers 6,24-26) in the Qumranite *Community Rule* (1QS)," *Bib* 89 (2008): 389–96 (396).

52. Patrick A. Tiller, "The 'Eternal Planting' in the Dead Sea Scrolls," *DSD* 4 (1997): 312–35 (334).

53. Other dimensions of this appropriation of elements of Israel's identity by the Qumran sect are explored in James C. VanderKam, "Sinai Revisited," in *Biblical Interpretation at Qumran*, ed. Matthias Henze, SDSSRL (Grand Rapids, MI: Eerdmans, 2005), 44–60.

54. This interaction and overlap is evident in collections like D. C. Harlow, K. M. Hogan, M. Goff and J. S. Kaminsky (eds), *The "Other" in Second Temple Judaism: Essays in Honor of John J. Collins* (Grand Rapids, MI: Eerdmans, 2011), and A. Gagne, A. Gignac, and G. Oegema (eds), *Constructing Religious Identities during the Second Temple Period/Construction des identités religieuses à l'époque du Second Temple*, Biblical Tools and Studies 24 (Leuven: Peeters, 2016).

55. Bradley L. Crowell, "Postcolonial Studies and the Hebrew Bible," *CBR* 7, no. 2 (2009): 217–44.

56. Antony Smith, "Migrancy, Hybridity, and Postcolonial Literary Studies," in *The Cambridge Companion to Postcolonial Literary Studies*, ed. N. Lazarus (Cambridge: Cambridge University Press, 2004), 241–61.

the ways that the biblical materials interact with colonial and imperial ideologies.[57] In addition to this focus on colonial aspects of textual *production*, postcolonial readings also shed light on imperial and colonial aspects of the *reception and interpretation* of these texts.[58] Since postcolonial reading is "an avenue of inquiry rather than a monolithic theory," it cannot be summarized or defined in terms of a neatly delineated method.[59] Similarly, because it draws on a wide variety of concepts and disciplines, including "nationalism, ethnicity, gender, colonial relations and political asymmetry," its points of contact with academic study of the HB/OT are often indirect.[60] All the same, a plethora of recent publications related to HB/OT, Second Temple Judaism, and New Testament studies demonstrate that its contact with these fields is as significant as its origins are complex.[61] Notably, in some cases, postcolonial reading is integrated with other hermeneutics, yielding an interdisciplinary, multi-perspectival approach in which each perspective nuances and informs the others.[62]

This constellation of interdisciplinary cross-pollination, textual rhetoric and ideology, and cultural and philosophical perspectives (including many not explicitly mentioned here) lies behind the decision of the Israelite Prophetic Literature Group of the Society of Biblical Literature to give sustained attention to the phenomenon of otherness or alterity.[63] The final form of the prophetic texts of the HB/OT presents a new, stable world that emerges from the aftermath of Israel/Judah's turbulent historical experience. Against the backdrop of past failures traced in different ways

---

57. R. S. Sugirtharajah, "A Brief Memorandum on Postcolonialism and Biblical Studies," *JSNT* 73 (1999): 3–5 (4).

58. R. S. Sugirtharajah, *Exploring Postcolonial Biblical Criticism: History, Method, Practice* (London: Wiley-Blackwell, 2011); Brett, *Decolonizing God.*

59. Sugirtharajah, "A Brief Memorandum," 5.

60. Crowell, "Postcolonial Studies," 219.

61. Varied appropriations of postcolonial reading can be found in Gossai, *Postcolonial Commentary and the Old Testament*; Fernando F. Segovia and R. S. Sugirtharajah (eds), *A Postcolonial Commentary on the New Testament* (London: Bloomsbury/T&T Clark, 2007), while Maxine L. Grossman surveys the same with respect to Second Temple Judaism more broadly in "Is Ancient Jewish Studies (Still) Postmodern (Yet)?," *CBR* 13 (2015): 245–83. For an attempt to trace its various points of contact with Biblical Studies, see Perdue, *Reconstructing Old Testament Theology*, 280–339.

62. Crowell, "Postcolonial Studies," 236–7.

63. Other points in this constellation, including literature, aesthetics, and architecture, are explored by Genoni, "Otherness, History of." The intersections of philosophy and identity are explored by Ramsey, "Philosophical History of Identity."

to the people's inability to maintain their identity as YHWH's people, the future sketched by the prophetic books presents Israel/Judah as a coherent community marked by a clearly determined identity and in pursuit of a singular goal. The ideal of stability, whether implicit in the accusations of past failings or envisaged in the future, depends upon an invisible but real line of demarcation between insiders and outsiders. The subtle and not so subtle rhetoric of otherness appears in varied forms such as space, race/ethnicity, gender, religious activity, and other identity markers that appear singly or intersect with one another. These intersections illustrate complex and sometimes contradictory representations of otherness in which alterity blurs the boundaries of constructed identities. A number of prophetic texts are simultaneously a means of opposition against entrenched and oppressive powers and a forceful exercise of exclusion against those whom the authors view as Other. The richness and complexity of these texts are further augmented by the fact that between the poles of Self/Other lie intricate mechanisms of identity and alterity that render the texts' constructions fluid in their appearance and in their impact on the reader.

Most of the essays that follow were originally presented in the Israelite Prophetic Literature Group's sessions, one focused on "Prophetic Otherness" (2014) and another dedicated to "Representations and Metaphors of Otherness" (2015). The essays describe and analyze the production of the various categories of otherness in ancient Israelite prophetic literature. They also reveal the complex and contradictory nature of otherness in prophetic literature, particularly because these texts emerge from communities that are themselves considered to be other. The essays exemplify diverse analysis of otherness with the aid of various theories (some more explicitly, some less so) in order to capture the highly textured nature of these representations of the ancient Israelite, Judahite, or Yehudite self and of the Other. Since the collection pays attention to the material and metaphorical constructions of otherness, the essays' collective scope captures the varied nature and complexity of the seemingly simple Self/Other binaries present in the final form of the prophetic corpus of the HB/OT.

Key Issues and Questions in the Essays

Although brief synopses of the essays follow immediately below, we note here some of the key issues and questions that they raise. To begin with a simple but fundamental point, virtually all of the essays demonstrate a well-known dictum: to *define the Self is to define the Other*, and vice versa. This does not mean that all efforts and mechanisms of identity are nefarious, but it does bring to the fore the relational nature of identity, or the inevitability of perceiving "the self as a member of a social category."[64] This reality is particularly interesting in the two-sided nature of some of the oracles studied. Although their subject matter is doubtless the nations outside Israel/Judah, they have significance for the Israel/Judah of which the author is part, as Davidson in the chapter on geography and Landy show. Indeed, in the end, Israel/Judah cannot be separated from the nations, as we see from Landy and Timmer.

Second, *otherness admits of degrees*. Essays like those of Irudayaraj, Kim, and Timmer note, rather ironically, that efforts to distinguish the Self from the Other are sometimes most ardent when the Other is perceived as being proximate rather than distant. But even the sharpest distinctions between the Self and the Other preserve a degree (however small) of similarity or comparability. It would appear, therefore, that all Self/Other relationships involve a limited degree of difference and so involve some measure of hybridity or permeability.[65]

Third, *otherness can be (at least partially) undone or overcome*. In some cases, this is evident in an oscillation between attraction and repulsion as Erickson shows, while other cases involve an ambiguous discourse regarding the Self–Other relationship as we see from Graybill and Irudayaraj. In still other cases, a relationship that is primarily one of difference or alterity at the outset is predicted to become, at some future time, one in which identity or commonality predominates, the view we get from Davidson on geographies of otherness, Landy, and Timmer. This movement is particularly interesting given the universalistic interest that appears in many parts of the HB/OT.[66]

Fourth, in several cases *the Israelite/Judahite Self or non-Israelite Other is bifurcated* or the group's *boundaries are found to be permeable*. In the case of bifurcation, the author (sometimes implicitly, sometimes explicitly) creates an ideal Self of which only some of the ostensible Self is part (cf. an "adopted We" or an "internal Other"). Erickson, Kim,

---

64. Jan E. Stets and Peter J. Burke, "A Sociological Approach to Self and Identity," in *Handbook of Self and Identity*, ed. M. R. Leary and J. P. Tangney (New York: Guilford, 2003), 128–52 (145–6).

65. The overlap of these terms with the semantic field of postcolonialism is not coincidental, and intimates the conceptual compatibility of the two fields. Cf. Abmet Atay, "Hybridity," in Jackson (ed.), *Encyclopedia of Identity*, 338.

66. See Jon D. Levenson, "The Universal Horizon of Biblical Particularism," in *Ethnicity and the Bible*, ed. M. Brett, BibInt 19 (Leiden: Brill, 1996), 143–69.

and Davidson on the issue of geography explore this phenomenon. A relatively common example of this is the Israelite/Judahite remnant as explored in Timmer's essay. When a group's boundaries are porous, the possibility arises that members of one group might come to share enough of the identity of another group that they are considered to be part of the latter. Examples of this phenomenon, or one like it, are evident when non-Israelites recognize and worship YHWH as sovereign (e.g., Isa. 19:18-25).

Finally, essays like those from Graybill and Erickson deal with the *relation of gender to othering*. Here the parity of the female/male binary is subjected to scrutiny, not least because of a number of instances of violence against female characters in the text (usually in a representative role, i.e., standing for a nation or city). Despite this arresting feature, some of these female characters show a mix of revulsion and attraction for the male entities with whom they interact, as seen in Erickson's work on Ezekiel 23. Also of interest in this perspective are the different roles assigned to male and female characters and their relative importance or value in the eyes of the author. Lastly, cases in which YHWH takes on roles normally reserved for female characters (e.g., bringing children to birth) prompt reflection on the relevance, suitability, or significance of gender identification for YHWH, as Graybill points out.

The Essays in Brief

Ahead of the programmatic essays, Steed Vernyl Davidson discusses what it means to think through otherness and how these thinking shapes our reading of prophetic literature. He demonstrates how theories from several academic disciplines have shaped the discourse of Self/Other while explaining these theories. Framed through the work of Stuart Hall and Sarah Ahmed, Davidson explores the essential question of this volume, namely, what accounts for the Judean view of other people that is present within prophetic literature. This largely negative view of others, foreigners, women, and other religious expressions, appears not only in the texts of the prophets but has become the bedrock for some modern views. Davidson shows that the historical questions that shape prophetic literature are as important as the contemporary theories of the Other that help account, in part, for the continued reading of these texts. The remaining chapters fall into two groups. The first five are principally concerned with metaphors of otherness, which the last two are primarily interested in representations of otherness.

The first study, by Dominic S. Irudayaraj, explores the image of the trampling warrior depicted in Isa. 63:1-6 and the significance of Edom as the warrior's point of departure. Noting the tension between Edom's genealogical and geographic proximity to Israel on the one hand and the animosity toward Edom that appears in some biblical traditions on the other, Irudayaraj deploys Social Identity Theory and the category of the "proximate other" to challenge interpretations of Isaiah 63 that find in it only animosity against Edom. As used here, these perspectives draw attention to the ways that proximity between groups complicates the articulation of their distinct identities. While the categories of Self and Other persist, the boundary between them is frustratingly permeable and their discourses exhibit ambivalence.

After briefly exploring the rhetoric of Isa. 63:1-6 and permeable geographic, kinship, and religious boundaries between Israel/Judah and Edom, Irudayaraj situates his reading of the passage, and particularly of YHWH's roles in it, at that conflicted and complex boundary. He also notes the ambiguity created by the trio of passages in Isaiah that deal with Edom and resist any monochromatic depiction of its identity and destiny (Isa. 21; 34; 63:1-6; 11:14 mentions Edom only in passing). A similar ambiguity appears in the arrival of the "outsider" warrior from Edom. His mix of astonishment and resolve, of stooping and power, reveal that he shares the experience of his exiled and returned people. This identification transforms a perceived outsider into "*the* insider" who will redeem Israel. Edom's persistence as a nation in a passage that also describes divine violence against it leaves the border between post-exilic Israelites and Edomites permeable and the tenor of the prophetic discourse ambivalent even as it reconstructs Yehudite identity.

Rhiannon Graybill's engagement with Isaiah takes up issues of gender and otherness in Isaiah 56–66. With a nod to Mieke Bal and Luce Irigaray, she employs a "Clytemnestra hermeneutic," in which violence is committed by and against the maternal figure, in order to explore the textual "erasure of the female body" and the "conjunctions of violence, maternity, and the deity" in dialogue with otherness. Graybill begins by noting the frequent connection in these chapters between female characters or images and moral wrong (e.g., 57:3, 7-10), but also the positive images of female figures that appear in sections dealing with restoration (e.g., 62:2-5; 66:7-9).

She then examines the "*crisis* of maternal-feminine imagery" as a binary element, especially in the female/male opposition. Following Irigaray's suggestions that "the feminine is used by the masculine to represent itself" and that maternal imagery limits female characters to a purely reproductive role, she argues that the prominence of childbirth as a female role in Isaiah 56–66 is a patriarchal representation. These images are complemented by several in which YHWH is depicted in the same role (66:7-9, 12-13).

Graybill then considers the elasticity of some of these categories. On the one hand, YHWH sometimes takes on motherly roles or is associated with blood, which Irigaray suggested is uniquely feminine. Conversely, Clytemnestra herself is presented as "a woman who thinks like a man" and exercises violence. Graybill concludes that while Isaiah 56–66 contains "little explicit *gender* violence," these chapters employ a "masculine appropriation of the female body" and evince "the impossibility of representing women or the feminine under a masculine economy of representation" and the erasure of relations between women. The association of both YHWH and Clytemnestra with power and violence adds "gender instability" to the discourse while drawing some close parallels between these two figures.

In a third essay on Isaiah, Francis Landy reflects on the metaphorical nature of much of the book and the significance of that language for three key Self/Other relationships in Isaiah's oracles concerning the nations: Judah/Israel vis-à-vis the nations, the prophet as spokesman for God and as spokesman to the people, and the present vis-à-vis the age to come. Landy begins by exploring the aural features of Isaiah 22, where sound often trumps semantics and expresses the strangeness of the nations. He finds similar mechanisms at work in the "surplus of speech over signification" in the non-referential aspect of the poetry in Isaiah 16. Landy carefully traces how these oracles occasionally but insistently draw the nations into proximity to YHWH and to Judah/Jerusalem (e.g., 16:5; 18:3, etc.), while the prophet's speech and silence constitute a delicate interplay at the border of language.

Landy contends that while in the present the nations are condemned to judgment, the new age, the "post-destruction era," sees (some of) them emerge from the previous era to experience the same utopian fate promised to faithful Judah (e.g., 18:7). Such images wed the distant and the proximate, the estranged and the intimate, and so express "the dialectic" of the oracles. He concludes that the "nations are Israel writ large," which offers metaphorical glimpses of its fates that they themselves will share.

Brittany Kim examines Ezekiel's presentation of Egypt in Ezekiel 29–32. She sets Ezekiel's treatment of Egypt and the Pharaoh in the context of Judah's struggle to maintain its identity in the face of Egypt's prowess, whether real or imagined. Her use of alterity theory includes the recognition that (among other things) the Self and the Other may in fact be quite similar, and that some Others are "internal" while some Selves may be "adopted." Kim argues that Ezekiel stresses the danger that Egypt poses to Israel as a potential source of religious corruption, a danger evident in Israel's interaction with Egypt in the past. Indeed, "at heart, the people of Judah are deceptively similar to the Egyptians," trusting in temporal and military power rather than in YHWH. Yet like Judah, Egypt's judgment will be followed by its restoration, establishing a unique parallel between these two nations.

Kim's examination of Ezekiel's depictions of the Pharaoh elaborates on this critique of Egypt and its ideology while preserving the intriguing similarity of the two nations. In each case she considers the ancient Near Eastern and Egyptian as well as the Hebrew Bible's backgrounds of the image before reflecting on Ezekiel's development of the image. Although in Egyptian royal ideology the image of the Pharaoh as a dragon (and, in ch. 32, as a lion) conveyed his might, the *tannin* in the HB/OT is a mere creature that YHWH controls, and Ezekiel affirms that YHWH will trap him in a net (32:3). Similarly, the depiction of the Pharaoh as a reed staff warns Judah (whose Davidic rulers are ideally "strong branches," Ezek. 19:11) against trusting in Egypt's strength rather than in YHWH. The metaphor of the Pharaoh as a magnificent cedar (cf. Judah as a cedar in Ezek. 17) recognizes Egypt's comparatively greater splendor and power, but since it owes its existence to YHWH, his punishment of its pride will bring it down to Sheol. The mix of similarity and difference in these oracles warns Judah against following Egypt (alterity), but also emphasizes that Judeans, like Egypt, are constantly tempted to trust someone or something other than YHWH (identity). Only the adoption of the ideal Self, by heeding this warning, enables Judah/Israel to endure the challenges of exile and beyond.

Diandra C. Erickson contributes a second essay dealing with Ezekiel. She focuses on the ambivalent identity of the Judean exiles in Babylon in Ezekiel 23, where the juxtaposition of oppression and resistance parallels dialectical pairs of power and powerlessness and of desire and repulsion. Erickson adopts a postcolonial lens that explores connections between Ezekiel's theological claims and the exiles' "experience of colonization" and "subsequent desire for agency." She argues that the initial hierarchy of Babylon over Judah gives way to a second, that of the prophet and the exilic community over both Jerusalem and Babylon, but notes that these identities are not binary or static. These fluctuating identities are reflected in the possibility that the Judean exiles might identify with YHWH *and* with Oholah and Oholibah, and thus with power and powerlessness. Erickson sees in this polyvalence a permeable boundary between the self and the other and between subject and object.

The balance of the essay explores the relationship between the patriarchal hierarchy of the book's male scribes and audience over its metaphorically female subject in dialogue with the imperial hierarchy of colonizer over colonized. Erickson attends to the gendered nature of the passage's colonial imagery, and proposes that the subjugation of the female bodies in the passage is a male response to the exilic loss of social dominance. This dynamic is complemented by the ambivalence of the female response to the colonizer, which integrates both attraction and repulsion. These dialectics and tensions capture the exiles' "precarious position as colonized entities."

Daniel C. Timmer's essay studies how othering is done and undone in Amos, Nahum, and Malachi. Several theses, most of which are used elsewhere in the volume, are important for his analysis: othering should not be conceived of as a binary process (an absolute Self–Other distinction) but rather as a spectrum that allows significant similarity between Self and Other; some aspects of alterity or identity can be more significant than others; and it is possible for a relationship that is primarily one of alterity to be transformed into one in which identity predominates.

Timmer first traces the status of the non-Israelites nations diachronically across the book of Amos. Their initial role as the enemies of Israel underlines their alterity (Amos 1:3–2:3), but near the end of the book Israel's alterity with respect to them is increasingly minimized (cf. 9:7). This movement reaches a climax after a future judgment of Israel, when some of the nations whom YHWH calls his own, as he did Israel, come under the control of the restored Davidic dynasty (9:11-12). These criteria of identity make the final relationship between restored Israel/Judah and some of the nations primarily one of religious identity, juxtaposed with political and ethnic alterity.

Timmer's study of Nahum contends that although much of the book focuses on the extreme alterity of the Neo-Assyrian Empire, which is presented as religiously, morally, and spiritually repugnant, the book's opening hymn (1:2-8) presents a different but complementary polarity. Noting the absence of cultural, ethnic, and geopolitical identifiers there, Timmer argues that the superlative, final othering this passage sketches is one in which religious/spiritual identity is the definitive, and indeed only, dimension of identity (esp. 1:7-8). Timmer finds a similarly complex perspective on alterity and identity in Malachi. Edom, as a result of its resolute opposition against YHWH and his people, will be destroyed (1:2-5). However, the "Israel" that Malachi presents is an ideal, as shown by the book's acerbic attack on corrupt priests and other members of Yehudite society (1:6–3:21[4:3]). This bifurcation of Yehudite society is matched by Malachi's bifurcation of the nations, some of whom will worship YHWH acceptably in their homelands (1:11, 14). Timmer concludes by reflecting on the varying distance the texts imagine between these mechanisms of othering and the exercise of social and political power.

The volume's final essay, by Steed Vernyl Davidson, uses insights drawn from cultural and especially postcolonial geography to demonstrate the significance of physical geography for othering and thus for interpretation of oracles concerning the nations. Noting the general absence of any explicit relationship between the nations and Israel/Judah in the oracles, he first explores oracles concerning the nations as ideologically constructed maps. Much like an empire's maps represent visually its "conquests either completed or in process," the oracles furnish an overview of territory that has been or will be "subdued and brought under divine influence." The ideological significance of these quasi-maps depends on the spaces and territories that they represent being filled in "with bodies, with cultural and religious practices, with histories" and the like. These forms and content constitute the "basis of otherness."

Davidson then considers the divine point of view inherent in these oracle-maps. Their "God's-eye view" encourages the reader to occupy the same moral and epistemological ground as YHWH, which is at the same time "the insider position of Judah." All other spaces are "other," and their moral otherness in particular provokes the divine intervention that is the oracles' dominant discourse. A glance at Jeremiah 46 illustrates these points, which Davidson summarizes as naming the nation, describing its use of its space in a general way, and then showing how divine intervention would "reconstitute a more acceptable space" (including the people in it).

The balance of Davidson's essay deals with how geographical-cultural otherness is overcome (rather than preserved) in prophetic oracles of the HB/OT. While on one level oracles concerning the nations typically undo rather than transform the nation concerned, Davidson suggests that we can see in the imagined and remade world that these oracles foretell Judah's construction of its "othered Self." Yet the project remains incomplete, since the geographic distance between Israel/Judah and the nations leaves both Israel/Judah and the nations in a liminal position. This liminality overlaps with Judah's literally diasporic existence in the Persian period, but does not fully resolve the tension between the real world in which Diaspora Jews live and the world envisioned by the oracles. Inevitably, Judah's othering of the nations in the oracles reveals that its identity and fate are bound up with theirs.

Chapter 2

Thinking with Otherness to Read Prophetic Texts

Steed Vernyl Davidson

Difference occurs naturally. The representation of difference emerges from social and cultural practices. Reflections on this reality, as well as the systems and their productions of the languages that sustain difference, date as far back as Plato in the Western academic tradition. In *The Sophist*, Plato thinks through the implications of being and by consequence non-being. For Plato existence assumes co-existence and while the available language may lack a term for or render the notion of "non-being" unintelligible, Plato conceives of otherness as related to "being" but of a different ontology.¹ The connections of ontology and alterity come into sharper focus in the twentieth century when the discussions are not merely abstractions but related to flesh and blood human beings. The atrocities of human history such as the Transatlantic slave trade, the Holocaust, and wars of genocide in the former Yugoslavia and Rwanda foreground the operations of alterity—the mere fact of being different. Despite the centuries-long debate and the myth of human progress, human interaction, as John Jervis acknowledges, shows that, "The evolution of modernity has always involved strategies of exclusion."²

---

1. Nestor-Luis Cordero, "Du non-être à l'autre: La découverte de l'altérité dans le Sophiste de Platon," *Revue Philosophique de la France et de l'Étranger* 130 (2005): 182.

2. John Jervis, *Transgressing the Modern: Explorations in the Western Experience of Otherness* (Oxford: Blackwell, 1999), 1.

Western theories of otherness that stretch back to debates in ancient Greece were concerned more with things than people. The debates, though, used people to discuss different forms and in the process set in place structured ways of thinking about difference. In *The Sophist*, a work that takes the form of a dialogue, Plato includes different participants, among them being the character named Zeno. English translations of the work have rendered Zeno (Χενος) as the Stranger, reading him as the outsider brought in to explore the notion of what is and what is not. Plato's philosophical reflection on forms that engage being and non-being is a realization of the edges of human experience. Just as in the ancient world the stranger represented the limits of the community's knowledge, so too non-being touches upon the limits of being. This, at least, is how Plato thinks of it. However, Sara Ahmed considers that the capacity to identify the stranger reflects some prior knowledge "that recuperates all that is beyond the human into the singularity of a given form."[3]

The striking aspect of Plato's work is that he draws conceptions of form and being together to highlight the existence of the other. Not only does Plato's voice remain mostly silent in the work, strategically, the Stranger raises the question of otherness. By bringing the Stranger to voice, Richard Kearney views Plato as making the point that if the other does not exist then strangers cannot prove their own existence. In effect, strangers cannot exist as a category different from the local if the local is all that exists. Kearney offers that the Stranger's voice on this matter has implications for the notion of otherness as well as ideas such as right and wrong: "For if being is all that exists and there is nothing other than being—e.g. a non-being in which words, images and things might also have some part—then one cannot explain the possibility of falsehood or error (which confounds what is and what is not)."[4]

The discovery of the stranger in the ancient world and the struggles around foreigners in a bordered world make the analysis of otherness an important point for reading ancient prophetic texts in our current contemporary realities. As Western societies have developed, categories of difference have multiplied. While on the one hand, ancient texts may appear to contain simple distinctions and on the other hand, the modern scene is seemingly marked by the complexities of diversity, critical readings of prophetic literature reveal a much greater range of differences

3. Sara Ahmed, *Strange Encounters: Embodied Others in Post-Coloniality* (London: Routledge, 2000), 2.
4. Richard Kearney, *Strangers, Gods and Monsters: Interpreting Otherness* (London: Routledge, 2003), 14.

that go beyond simple binaries. In fact, the apparent binary of insider/outsider in reality does not exist, as the systems of representation cannot hold these categories apart with any precision. Also, the starkness of the binaries is a way to avoid acknowledging descriptions such as Ahmed's, who defines the alien as "the outsider inside,"[5] and that of Patricia Hill Collins, who describes the alien as the "outsider within."[6] From this perspective, otherness emerges not so much as an ontological reality that derives from inherent properties, but otherness is something given meaning and therefore an ontology by systems of representation. As Ahmed indicates, the category "alien" only makes sense "within a given community of citizens or subjects."[7]

Despite being represented in various socially constructed categories, otherness does exist in actual reality. Differences are given meaning in social contexts that shape the experiences and consciousness of persons negatively impacted by those ideas, which Hill Collins articulates is a defining feature of African American women's lives.[8] Whole groups of people seen as outsiders are systematically excluded and oppressed in real-life situations. Discussions on otherness can easily tend to the abstract and miss the encoding that occurs on real bodies. To take seriously the systems of representation means also to take seriously their powers to construct whole groups of people based upon stereotypes as well as the rhetorical force to entrench these ideas and the consequences that they set in motion. Rhetorics of otherness have given rise to actual systems of persecution that Kearney lists as including "the recurring phenomena of witch-hunting, xenophobia, racism and anti-Semitism."[9] These systems do not merely represent animus against a particular group. As Lisa Isherwood and David Harris offers, these groups are named and produced by mechanisms of otherness and subsequently excluded and oppressed. Isherwood and Harris refer to the tendency within Christianity to articulate intolerance for difference and the ways in which this intolerance helped to create "black people, witches, homosexuals, indigenous

---

5. Ahmed, *Strange Encounters*, 3.
6. Patricia Hill Collins, "Learning from the Outside Within: The Sociological Significance of Black Feminist Thought," *Social Problems* 33 (1986): 14.
7. Ahmed, *Strange Encounters*, 3.
8. Hill Collins explains how the ideas and practices of racial segregation, even though they change from one generation to the next, create a common set of experiences for African American women. Hill Collins, "Learning from the Outside Within," 23–4.
9. Kearney, *Strangers, Gods and Monsters*, 38.

folk, and transgendered and transsexual people."[10] The "creative" capacity of rhetorics of otherness is matched by the destructive potential of these ideas in real life. These potentials, though, lack ontological capacities. They contain instead the power to mark, name, define, enforce, and regulate the character of the insider/outsider or what belongs to "home."

In this chapter, I explore various ways to think about how the other is produced in prophetic literature. My initial concern, though, stems from the question of what accounts for the vitriol against the outsider that appears in overt and subtle ways in prophetic literature. Whatever representational regimes we may discover in these texts may only supply a partial answer to that question. Nonetheless, I find Stuart Hall's thinking around representations of otherness a useful foundation to attend to reproduction and circulation of these ideas within and through the prophetic corpus. The negative depiction of outsiders as foreigners or even distant entities that must be controlled by the lethal divine power calls attention to Ahmed's understanding of the stranger. Ahmed helps to make sense of the processes that can lead to exclusion of folk already known but assessed as dangerous. In the first section, then, I discuss how Hall and Ahmed establish these twin concerns of representation and production of otherness as critical to a postcolonial optic. In the next major section, I explore several moments in the Western academic tradition and the questions they generated as a means of highlighting the postcolonial perspective on otherness. From there, in the third section I analyze how Biblical Studies has engaged the notion of the other. The section consists of a brief description of monographs that use otherness as a category of enquiry. The chapter closes with a broad sketch of representations of otherness in prophetic literature and ground that this volume sets out to explore.

Representation and Production of Otherness

The ideas that support the production of otherness can suggest that the other is both a natural product and one that comes out of nowhere. Both get at origins even though they are seemingly facile explanations. This volume is as much interested in understanding otherness as it is about accounting for its origins and reproduction in modern life. Stuart Hall's concerns with representation takes us to language and other discursive sources to understand the origination of otherness within regimes of

---

10. Lisa Isherwood and David Harris, *Radical Otherness: Sociological and Theological Approaches* (Durham, UK: Acumen, 2013), 17.

representation. Sarah Ahmed, on the other hand, accounts for otherness within existing human relationships. These two positions are neither mutually exclusive nor contradictory, since Ahmed is not concerned so much with regimes of representations. Ahmed provides a way for us to witness the operations of mechanisms that render people as other. These two perspectives serve useful purposes for prophetic literature to the extent that they open up the spaces to consider prophetic texts *qua* texts but, more importantly, as cultural products that communicate and teach language regarding those who do not belong to the community of the restored Judah. To the extent that we believe that prophetic texts have taken on lives beyond their ancient contexts, the legacies of these texts in sustaining practices of naming and exclusion of those considered other provide insight into the power of these texts.

Theories of representation offer interesting possibilities when considering prophetic texts with their limited circulation as a result of the small readership for these texts. These texts do not feature any visual representations, nor do they presuppose a steady recitation of their contents to ensure their perpetuation across generations and space. At best, we can surmise that these texts record words already uttered. While the full impact of these words may not be as huge as we imagine, the fact that they exist points us to a cultural production with striking notions of otherness. Hall's perspective that representation is about the exchange of meanings within a "circuit of culture"[11] draws attention to the potential of edited scrolls to function as a symbol of and producer of identity. Even more as these scrolls circulate across time and space, the meanings of these products evolve. Therefore, our concerns about the meanings of these texts can focus on specific or all periods of the lives of these texts. I raise the range across which meaning stretches to draw out the heuristic value of Hall's thinking on representation with regards to prophetic texts. As a corpus the meaning of these texts is not fixed, and neither is that meaning singular even when examined at a specific moment in time. Essentially, Hall helps us to name that prophetic texts have been involved in meaning-making regarding those considered other from the inception of these texts.

Hall adopts the "constructionist approach"[12] to meaning, where language is a system of ideas and symbols. From this perspective, meaning does not simply inhere in the words or mechanisms of communications. Rather,

---

11. Stuart Hall, "Introduction," in *Representation: Cultural Representations and Signifying Practices*, ed. Stuart Hall (London: Sage, 2003), 4.

12. Stuart Hall, "The Work of Representation," in Hall (ed.), *Representation*, 25.

meaning occurs through the actions of social forces that deploy and replicate language to communicate ideas. A text and a text collection such as the prophetic texts perform this work, and whether they actually speak to an audience or not prophetic texts consist of language designed to construct meaning through a system of representation. Hall acknowledges the slight differences he has with the way Michel Foucault thinks about representation. While representation and related discursive systems are "about the production of knowledge through language"[13] for Foucault, Hall draws representation in line with meaning.[14] The distinction may be slight. Nonetheless, Foucault's power/knowledge, even though providing a vibrant accounting for systems of oppression, does not capture an essential feature that Hall draws out with his emphasis on meaning: belonging. Hall shows how meaning "gives [a community] a sense of… identity"[15] that derives from discursive representations involved in "the production and exchange of meanings."[16] He shows how one form of representation—stereotyping—"is central to the representation of racial difference."[17] Prophetic literature is concerned about the restored Judean community and who belongs to that community in order to safeguard the community's integrity. From this perspective, therefore, Hall helps us to think about the capacity of representation through language to develop, confirm, and perpetuate mental maps about the community. These maps, in part, define insiders and outsider, self and other.

The production of the subject position of other does not materialize in a vacuum. Hall draws upon Foucault's work in relation to the subject and power to point out that representation functions as a twin act of power and empowerment. Representation communicates an identity that defines the subject within cultural discourses. The discursive systems give the subject a place from which to make meaning within the discourse. The seeming empowerment of the subject, though, can ignore the fact that its existence within the discourse participates in the knowledge produced by the discourse. Subjects, then, are not so much autonomous agents as they are "bearers of [a particular discourse's] power/knowledge."[18] Regimes

---

13. Ibid., 44.
14. "Representation is the process by which members of a culture use language (broadly defined as any system which deploys signs, any signifying system) to produce meaning." Ibid., 61.
15. Hall, "Introduction," 8.
16. Ibid., 7.
17. Stuart Hall, "The Spectacle of the 'Other,'" in Hall (ed.), *Representation*, 267.
18. Hall, "The Work of Representation," 56.

of representation create places for subjects—insider/outsider—intelligible to those subjects who submit themselves to the "meanings, power and regulation"[19] of discursive systems. Understandably, a body of texts, like the prophetic corpus, constructs its readers as subjects presumably to take the position of Judean insiders as the position that makes sense over and against the outsider produced in various forms as foreigner, sinful, unrighteous, woman, and so on.[20] To construct the preferred subject position assumes knowledge of the language that structures us/them as facilitated through some form of prior contact.

The other is more a stranger than unknown; more like us than unlike us. Ahmed engages the uncomfortable truth that runs through several theories of otherness: the other is quite like the self. Her preferred exploration of the stranger helps us understand the allergy to otherness that pervades prophetic literature. Her work offers a "rethinking [of] the primacy of the encounter over ontology."[21] She defines the stranger as "the one whom we have not yet encountered, but the one whom we have already encountered, or already faced."[22] Recognition of the stranger therefore amounts to a form of knowing again, as suggested by the semantic meaning of the word "recognize." For Ahmed, this recognition works with histories of "regimes of difference"[23] that produce the body and text of the stranger as out of place and therefore the necessity to create boundaries in order to mark place. Ahmed thinks of the production of the stranger as other in various settings of modern life as having a long genealogy. In part, she rejects the

---

19. Ibid.

20. Ehud Ben Zvi offers that biblical texts contain "quite complex grammars of constructing 'others' that were far more advanced than a simplistic binary of Us = good, male, able-bodied, righteous, and pure that included a Them = bad, female, not fully able-bodied, unrighteous, and impure." Ehud Ben Zvi, "Othering, Selfing, 'Boundarying' and 'Cross-Boundarying' as Interwoven with Socially Shared Memories: Some Observations," in *Imagining the Other and Constructing Israelite Identity in the Early Second Temple Period*, ed. Ehud Ben Zvi and Diana V. Edelman, LHBOTS 591 (London: T&T Clark, 2014), 22. I agree that as a totality the Bible is not unequivocal in this regard. Although there are places where individual foreigners such as Ebed-Melech in Jer. 38 are represented in positive ways, these may be cases of exoticization. See Steed Vernyl Davidson, "'Exoticizing the Otter': The Curious Case of the Rechabites in Jeremiah 35," in *Prophecy and Power: Jeremiah in Feminist and Postcolonial Perspective*, ed. Christl M. Maier and Carolyn J. Sharp, LHBOTS 577 (London: Bloomsbury T&T Clark, 2013), 189–207.

21. Ahmed, *Strange Encounters*, 10.

22. Ibid., 21. Ahmed admits: "'the other' is held in place as 'the stranger.'" Ibid., 165.

23. Ibid., 13.

historical narratives of European colonialism as the creation of modernity[24] and in the process she destabilizes the inclination to think of colonialism as the historical explanation for the development of the Western preoccupation with the other. Ahmed offers that "colonial encounters...involve, at one and the same time, social and spatial relations of distance and proximity."[25] In other words, the figure of the other—the colonized other, the alien, the stranger, and so on—emerges not so much from without but from within. Through the figure of the stranger, Ahmed then is able to explore a range of contexts that include Neighbourhood Watch programs for the practices that result from the construction of otherness.

I turn to Ahmed because both the body and performances of the stranger stand out in her work. She takes us beyond abstractions to explore real-life encounters that from time to time occur through bodies. Even though Ahmed recognizes that the body can serve as text and therefore be represented—readable, rendered intelligent, given meaning, as Hall shows us—her interests lie in figuring out how bodies "come to take certain shapes over others, and in relation to others."[26] The visceral reaction that she evokes makes real for us as readers of prophetic texts "that there is always *some-body* at stake."[27] Representations of Judeans therefore have implications for them as well as others in the same way the depictions of foreigners in negative terms pose benefits to Judeans.

For Ahmed, both body and performance are crucial for understanding how the stranger figures in the fiction and narratives of communities and by extension the actions that follow in the wake of those narratives. In Ahmed, the word "skin" stands quite often for a popular conception of "body," a preference that she explains moves us beyond the visual and to engage affect and "a process of materialization." In this way, she does with bodies, as we see below, what Levinas does with faces, by calling attention to the fact that bodies touch each other at the level of the skin. The skin also operates as the boundary where bodies affect one another.[28] As the skin serves as the container of bodies in several ways, Ahmed examines how social spaces are regulated, in this case not through proximity, but through separateness. By creating exclusionary zones—Neighbourhood Watch programs, immigration regulations, for example—skin as a surface marks bodies through race, ethnicity, gender,

24. Ibid., 11.
25. Ibid., 12.
26. Ibid., 41.
27. Ibid., 40 (emphasis in the original).
28. Ibid., 45. Ahmed also uses the expression "eye-to-eye" to talk about body encounters.

ability, and so on. These markings are essentially borders creating "the constitutive outside" that enables the self, what Ahmed refers to as "the body-at-home."[29] The self, contained at home, essentially becomes the marked-off space of exclusion "from which other beings are expelled."[30] In this sense, the stranger as other not only belongs to no home and is therefore not worthy of life but also cannot be permanently absorbed into the self or the home in Ahmed's categories.

Precisely the group or communal nature of exclusion of actual bodies that Ahmed references interests me in this chapter. This interest, though, emerges because texts and more particularly biblical texts organize themselves around flesh-and-blood communities. Whether those communities belong to the earliest tradents of the texts or contemporary readers, texts like the prophetic corpus socialize readers into a language. The language of the texts offers representations of righteousness/unrighteousness, virtue/evil, or preferred/not preferred. As Hall puts it, there is "power in *representation*; power to mark, assign and classify; of *symbolic* power; of *ritualized* expulsion."[31] As I turn in the next section to how Western thought has constructed the self/other from a highly individualistic perspective, the potential of texts to organize community, shape attitudes, and empower practice needs to be remembered. At times these theoretical interventions seem like personal angst and white anxieties. And to the extent that they are, Ahmed situates this concern for me within the broader realities of colonial relationships. These "relationships of knowledge"[32] do not merely exist as colonial encounters but as mechanisms that name, categorize, and position people as outside of the group. These mechanisms are more than simply the developing awareness of subjectivity, but they speak to the ways particular subjectivities emerged to embody the other in the stranger.

The Self/Other in Western Thought: A Postcolonial Intervention

Various cultures have multiple ways of representing those persons, things, and ideas that are different. The different has been a consistent source of fascination across time and cultures. While the forms of the appeal may change over time and place, the underlying motivations consist of simply sorting out reality. As Toni Morrison indicates, this sorting process is never neutral: "Descriptions of cultural, racial, and physical differences

---

29. Ibid., 48.
30. Ibid., 52.
31. Hall, "The Spectacle of the 'Other,'" 259 (emphasis in original).
32. Ahmed, *Strange Encounters*, 57.

that note 'Otherness' but remain free of categories of worth or rank are difficulty to come by."[33] The seeming simplicity of in/out is belied by the complex processes, systems, and difficulty of taming the unruliness of life. Complexities make for good philosophical reflection. Different theoretical perspectives offer disparate, though related ways of thinking about otherness. Among these theoretical interventions, the attempt at being either complete or sufficient soon fails. In effect, they are like one of the six men examining a part of the proverbial elephant under the mistaken notion that they have a grasp on the whole.

I make this turn to explore a select number of Western theories of otherness to situate the postcolonial intervention that I bring through Hall and Ahmed and later through the work of Fanon and Bhabha. This intervention into the theoretical ground becomes necessary not only because this work is normative in Western academic spaces, but I find it important to expand the theoretical range from the highly individualistic way these theories are understood and to position them within colonialist discourses. In doing so, I show that the thinking about otherness is not simply a reflection upon an innate response but one that tries to make sense of otherness that has already been embodied as a subject. Therefore, these theories are not so much about otherness that resolves the Cartesian doubt around subjectivity. They are more responsive to questions raised by intersubjectivity in a world that has been marked by difference. These theories do not explain the origins of otherness as much as they provide a window into how Western thinkers have tried to make sense of dominant white subjectivity as this has been challenged over time with increasing encounters with those categorized as not the same. As Ahmed helpfully points out, the postcolonial intervention here also consists in disrupting colonialism as the historical irruption and origin that explains Western theorizing on otherness.

As much of the twentieth-century work on otherness has shown, transdisciplinarity offers expanded ways of reflecting on the other. In this regard Sigmund Freud's psychological notions are pushed further by Jacques Lacan, who helps to shape a philosophical enquiry that is psychologically inflected. Lacan's impact can be seen on Frantz Fanon who in turn influences postcolonial thought. René Girard works through the idea of the other from anthropological categories along with philosophy and literary criticism. The notion of the other in literary studies has gained momentum from postcolonial studies which itself, in part, owes its place

---

33. Toni Morrison, *The Origin of Others* (Cambridge, MA: Harvard University Press, 2017), 3.

among the disciplines of the humanities to, as well as being an, offspring of postmodern, poststructural, and Marxist thought.

I select three disciplinary areas to set up the postcolonial intervention that I follow through Hall and Ahmed. This repositioning I then use to think through the implications for prophetic literature. I draw a thread through psychology, anthropology, and phenomenology, as these in various ways—explicit and implicit—impact Fanon and subsequently Bhabha who prove critical for postcolonial studies. At the same time, Ahmed's critique of Fanon/Bhabha prove important for unsettling historiographies of colonialism that privilege Europe. The link between psychology and phenomenology immediately appears in the ways Fanon engages Freud and Hegel. The anthropological connections are less apparent. I include anthropology here since it operates in the background of several disciplines and ideas rather than being referenced explicitly.

The Self and the Other—The Psychological Turn

Through his work in psychoanalysis, Sigmund Freud sets in play conceptions of the self rooted in consciousness and explained by means of psychological theory rather than philosophy.[34] Freud delineates human awareness between the ego, id, and superego. More than a mental state, Freud insists on the ego as "a bodily ego," likening it to certain functions of the cortex.[35] He invests it with not only the control of various bodily functions and drives but importantly with self-preservation.[36] This understanding of the ego differentiates it from the id that Freud conceives of in

---

34. Jacques Lacan contrasts Descartes and Freud on their reflections on the formulation "I think." Lacan shows that, unlike Descartes, Freud engages doubt, aware of "the certainty of the unconscious," while Descartes is thrust into reliance on truth as stemming from a source as complete as God. The difference that Lacan raises here is between Freud's use of bodily functions like dreams and Descartes explorations of the abstract. Jacques Lacan, *The Seminar of Jacques Lacan: Book XI, The Four Fundamental Concepts of Psychoanalysis*, ed. Jacques-Alain Miller, trans. Alan Sheridan (New York: Norton, 1978), 36. In Lacan's perspective the unconscious is a part of the body, an element that "these people who call themselves philosophers has ever dreamt of producing." Jacques Lacan, *The Seminar of Jacques Lacan: Book V, Formations of the Unconscious*, ed. Jacques-Alain Miller, trans. Russell Grigg (Cambridge: Polity, 1998), 160.

35. Sigmund Freud, *The Ego and the Id*, trans. Joan Riviere, rev. and ed. James Strachey (New York: Norton, 1960), 16.

36. Sigmund Freud, "An Outline of Psycho-analysis," *International Journal of Psychoanalysis* 21 (1940): 28.

categories that resemble Plato's otherness. Freud speaks of the id as archetypal forms of human conditioning that are genetically acquired. As the template of human consciousness, Freud thinks of the id as the original from which the ego develops to create unique human individuals.[37] Again, his thinking falls within the binary of the Self/Other. However, Freud introduces the third notion of the superego. While seen as a third term, the superego navigates between the ego and id in the form of socialization from sources as varied as parents, teachers, influential public figures, and other life experiences. At times, Freud refers to the superego as the "ego ideal."[38] In this regard, the superego reflects a "higher nature" that mirrors for the ego the ideals that come from sources such as "religion, morality and a social sense."[39] The superego, in Freud's thought, acts as the interface between the ego and the id, between inner and outer worlds.

Freud lays the groundwork for understanding consciousness of the self from a psychological point of view. A deep biological essentialism marks his work even though he leaves room for social factors. Jacques Lacan adopts Freud's work to produce insights useable in postmodern thought. Beginning with the notion of the "mirror stage," Lacan poses the question prior to Freud's intervention, How is human consciousness formed? Through a mix of Freud's psychanalytic theories and other influences, Lacan thinks of consciousness as something resembling the projection of the body's image in a mirror. However, this sight is disembodied, representing what Lacan thinks of as the "imaginary other;" the other from which the "I" is alienated and subject to misrecognition. Lacan describes the tension between what he refers to as the "I" ("*Je*") and the other created by the mirror image this way:

> But the important point is that this form situates the instance of the *moi*, from before its social determination, in a fictional line, eternally irreducible for the single individual—or rather, an instance which will only asymptotically rejoin the becoming of the subject, whatever may be the success of the dialectical syntheses by which the subject is to resolve as *je* his discordance with his own reality.[40]

---

37. Ibid., 27.
38. Freud, *Ego and the Id*, 26.
39. Ibid., 27.
40. Jacques Lacan, *The Language of the Self: The Function of Language in Psychoanalysis*, trans. Anthony Wilden (Baltimore: The Johns Hopkins University Press, 1968), 135.

Lacan's overdependence upon vision as a step in the development of consciousness contains obvious ableist assumptions among other deficiencies.[41] Nonetheless, he reveals a co-existent relationship between the Self/Other where consciousness is formed via the other. Unlike Freud where "other" refers to another person, in Lacan, "other" is a projection of the ego, in this case an idealization divided from the self. This imaginary "other" is critical to the integration of the self as it holds out the promise of wholeness.

Lacan's conception of the other goes further with a capitalization of the term. He refers to this as "the duality of the Other with a big O and the other with a little o."[42] The big O shows his dependence upon Freud, as he thinks of this in part as the resolution of the Oedipal impulses in relation to the mother and the developing child's desire for the mother.[43] In the child's overly dependent relationship on the mother, the mother becomes the all-powerful and all-knowing source. Lacan puts it this way: "the capital Other (*le grand Autre*), the locus of speech and, potentially, the locus of truth."[44] In this sense, Lacan uses Other to refer to parents, other authority figures, and systems to evoke the idea of how structures overdetermine the unconscious. Language serves as one of the more determinative structures for Lacan, as seen in his formulation: "*the unconscious is the discourse of the Other.*"[45] The conventions of law and social functioning serves as language embeds upon the unconscious. As such the Other represents radical alterity in that it cannot be assimilated into the self. Systems and conventions such as language exist outside of the ego and cannot be consciously controlled. As Lacan puts it, "the discourse of the Other that is to be realized, that of the unconscious, is not beyond the closure, it is *outside.*"[46]

---

41. See Anthony Wilden, "Lacan and the Discourse of the Other," in *The Language of the Self*, 160.

42. Lacan, *Formations of the Unconscious*, 6.

43. Ibid., 175.

44. Lacan, *The Seminar of Jacques Lacan*, 129. Lorenso Chiesa indicates that in this move to the capitalized form Lacan pulls together three influences (1) the idea of language as a structure, (2) the symbolic order of the way human culture is organized around laws, and (3) Freud's notion of the unconscious. Lorenzo Chiesa, *Subjectivity and Otherness: A Philosophical Reading of Lacan* (Cambridge, MA: MIT, 2007), 35.

45. Lacan, *The Seminar of Jacques Lacan*, 131 (emphasis in the original). Lacan though limits this assertion with, "The unconscious discourse is not the last word of the unconscious." Lacan, *Formations of the Unconscious*, 240.

46. Lacan, *The Seminar of Jacques Lacan*, 131 (emphasis in the original).

An inherent biologism lies at heart of the work of both Freud and Lacan but to different degrees. While Freud articulates the notion of the ego and ultimately the distinctions of self/other in the body, Lacan views the construction from the perspective of social imprinting upon the body. In both cases, they subscribe to rigid systems of demarcation. For Freud the ego (self) as distinct from the id (other) produces a subject set apart from other people that are distinctively different. Lacan, on the other hand, thinks of an ego overdetermined by the Other forced into communicating with others as the path towards subjectivity. Both Freud and Lacan explore subjectivity not simply within the limited space of a one-to-one encounter between isolated individuals. Rather, they think through the question of consciousness in relation to whole communities and the ways in which social formations structure individual subjectivity. Fanon notices this feature of Lacan's work and readily identifies that as part of the process of racialization that cannot be separated from white subjectivity. To the extent that subjectivity develops within the lived world, then it happens in a world marked by racial categories, therefore "the real Other for the white man is and will continue to be the black man."[47]

Psychology serves as the field to think through the existential question that preoccupies Western thinkers such as René Descartes and Jean-Paul Sartre: does individual subjectivity exist? By attaching the formation of individual subjectivity to the body, the psychoanalytical perspective of Freud and Lacan appears to naturalize and fix subjectivity as outside of the control of consciousness. To the extent that this is thought of as a natural process, psychology could be seen as affirming that binary distinctions are also natural. In fact, social formation is also occurring and the self is not merely coming to consciousness in relation to one but to many who would contain several characteristics that may or may not be the same as the self. Even more, the true self relies upon the other (whether small o or capital O) for anything that comes close to resembling stability. Otherness becomes that essential ingredient needed for completion that can never be fully realized. This split helps psychoanalysts explain neuroses, though no one is completely integrated. As Stuart Hall points out, through the work of Fanon, this split creates the space for "projecting on to others the 'bad' feelings one cannot deal with,"[48] as demonstrated in racial imperialism.

---

47. Frantz Fanon, *Black Skins White Masks*, trans. Richard Philcox (New York: Grove, 2008), 124.

48. Hall, "The Spectacle of the 'Other,'" 238.

Sociology of Difference – Anthropology as the Background

Anthropology presents another perspective that thinks through the notion of otherness as a natural phenomenon. The other in anthropological perspective is essentially an alien or a stranger; someone who differs from the normative humanity as defined by the community. In fact, as a discipline, anthropology, in its earliest phases, understands the human norm from the perspective of Western culture. Non-Western humans served as "living fossils," as they are thought to represent the prior stages of development through which Western culture had already progressed. In one sense, difference serves as the basis for understanding the other. Difference, though, is not a sufficient enough basis for understanding how otherness works in human societies, since the distinctions are not merely between humans and vegetation. Anthropology, therefore, investigates the processes at work within human communities that mark certain groups as being other.

René Girard's work with anthropological data seems useful for my exploration here. Although Girard is not an anthropologist, in the strictest sense, his work has been of interest to a wide range of disciplines, including "literary critics…cultural anthropologists, cognitional theorists, psychoanalytic critics and theologians."[49] Girard's interaction with Freud's conception of desire offers a starting point to understand how otherness works within communities. He comes at the pressing question of subjectivity not merely from another disciplinary angle but from a slant, in that he does not really set out to answer the question of the subject. What Girard offers us, though, are ways of thinking through human interaction particularly the conflictual aspects of human interaction. For Girard, human subjectivity—the awareness of the difference between the self and the other—can be located in desire. Contrary to Freud's reading of *Oedipus the King*, Girard conceives of desire as emanating from the imitation of a model rather than the unconscious competition with the father figure as Freud has it.

Girard offers an understanding of the construction of human communities and of "human interrelationship in terms of mimesis."[50] The source of this desire is not so much another human being as a thing—a third party—an important aspect for Girard, who stresses the location as external to the individual.[51] Girard draws his thinking from several

---

49. Diana Culbertson, "'Ain't Nobody Clean': The Liturgy of Violence in *Glory*," *Religion and Literature* 25 (1993): 38.

50. Ibid., 39.

51. René Girard, *Mimesis and Theory: Essays on Literature and Criticism*, ed. Robert Doran (Stanford, CA: Stanford University Press, 2008), 246.

sources, among which are anthropological investigations, but importantly several texts from the ancient Western literary canon—read here ancient Greek sources.[52] These sources reveal to Girard that mimetic desire arises from two people's shared interest in an object. These competing interests make the object more valuable than it would have been previously. The object becomes valued and therefore desirable precisely because someone else wants it: *"the subject desires the object because the rival desires it."*[53] The interest in the object generates conflict not because of the relationship between the two individuals but because one person is imitating the other or modeling the other, "not only in regard to such secondary matters as style and opinions but also and more essentially, in regard to desires."[54] Girard uses this generic scenario and not the familial context that Freud and others in the psychoanalytic world rely upon to formulate a theory of intersubjective relationships. He thinks of this as "a primary impulse of most living creatures,"[55] as a sharp rejection of the tendency to assign a significant role to the unconscious to account for how humans distinguish themselves from others.[56]

The mentoring relationship that facilitates the development of the self also produces the other. Girard conceives of the process as inherently conflictual since the implicit invitation "imitate me!" also carries with it the prohibition "don't imitate me!" The prohibition places the one striving to imitate the rival in the position of responding or not responding to that prohibition. In either case this creates what Girard calls "the *double bind*."[57] Girard accounts for the conflict inherent in this process with the observation that "opposition exasperates desires."[58] The double bind becomes even more pressing when the desired thing is not simply a thing but existence. Ultimately, the matter of interrelationships reflects the desire of being, and the self recognizes that "something he himself lacks and which some other person seems to possess." The other then becomes the source through which to acquire that which is necessary for being and

---

52. Girard refers to mimesis as "an ancient notion" and further notes that dramatists understood the struggle around desire. René Girard, *Violence and the Sacred*, trans. Patrick Gregory (London: Continuum, 2005), 155.
53. Ibid., 154 (emphasis in the original).
54. Ibid., 155.
55. Ibid., 156.
56. Girard critiques Freud's understanding of mimetic desire as "his mimetic intuitions are incompletely formulated." Ibid., 179.
57. Ibid., 156 (emphasis in the original).
58. René Girard, *I See Satan Fall Like Lightning*, trans. James G. Williams (Maryknoll, NY: Orbis, 2001), 10.

self-actualization. The competitive impulse increases if the self thinks in terms superior to the other, so that "the object must surely be capable of conferring an even greater plenitude of being."[59] Girard admits that at its best, this process results in antagonistic relationships.[60]

The value of Girard's work for this volume lies in its application of the development of lines of difference that are sustained by particular mechanisms that result in categorizing the other as fit for violence. This notion helps to think through more critically the searing violence and revenge fantasies present in prophetic literature.[61] Although Girard is concerned about the application of violence, as he indicates, certain social and other conventions regulate the antagonisms that derive from mimetic violence in human societies. The emergence of the self out of the imitation of the other results from actual human interaction rather than an unconscious process. Imitation represents the drive to achieve selfhood but at the same time, selfhood operates to build an identity over and against someone else. Girard describes this reality as "the more ego-centeredness increase, the more likely it is to turn into an underground 'other-centeredness.'"[62] Yet for all that "extreme openness,"[63] this preoccupation with the other is not unselfish but in fact manifests as "failed selfishness."[64] The competitive relationship means that the other presents as "mimetic doubles"[65] or a "monstrous double."[66] These are degrees of the same category in Girard's thought that express ways

59. Girard, *Violence and the Sacred*, 155.
60. Culbertson, "'Ain't Nobody Clean,'" 39.
61. For discussion on revenge fantasies in prophetic literature, see Amy Kalmanofsky, "'As She Did, Do to Her!': Jeremiah's OAN as Revenge Fantasies," in *Concerning the Nations: Essays on the Oracles Against the Nations in Isaiah, Jeremiah and Ezekiel*, ed. Else K. Holt, Hyun Chul Paul Kim and Andrew Mein, LHBOTS 612 (London: Bloomsbury T&T Clark, 2015), 109–27.
62. Girard, *Mimesis and Theory*, 256.
63. Rebecca Adams and René Girard, "Violence, Difference, Sacrifice: A Conversation with René Girard," *Religion and Literature* 25 (1993): 24.
64. Girard, *Mimesis and Theory*, 256.
65. Williams (Girard's translator) defines Girard's notion of the mimetic doubles as forming from the preoccupation with each other where they are alike but see sharp difference between them. See Girard, *I See Satan Fall*, 22.
66. Girard understands the monstrous double as the result of the ability to conceive of existence outside of the self that at first recognizes the other as "not me" and therefore a double. That which is "not me" is seen as so different and unfamiliar that it cannot belong to the same world and therefore is assessed as foreign or alien. Girard, *Violence and the Sacred*, 174.

in which difference and antagonism manifest in the relationship. While the mimetic doubles produce sameness that requires distinction, the monstrous double, as a product in literature, enables Girard to conceptualize how an "encounter [between] an 'I' and an 'Other'" generates differences and in turn produces violence.[67] In a sense, the differentiation of the self from the other seems like an obvious path of human development. Yet Girard's work deals with more than simply an individual but rather with communities. What Girard enables us to acknowledge is that this production of the "I" occurs through rendering the other as different to the point of being fit for violence and how that spreads as a contagion through the community. Morrison puts it this way in relation to scientific racism, which she describes as the need "to identify an outside in order to define one's self."[68] Certainly, the conceptions that Girard offers can produce different gradations of violence. The over and against nature that lies at the heart of mimesis means that intersubjectivity is marked by struggle; a struggle that can vary from the respectful engagement with others who are different to antagonistic competition.

Girard's work with communities helps our understanding of the construction of otherness as a systemic product. More than simply a deep dive into the subjectivity of the individual that seemingly occurs in Freud, Girard's focus on the community and its practices illustrates how mimetic violence operates through what he calls the mimetic contagion. Like a disease spread among a group, mimetic contagion is the group's fascination and acceptance of mimetic rivalry. As the subject models itself after the rival, so too the group, in Girard's words, "borrows" from their models. This borrowing "is a mass of behaviors, attitudes, things learned, prejudices, preferences, etc."[69] The contagion spreads to the group (the community) and individuals within the group act out the traits of the contagion. Girard makes a careful distinction to avoid branding communities as inherently possessing particular traits. For instance, he rejects what he terms the "medieval anti-Semitism" that reads the persecution and the death of Jesus as a particularly Jewish trait to kill prophets. He offers instead that what unites the persecution of the Hebrew prophet and Jesus's crucifixion "is clearly mimetic contagion that explains the hatred of the masses for exceptional persons, such as Jesus and all the prophets; it is not a matter of ethnic or religious identity."[70] Girard's insistence on

---

67. Ibid.
68. Morrison, *The Origin of Others*, 6.
69. Girard, *I See Satan Fall*, 15.
70. Ibid., 26.

modeling as the basis for the development of subjectivity—individual and group—suggests that social forces more than the biological attributes account for the construction of otherness. As Morrison observes, "one learns Othering not by lecture of instruction but by example."[71]

Dialectics of Master/Slave—The Philosophical Perspective

Much philosophical thought around otherness as a binary construction stems from G. W. F. Hegel's dialectic of "lordship and bondage,"[72] more popularly known as the master/slave dialectic. Hegel's dialectic animates the shape of several forms of thinking on otherness. His work fuels philosophical traditions like phenomenology on the matter of otherness. Karl Marx's use of the dialectic as well as his ideas of the generation of consciousness introduces the Hegelian conception of otherness to Marxist thought and several of the derived postmodern theories that rely upon Marxism. Lacan represents a unique fusion of Freud, Marx, and Hegel. Essentially, the Western philosophical tradition reflects Hegel's deep impact in one way or another.

In his book, *Phenomenology of Spirit*, Hegel purports to deal with the issue of the human spirit through a history of consciousness. He sets up an imaginary scenario of a spirit split between what can be labelled master and enslaved. Hegel's use of the categories of master/enslaved are neither accidental nor abstract. As Susan Buck-Morss indicates, Hegel's affinity for the work of Adam Smith and other early economists, as well as his fascination with the Haitian Revolution, provides "the theoretical hinge that takes Hegel's analysis out of the limitlessly expanding colonial economy and onto the plane of world history which he defines as the realization of freedom—a theoretical solution that was taking place in practice in Haiti at that very moment."[73] Although read as a conjectural thought game or metaphor, Buck-Morss recognizes how slavery functioned as "the root metaphor of Western political philosophy, connoting everything that was evil about power relations"[74] by the eighteenth century in ways that inform Hegel's narration of lordship and bondage. Despite the prevalence of the metaphor of slavery during the period of the European practice of racial enslavement, political philosophers make little direct reference to

---

71. Morrison, *The Origin of Others*, 6.
72. G. W. F. Hegel, *Hegel: The Phenomenology of Spirit*, trans. Michael Inwood (Oxford: Oxford University Press, 2018), 76.
73. Susan Buck-Morss, *Hegel, Haiti, and Universal History* (Pittsburgh, PA: University of Pittsburgh Press, 2009), 12.
74. Ibid., 21.

enslaved Africans in their works. The apparent silence about slavery and the absence of the enslaved Africans as explicit subjects in their work belies a preoccupation of these philosophical traditions with African enslavement. Buck-Morss shows a connection exists between the Haitian Revolution and Hegel's development of the master/slave dialectic.[75]

Like other thinkers, Hegel struggles with the notion of self-consciousness in the context of interrelatedness. For him this is important in order to avoid the "motionless tautology of: I am I."[76] Starting with the acknowledgement that the entities mutually recognize each other, he admits that the mutual recognition in not equal since the subject is more concerned about itself and views the other negatively. This self-regard also generates a certainty of the self and the necessity to show an independent existence through the death of the other and the preservation of its life. These two then enter into a life and death struggle to ensure the death of the other in order to "elevate their certainty of themselves." By entering into the struggle there is a risk of death but the embrace of this threat of death serves as the path to freedom. Hegel describes freedom here not merely as knowing oneself as a person but as "recognition of an independent self-consciousness." Driven by pure self-interest to kill the other, the subject manifests a higher value of itself over the other. Precisely in the openness to death, the subject embraces the reality that "death is the *natural* negation of consciousness, negation without independence."[77] In the surrender to death, the other yields recognition to the subject by giving up on consciousness and independence. In the struggle one was prepared to let go of independence and to be open beyond itself.

From the experiences of the struggle, Hegel goes on to draw a line between self-consciousness and pure self-consciousness. The difference consists of consciousness open beyond itself and consciousness drawn into itself. He describes "the independent consciousness for which the essence is Being-for-itself" as "the *lord*." And the "dependent consciousness for which the essence is life or Being for another" as "the *bondsman*."[78] Hegel conceives of the lord as the consciousness that is both for itself and facilitated through the consciousness of another, in this case the enslaved. The descriptions of the lord reflect expected categories of independence, dominance, acquisitiveness, control, and superiority. The enslaved on the other hand demonstrates dependence, sublation, and the capacity to

---

75. Ibid., 59.
76. Hegel, *Hegel*, 73.
77. Ibid., 78 (emphasis in the original).
78. Ibid. (emphasis in the original).

mediate recognition and things, that is produce things, for the lord. This obviously creates an asymmetrical relationship where the lord derives benefits from the enslaved's production of goods. The enslaved eschews any interests or pleasure in goods, just as it lets go of recognition.

As Hegel tells the parable, it seems that up to this point he describes what seems to be the reality of uneven and unequal relationships of dominance. However, as Buck-Morss points out, the successful revolt of enslaved Africans in Haiti marks a development in Hegel's thinking that brings "the dialectical logic of recognition" to the forefront.[79] Hegel articulates how the hard-won recognition of the lord stands upon the consciousness of the enslaved who already sees recognition as not that important. Further, the enslaved's production of goods and dependence reveals the nature of consciousness built upon the creation of goods distinct from itself. That is to say, the recognition of the value of labor in produced goods gives the enslaved its self-consciousness. If this then is the basis of the enslaved's recognition of the lord, then what was previously thought of as independent consciousness is in fact dependent. Hegel summarizes this as "a recognition that is one-sided and unequal."[80] In fact, Hegel admits that "the servile consciousness" is independent consciousness since it turns into itself. By comparison, the lord's consciousness is not as pure as once thought, but rather an inversion of what it could be: dependent and not self-consciousness. Hegel's examination of the enslaved's consciousness leads him to acknowledge the power of the enslaved. Facing the fear of the death of the lord on whom the enslaved's existence and sense of truth hang, the enslaved engages with "the absolute liquidization of all subsistence," which Hegel thinks of as the essence of self-consciousness. Further, Hegel notes that the enslaved, by producing things, gains detachment from goods and is able to recognize itself because the enslaved can now perceive as a subject that transforms objects into goods. The enslaved as a result becomes turned towards itself rather than merely being for others. Hegel concludes, "the working consciousness arrives at the intuition of independent Being *as of its own self.*"[81] The enslaved recognizes itself as a being, and can claim that freedom through death. This self-recognition comes through fear and service and not as a result of the lord's consciousness. Hegel comes to these conclusions when he considers servile consciousness "in and for itself."[82] The result

79. Buck-Morss, *Hegel, Haiti, and Universal History*, 59.
80. Hegel, *Hegel*, 80.
81. Ibid., 81 (emphasis in the original).
82. Ibid., 80.

of this recognition, though, does not lead to mastery or dominance, so there is no fear here of the reversal of positions. The enslaved achieves self-consciousness outside of itself and independent of the lord, a feat that the lord does not accomplish.

The processes of thesis, antithesis, and synthesis that Hegel follows leads him to the realization of the power of the enslaved, particularly that the enslaved possesses self-awareness "that *thinks* or is free self-consciousness." Hegel describes the capacity to think as not merely the ability for abstraction but rather the perception of the self as an "I," as in the concretizing of the self as an object.[83] In Buck-Morss's perception, Hegel comes to terms with this reality in the success of the Haitian Revolution, a moment, she offers, when "theory and reality converged."[84] Hegel's experience shows us the crisis that occurs in Europe's self-conception when the place of other human beings within a reordered world has to be acknowledged. Whether this crisis stems from facing the hollowness of liberal values as articulated throughout European and the United States as products of the so-called Age of Enlightenment or the present limits that face Western democracies, the Western philosophical tradition reflects the engagement of what to make of those named as stranger and the implications for their being upon the European self.

I rehearse Hegel's theory in this essay to call attention to its breadth and complexity. There is a sense in which the conclusion that Hegel reached through the parable destabilizes the automatic perception that otherness equals an inferior ontology. Sharp distinctions of otherness may indeed mask the powerful potential of the term placed in the inferior position as Hegel's work show us. If anything, Hegel's work reveals the interconnectedness of the self and the other, the interconnectedness of humans. Postcolonial thinkers will find Hegel useful to call attention to the potential of the other to destroy the self. For instance, Achille Mbembe offers a Hegelian tinge in his reading of the logic of martyrdom as demonstrated by the suicide bomber: "the lowest form of survival is killing... resistance and self-destruction are synonymous."[85] My other purpose for including Hegel comes from his influence upon postcolonial thought. Buck-Morss indicates how the Haiti–Hegel connection has been largely overlooked in white scholarly circles due to racism and racist tendencies to center Europe as constituting universal history.[86] In invoking Hegel, I

---

83. Ibid., 82.
84. Buck-Morss, *Hegel, Haiti, and Universal History*, 60.
85. Achille Mmembe, "Necropolics," *Public Culture* 15 (2003): 36.
86. Buck-Morss, *Hegel, Haiti, and Universal History*, 57.

draw attention to the reality that his theoretical engagement already comes fashioned with categories of dominance and servitude that do not derive exclusively from the Transatlantic slave system. Socially and otherwise Hegel is already primed to represent the binary. The other rather than being unknown is simply recognized in the various representations of the age.

The function of recognition in Hegel's thinking leads me to consider Emmanuel Levinas's theory next. Several strands connect Levinas to Hegel, mostly the thread of phenomenology. As Hegel conceives of the duality as an encounter where recognition facilitates consciousness, Levinas grounds his thinking around the relation between the subject and the other "as a *face to face*."[87] The transition from Hegel to Levinas not only represents a few centuries but also an open acknowledgement of the practice of otherness and its deleterious impact. While Hegel subsumes the European enslavement of Africans as the central economic project of modern Europe, Levinas centers the Jewish Holocaust in his conception of the other.[88] This open acknowledgment of human wickedness influences Levinas in his development of what he regards as ethics. For him, ethics is about responsibility as much as it is about a disciplinary distinction. Levinas in many ways creates a different lane on the question of otherness. Although he engages with psychology, his deepest interactions take place with phenomenology, where he creates a distinction between philosophy and ethics.[89] Ultimately, for Levinas, the concepts are not abstractions since he grounds his thinking in human interactions.

The other in Levinas stands apart from the subject as decidedly different. However, the difference is not an ontological one or even one of degree. Levinas offers, that the other is different "like the bread I eat, the land in which I dwell, the landscape I contemplate."[90] Despite using non-human metaphors, Levinas shows the other as diversity within the same species, but not diversity that results from inherently different

---

87. Emmanuel Levinas, *Totality and Infinity: An Essay on Exteriority*, trans. Alphonso Lingis (The Hague: Martinus Nijhoff, 1979), 39 (emphasis in the original).

88. John Drabinski confronts the gaps in Levinas's work as a post-Shoah thinker around contemporary debates on decolonization and the attendant legacies of slavery in relation to European empire. John E. Drabinski, *Levinas and the Postcolonial: Race, Nation, Other* (Edinburgh: Edinburgh University Press, 2013), 128–64.

89. In its simplest way, Levinas differentiates philosophy as a system that resolves the other into the same, while he presents ethics as regarding the other as irreducible. Levinas, *Totality and Infinity*, 47.

90. Ibid., 33.

biological traits.⁹¹ Levinas stresses the separateness of the other, what he describes as "rigorously other,"⁹² in order to distinguish his thought as based upon the external process of the face-to-face encounter. By stepping back from the interiority of Freud and the psychoanalytic school or recognition as the phenomenologists have it, Levinas foregrounds the fact that "self-consciousness…rest[s] on the unrendable identity of the I and the self."⁹³ The other is not subject to change by the self. The other is not subsumed into the self. The individuality of the other remains vital for a meaningful interaction of mutuality in the face to face encounter.

The face-to-face encounter takes place between what Levinas calls the same and the other. The two stand at a distance from each other. Levinas insists on thinking of this distance as having several properties. First, it is not hierarchical. Secondly, the distance makes clear that the other transcends the same as "a being that lives *somewhere*."⁹⁴ Thirdly, the separation is not based upon a negative evaluation of the two parties. The validity of the encounter as a meeting of two parties relies upon the separation. Separation facilitates rather than destroys the relationship, since this means that two distinct parties are meeting rather than "an implantation in the other and a confusion with" the same.⁹⁵ As a result, Levinas conceives of the encounter as value neutral where the differences of the other are respected and not marked in any way by the recognition of the other.⁹⁶ The face of the other in the encounter remains unchanged and in fact does not affect the same either. Levinas describes the encounter with the face of the other as an invitation into relation. The idealism present here leaves the space open for Levinas to make the point about language. Language facilitates the relationship and at the same time maintains the separation between the same and the other.⁹⁷ Additionally, the value neutral encounter helps Levinas to insist that no prior natural, psychological, cultural, or other factors shape this encounter in a way that gives priority to the same or the other.

---

91. Ibid., 214. Levinas rejects thinking of the other as produced by biological factors, as presented by racist biologism like Nazism. Ibid., 215.

92. Ibid., 39.

93. Ibid., 37.

94. Ibid., 216 (emphasis in the original).

95. Ibid., 42–3.

96. Ibid., 195. Although this may seem idealistic, Drabinski acknowledges that Levinas demonstrates a fair sense of embodiment and the implications of embodiment in his work even though this at best appears "ambivalent." Drabinski, *Levinas and the Postcolonial*, 33.

97. Levinas, *Totality and Infinity*, 39.

Of course, in real life these encounters occur quite differently than how Levinas makes them seem. Values are placed upon the other. The other is forced into the knowledge categories of the same. Mechanisms to explain the being of the other emerge. Levinas assigns these actions to Western philosophy and its preoccupation with ontology. As systems of interrogation, Levinas thinks of philosophy as dealing with problematic ontology and the development of generalizations and schemas. These structures he thinks permit "the priority of *Being* over *existents*,"[98] that is, the universal over the particular; abstractions instead of embodiment; philosophy without ethics. As a result, experience and relationality do not lead to philosophical thought that highlights responsibility, but instead sanctions ignorance regarding the knowledge that being is supposed to explore: the other. These failed moves permit the human atrocities such as the Shoah. Levinas indicts philosophy as responsible for evils from "imperialist domination, to tyranny."[99] He suggests ethics as a corrective to the tendencies in philosophies not merely as a disciplinary turn but as a path of responsibility to the other. Ethics, he offers, admits to the irreducibility of the other. Ethics accepts the strangeness of the other and refuses the way of possession that makes the other into the same. Instead, he proposes "a non-allergic relation, an ethical relation" characterized by welcome and conversation.[100] Ahmed helpfully summarizes ethics as "how one encounters others *as* other (than being)."[101]

Levinas offers a conception of otherness that emphasizes radical difference. While he acknowledges that social thought invests these differences with negative meanings, he presents the other as that which is different. That the different is not negative or threatening comes across in his choice of the face as his central metaphor. The human face at once reveals difference and the lack of menace unlike, say, the human arm. The arm does not contain the same level of physical differentiation as the face and is the critical limb through which humans wield weapons. The face indicates the separateness, uniqueness, and independence of the other.[102] By turning to each other face to face, Levinas conceives of this encounter as one that does not change the other in the way Hegel thinks of the struggle between the lord and the enslaved. Instead, Levinas conceives

---

98. Ibid., 45 (emphasis in the original).
99. Ibid., 46.
100. Ibid., 51.
101. Ahmed, *Strange Encounters*, 138 (emphasis in the original).
102. Levinas, *Totality and Infinity*, 89. In fact, Levinas speaks of the turning to face each other as taking place with "empty hands." Ibid., 50.

of the turning as freedom "to maintain oneself against the other despite every relation with the other to ensure the autarchy of an I."[103] The other possesses no trait that negates the "I." This proves an important point for Levinas, since to think of the other as owning some characteristic that differs from other humans then makes alterity null and void.[104] At that point, what we are dealing with are incomparable beings.

Lumping Levinas with other theorists who ignore the social constructions may do a disservice to his work. Levinas pays attention to particularities even though he appears to be uncomfortable with valuing those particularities that jumps swiftly in to ontological categories. As Ahmed indicates, Levinas is caught in the bind of trying to "rescue the other from philosophy through philosophy."[105] For her, the nomenclature *the* other already performs this work based as it is on "both ethical asymmetry and on phenomenological symmetry: the other is radically other than me, but as his being is characterised by such otherness, he is, like me, a being."[106] To get at the value-neutral encounter that Levinas imagines, Ahmed suggests focusing on the particularity of the modes of encounter, which has the effect of reducing the preoccupation with the characteristics of the parties and instead enfleshes participants in a way that "*differentiates others from other others.*"[107] The inability of Western theorizing to acknowledge the prior move of theory inflected, and perhaps infected, by social categories means that we have theories about the neutral self that in effect center white subjectivities.

I now turn to Jacques Derrida because Derrida helps to name the limits of Levinas's work that is partially useful for the postcolonial intervention. Derrida provides a wealth of ideas on otherness, but it is his analysis of Levinas that proves important at this point. Derrida questions what he regards in Levinas as "absolute singularity."[108] For Derrida, Levinas stresses the uniqueness of the other so much that it makes the responsibility that Levinas anticipates should flow from the encounter a "paradox, scandal, and aporia."[109] In other words, if everyone is unique

---

103. Ibid., 46.
104. Ibid., 194. Levinas goes further to rule out "psychological dispositions" as a basis for establishing difference. Ibid., 215.
105. Ahmed, *Strange Encounters*, 142.
106. Ibid., 143.
107. Ibid., 144 (emphasis in the original).
108. Jacques Derrida, *The Gift of Death*, trans. David Wills (Chicago: University of Chicago Press, 1995), 84.
109. Ibid., 68.

in radical ways, then a general ethics to hold anyone accountable for the performance of responsibility is no longer possible.[110] As Derrida examines the issue of otherness, responsibility through the performance of duty becomes almost impossible. In fact, he thinks that this leads to overlooking other others.

Derrida considers otherness within the context of God as "the absolute other as other."[111] In responding to Levinas's construction of the other as a unique and particular being, Derrida thinks of God as wholly separate and that God relates to individual humans in that way, as separate beings distinct from God. Therefore, for Derrida "a radical heterology" consists in the human interactions that mirror relationships which require each human being to take the distinctiveness of another person seriously.[112] Derrida similarly situates human responsibility in the context of God's duty to each individual: "I am responsible to the other as other."[113] But this space of responsibility also creates what Derrida terms the "risk of absolute sacrifice."[114] Recalling Derrida's sense that the uniqueness of everyone makes generalizations impossible, he raises a comparable concern in relation to sacrifice. If all situations of need are special and unique then one can only respond to a finite number of situations. The exercise of the responsible thing in one case results in an act of irresponsibility that ignores the uniqueness of someone else. The problem that Derrida identifies lies in what he points out as Levinas's integration of responsibility with absolute singularity. In the process of engaging with the other through responsibility—read here valuing the other's ontology equally—other others are created. That is to say, people whose need does not rise to the same level of concern or whose being is considered as less worthy of attention.

---

110. Ibid., 84.
111. Ibid., 68.
112. Ibid., 82. The consideration of the gap between humanity and divinity leads Derrida to play with different formulations of the phrase: "every other (one) is every (bit) other," as an alternative, "Every other (one) is God," or "God is every (bit) other." In the end, Derrida raises the possibility that the properties of otherness could be assigned to God and divinity to the other. Ibid., 87.
113. Ibid., 68.
114. Derrida uses the story of Abraham's near sacrifice of Isaac to illustrate the risk of absolute sacrifice. Abraham is caught between his duty to God and his duty to his son and he cannot faithfully perform one without failing in the other. Ibid., 86.

I do not consider that Derrida offers so much of a corrective to Levinas as much as exposing the difficulties in theorizing otherness. In one sense, Levinas can be read as trying to find a way to reduce the violence and oppression that arises as a result of inherent differences, given socially constructed meanings and other forms of differences that societies develop to mark themselves. My purpose here is not so much to forge a path for the eradication of difference or the dismantling of the systems of meaning that produce these differences, as salutary goals as those may be. Levinas helps me to demonstrate that alterity need not be a problem and that alterity evolves into the evils that mark human history in part because of the failure to halt the processes that generate systems of meaning around difference.

The Differences of Power—The Postcolonial Perspective

Among several of the postmodern forms of critical inquiry, postcolonial studies pays attention to the notion of otherness. Undoubtedly, the ideas of a Western European sense of supremacy were enacted and continue to arise in Western imperial practices. Therefore, to analyze modern imperialism is to confront the specter of otherness not only in the practices of empire but in the ideas that support and maintain those practices. The simple binary construction of self/other with the inevitable unequal values suggested by the pairing[115] structures Fanon's thinking and in turn frames aspects of postcolonial studies. Additionally, the Marxist appropriation of Hegel's work around the consciousness of the enslaved and other aspects of Hegel's thought make their way into postcolonial studies. In this section, I look mostly at Fanon and the way that Homi Bhabha appropriates Fanon.[116] Ahmed ruptures the conception of the postcolonial in ways that destabilizes what at times appears as the transgressive binary of colonized/colonizer in Fanon and Bhabha. Instead of thinking of the colonizer/colonized relationship as a product of the historical fact of colonialism, Ahmed conceives of the binaries as the result of "a series of discontinuous encounters between nations, cultures, others and other others."[117]

---

115. Hall, "The Spectacle of the 'Other,'" 235.
116. The philosophic genealogy of Freud–Fanon–Bhabha is not without concerns within postcolonial studies. Rey Chow shows how Fanon picks up Freud's Oedipal construction to frame native people as characterized by lack in the way that Freud thinks of women. Rey Chow, "Where have all the Natives Gone?," in *Feminist Postcolonial Theory: A Reader*, ed. Reina Lewis and Sara Mills (New York: Routledge, 2003), 327.
117. Ahmed, *Strange Encounters*, 11.

Colonialism creates a crisis of identity, as Fanon reads history. He offers that colonialism as an historical event built upon the disavowal of the colonized generates a psychic rupture: "Because it is a systematic negation of the other person and a furious determination to deny the other person all attributes of humanity, colonialism forces the people it dominates to ask themselves the question constantly: 'In reality, who am I?'"[118] In Fanon, this crisis of identity takes shape along an axis of recognition. With no Levinasian face, Fanon contends with the Hegelian recognition that generates self-consciousness and the Freudian legacies of misrecognition. For the most part, Bhabha notes that Fanon would find Lacan's notion of the other as more suited to the colonial context than Hegel.[119] In Fanon, recognition means foregrounding the grotesqueries of racist constructions of a "suffocating reification" through the interpellation, "Look! A Negro!"[120] Such hailing structures the gaze of the colonizer in the production of stereotypes. Fanon describes Lacanian misrecognition in the categories of Hegelian recognition. The result is not only a sharp division that places what we have been thinking of as the other within a zone of negation, but also self-alienation.

The mechanisms of constructing the colonized, who Fanon names as "the Negro," given the historical context, lie more in their power to evacuate the colonized of a past and in the process to produce racial stereotypes. Fanon offers that the myth of the lack of history performs a dialectic function, where the colonized turns to the colonizer as the model upon which to construct an identity.[121] Representing the paternalism of the psychological models, Fanon depicts the operations of a logic that convinces the colonized as "sub-men to become human, and to take as their prototype Western humanity as incarnated in the Western bourgeoisie."[122] Unlike the psychological models that understood a process of maturation of persons within the human family, Fanon invokes much of

---

118. Frantz Fanon, *The Wretched of the Earth*, trans. Constance Farrington (New York: Grove, 1963), 250.

119. Homi Bhabha, *The Location of Culture* (London: Routledge, 1994), 47. Bhabha goes further to describe the influences upon Fanon as "a Hegelian–Marxist dialectic, a phenomenological affirmation of Self and Other and the psychoanalytic ambivalence of the Unconscious." Ibid., 58.

120. Fanon, *Black Skins*, 89.

121. Fanon, *Wretched*, 210.

122. Ibid., 162. Given the power of imperialism, Fanon regards assimilation not only as the acquisition of white culture but also as the misguided belief of whiteness as the path to "becoming a true human being." Fanon, *Black Skins*, 2.

the imperialist rhetoric of the inhumanity of colonized people to position the colonized other as radically different. Fanon's descriptions of the binaries of colonizer/colonized or Black/white speak to "a world divided into compartments, a motionless, Manicheistic world."[123]

Let me clarify that Fanon examines the Manichean split between whiteness and blackness as more than simply consisting of ideas. Fanon writes in a visceral way that makes clear that blackness as otherness is more than a discursive or conceptual reality. Blackness as embodiment resonates clearly in Fanon's work. Even more for Fanon is the colonial disciplinary regimes than entrench hate and self-hate upon Black bodies: "In the white world the man of color encounters difficulties in the development of his bodily schema. Consciousness of the body is solely a negating activity."[124] The construction of the other in a racist colonial society releases disciplinary regimes that condition the performances and spaces of Black bodies. Fanon speaks of the "body schema" that accompanies the "historical-racial schema" of white racism.[125] He does so to make the point of the inadequacies of philosophical thought that engages in abstraction with no attention to the real-world experiences. With gestures to Hegel, Fanon indicates that ontology cannot come to terms with blackness as a lived experience. In fact, he uses Hegel's conclusion of the other as determinative of the self to point to the Black self constructed by colonialism. And at the same time, he shows the ambiguity of Hegel's ideas, particularly as they pertain to any real-life experience. He writes of "the Other" that at once has the power to regulate social space and to appear as a phantasm.[126] Fanon further engages with Hegel through a recitation of the parable of lordship and enslavement. For the most part, he accepts Hegel's formulation of the centrality of recognition that leads him to the strange notion that since enslavement ended as a result of white generosity there is a lack of the necessary recognition of the humanity of Black people in the period after slavery.[127]

---

123. Fanon, *Wretched*, 51.
124. Ibid., 258.
125. Fanon, *Black Skins*, 91. At this point in the book, Fanon describes the contorted moves that a Black person needs to make in relation to white people.
126. Here Fanon capitalizes "the Other." He uses the construction: colonialist Other and colonized Self. He uses lower case to refer to another generic human being. Ibid., 92. For Bhabha, Fanon rejects the Hegelian–Marxist dialectic that resolves into a more just universal order, particularly the way Black people can be construed through a strict reading of Hegel. Bhabha, *Location of Culture*, 341.
127. Fanon, *Black Skins*, 194–5.

In the end, Fanon suggests a strident assertion of Black identity as the means to break through the myth of otherness, or as Bhabha puts it, "their ethnocentric margin."[128] The path of recovery lies in "disalienation."[129] As Fanon offers, "Since the Other was reluctant to recognize me, there was only one answer: to make myself known."[130]

The ambivalences of colonial identity provide the space for me to bring Bhabha closer to the center of this exploration. Bhabha makes generous use of Fanon in his writings, as seen in his essay "Interrogating Identity," which takes its point of departure from Fanon's narration of Black life under the white gaze. More than simply the abstract view of two parties, Bhabha indicates that the implication of the colonizer's gaze is the production of the fractured being of the colonized: "The white man's eyes break up the black man's body." He reads Fanon as inveighing against the Western philosophic constructs of humanity and the way these constructs do violence to Black bodies, what he regards as an "act of epistemic violence." Sutured through with negative stereotypes, the Western intellectual tradition falls under its own weight, "its own frame of reference is transgressed, its field of vision disturbed"[131] by the colonial context. Given how he reads Fanon's indictment of colonialism and the Western philosophic tradition, Bhabha pursues his interests in both sides of the binary.

Bhabha highlights the implications of Fanon's thought regarding the identity of the colonizer. The racist constructions of colonial society are not without their impact upon the colonizer, despite the pretense to the contrary. Bhabha characterizes the legacies of colonial oppression as "a perversion" where the figure of the colonized, the "dark reflection," haunts the colonizer and "distorts his outline, breaches his boundaries, repeats his action at a distance, disturbs and divides the very time of his being."[132] The issue of otherness that Bhabha picks up, following Fanon, therefore is not the opposition of self and other but rather what Bhabha considers as "the otherness of the Self inscribed in the perverse palimpsest of colonial identity." That is to say, the aspects of white identity that emerge as a result of colonialism as a regime of oppression that effectively leads those colonized to embrace their secondary status.

---

128. Bhabha, *Location of Culture*, 340.
129. Fanon, *Black Skins*, 206.
130. Ibid., 95.
131. Bhabha, *Location of Culture*, 60.
132. Ibid., 62.

Bhabha has an eye to the way subjectivity becomes intersubjectivity, and, therefore, is alert to the fact that colonizers suffer from colonialization. The axes of identity that operate in colonized society turn both ways. Therefore, the distortion of Black identity has corresponding effects upon white identity. Bhabha explains this process of identification by way of three principles. First, that being is always navigated in relation to an otherness. Secondly, these relational negotiations caught up with demand and longing produce an identity that is split. And thirdly, identity is not fixed or even inherent but produced in relation to otherness.[133]

Bhabha captures the Hegelian contours of Fanon's foregrounding of blackness as an interpellation. While Fanon moves to the point of the assertion of blackness as a resistant mode, Bhabha examines the limits of white colonial societies' construction of blackness. Inherent in the demand to code blackness in its recognizable stereotypes—or even to desire the invisibility of blackness—lies what Bhabha regards as "the subject's *transitive* demand for a *direct* object of self-reflection."[134] The self cannot exist without the other! This reality, though, can be lost upon the self that imagines an analogous relation with the other where the appearance of self-sufficiency, and perhaps superiority, informs what Bhabha draws from Roland Barthes as "symbolic consciousness."[135] Bhabha shapes his concerns, though, in the direction of discursive strategy, since the real issue is not "an ontological problem of being."[136] In the turn to literary production, Bhabha pays attention to the binary of the image and reality in the representation of the other. Language and articulation supply the details of the need for knowledge of the other. Bhabha presents this split as a spatial one, where text/image "makes *present* something that is *absent*."[137] The image must be seen for what it is, a substitute, an artifice, a symbol. Otherwise, this image overtakes reality and consequently overdetermines the other. In the end, the construction of the other through discursive practices satisfies the colonizers need for an other in order to stabilize its own identity. Bhabha concludes: "Identification, as it is spoken in the *desire of the Other*, is always a question of interpretation, for it's the elusive assignation of myself with a one-self, the elision of person and place."[138]

---

133. Ibid., 63.
134. Ibid., 67 (emphasis in the original).
135. Ibid., 69.
136. Ibid., 71.
137. Ibid., 73 (emphasis in the original).
138. Ibid., 74 (emphasis in the original).

Ahmed's work on the stranger exceeds the masculinist range of either Fanon or Bhabha as she considers global women of color subsumed under universalist feminist approaches. She uses the experiences of women to show how distance and silence reproduce global women of color in colonialist assumptions of otherness. Therefore, the veiled woman reads only as oppressed because she is unlike the emancipated Western woman. Never mind the historical knowledge and varied subjectivities of women who choose to veil that can reveal greater diversity and complexity of women's agency. Being unlike the liberated Western woman means that veiled women are both recognizable (this is what we once we were) and strange.[139] Ahmed's evocation of stranger confronts the Hegelian preoccupation around recognition. In this regard, she resonates with Fanon and Bhabha in their awareness of how the gaze structures otherness. Ahmed uses surveillance as a security apparatus to think through otherness; in this case the figure of the stranger. On this point, Ahmed expands the range of the colonial and arguably postcolonial condition as Fanon and Bhabha conceive it. Rather than discrete historical encounters in the modern European colonialism of Fanon and Bhabha, she presses further backward and forward to interrogate prior encounters as well as the mode of encounters. The limited historical wells that Fanon and Bhabha draw from restrict the ways they conceive the problem as belonging to discrete historical moments and participants. In fact, the social organizations and constructs already prepare the ground for the encounters.

Ahmed's work helps me to situate the other within the swirling vortex of postcoloniality that plays out in contemporary communities through state and community disciplining of racially marked bodies. The figure of the stranger remains evocative in Western societies increasingly under the siege of white anxieties that direct their vitriol to immigrants and racialized others. The impact of the externalization of such violence, Ahmed reminds us, serves to make the danger from within unintelligible, since danger is exclusively seen as coming from the outside. Therefore, the equipping power of patriarchy along with other home-grown oppressive ideologies that render domestic actors into "monsters" or "strangers," or whatever term that rhetorically sets them outside of normative society, remain unexamined since "the ultimate violent strangers are hence figured as immigrants."[140]

---

139. Ahmed, *Strange Encounters*, 166.

140. Ibid., 36. José Ramírez Kidd sets a useful path to understand the figure of the stranger in biblical texts. He examines the use of the term גר in legal texts and shows how the figure of the stranger as embedded in the term גר applies to persons outside and inside of the community (11). He concludes that ancient Israel as a corporate

Theorizing otherness for reading biblical texts requires asking more than simply how or why the other is reproduced in the ways they are in these texts. The burden of the question more often than not gets at the ontology of the other rather than the encounters—across diverse temporal and spatial locations—that shape the recognition that this body already is not like us. Ahmed presents this reality as a source of anguish for the self because the stranger, as distant as the self would wish it to be, remains close by. The stranger haunts the self, forcing the self to open up to the world in ways that cannot be fulfilled. Ahmed's stranger is neither Hegel's dialectic pair that resolves in an asymmetrical inversion, nor yet Girard's mimetic double, or even Lacan's misrecognized other. Somewhat closer to Fanon and Bhabha, Ahmed's stranger becomes a source of frustration for the self: "the self becomes an opening, a boundless space of torment, the tiredness of being by the other, and of being with and for that which is *not yet*."[141] In naming the prophetic corpus' preoccupation with the other, the postcolonial intervention becomes necessary to trace ways in which the other as subject is produced in these texts. That exploration also gets at the historical relationships that remain obscured and hidden by the reproduction of the other as a previously unknown entity.

Otherness and Prophetic Literature

Perhaps due to the intractability of critical theory but more to the point the inapplicability of modern theoretical models to the ancient world, biblical scholars shy away from full-on use of theory to read otherness in biblical texts. Authors instead opt for the stripped-down notion of the other as the negative element in a pair as the basis for their reading.[142] My point here is not so much about the use of non-use of critical theory in biblical studies. There are others who warn against both the use and overuse of theory, and even advocate for a new use of theory.[143] Deploying theory

---

entity takes on the identity of the stranger based upon the experiences of individuals (133). In other words, the stranger not only lies within but participates in facilitating greater social cohesion. José E. Ramírez Kidd, *Alterity and Identity in Israel*, BZAW 283 (Berlin: de Gruyter, 1999).

141. Ahmed, *Strange Encounters*, 139 (emphasis in the original).

142. One notable exception is Dominic S. Irudayaraj, *Violence, Otherness, and Identity in Isaiah 63:1-6: The Trampling One Coming from Edom*, LHBOTS 633 (London/New York: Bloomsbury T&T Clark, 2017). I do not treat this work here, as Irudayaraj's essay in this volume provides a representative version of the book.

143. See Stephen D. Moore and Yvonne Sherwood, *The Invention of the Biblical Scholars: A Critical Manifesto* (Minneapolis, MN: Fortress, 2011), 15. Stephen Moore highlights how post-poststructuralism offers a use of theory in a turn away

differently demonstrates how biblical texts can highlight interconnectedness as a result of modern colonialism previously missed in the way that Mary Mills does in her examination of the ties between the prophet and the land.[144] The inclusion of the land and other aspects of creation can help make the point that the stranger is already known.

The essential claim of the prophetic corpus rests with the creation of a better self. This call to amelioration imagines the state of apostasy as a state of otherness, an alienation from the true self. The true self does not exist in the past—except perhaps in mythical contexts such as wilderness as imagined by Jeremiah's presentation of the dutiful bride (2:2)—but in the future. The present that the prophetic literature depicts engages with otherness in multiple ways. Numerous images and reference points are used to depict sin as an intolerable form of difference. The images and references used in prophetic literature run the gamut from appropriate to uncomfortable, from rhetorically effective to opportunistic, and also from the sublime to the outrageous. Images, statements, or even inferences of otherness do not simply appear but form out of systems of value reflecting the material relations of their time.

Prophetic literature splits along several binaries in addition to the sinful/ redeemed axis.[145] As the main paradigm for the prophetic corpus, the axis of sin lines up groups of people—inside and outside of Israel/Judah—on different sides. Gender and nationality serve as the most notable dividing line. Women—whether native or not—in all their threatening foreignness are a source of anxiety and targets of violence. Gomer as Hosea's wife and the other purported wives of the book of Hosea, presumably Israelite, are as vilified and the subject to violence as the foreign-born unnamed woman of Ezekiel 16. The being and body of the outsider also represent a site of disquiet. Second Isaiah particularly singles out Babylonian deities and their religious systems for scathing ridicule (particularly Isa. 44:9-20).

---

from language and therefore a focus on the non-human. Stephen D. Moore, *Gospel Jesuses and Other Nonhumans: Biblical Criticism Post-poststructuralism*, SemeiaSt 89 (Atlanta, GA: SBL, 2017), 3.

144. Mary Mills uses Charles Taylor's *Sources of the Self* to delineate three streams of European self-identity: theistic, rationalism, and expressivism, in order to pursue two main concerns: the spatiality and the body in space as expressions of the other (21). She shows how the prophets as agents of the divine have to navigate space even as their bodies are the colonized spaces upon which the nation's resistance and its future are staged. Mary E. Mills, *Alterity, Pain, and Suffering in Isaiah, Jeremiah, and Ezekiel*, LHBOTS 479 (New York: T&T Clark, 2007), 28.

145. Notably, Ben Zvi offers a ternary rather than a binary structure as present within biblical texts; us, them, and an in-between. Ben Zvi, "Othering," 21.

Foreign lands and their culture are devalued, as seen in the oracles against the nations. Ezekiel focuses attention on the Egyptian pharaoh as well as Egypt in extended oracles (Ezek. 29–32). Tyre also gains Ezekiel's attention with a volume of words that outweighs its geographical size but not its geopolitical importance (Ezek. 26:1–28:19).

Foreign people, land, religion, and their military structures occupy notable spaces in prophetic literature, and are all coded as strange in ways that mark what Ahmed presents as the fact that they do not seem to bring a reasonable purpose to their presence. Ahmed's conception of the stranger as other helps us to see how foreignness functions in prophetic literature. Ahmed highlights one aspect of the definition of the stranger as those that *"do not enter into exchanges of capital that transforms spaces into places."*[146] Strangers are takers rather than makers and therefore they do not belong. Whether their contributions are measured in economic or religious values as the prophetic texts may indicate, strangers, unless they are what Ben Zvi regards as being "Israelitized,"[147] are an unwelcome presence in places that become allergic to differences, particularly differences that diverge from what are seen as the norms that define the community. Particular prophetic texts represent this tension over the outsider. The marked difference over the foreigner's place in the pilgrimage stands out in the shared peace poem in Isaiah and Micah (Isa. 2:1-4; cf. Mic. 4:1-5). The additional verses in Micah (vv. 4-5), missing in Isaiah, indicate a different conception of the outsider's relationship with Jerusalem. While Isaiah imagines the global excursion from a universalist perspective, Micah depicts it as a diverse gathering of peoples where differences remain intact. Zechariah's conception of a global journey to Jerusalem similarly takes on Isaiah's perspective, where pilgrims will observe the festival of Succoth (Zech. 14:16-19). Of course, there is more than one perspective on this matter in the prophetic books, making an unequivocal position difficult to determine. However, the presence of different positions on religious participation or diversity in these texts may reveal both a struggle to come to terms with otherness as well as the reality that the prophetic corpus conveys a mechanism that marks, values, and regulates strangers.

Women serve as another preoccupation with otherness in prophetic literature. Women are named—Gomer (Hos. 1:2-3), Oholah and Oholibah (Ezek. 23:4)—but mostly unnamed in prophetic texts. Naming garners women greater notoriety as seen in the differences between the unnamed

---

146. Ahmed, *Strange Encounters*, 31 (emphasis in the original).
147. Ben Zvi, "Othering," 27.

woman in Ezekiel 16 and the sisters of ch. 23. In any event, gendering, whether women *qua* woman, spaces, or places, creates bodily representations that, Ahmed offers, invokes the skin as a site of contact in order to point out the threat posed by strange bodies.[148] In the case of women or the feminization of cities, the skin of bodies as sites of sexual contact hovers in the text as a reminder of the danger of this other and othered body. Women in these prophetic texts, women as sexual objects—particularly their body parts—stand as the ultimate stranger inside. Their proximity and intimacy in all the productive functions of home—whether the household or the city—means that they hover in the space of menace as Bhabha would have it and the space of encounter in a Lacanian fashion.

The skin functions in prophetic literature as the marker of gender as danger. Figures of women appear in these texts as mostly sexual actors. Jeremiah directs recognition to spaces sexualized by the practices of the female body (Jer. 3:1-3) in a conflation that devalues both space and the woman. The text offers a striking face-to-face encounter with the woman that immediately presents negative judgement upon her. With "the forehead of a whore" (Jer. 3:3, NRSV), the encounter with this face equates alterity with ontology. In the case of Nahum, femininized Nineveh's body deserves exposure and humiliation (Nah. 3:5). The narrative of her misdeeds inscribed upon her body fixes the body in the popular gaze as recognizably other. Both these women as well as other women and depictions of women in prophetic texts use the skin of women to mark them as decidedly separate. The standard term in the prophetic texts for these women, *zōnah* is used "to describe female characters and their sexual actions."[149] As Rhiannon Graybill goes on to observe, women's bodies serve as representative geography of a variety of open spaces—land, cities, fields—as sites upon which prophetic messages are written.[150] Such inscription amounts to catachresis as Gayatri Spivak understands it—"a metaphor in abuse."[151] Through the metaphor, prophetic texts imply an idealized woman behind these negative portrayals of women.

Women appear in other non-sexualized guises in prophetic literature that are equally problematic. In these instances, to mark women's bodies is to foreground danger. The encounter between Jeremiah and the women in the refugee community in Egypt offers a telling example of the danger

---

148. Ahmed, *Strange Encounters*, 46.

149. Rhiannon Graybill, *Are We Not Men? Unstable Masculinity in the Hebrew Prophets* (New York: Oxford University Press), 53.

150. Ibid., 51.

151. Gayatri Chakravorty Spivak, *An Aesthetic Education in the Era of Globalization* (Cambridge, MA: Harvard University Press, 2012), 70.

of female bodies (Jer. 44). In this story the women silenced and erased in various ways in the book talk back to Jeremiah, or as Fanon puts it in reference to protesting racism, "to shout my blackness."[152] This narrative invokes earlier references to women's bodies in ritual spaces where women's leadership and participation are coded in negative ways (Jer. 7:17-18). Foreign space combines with non-normative gender performances to make for an explosive mix that the logic of the narrative twists into a win for Jeremiah (Jer. 44:20-22).[153] The text's potent force repeats rhetoric seen in earlier parts of the book of Jeremiah but this time singles out women for special mention in order to call out their problematic presence. In fact, this call out of women attempts to close them off, unlike the openness of women that Graybill refers to as peculiar to prophetic texts. To close off vocal and dissident women further splits the representation in an attempt to populate negative stereotypes with further details.

Hall provides a useful summary of fetishism from three different perspectives that apply to the appearance of the other in prophetic texts. From an anthropological position, Hall thinks of fetishism as the substitution of divinity for ordinary things that can acquire the power of the divine. Therefore, the danger of women to supersede what is seen as the divine patriarchal order or even to render reality uncertain makes them threats both to ritual life and the absolute monotheistic view that suppressed the goddess. Foreigners, with their binary theism, serve a similar threat in need of control. As a Marxist concept, Hall interprets fetishism as the capacity of the worker's labor to transform products that can be purchased that gives workers the awareness of their independence. To release women and foreigners from the disciplinary regimes that control their bodies and spaces those bodies occupy flattens the world and calls for a type of responsibility unlike the type of violence that prophetic texts advocate as solutions to intractable problems. Then thirdly, Hall points out that the psychological conception of fetishism is that of the displaced sex drive from the penis that leads to the eroticization of another body part. The hypersexual presentations of women and in some instances of foreign men (e.g. Ezek. 23:12-21) suggest sexual fascination that belies their denunciation.[154]

---

152. Fanon, *Black Skins*, 101.

153. See Steed Vernyl Davidson, "'Every Green Tree and the Streets of Jerusalem': Counter Constructions of Gendered Sacred Space in the Book of Jeremiah," in *Constructions of Space IV: Further Developments in Examining Ancient Israel's Social Space*, ed. Mark K. George, LHBOTS 569 (New York: Bloomsbury, 2013), 128–9.

154. Hall, "The Spectacle of the 'Other,'" 267.

From any of these three perspectives, prophetic texts reveal the fear/desire of the other. Binaries may not ultimately hold, as the apparent animus may in fact reveal histories of encounter and relationships that are masked in the texts. Ahmed notes how stranger fetishism traffics in tropes and images that hide prior and perhaps existing relationships. Prophetic texts may well indicate much more commerce—financial, social, and otherwise—between ancient Israel and its neighbors both far and near. Possibly the names and characterizations of the named entities may be meaningless and not reflective of actual histories. This raises the question Ahmed asks in relation to the modern stranger fetishism, "what are the social relationships (involving both fantasy and materiality) that are concealed."[155] Randall Bailey studies the number and nature of references to African nations in the Hebrew Bible. In doing so, he not only points to histories not fully explored in the texts and exegesis of these texts, but to the type of encounters that represent "these nations as standards against which to evaluate Israel."[156] The intermingled modes of sexual, ethnic, geographic, and religious otherness that appear in these texts hint at the circulation of difference in the world behind these texts. Prophetic texts seemingly participate in what Bhabha refers to as "a narrative economy of voyeurism and fetishism."[157]

The neat fiction of the containment of the other through the pursuit of righteousness ultimately proves to be fictive. The other is not as far removed as the representation may indicate. The self is not as independent and autonomous as it would like to imagine, much to its own horror. Instead, the preoccupation with the other reveals a narcissism like that which Ahmed notes in Western feminism. The other serves to indicate what the self once was and functions as a point of reference.[158] Such narcissism can fuel the message of prophetic texts to call the self away from what it was. The other serves as a convenient device to illustrate what not to be. In this regard, like other systems prophetic texts betray the fear/desire of the other. Far from eliminating otherness, prophetic texts require those forms of difference to persist in order to generate meaning.

---

155. Ahmed, *Strange Encounters*, 5.
156. Randall C. Bailey, "Beyond Identification: The Use of Africans in Old Testament Poetry and Narratives," in *Stony the Road We Trod: African American Biblical Interpretation*, ed. Cain Hope Felder (Minneapolis, MN: Fortress, 1991), 178.
157. Bhabha, *Location of Culture*, 98.
158. Ahmed, *Strange Encounters*, 166.

Conclusion

The long life of the critical conception of otherness means that prophetic texts may contain more intentional reflective thought on the construction of otherness that we are initially inclined to offer. Naturally, the categories of self/other do not appear in the language of the texts. These categories appear to us in starker relief through the help of the various theories I explore here, as well as others not looked at here. We know for a fact that the prophetic tradition used the stranger, the foreigner, or the other as a means to warn and encourage hearers. The diversity of representations suggests the multiple ways available in the ancient world and across human history to construct otherness. Rather than a fixed category, the other becomes what is needed as determined by context. The malleability of the figure of the other facilitates its various spatial, temporal, and other representations. Texts like the prophetic corpus that blur time can make the other appear in whatever form possible. The elasticity of representation is only mirrored by the numerous theoretical conceptions that offer readers several interpretative possibilities for the reading of prophetic literature.

Chapter 3

Edom, the Proximate "Other": A Social Identity Reading of Isaiah 63:1-6*

Dominic S. Irudayaraj

Introduction

Within Isaiah 56–66, an explicit "prospect of great salvation" in Isaiah 60–62 is flanked by "two words of doom" in the two warrior panels in chs 59 and 63.[1] Of these two panels, the present chapter's focus is on the second one. If words of doom are disturbing, equally disconcerting are some of the depictions of God and the "other" in the Bible. The description of the Trampling One in Isaiah 63 is an illustrative instance. The text presents the *Trampling One* in blood-stained garments as he comes after treading the winepress alone (v. 3) and trampling the people in anger (v. 6). And he is identified as the *One Coming from Edom* (v. 1). Why Edom?

---

* I gratefully acknowledge Professor Steed V. Davidson for the opportunity to partake and learn from the two SBL sessions on *Prophetic Otherness*. See Dominic S. Irudayaraj, "Edom, the Proximate 'Other': Persisting Category and Permeable Boundary: A Social Identity Reading of Isaiah 63:1-6," presented to the 'Israelite Prophetic Literature' section (SBL Annual Meeting, San Diego, CA, 2014). The same paper evolved and became part of my doctoral thesis, which is now a monograph: *Violence, Otherness and Identity in Isaiah 63:1-6: The Trampling One Coming from Edom*, LHBOTS 633 (London: Bloomsbury T&T Clark, 2017). Reused with the kind permission of T&T Clark, an imprint of Bloomsbury Publishing Plc.

1. On the said contrast, see Jan L. Koole, *Isaiah, vol. 3*, HCOT (Leuven: Peeters, 2001), 328.

Edom's prevalence[2] in the Old Testament can hardly be missed even by a cursory reading. Starting from Genesis and going up to Malachi, Edom makes its presence felt in every major section of the Old Testament. Within the book of Isaiah, Edom appears first in ch. 11. In the description of the ingathering of the dispersed (11:12), the nations are presented as the objects of plunder for the returnees. Edom is one of them (see 11:14).[3] Edom features again in ch. 34. The LORD summons the nations so that they may witness a sweeping catastrophe that awaits Edom. Finally, ch. 63 presents the Trampling One as "coming from Edom" (63:1). Thus the plunder foretold in ch. 11 and the anticipated destruction in ch. 34 find fulfillment by the divine warrior's march from Edom.[4] They together present a complete (perhaps, a completed) story, but a troubling story.

Why is Edom singled out? Neither in Isaiah 63 nor elsewhere in the Bible is there any consensus as to why Edom was the object of unrelenting animosity.[5] Scholars have proposed various reasons, including: (1) Edom's anti-Judean attitude and acts during the Babylonian conquest and the subsequent exile (see Ps. 137:7; Obad. 8-15);[6] (2) the Edomite

---

2. Edom occurs 98 times, Edomite 7 times, and Edomites 13 times. See C. W. Lyons and Thomas Deliduka, *The Catholic Bible Concordance: Revised Standard Version, Catholic Edition* (Steubenville, OH: Emmaus Road, 2009), 514–15.

3. Patricia Tull avers that the list is a recollection of the "the neighboring lands that David once subdued—Philistia, Edom, Moab, and Ammon." See Patricia K. Tull, *Isaiah 1–39*, SHBC (Macon, GA: Smyth & Helwys, 2010), 236. Childs suggests that this harsh and nationalistic tone needs to be "understood as part of the righteous rule" (11:4ff.). See Brevard Childs, *Isaiah: A Commentary*, OTL (Louisville, KY: Westminster John Knox, 2001), 106.

4. See Shalom Paul, *Isaiah 40–66: Translation and Commentary*, ECC (Grand Rapids, MI: Eerdmans, 2012), 562: "The motif of God coming from Edom is found in other biblical traditions as well" (see Deut. 33:2; Judg. 5:4; Hab. 3:3). Drawing from various scholars, Koole observes that "God comes precisely from this direction to give his people victory." See Koole, *Isaiah*, 3:332. Yahweh's "March in the South" theophany tradition includes Judg. 5:5; Ps. 68:9, 18; Deut. 33:2; and Hab. 3:3-4. "The arguments in favor of the antiquity of the poems" were proposed by W. F. Albright. The same arguments were then expanded by Cross, Freedman, and Miller. For relevant sources, see Thomas B. Dozeman, *God at War: Power in the Exodus Tradition* (New York: Oxford University Press, 1996), 82 n. 85.

5. Bruce Cresson's summarizing phrase captures such animosity: it is a "damn Edom theology." Bruce C. Cresson, "The Condemnation of Edom in Post-Exilic Judaism," in *Use of the Old Testament in the New and Other Essays: Studies in Honor of William Franklin Stinespring*, ed. James M. Efird (Durham, NC: Duke University Press, 1972), 125–48. As quoted in Tull, *Isaiah 1–39*, 521 n. 19.

6. See R. N. Whybray, *Isaiah 40–66*, NCBC (Grand Rapids, MI: Eerdmans, 1984), 253; Koole, *Isaiah*, 331.

incursion into Judean land[7]; (3) the redemption of Zion comes only after the judgment of her enemies—Edom included; and (4) Edom is merely a representative of the nations.[8] Recent scholarly observations situate the animosity in the context of a dual relation, that is, Edom as Israel's enemy and brother.[9]

Edom was Israel's closest neighbor in more than one way. This essay argues that the Isaian depiction of Edom in 63:1-6 can be correlated to the proximity between them. For this purpose, a socially cued reading may prove profitable. Some of the key findings of a Social Identity Approach[10]

---

7. Textual as well as archaeological witnesses are adduced to underscore this claim. As regards the textual, Dicou sees such pointers in Ezek. 35:10; Obad. 19–20; Amos 9:12. See Bert Dicou, *Edom, Israel's Brother and Antagonist: The Role of Edom in Biblical Prophecy and Story*, JSOTSup 169 (Sheffield: Sheffield Academic, 1994), 186. For archeological evidences, see Alexander Fantalkin and Oren Tal, "Redating Lachish Level I: Identifying Achaemenid Imperial Policy at the Southern Frontier of the Fifth Satrapy," in *Judah and the Judeans in the Persian Period*, ed. O. Lipschits and M. Oeming (Winona Lake, IN: Eisenbrauns, 2006), 167–97 (178–9). See also Itzhaq Beit-Arieh, "The Edomites in Cisjordan," in *You Shall Not Abhor an Edomite for He Is Your Brother: Edom and Seir in History and Tradition*, ed. D. V. Edelman, ABS 3 (Atlanta, GA: Scholars Press, 1995), 33–40. See further in John W. Wright, "Remapping Yehud: The Borders of Yehud and the Genealogies of Chronicles," in Lipschitz and Oeming (eds), *Judah and the Judeans in the Persian Period*, 87.

8. Whybray, *Isaiah 40–66*, 253; Matthew J. Lynch, "Zion's Warrior and the Nations: Isaiah 59:15b–63:6 in Isaiah's Zion Traditions," *CBQ* 70 (2008): 256–7; Gary V. Smith, *Isaiah 40–66*, NAC 15B (Nashville, TN: B&H, 2009), 657. On the ideological and theological significance of the hostility towards Edom, see Elie Assis, "Why Edom? On the Hostility towards Jacob's Brother in Prophetic Sources," *VT* 56 (2006): 1–20. Assis's recent work is a further adumbration of how identity and chosenness inform such an animosity. See Elie Assis, *Identity in Conflict: The Struggle between Esau and Jacob, Edom and Israel*, Siphrut: Literature and Theology of the Hebrew Scriptures 19 (Winona Lake, IN: Eisenbrauns, 2016).

9. Drawing from such a scholarly trend, Childs wonders if "Third Isaiah's use of Edom addresses another aspect of his understanding of the continuing sharp polarity within the household of Israel." See Childs, *Isaiah*, 516. For an extensive survey of the scholarly views on the animosity towards Edom, see Dicou, *Edom, Israel's Brother and Antagonist*.

10. The Social Identity Approach (SIA) has made a recent entry into the horizon of biblical exegesis and has been employed to study the New Testament (e.g.: Galatians) and Dead Sea Scrolls (e.g.: *pesharim*). See Jutta Jokiranta, "Social-Scientific Approaches to the Dead Sea Scrolls," in *Rediscovering the Dead Sea Scrolls: An Assessment of Old and New Approaches and Methods*, ed. Maxine L. Grossman (Grand Rapids, MI: Eerdmans, 2010), 246–63.

together with the concept of a heuristic category *proximate "other"*[11] are employed here not only to situate the unrelenting animosity but also to underscore the prophetic revival of identity.

Proximate "Other": A Heuristic Category

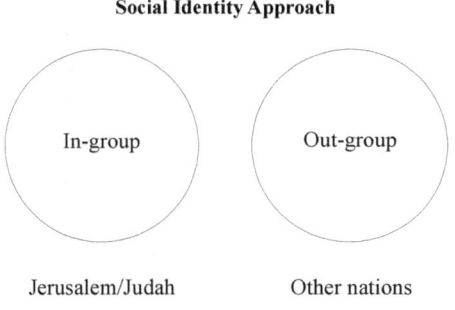

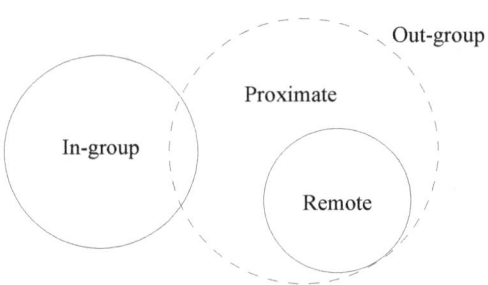

Figure 1. The Proximate "Other"[12]

11. For details, see Jonathan Z. Smith, "What a Difference a Difference Makes," in *"To See Ourselves as Others See Us": Christians, Jews, "Others" in Late Antiquity*, ed. Jacob Neusner, Ernest S. Frerichs, and Caroline McCracken-Flesher (Chico, CA: Scholars Press, 1985), 3–48. For an application of proximate "other," see Nathaniel Deutsch, "The Proximate Other: The Nation of Islam and Judaism," in *Black Zion: African American Religious Encounters with Judaism*, ed. Yvonne Patricia Chireau and Nathaniel Deutsch (New York: Oxford University Press, 2000), 91–117.

12. Whereas a cursory reading of the biblical depiction of Jerusalem/Judah vis-à-vis the other nations may point to two clearly demarcated boundaries (see the left panel of the figure), a closer scrutiny—especially in the case of Edom—may point to a porous boundary (as indicated by the dotted circle). See the subsection "3.3 The Permeable Boundary" below.

The Proximate "Other"[13]

Jonathan Z. Smith has aptly observed that in inter-group and inter-personal interactions, often "the problem is not alterity, but similarity—at times, even identity."[14] Every attempt to plot the contours of "self" is inevitably achieved in tandem with a theory of "other." Often, the "other" serves merely as a counterfoil to the "self." Going beyond the traditionally held binaries of "they" and "we," Smith has introduced further nuances: "the 'other' may be perceived as being either LIKE-US or NOT-LIKE-US, he [sic] is, in fact, most problematic when he [sic] is TOO-MUCH-LIKE-US, or when he [sic] claims to BE-US."[15] In short, the "other" may be perceived as either a proximate or a remote other (see Figure 1).

Of these two, "the proximate 'other' is problematic, and hence of supreme interest."[16] While the proximate other's closeness makes it attractive and calls out for active engagement, its NEAR-IDENTITY-TO-US challenges us. Responses in such situations are formulated with great urgency—an urgency which is not so much motivated by our desire to place the "other" as by our longing to situate ourselves. In other words, responses are not aimed at "expulsion" of the "other" but are typically marked by "adjustment."[17]

Theorists of social identity[18] have also noted that identity can be "threatened by...groups that are [very] similar to one's own group,

---

13. Jonathan Smith, a theorist of religion, has helped popularize this term. Interestingly, his elucidation encompasses two illustrations from two unlikely—even unrelated—areas: taxonomy in the history of parasitology and the "discovery" of America (Columbus trying to understand the new in terms of the old). See Smith, "What a Difference a Difference Makes," 251–302. Smith's phrase (proximate "other") is quite appealing because the term aptly brings out the odd juxtaposition of contrasting features. This chapter follows Smith's convention.

14. Ibid., 275.

15. Jonathan Z. Smith, *Relating Religion: Essays in the Study of Religion* (Chicago: University of Chicago Press, 2004), 275.

16. Ibid., 253.

17. Smith uses C. Lévi-Strauss's 'micro-adjustment' to explain this dynamic. See Smith, *Relating Religion*, 301 n. 186.

18. Henri Tajfel, the founder of Social Identity Theory, formulated his questions on identity and intergroup bias by drawing from his experiences during and after the World War II. Tajfel, a Polish Jew studying in France, was summoned to fight during the war. He was captured, but because he was thought to be French, he ended up in a prisoner of war camp rather than a concentration camp. His post-war work among the war refugees propelled him to bring his experience-based insights in conversation with the prevailing social psychological views of his time, particularly those of Floyd Allport. Tajfel found the latter's views to be wanting, especially in delineating adequate explanation to Tajfel's experience. Tajfel therefore quizzed "How

motivating differentiation and possibly also discrimination."[19] This is so because the proximate "other" frustrates the search for distinct identity. For our purpose of reading the Isaian text, these observations are grouped under three aspects of proximate "other": (1) Edom as Israel's "other" *persists*; (2) the boundary between Israel and Edom is anything but impermeable; (3) as a result, ambivalence abounds in such discourses. Further, such discourses of the "other" stem from the agonistic setting where identity construction and revival are earnestly pursued. These categories (see Figure 2) serve as heuristic guideposts to situate the anti-Edomite sentiments within the identity-reviving vision of the prophet.

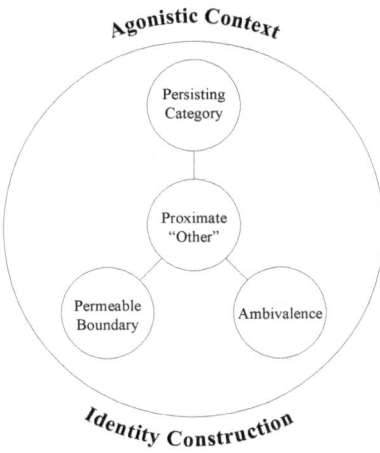

Figure 2. Proximate "other": A Conceptual Schema

people who had been living together as neighbors…could come to see each other as dangerous enemies even when there were no rational or objective reasons to do so." For details, see Naomi Ellemers and S. Alexander Haslam, "Social Identity Theory," in *Handbook of Theories of Social Psychology, vol. 2*, ed. Paul A. M. V. Lange, A. W. Kruglanski, and E. T. Higgins (Thousand Oaks, CA: SAGE, 2012), 380. For a short overview of Tajfel's life and ideas, see John C. Turner, "Henri Tajfel: An Introduction," in *Social Groups and Identities: Developing the Legacy of Henri Tajfel*, ed. W. P. Robinson, International Series in Social Psychology (Oxford: Butterworth-Heinemann, 1996), 1–23. On Allport's view, see Floyd H. Allport, *Social Psychology* (New York: Houghton Mifflin, 1924), 4.

On the relevance as well as the limitations of SIA for reading some of the ancient texts—including biblical and Qumran—see my comments in *Violence, Otherness and Identity in Isaiah 63:1-6*, 39–53.

19. See Russell Spears, "Social Identity, Legitimacy, and Intergroup Conflict: The Rocky Road to Reconciliation," in *Social Psychology of Intergroup Reconciliation*, ed. A. Nadler, T. E. Malloy, and J. D. Fisher (New York: Oxford University Press, 2008), 327.

Edom, the Proximate "Other":
A Social Identity Reading of Isaiah 63:1-6

The Babylonian onslaught in 587 BCE dealt fatal blows to Judah's centralizing aspects, such as kingship, land, and temple. The subsequent exile was by no means less unsettling. Israel in exile was Israel in trauma. As a result, the exiled community had to face deep-seated and lingering questions. Those questions included the role and relevance of their God and also the community's identity as God's covenant people ("My people and your God"; Isa. 40:1). The arrival of Cyrus and his edict (see 2 Chron. 36:22-23) may have revived some hope (see Isa. 45:1). But the return to the 'homeland' was not as impressive a reversal of fortunes (for example, Isa. 43) as the returning community would have expected. The discourses and the texts of this time are marked by traces of the community's continued struggle.

While it is hard to determine the exact composition of the community in the Persian province of Yehud, there are nonetheless enough indicators to allow us to reconstruct the atmosphere that must have prevailed in the post-exilic community. The situation was anything but amicable. "The polemic oracles of Third Isaiah"[20] (see 57:3-13; 65:1-7, 11-15; 66:3-4, 17) are considered to be echoes of the internal divisions in the community.[21] As Paul Hanson observes, it was "a community that, even after having returned to Judah, continue[d] to suffer economic and legal deprivation and subjugation under foreign powers."[22] Naturally, such experiences express themselves and leave agonistic[23] traces behind. And Isa. 63:1-6 is imprinted with such traces, to some of which we now turn.

---

20. See Brooks Schramm, *The Opponents of Third Isaiah: Reconstructing the Cultic History of the Restoration*, JSOTSup 193 (Sheffield: JSOT, 1995), 174.

21. Paul Hanson has argued that it was a division between "the hierocrats and the visionaries." Brooks Schramm, however, has proposed that the dissention was between "the official and traditional religious practices." See John T. Strong, review of *The Opponents of Third Isaiah: Reconstructing the Cultic History of the Restoration*, by Brooks Schramm, *CBQ* 58 (1996): 334. For Hanson's views, see Paul D. Hanson, *The Dawn of Apocalyptic: The Historical and Sociological Roots of Jewish Apocalyptic Eschatology* (Philadelphia: Fortress, 1979). And for Schramm's argument, see Schramm, *The Opponents of Third Isaiah*.

22. Paul D. Hanson, *Isaiah 40–66*, Interpretation, a Biblical Commentary for Teaching and Preaching (Louisville, KY: Westminster John Knox, 1995), 234.

23. Here, Chantal Mouffe's description of agonism, in contradistinction to antagonism, is instructive: "Contrary to the antagonistic friend/enemy relation in which… the different sides aim at eliminating their opponent, in an agonistic relation the adversaries share a common symbolic space and they recognize, at least to some degree,

Agonistic Traces in Isaiah 63:1-6

¹ "Who is this coming from Edom,[24]
   from Bozrah in garments of glowing colors?
   Who is this so splendidly robed, stooping (צעה) in his great might?"
   "It is I, announcing vindication, mighty to save."
² "Why is there red on your robes,
   and your garments like theirs who tread the wine press?"
³ "I have trodden the wine press alone,
   and from the peoples no one was with me;
   I trod them in my anger and trampled them in my wrath;
   their juice spattered on my robes,
   and I stained (אגאלתי) all my robes.
⁴ For the day of vengeance was in my heart,
   and the year of my redeeming (גאל) (work) had come.
⁵ I looked, but there was no helper;
   I was appalled (אשתומם), but there was no one to sustain;
   so my own arm brought me victory,
   and my wrath sustained me.
⁶ I trampled down peoples in my anger,
   I made them drunk in my wrath,
and I poured out their lifeblood on the ground."

The Question

A tone of contestation marks the beginning of the divine warrior pericope. The passage begins with an interrogative (מי־זה; v. 1a). The identity of the arriving one is demanded by an inquirer. Strangely, however, the inquirer is already aware of the coming one's originating locus as "Edom" (v. 1a). The inquirer even goes on to give further descriptions of the arriving one: "garments in glowing color" (v. 1a), "splendidly robed," (v. 1a), and "stooping in his great might" (v. 1a). If so much is already known and seen, one might wonder, why should there be any need to ask the "Who" question at all? Perhaps because there is so much that was known, seen, and taken note of, the question had to be posed. In any case, an identity-demanding query is made.

---

the legitimacy of the claims of their opponents." Chantal Mouffe, "An Agonistic Approach to the Future of Europe," *New Literary History* 43 (2012): 632–3. Though stemming from the current European contexts, Mouffe's study nonetheless focuses on group identities, which is relevant for the present purpose.

24. The translation of Isa. 63:1-6 here and elsewhere in the essay are mine. Translations of other biblical texts are from NRSV.

The Response

If the intention of the inquirer were to know the identity of the arriving one by name, the response in v. 1b falls disappointingly short. No name is given. The coming one merely identifies himself as the one "announcing vindication" and "mighty to save" (v. 1b). Refusal to identify oneself by name is not uncommon in the biblical tradition. Further, a name can hardly describe a person completely and much less God. True, the coming one does not reveal his identity by name, but the descriptions do. As Walter Brueggemann observes, "The approaching one is marked by Yahweh's most characteristic terms of 'vindication' (*ṣedeqāh*) and 'salvation' (*yšʿ*)."[25] In addition, the description of him as "coming from Edom" brings to mind the motif of God coming from the South.

Second Question and Response

The agonistic contestation continues by means of a second question, which concerns "the red" on the garments of the coming one (v. 2). Once again, the inquirer sees and says more: the "red" on the robe is compared to that of a wine-treader. An elaborate response follows (vv. 4-6). The response begins by continuing the wine-treading image (see v. 2b || v. 3a) but soon changes into something more intense and severe: "treading in anger and wrath" (vv. 3, 6).

Drawn from the athletic context, the Greek root of *agonistic* underscores that in the *agon*, a keenly engaged contestation is given greater significance than the final outcome (victory/defeat). Against this background, it is reasonable to count the dialogue between the inquirer and the Coming One as agonistic:[26] by the role of questioning and the knowledge of the

---

25. The same word pair also occurs elsewhere in Isaiah (see 61:10; 62:2). See Walter Brueggemann, *Isaiah: 40–66*, 1st ed., Westminster Bible Companion (Louisville, KY: Westminster John Knox, 1998), 226.

26. In the ancient Near Eastern context, where honor and shame played key roles, "question and answer" often served purposes that went beyond information furnishing. Bruce Malina, for instance, views them as "challenge and riposte." A question, as such, is a challenge which makes claim to the social space of the one who is questioned, thus undermining the latter's honor. The riposte, therefore, is the respondent's attempt at regaining one's social space and the attendant honor. See Bruce J. Malina, *The New Testament World: Insights from Cultural Anthropology*, rev. ed. (Louisville, KY: Westminster John Knox, 1993), 35, 40 (passim). For an illustrative study of Second Isaiah which takes recourse to these honor and shame categories, see Sarah J. Dille, "Honor Restored: Honor, Shame and God as Redeeming Kinsman in Second Isaiah," in *Relating to the Text: Interdisciplinary and Form-Critical Insights on the Bible*, ed. T. Sandoval and C. Mandolfo (London: T&T Clark International, 2003), 232–50.

Coming One's origin, the inquirer displays initial advantage; but by the responses that reveal his identity not in name but in redeeming deeds and in the transformation of the grape-treading image, the respondent appears to be equally advantaged. Further, the text does not limit itself to responding to these two explicit questions. The text has also, in the process, laid to rest two other questions that were posed elsewhere in Isaiah. An example of this is the 'hand'||'arm' motif.[27]

Motif of 'hand'|| 'arm'

Lena-Sofia Tiemeyer observes that the "arm" motif is found in Isa. 40:10a; 48:14; 59:16 || 63:5; 62:8a. She underscores how in the book of Deuteronomy the 'hand'||'arm' parallel "function[s] as shorthand for recollecting the Exodus event" (see 4:34; 5:15; 7:19; 11:2; cf. Exod. 15:16).[28] Elsewhere in Isaiah, it is this redeeming/delivering hand that is called into question: "Is my hand shortened, that it cannot redeem? Or have I no power to deliver?" retorts Israel's God in Isa. 50:2. Implied in these words are the deep-seated questions of the post-exilic community concerning the relevance of God. Such contesting questions find a fitting response in Isa. 63:5. The verse recounts the singularity of agency in the trampling act—that the divine warrior was alone (לבדי). If it were possible to miss its significance, the author adds a reiterating parallel phrase "no one" (אין־איש).[29] As such, in this doubly solitary act, it is his "arm" (זרע) which is said to have brought victory. In short, the challenging query in Isa. 50:2 gets a reassuring response in 63:5.

Edom, the Persisting Category

As noted above, Edom is ubiquitous in the Old Testament. Within Isaiah, the pair "Edom-Bozrah" appears twice. The first occurrence is in ch. 34. There, the gory description of a sword "sated with blood" (v. 6) is matched by the garments spattered with blood in 63:3. In ch. 34, the

---

27. The other question concerns the theme of *Coming* (בא) *Salvation.* See Irudayaraj, *Violence, Otherness and Identity in Isaiah 63:1-6*, 76.

28. However, the "hand"||"arm" motif does not in every place indicate good tidings. In Jer. 21:5, a striking inversion occurs where the arm and the hand come combined with anger, fury, and wrath against Zedekiah and Jerusalem. See Tiemeyer, "Continuity and Discontinuity in Isaiah 40–66: History of Research," in *Continuity and Discontinuity: Chronological and Thematic Development in Isaiah 40–66*, ed. L.-S. Tiemeyer and H. M. Barstad, FRLANT 225 (Göttingen: Vandenhoeck & Ruprecht, 2014), 30.

29. For Paul, this "negative parallelism לבדי / אין־איש ('alone/no one') emphasizes God acting alone in the destruction of the adversary." See Paul, *Isaiah 40–66*, 564.

actor is the LORD, the objects of the LORD's rage are the nations (v. 2), but then Edom is singled out (see vv. 5ff.). In contrast, ch. 63 does not provide as much detail. The identity of the questioner is not revealed nor is the identity of the Coming One. The locus of the dialogue also remains elusive. But amidst all these hazy descriptions, Edom is mentioned. Lest one miss its persistence, the text mentions Edom's chief city Bozrah as well. And in the end, the one coming to announce vindication and salvation is identified as "coming from" this "Edom and Bozrah" (see 63:1). The explicit mentioning of Edom with its chief city in a text with its otherwise elusive details tell the tale of Edom as a persisting category.

Permeable Boundary

Geographic Boundary

Biblical tradition narrates the story of shared boundaries between Israel/Judah and Edom. The book of Joshua recounts that the "lot for the tribe of the people of Judah…reached southward to the boundary of Edom" (Josh. 15:1; also v. 21). During the monarchic period, the boundary between these two neighboring nations was sharply contested. Further, Edomite presence in southern Judah is well attested. For example, although Edom lay to the south-east of Judah, "[a]n Edomite ostracon, which includes a reference to their chief god Qos was found at Ḥorvat 'Uza, near Arad."[30] Based on the material evidence, Itzhaq Beit-Arieh affirms that "the Edomite presence in the eastern Negeb is an objective fact" towards the end of Israelite monarchy.[31] Scholars have suggested a similar scenario in the ensuing centuries as well. According to this proposal, the Edomite incursion into and their presence in southern Judah could have been due

---

30. See Bruce C. Cresson, "Edom," in *Eerdmans Dictionary of the Bible*, ed. David N. Freedman (Grand Rapids, MI: Eerdmans, 2000), 373. For an extensive historical survey based on material and textual witnesses, see John R. Bartlett, *Edom and the Edomites*, JSOTSup 77 (Sheffield: Sheffield Academic, 1989), 163–86; MacDonald concurs with Bartlett based on the "Edomite names in ostraca, written in Aramaic, [which]…number about one hundred and date to the late fifth century BCE." See B. MacDonald, "Edom, Edomites," in *Dictionary of the Old Testament: Historical Books*, ed. B. T. Arnold and H. G. M. Williamson (Downers Grove, IL: InterVarsity, 2011), 234.

31. Beit-Arieh, "The Edomites in Cisjordan," 38. The time under consideration is around 600 BCE. See Itzhaq Beit-Arieh, "New Data on the Relationship between Judah and Edom toward the End of the Iron Age," in *Recent Excavations in Israel: Studies in Iron Age Archaeology*, ed. Seymour Gitin and William G. Dever, AASOR 49 (Winona Lake, IN: Eisenbrauns, 1989), 125.

to the Arab pressure on the Edomites and/or the Babylonian exile and the resultant vulnerability of Judean land.[32] So the post-exilic Judean context presents a situation where the geographic boundary between these two not-so-friendly neighboring nations was far from impermeable.

Kinship Boundary

A canonical reading of the relation between Judah and Edom goes as far back as their eponymous ancestors Esau and Jacob.[33] Genesis 26 presents Easu as the closest possible kin, Jacob's twin. The parallel motif of "Edom as Israel's brother" is repeatedly found in the biblical tradition[34] (for example see Deut. 23).[35] But their story has been a story of crossing this kinship boundary especially when it pertained to land and possession. Such violations find echoes in their ancestral stories. Jacob violated the kinship boundary by craftily stealing the blessing and birthright from Esau, the first born son who should have received it.

Religious Boundary

The affinity between Yahweh and Edom/Seʻir is both textually and materially attested. Textually, the Song of Deborah (Judg. 5:4) and the blessing of Moses (Deut. 33:2) speak of Yahweh as coming from Seir, that is, Edom.[36] Materially, an Egyptian inscription from the time of Ramesses II mentions "Shasu of Seʻir" alongside a proper name "Shasu

---

32. George L. Kelm, "Edom/Edomites/Idumaea," in *Mercer Dictionary of the Bible*, ed. W. E. Mills and R. A. Bullard (Macon, GA: Mercer University Press, 1990), 233.

33. Scholars find this story of twin-brothers to be "a clear case of seventh century perceptions presented in more ancient costume," which served as "a divine legitimacy for the political relationship between the two nations in late-monarchic times." See Israel Finkelstein and Amihay Mazar, *The Quest for the Historical Israel: Debating Archaeology and the History of Early Israel*, ed. B. B. Schmidt, SBL Archaeology and Biblical Studies 17 (Atlanta, GA: Society of Biblical Literature, 2007), 47.

34. "Brotherhood" does not always imply an amicable relation. So, Coggins and Re'emi opine, "It is impossible to treat as strict history the idea that Jacob and Esau were literally the founders of the two nations, all of those people were descended from them." See R. J. Coggins and S. P. Re'emi, *Israel Among the Nations: A Commentary on the Books of Nahum, Obadiah, and Esther*, International Theological Commentary (Grand Rapids, MI: Eerdmans, 1985), 70–1.

35. Bartlett, *Edom and the Edomites*, 182.

36. See Finkelstein and Mazar, *The Quest for the Historical Israel*, 71, 95. See also Mark S. Smith, *The Origins of Biblical Monotheism: Israel's Polytheistic Background and the Ugaritic Texts* (New York: Oxford University Press, 2003), 145–6.

Yahwi." However, identifying Edomite religion[37] has so far proved to be a frustrating pursuit. Yet, as John Bartlett argues, within the biblical tradition, which is highly critical of people who worshipped abominations, the silence[38] regarding the god of the Edomites and their worship patterns demands explanation. This silence, in addition to the textual and material witnesses, may indicate that in the eyes of the Israelites, the Edomites might have been seen as "co-religionists."[39] These pointers therefore suggest the possibility of a blurred boundary between Judah and Edom in terms of their religious affinity.

Isaiah 63:1-6: A Dialogue at the Boundary?

Shalom Paul proposes to read Isa. 63:1-6 against the backdrop of Isa. 21:11-12. The latter text depicts the One calling from Seʻir, questioning a watchman. Accordingly, Paul finds in the divine warrior pericope a watchman seeing "a rapidly approaching figure and demand[ing] that he identifies himself."[40] In somewhat similar sense, John Sawyer suggests reading 63:1 with 62:6-7. The latter text depicts sentinels on the walls of Jerusalem who will not be silent and will not give rest to the LORD until he re-establishes Jerusalem.[41] Common to both these suggestions is the strong allusion to an image of a sentinel or a watchman. If we assume such a scenario in 63:1, reading our text against the backdrop of shared/blurred boundaries between Edom and Judah makes the story all the more intriguing.

Sentinels typically worked at the border or at boundary locations. At those boundaries an "insider" was differentiated from an "outsider." Precisely at this point, an "outsider" may be granted an "insider" status or vice versa. In short, borders/boundaries—the places at which sentinels work—are at once a dividing symbol and also a point of interaction and

---

37. While the term "religion" can typically connote a complex phenomenon, its use here is limited to cultic places and practices. In this sense, the Edomite "religion" has far less data to offer than those of their neighbors.

38. The only probable exception is 2 Chron. 25:5-24. See Bartlett, *Edom and the Edomites*, 195.

39. Ibid., 185. However, Mark Smith opines that monotheistic belief is not "translatable" to other cultures. See Mark S. Smith, *God in Translation: Deities in Cross-Cultural Discourse in the Biblical World* (Grand Rapids, MI: Eerdmans, 2010), 149–80.

40. See Paul, *Isaiah 40-66*, 561. Others also presuppose a sentinel/watchman as the questioner. See for example Childs, *Isaiah: A Commentary*, 516.

41. See John F. A. Sawyer, *Isaiah, vol. 2*, The Daily Study Bible Series (Louisville, KY: Westminster John Knox, 1986), 196. Koole also reads the chosen text together with Isa. 62:6f. See Koole, *Isaiah*, 3:330–1.

exchange. They are the points of intense contestation and yet creative exchanges. These initial reflections prompt the reader to examine the sentinel's cry in Isaiah 63 for such creative exchanges.

Scholars who support the textual emendation (from צעה "stooping" to צעד "marching") in v. 1 do so because "stooping" does not align well with the description of the Coming One in the rest of the pericope (for example, "greatness of his strength"; v. 1). But Sawyer has argued for retaining צעה ("stooping") because it fits well with other Isaian images, such as "Yahweh as a woman in labor (42.14), an apologetic husband (54.7-8) and a midwife (66.9)."[42]

The only other use of צעה ("stooping") in Isaiah occurs in the context of God's promise of deliverance to the "cowering" ones (exiles?; see 51:14).[43] So, following Sawyer, if the text is retained as it is, we see here a God who is perceived as bearing the mark of the exiles. Nevertheless, it is this "stooping" One who is shown to be coming in "his great strength" in order to announce "deliverance." Thus, "stooping" and "coming in his great strength" need not be construed as divergent descriptions. At the boundary, these disjunctive descriptions are held together. And it is in that odd juxtaposition that the prophetic text locates Israel's Redeeming One. An audacious prophetic imagination depicts its God in terms of the people's past experiences. Such imagination is not limited to the juxtaposition of "stooped" and "greatness of strength," as the next subsection on ambivalence underscores.

Ambivalence

The biblical history narrates a colonial relation between Israel and Edom. Because colonial discourses have been shown to be ambivalent,[44] it is no

---

42. See John F. A. Sawyer, "Radical Images of Yahweh in Isaiah 63," in *Among the Prophets: Language, Image and Structure in the Prophetic Writings*, ed. P. R. Davies and D. J. A. Clines, JSOTSup 144 (Sheffield: JSOT, 1993), 72. Along similar lines, Paul Kim avers that "this portrayal of YHWH whose clothes are spattered with blood may point to the anthropomorphic vulnerability of God." See Hyun Chul Paul Kim, *Reading Isaiah: A Literary and Theological Commentary,* Reading the Old Testament (Macon, GA: Smyth & Helwys, 2016), 284.

43. According to John Oswalt, "'the stooped' are those bent over in chains… [And] the experience of the exile…provide[s] the main stock of images for this section." See John Oswalt, *The Book of Isaiah: Chapters 40–66*, NICOT (Grand Rapids, MI: Eerdmans, 1998), 347.

44. For instance, see Homi K. Bhabha, "Of Mimicry and Man: The Ambivalence of Colonial Discourse," in *The Location of Culture*, 2nd ed. (New York: Routledge, 2004), 121–31. The work of Diandra C. Erickson, in this volume, attends to the "ambivalences" in the construction of the Judean inhabitants as "the other" in

surprise that ambivalence abounds in Judah's depiction of Edom.[45] The historical books recount how Edom was a defeated and subservient entity during part of the monarchic period (see 2 Sam. 8; 2 Kgs 8). Later, Edom revolted (see 2 Kgs 8:20-22) and broke free, and a narrative description adds, "Edom has been in revolt against the rule of Judah to this day" (2 Kgs 8:22).[46] Such a description underscores Judah's (the colonizers') split vision: a vision that stereotypes the colonized nation's breaking free as a "revolt" and, in the process, tacitly asserts Judah's prerogative to rule.

Against this colonial backdrop, the Edomite incursion into and presence in Judah must have appeared to the returning community as nothing less than an audacious act of their once colonized subjects. Edom dared to move into the land of its former colonizer. Colonial relations often stem from and are centered on land/territory. Therefore, colonial ambivalences abound in territory-related discourse. The depictions of Edom in the prophetic literature are often accompanied by the themes of land, possession, and dispossession. For example, an arresting depiction occurs with regard to land in Malachi: the Lord's love for Jacob is to be proved through his perpetual tearing down of the land of Esau (see Mal. 1:2-5).

Closely related to the theme of land is the 'possession' motif. "Isaiah uses the term ירש almost exclusively with reference to Israel's relationship to the land of promise; one exception is the reference to Edom's dispossession (see 34:11, 17)."[47] Despite the catastrophic dispossession that Edom is expected to undergo, Isaiah 34 nonetheless leaves behind a trace of its split vision. As Göran Eidevall perceptively observes:

> In the imaginary universe conjured by Isaiah 34, all that remains is a name, "Edom," attached to a waste land. The Edomites are gone. However, the text does not manage to eradicate their memory altogether. Perhaps inadvertently, the author of v. 12 proclaims… "they shall proclaim no kingdom there, and all its princes will become nothing." Thus *a counter image emerges*, suppressed yet discernible, of Edom as a place for kings and princes.[48]

33:23-29 and 11:14-21. [Reference to Diandra's work in this volume, with a particular focus on ambivalence, will be indicated here.]

    45. See Tull, *Isaiah 1–39*, 511.

    46. The expression is indicative of Israel's inability "to subdue Edom wholly." See Lissa Wray Beal, *1 & 2 Kings*, ApOTC (Downers Grove, IL: InterVarsity, 2014), 418.

    47. Bradford A. Anderson, *Brotherhood and Inheritance: A Canonical Reading of the Esau and Edom Traditions*, LHBOTS 556 (London: T&T Clark International, 2012), 195–6.

    48. Göran Eidevall, *Prophecy and Propaganda: Images of Enemies in the Book of Isaiah*, ConBOT 56 (Winona Lake, IN: Eisenbrauns, 2009), 157 (emphasis in the original).

What light might attention to such ambivalent depictions shed on the divine warrior hymn in Isaiah 63? Bert Dicou has underscored that Isaiah 63 does not depict Edom's annihilation.[49] Also, as Eidevall observes, "the passage does not contain a clear-cut enemy image."[50] In addition, the answer to the question "Who is being judged?" remains unclear.[51] From this, it can be surmised that the three occurrences of Edom in Isaiah, although appearing to tell a complete story, actually present an ambivalent depiction. The nation singled out for destruction in Isaiah 34, followed later by the only named entity in the Grape Treader passage—a pericope in which the actor, the recipients, and the locus remain enigmatic—is charged with ambivalence. In the end, to a simple and straightforward question "Was Edom annihilated?" an emphatic "yes" can hardly be given. Israel's proximate "other" persists. And the ambivalence endures. Fortunately, however, ambivalences do not merely point to split visions; they can also narrate positive identity constructions. Not only does Isaiah 63 contain such ambivalences, but it uses them to construct identity.

Correlated and Revived Identities

Verse 5 states that the trampling one "looked" but there was "no help," and that he was "appalled" (אשתומם).[52] Other than the divine warrior's parallel text in 59:16, the root שמם occurs twice in Isaiah. Both occurrences are found in ch. 54. In the context of the return of Zion's glory, these words are used to describe Zion's earlier status as "desolate" (שוממה) and show how, in the reversal of her fortunes, her descendants will dispossess and settle in the "deserted (cites)" (נשמות) of her adversaries. Earlier in the discussion, we saw how the appearance of Cyrus may have revived the hopes of the exiles (for help?). But the expected glorious return was met with internal divisions.

From these pointers, it is possible to imagine that these descriptions ("stooped," "no help," and "appalled"/"desolate") effectively capture the lived experiences of Israel during and after the exile. Granting such a scenario, the description of the Coming One in these terms argues for an appealing Isaian vision to the people who have gone through similar experiences. Further, "stooping," "no help," and "appalled"/ "desolate" alone do not tell the entire story.

49. See Dicou, *Edom, Israel's Brother and Antagonist*, 192.
50. Eidevall, *Prophecy and Propaganda*, 158.
51. See Schramm, *The Opponents of Third Isaiah*, 149.
52. The *Hitpolel* form with the meaning of "appalled or astounded" fits the context better than the positive sense of "amazement." See Izaak J. de Hulster, *Iconographic Exegesis and Third Isaiah*, FAT 2/36 (Tübingen: Mohr Siebeck, 2009), 250.

The Coming One may be "stooping" (v. 1a) but he nonetheless comes "in the greatness of his strength" (v. 1a); he finds "no help" (v. 5a) but his own "arm" brought him victory (v. 5b); he is "appalled" (v. 5a) but his "wrath sustained him" (v. 5a); and, in doing these, all of his garments are "defiled" (v. 3b) and yet he appears "splendidly robed" (v. 1a). In as much as the prophetic depiction correlates the experience of the people with that of the divine warrior, it reiterates that the bringer of salvation is sharing in the "desolate" experiences of the people. And the converse is equally—if not more—significant. One could imagine the prophetic counter-story to the post-exilic community being narrated as follows: "In your exile, you 'stooped.' You looked up for help. A few signs did appear but none quite satisfying. So you were appalled. However, the one bringing vindication is here. He, while sharing in your experiences, is still 'mighty to save' (v. 1b). And the year of salvation has come (v. 4b)." The effect of such a narrative would have been striking. The outsider, whose identity was demanded at the boundary, has not just become *any* insider but *the* insider because he is none other than Israel's "redeeming" (גאל; v. 4a) and "Saving One" (להושיע; v. 1b).

Conclusion

Jutta Jokiranta observes, "Negative connotations…justify [an] [in-]group's existence and claims by juxtaposing the most *relevant* out-groups as the opposites of the in-group."[53] Every attempt at depicting—even caricaturing—the identity of the "other" is in turn a passionate plea to "situate" oneself. This chapter took up the task of underscoring one such connotation in the book of Isaiah. The divine warrior hymn has elicited unceasing scholarly interest because of its gory depiction of the Trampling One. Edom featuring in such a text contributes towards continuing the predominantly negative depiction of Edom in the Old Testament. This essay argues that there is more to this text than mere violence. The heuristic category of the proximate "other" with the chosen aspects of persisting categories, permeable boundaries, and ambivalence helps uncover identity-constructing dynamics in the text. The text's unrelenting animosity toward Edom should be situated within such a complex dynamic of identity revival.

The proposed reading is unapologetically sympathetic. This reading discloses the complex process of identity construction in the Yehud

---

53. Jutta Jokiranta, "Social Identity Approach: Identity-Construction Elements in the Psalms Pesher," in *Defining Identities: We, You, and the Other in the Dead Sea Scrolls: Proceedings of the Fifth Meeting of the IOQS in Gröningen*, ed. F. G. Martínez and M. Popović, STDJ 70 (Malden, MA: Brill, 2008), 96–7 (author's emphasis).

community. However, before closing, an additional note is appropriate. We underscore throughout this essay that Edom elicits predominantly critical appraisals in the biblical tradition. There are nonetheless some positive depictions interspersed among them. Unfortunately, in the post-biblical literature, Edom came to mean nothing but enmity, a code name for an archenemy and the epitome of evil.

A startling case occurs in rabbinic literature. Genesis 33 recounts the reconciling meeting between Esau and Jacob. The narrative portrays that upon looking up and seeing Esau coming, Jacob divides the children among his wives and maids. He himself goes ahead and bows himself to the ground seven times. But Esau runs to meet him, embraces Jacob, falls on his neck and kisses him, and both the brothers weep (vv. 3-4). However, in the rabbinic rendering, "the encounter is re-interpreted so that Jacob weeps because Esau has bitten his neck and Esau weeps because his teeth have been hurt by the biting."[54] The midrashists even changed one of the consonants in the Hebrew text, thus changing the verb from נשק ("kiss") to נשך ("bite").[55] As a result, an otherwise happy resolution of the Esau and Jacob story is reinterpreted in such a way that it presents a picture that is contrary to the biblical rendition. The midrash is a reinterpretation that keeps the animosity alive.

Such aberrations are one possible response to our proximate "other." In our earnest desire to situate ourselves, the other who is proximate to us is turned into an unbridled monster, an evil to be overcome, and a power to be subdued and possessed. But even as we do so, the proximate "other" endures. In its endurance, it extends a challenging invitation to peer into ourselves to perceive our misplaced judgments so that we not only acknowledge but also name them. After all, when we stare for a long time into the eyes of our proximate "other," our proximate "other" stares back at us![56]

54. Linda Haney, "Yhwh, the God of Israel...and of Edom? The Relationships in the Oracle to Edom in Jeremiah 49:7-22," in *Uprooting and Planting: Essays on Jeremiah for Leslie Allen*, ed. J. Goldingay, LHBOTS 459 (New York: T&T Clark International, 2007), 78–9.

55. In addition, the midrashists interpret Jacob's sevenfold prostration (v. 3) as given "to God, since it could not be to the wicked Esau." For relevant sources, see Christopher Burdon, "Jacob, Esau and the Strife of Meanings," in *Self, Same, Other: Re-Visioning the Subject in Literature and Theology*, ed. H. Walton and A. Hass (Sheffield: Sheffield Academic, 2000), 166.

56. These words are patterned after the quote from Nietzsche: "when you stare for a long time into an abyss, the abyss stares back into you." See Friedrich Nietzsche, *Beyond Good and Evil: Prelude to a Philosophy of the Future*, ed. Rolf-Peter Horstmann, trans. Judith Norman, Cambridge Texts in the History of Philosophy (New York: Cambridge University Press, 2002), 146.

Chapter 4

WHERE IS CLYTEMNESTRA WHEN YOU NEED
HER? GENDER, ALTERITY, AND THE MASCULINE
ECONOMY OF PROPHECY IN ISAIAH 56–66

Rhiannon Graybill

The final eleven chapters of the book of Isaiah (Isa. 56–66) pose a number of hermeneutical challenges to interpreters.[1] For interpreters interested in textual and source critical issues, these challenges are obvious: What is the relation of these chapters, also known as Third Isaiah or Trito-Isaiah, to Second Isaiah (Isa. 40–55), not to mention First Isaiah (Isa. 1–39)?[2] Who wrote Trito-Isaiah, and how many authors and layers of textuality does it contain?[3] Where does Trito-Isaiah begin,

---

1. The division of Isaiah into three units of text (Proto-, Deutero-, and Trito-, or First, Second and Third Isaiah) dates to Bernhard Duhm's 1892 commentary. Bernhard Duhm, *Das Buch Jesaia* (Göttingen: Vandenhoeck & Ruprecht, 1902). Duhm's division largely persists, though more as a result of tradition than a reflection of accepted scholarly consensus.

2. See e.g. Paul V. Niskanen, *Isaiah 56–66*, Berit Olam (Collegeville, MN: Liturgical, 2014), x; Hans M. Barstad, "Isaiah 56–66 in Relation to Isaiah 40–55: Why a New Reading Is Necessary," in *Continuity and Discontinuity: Chronological and Thematic Development in Isaiah 40–66*, ed. Lena-Sofia Tiemeyer and Hans M. Barstad (Göttingen: Vandenhoeck & Ruprecht, 2014), 41–62.

3. See e.g. Joseph Blenkinsopp, *Isaiah 56–66: A New Translation with Introduction and Commentary*, Yale Anchor Bible 19B (New Haven, CT: Yale University Press, 2011), 59. See also Paul Allan Smith, *Rhetoric and Redaction in Trito-Isaiah: The Structure, Growth, and Authorship of Isaiah 56–66* (Leiden: Brill, 1995).

anyway?[4] But though Third Isaiah attracts attention on these grounds, it has attracted less scholarly notice as a synchronic text, particularly with reference to its complicated and ambivalent representations of gender and gendered alterity. While feminist criticism has directed significant attention to Second Isaiah and its collection of maternal and marital imagery, Third Isaiah remains largely neglected, particularly as a body of text in its own right (and not simply the limping, halfhearted extension of Second Isaiah).

And yet there is much to explore concerning gender and alterity in Trito-Isaiah. The text contains an uneasy mix of feminine and maternal imagery and bloody violence, much of it perpetrated by Yahweh himself. Yahweh promises to re-marry his wayward wife (62:4-5), to bring an end to weeping (65:19), and to open wombs and bring forth children instantly and without pain (66:7-9). There are also darker images of women and female sexuality: children of witches and whores are condemned (57:3-4), promiscuous female sexuality is exposed and punished (57:7-10). At still other points, Yahweh seems to replace the mother or to assert his own power over the maternal body. These images are set against a series of violent and masculine representations of Yahweh. How is gender represented here? Do the fragmented figurations of the female body (through sexuality, through birth) point toward a (perhaps partial) reclamation of the feminine? What is the relationship between Yahweh's violence and his feminine and maternal moments (a tension that is also present in Second Isaiah, and that Third Isaiah continues and amplifies)?

In exploring these questions, this essay approaches Isaiah 56–66 through a "Clytemnestra hermeneutic." As the phrase suggests, I look beyond the biblical text to the story of Clytemnestra and to its legacy in the work of philosopher Luce Irigaray in order to interpret Third Isaiah. In Greek myth, Clytemnestra is the wife of Agamemnon and queen of Argos. Agamemnon sacrifices their daughter, Iphigenia, in order to gain favorable winds to sail to Troy. Upon his return, Clytemnestra murders him, along with the slave he has brought back with him, Cassandra. Her son, Orestes, subsequently murders her. Orestes is then pursued by the

---

4. See e.g. Ulrich Berges, "Where Does Trito-Isaiah Start in the Book of Isaiah?," in Tiemeyer and Barstad (eds), *Continuity and Discontinuity*, 41–62; William L. Holladay, "Was Trito-Isaiah Deutero-Isaiah After All?" in *Writing and Reading the Scroll of Isaiah: Studies of an Interpretive Tradition, Vol. 1*, ed. Craig C. Broyles and Craig A. Evans, Formation and Interpretation of Old Testament Literature 1, VTSup 70 (Leiden: Brill, 1997), 193–217.

Furies until Athena intervenes and ends the cycle of violence.[5] Across this cycle of events, Clytemnestra represents the force of maternal vengeance; the mariticidal mother stands at the nexus of violence, maternity, and the female body. Maternal vengeance is the essence of the Clytemnestra hermeneutic.

I am not the first feminist biblical interpreter to think with Clytemnestra. Of the book of Judges, a truly nasty text filled with dead and dismembered women, Mieke Bal asks the question: "Where is Clytemnestra?"[6] This question, posed to the biblical text, signals several meanings—Where are the mothers of the many murdered women of Judges? Where is the revenge? Why can Jephthah, for example, sacrifice (murder) his daughter with seeming impunity (Judg. 11), while Agamemnon pays for Iphigenia's life with his own? *Where is Clytemnestra when you need her?* As Bal suggests, this question offers ways of thinking through gender violence. A Clytemnestra hermeneutic—reading the biblical texts in relation to the myth of Clytemnestra—enables a critical distance from the passages to bring their gender dynamics into focus.

By invoking Clytemnestra to read biblical texts, I also draw on the work of feminist philosopher Luce Irigaray, who returns to Clytemnestra repeatedly in her work. Against Freud's description of the murder of the father as primal scene (described in *Totem and Taboo*, *Moses and Monotheism*, and other works), Irigaray argues for a primal murder of the mother, represented by Clytemnestra's death at the hands of her son Orestes.[7] The murder of the mother becomes the symbolic foundational

---

5. There are many iterations of the Clytemnestra myth across Greek literature; my summary here (and discussion in the essay) focuses on Aeschlyus's cycle of tragedies known as the *Oresteia*. The first play, *Agamemnon*, presents Agamemnon's return and murder at Clytemenstra's hands; Orestes' revenge comes in the second play, *The Libation Bearers*. His pursuit by the Furies, and the situation's eventual resolution by Athena, is the topic of the *Eumenides*. For the text, see Aeschylus, *Aeschylus: Agamemnon; Libation bearers; Eumenides*, trans. Alan H. Sommerstein (Cambridge, MA: Harvard University Press, 2009).

6. Mieke Bal, *Death and Dissymmetry: The Politics of Coherence in the Book of Judges* (Chicago: University of Chicago Press, 1988), 197.

7. Luce Irigaray, "The Bodily Encounter with the Mother," in *The Irigaray Reader*, ed. Margaret Whitford (Cambridge, MA: Blackwell, 1991), 34–46 (37–8), a version also appears in Luce Irigaray, *Sexes and Genealogies*, trans. Gillian C. Gill (New York: Columbia University Press, 1993), 7–22. See also Irigaray, *Sexes and Genealogies* 134, 189; Luce Irigaray, *Marine Lover of Friedrich Nietzsche*, trans. Gillian C. Gill (New York: Columbia University Press, 1991), 88–9; Luce Irigaray, *Thinking the Difference: For a Peaceful Revolution*, trans. Karin Montin (New York: Routledge, 2001), 9.

event for the establishment of culture (even as Clytemnestra is left dead and Electra, another daughter, is driven to madness by rage and grief).⁸ In Irigaray's reading, Clytemnestra represents both the crisis point—the *already murdered mother*—and the possibility of imagining otherwise, through the figure of the *avenging mother*. Irigaray thus uses the Clytemnestra myth to challenge and critique the masculine economy of representation, which dominates in both psychoanalysis and in Western culture more broadly. She poses the same question as Bal, *Where is Clytemnestra?*, but to a larger swath of tradition.

In this essay, I follow Clytemnestra in two ways: first, as she functions in Irigaray's theorization of the maternal body and the larger gendered economy of representation, and second, as a figure in her own right. Together, these reading strategies constitute the "Clytemnestra hermeneutic." Such a Clytemnestra hermeneutic directs attention to the erasure of the female body in the textual representations of maternity. It invites readers to interrogate questions of blood, violence, and revenge. And it opens new ways of exploring the conjunctions of violence, maternity, and the deity, while also attending to the workings of prophetic otherness.

As the Clytemnestra hermeneutic exposes, the maternal and feminine imagery in Third Isaiah does not represent a positive opening or transformation. Instead, it marks a symbolic murder of the feminine (an event Irigaray associates with the Clytemnestra myth), as well as a crisis of representing women or the female body. But while Third Isaiah positions the masculine Yahweh over and against the feminine, this opposition is not complete. As the final portion of the essay explores, Yahweh and Clytemnestra share similarities, which destabilizes the logic of opposition and opens new possibilities in reading alterity in Isaiah 56–66.

On Isaiah 56–66

Interpreters commonly describe Third Isaiah as derivative of, and inferior to, the rest of Isaiah, especially Isaiah 40–55. In particular, Third Isaiah fares poorly when compared with the much-praised artistry of Second Isaiah. Already in the middle of the twentieth century, Walther Zimmerli criticized the stylistic inferiority of Third Isaiah.⁹ In a similar vein, in *The Dawn of Apocalyptic*, Paul Hanson described Third Isaiah's "irregular, baroque style," including a penchant for "prosaic, list-like effect[s]"

---

8. Irigaray, "The Bodily Encounter with the Mother," 37–8.
9. Walther Zimmerli, "Zur Sprache Triojesaias," in *Gottes Offenbarung: gesammelte Aufsätze zum Alten Testament*, Theologische Bücher 19 (Munich: Kaiser, 1963), 217–33.

and "the grotesque mixing of metaphoric patterns."¹⁰ Even scholars who resist inferiorizing Third Isaiah note its challenges. For example, Grace Emmerson comments, slightly apologetically, "chs. 56–66 are likely to seem, at first sight, a bewildering medley of denunciation and promise, warning and hope, lament and confidence."¹¹ And even Jon L. Berquist, whose deconstructive reading of the book remains one of the best literary readings of Third Isaiah, concedes, "the text tone and style shifts repeatedly, and the reader discerns patterns only with difficulty."¹² Third Isaiah, it seems, is far from the best of biblical literature.

Recent scholarship on Third Isaiah has sometimes challenged accepted wisdom about the low literary merit of the text. In addition to Berquist's deconstructive reading, Paul V. Niskanen offers a literary commentary on the final form of the text.¹³ And taking up a sub-unit of Third Isaiah, its final two chapters, Michael J. Chan argues that "Isaiah 65–66 provides some of the Hebrew Bible's richest and most radical metaphors and images of Yhwh, Yhwh's servants, and Zion/Jerusalem."¹⁴ As Chan's comments indicate, literary reevaluations of Third Isaiah, whether as a whole or in parts, are often tied to an evaluation of its themes, which include a focus on universalism, hope, and the inclusion of the excluded. Even the eunuchs are included in the vision of the future to come (Isa. 56:4-5).

My own reading similarly embraces literary methods, but resists the assumption that if we read Third Isaiah as literature, we necessarily find it either good literature or literature containing positive content (note these are distinct categories). I also direct attention to the question of gender (most gender-oriented readings, like most literary readings, focus on 40–55 instead of 56–66).¹⁵ And from a literary perspective, the final ten

---

10. Paul D. Hanson, *The Dawn of Apocalyptic: The Historical and Sociological Roots of Jewish Apocalyptic Eschatology* (Philadelphia: Fortress, 1979), 59.

11. Grace Emmerson, *Isaiah 56–66* (London: T&T Clark, 2004), 15.

12. Jon L. Berquist, "Reading Difference in Isaiah 56–66: The Interplay of Literary and Sociological Strategies," *Method & Theory in the Study of Religion* 7 (1995): 23–42 (27).

13. Niskanen, *Isaiah 56–66*.

14. Michael J. Chan, "Isaiah 65–66 and the Genesis of Reorienting Speech," *CBQ* 72 (2010): 445–63 (445).

15. For example, Hanne Løland, *Silent or Salient Gender? The Interpretation of Gendered God-Language in the Hebrew Bible, Exemplified in Isaiah 42, 46 and 49*, FAT 2/32 (Tübingen: Mohr Siebeck, 2007); James Harding, "In the Name of Love: Resisting Reader and Abusive Redeemer in Deutero-Isaiah," *The Bible and Critical Theory* 2, no. 2 (2006): 14.1–14.15; Gerlinde Baumann, "Prophetic Objections to

chapters of Isaiah are a complicated and not always successful unit of text. While both first Isaiah (chs 1–39) and second Isaiah (ch. 40–55) are often praised on literary grounds, Isaiah 56–66 remains more challenging to appreciate. The text repeats images and themes from Isaiah 40–55, though with less coherence or intentionality, threatening to spin out of control. The representation of Yahweh vacillates between images of maternity and compassion and scenes of violence, escalating a tendency already present in the earlier chapters of Isaiah, though previously held somewhat in check.

The maternal and feminine images and moments in Third Isaiah are unevenly dispersed across the chapters. They vie for space with other images and divine pronouncements, many of them extremely violent. In a famous passage in 63:1-5, Yahweh appears, dripping with the blood of the people he has slaughtered (a scene of violence whose visuals are reminiscent of Brian de Palma's film adaptation of Stephen King's bloody classic *Carrie*). The book likewise ends not with peace or restoration but with a final glance at corpses: "They will go out and look at the bodies of the people who rebelled against me, for their worm will not die, their fire will not be quenched, and they will be an abhorrence to all flesh" (Isa. 66:24). This violence is set alongside images of divine power and general restoration.

There are also multiple images that involve women, maternity, and childbirth (sometimes together, sometimes separately). First, and perhaps least surprisingly, given the frequent and wide-ranging misogyny of the prophetic literature, there are a handful of passages in Third Isaiah that employ strongly negative images of women. This is the classic "woman as evil" motif that is familiar across the Hebrew Bible.[16] Women are used to signal bad actions, bad sexual and religious practices (which of course imply each other), and the danger of foreignness. In Isa. 57:3, the wicked are denounced as "children of a witch" and "offspring of an adulterer and whore." The wickedness of the people is concisely communicated via their relations to the mother, and to the mother as associated with

YHWH as the Violent Husband of Israel: Reinterpretations of the Prophetic Marriage Metaphor in Second Isaiah (Isaiah 40-55)," in *A Feminist Companion to Prophets and Daniel*, ed. Athalya Brenner, A Feminist Companion to the Bible (2nd Series) 8 (London: Bloomsbury T&T Clark, 2002), 88–120. The marriage metaphor that occurs in Isa. 62:4-5 is largely neglected by readers; as Niskanen notes, "the more systematic studies of marital imagery in the Bible generally give little or no attention to Isaiah 62:4-5," a "somewhat surprising" omission. Niskanen, *Isaiah 56–66*, 61.

16. Gale A. Yee, *Poor Banished Children of Eve: Woman as Evil in the Hebrew Bible* (Minneapolis, MN: Augsburg Fortress, 2003).

transgressive sex and witchcraft in particular. In 57:7-10, we find a more elaborated association between bad religious practice and bad female sexual desire:

> ⁷Upon a high and elevated mountain you have placed your bed;
>   Also there you went up to offer sacrifices.
> ⁸Behind the door and the doorpost you have put your symbol,
>   because when you deserted me, you uncovered your bed, you went
>   up to it, and you spread it out.
>   You have made yourself a bargain with them, you have loved their
>   bed, you have seen their genitals.
> ⁹You have gone down to Molech with oil and multiplied your perfumes,
>   You have sent your envoys far, even down to Sheol.
> ¹⁰You grew weary from your many ways but did not say I despair,
>   you found your strength increased so you did not weaken.
>   (Isa. 57:7-10)

The passage is redolent with sexual imagery, some of which is obscured in translation. In addition to the bed, with its suggestions of sex, the "symbol" (זכרון) in v. 8 has sexual overtones and likely suggests a phallic image of some sort (cf. Ezek. 16:17). The final expression in v. 8, יד חזית literally, "you have seen a hand," uses יד, "hand," as a euphemism for the penis.[17] Child sacrifice is also often grouped together with bad sexual practices, as in the description of the feminized Jerusalem playing the whore and engaging in child sacrifice in Ezek. 16:20, or the references to sacrificing to Molech in the Levitical incest laws (Lev. 18:21; 20:2-5).

Related to these figurations of women as evil, contemptible, or blameworthy, Third Isaiah makes use of the "marriage metaphor," familiar from elsewhere in the prophetic literature (Hos. 1–3; Jer. 3; Ezek. 16; 23). The basic form of the metaphor presents Yahweh as cuckolded husband and Israel as adulterous or whoring wife; the wife's lovers represent the other gods that Israel has worshipped (the basic association of the metaphor is between bad religious practices, the tenor, and bad sexual practices, vehicle). Israel uncovering her bed to her lovers in 57:7-8 is one brief use of the marriage metaphor. Later in the text, remarriage is used to signal the resolution of the adultery/idolatry crisis; Israel is bedecked as a bride

---

17. As in the Ugaritic text, "The Feast of the Goodly Gods," where we find "Does the 'hand' of El excite you?" with clear sexual implications. See discussion in Mark S. Smith, *The Rituals and Myths of the Feast of the Goodly Gods of KTU/CAT 1.23: Royal Constructions of Opposition, Intersection, Integration, and Domination*, Resources for Biblical Study 51 (Leiden: Brill, 2006), 79.

and bridegroom (61:10)—though, of course, marriage is no guarantee against either unhappiness or violence. The metaphor is more explicit in 62:2-5, which includes both remarriage and renaming:

> ² The nations will see your righteousness, and all of the kings your glory
>   You will be called by a new name that the mouth of Yahweh will establish.
> ³ You will be a crown of beauty in the hand of Yahweh,
>   and a royal tiara in the palm of your God.
> ⁴ You will no longer be called Forsaken, and your land will not be called Desolate,
>   because you will be called My Delight Is In Her and your land, Married,
>   because Yahweh delights in you, and your land will be married.
> ⁵ As a young man marries a young woman, your sons will marry you,
>   and as a groom rejoices over a bride, your God will rejoice over you.

Other passages make use of the imagery of labor, birth, and infancy. The restoration of the nation brings an end to infant mortality and to vain or difficult labor (65:20-23). Yahweh, who controls the opening and closing of the womb, promises childbirth without pain and indeed without effort (66:7-9).

Little surprise, then, that weeping and the cry of distress are banished from the land (65:19). Though Yahweh is described as father (63:16), he also takes on the role of mother: "Like a mother comforts, so I will comfort you; you shall be comforted in Jerusalem" (66:13). Elsewhere, he promises the nation that "You will suck the milk of nations and you will suck the breast of kings" (60:16). Here, as at other moments in both Second and Third Isaiah, the deity associates himself with the economy of fluids that is otherwise chiefly associated with the female body. Chief among these fluids are the fluids of birth and blood.

Gender and/as Alterity in Isaiah 56–66

One way of reading the images of the female body in Isaiah 56–66 is as structuring figures in a series of binary oppositions that delineate appropriate Israelite beliefs and practices. The marriage metaphor, for example, sets the bad, adulterous wife (Israel pursuing other gods) against the good, virtuous wife (Israel loyal to Yahweh and the covenant). The remarriage that occurs in ch. 62 represents the restoration of the covenant and the shift from the bad mode of subjectivity—adultery/idolatry—to the desired faithfulness. The chapters also offer a recurring opposition between bad mothers and good mothers—evil Israelites are the children of sorceresses and whores, while the restoration of order is described as a return to "good" forms of maternity, including an easy birth (66:7-9). Indeed, Yahweh himself becomes maternal, comforting the people and suckling the nation (60:16; 66:13). The images in chs 56–66 also distinguish between a "bad" past time—associated with both negative forms of female sexuality and difficulty in childbirth and infancy—and a "good" coming time, which includes the restoration of marriage, the assertion of control over childbirth and the womb, and divinely ordained biopolitics.[18]

This kind of binary analysis has done much to advance feminist studies of biblical texts. Showing how women and the feminine "work"—or, more properly, *are worked with* by dominant structures of meaning—helps open questions of gender and power in and around texts. Thus J. Cheryl Exum's classic reading of the Samson story traces out a series of binaries constructed by the biblical text.[19] Many studies of the marriage metaphor in particular have taken a similar approach, directing attention to the ways the texts construct gendered binaries (good husband, bad wife) or binaries within a single gender category (good wife, bad whore).

Even the term for female, נקבה, has been analyzed for its binary relationship to the masculine: as Athalya Brenner notes, נקבה means hollow or pierced; it describes a body acted upon by the male/phallus/penis.[20]

However, instead of extending this sort of binary analysis, I pursue another approach here. I suggest that dualism, while useful in many ways at getting at the gender difficulties in biblical texts, fails as an approach to gender, the body, and alterity in Isaiah 56–66. Instead, I propose reading the text through Irigaray, as a way of highlighting the *crisis* of maternal-feminine imagery in the text. The maternal and feminine imagery in Third Isaiah does not stand as a stable (if misogynistic) half of a binary. Rather, it signals the larger impossibility of representing women or the female body, however the text—or criticism of it—might attempt to do so via binary thinking. I am interested in what Irigaray names "the Blind Spot in

---

18. For an analysis of biopolitics and divine surveillance, see Erin Runions, "Political Theologies of the Surveilled Womb?," *Political Theology* 16, no. 4 (2015): 301–4 and "Biobible: Biblical Provocations to Biocapital in the US Culture Wars," *The Bible and Critical Theory* 12, no. 2 (2016): 1–23.

19. J. Cheryl Exum, *Fragmented Women: Feminist (Sub)Versions of Biblical Narratives*, JSOTSup 163 (Sheffield: JSOT, 1993).

20. Athalya Brenner, *The Intercourse of Knowledge: On Gendering Desire and Sexuality in the Hebrew Bible*, BibInt 26 (Leiden: Brill, 1997).

an Old Dream of Symmetry."[21] This "old dream of symmetry" is the idea of symmetry between male and female (we might trace biblical analogues in the Gen. 1 account of creation); the blind spot is the way that this dream in fact ignores the specificity of the feminine, treating it, instead, as a mirror for the masculine, as well as a vessel for its use.

Of course, the dream of symmetry is an illusion; it is an illusion, moreover, in the service of the masculine (as Irigaray titles another of her famous essays, "Any Theory of the 'Subject' Has Always Been Appropriated by the 'Masculine'"[22]). It is impossible to represent the feminine under the masculine economy of representation. Instead, the feminine is used by the masculine to represent itself (often via binary logics), forced into what Irigaray terms "a certain game for which she will always find herself signed up without having begun to play."[23] Much of Irigaray's work is dedicated to unraveling this game, to challenging its terms, and to finding a different way for women to speak "among ourselves." In *Speculum of the Other Woman*, Irigaray reads Plato's cave and Freud's reflections on women against the source texts, revealing a narrative of the suppression of women while also gesturing at an alternate economy of representation. Her reading of the Clytemnestra myth—under and against the Greek, biblical, and Freudian myths of the murder of the Father—performs similar work.

Another part of Irigaray's project involves rethinking the mother. She suggests that under the patriarchal economy of representation, woman is reduced to the position of the mother and even more drastically to the womb/earth/substratum. Woman becomes "Matrix—womb, earth, factor, bank—to which the seed capital is entrusted so that it may germinate, produce, grow fruitful, without woman being able to lay claim to either capital or interest since she has only submitted 'passively' to reproduction" as *Speculum* has it.[24] Because woman is represented as place and ground for the male, she is denied subjectivity.[25] Given this state of affairs, it is impossible for women to speak among themselves, or to think seriously about relations between women. Speaking of psychoanalysis, she writes, "I might nevertheless point to one thing that has been singularly neglected, barely touched on, in the theory of the unconscious:

---

21. Luce Irigaray, *Speculum of the Other Woman*, trans. Gillian C. Gill (Ithaca, NY: Cornell University Press, 1985).
22. This essay is contained in ibid., 133–46.
23. Ibid., 22.
24. Ibid., 18.
25. Ibid., 227.

the relation of woman to the mother and the relation of women among themselves."[26] This extends to the relation between mother and daughter.[27] A significant part of her project, including her use of the Clytemnestra myth, is dedicated to opening and reimagining this question of the relation to the mother.

As even this brief summary should suggest, Irigaray's work presents a valuable resource for reading prophetic literature in the Hebrew Bible. The density of imagery, the mix of violence and beauty, and the thickly textured ambiguities of biblical prophecy converge to invite Irigarayan readings. In the case of Isaiah in particular, the text contains a number of maternal images, along with the partial and often fragmented representations of *mothers*. These further call Irigaray and her writing on the "bodily relation to the mother" to mind. In fact, given the substantial overlap between Irigaray's own interests—structures of meaning, poetic language, violence against the feminine, questions of the divine, rereading and reimagining ancient texts, fractured maternity—and those of feminist biblical studies, it is remarkable how little her work has been engaged in reading biblical texts. This neglect of Irigaray is lamentable, especially given the resources her work provides for thinking through gender, alterity, and the female body in biblical texts.[28]

Irigaray's focus on maternity and the female body provides a useful entry to read the book of Isaiah, the Hebrew prophet with the greatest density of female imagery other than the marriage metaphor. Elsewhere, I have used Irigaray, with particular emphasis on her description of the vampire, to read Isaiah 40–55.[29] Like the chapters considered here

---

26. Luce Irigaray, *This Sex Which Is Not One*, trans. Catherine Porter (Ithaca, NY: Cornell University Press, 1985), 124 (emphasis in the original).

27. Irigaray writes, "When I speak of the *relation to the mother*, I mean that in our patriarchal culture the daughter is absolutely unable to control her relation to her mother. Nor can the woman control her relation to maternity, unless she reduces herself to that role alone." Ibid., 143 (emphasis in the original).

28. There are some scattered counterexamples to this neglect; Julie Kelso provides a compelling example of the uses of *O Mother, Where Art Thou? An Irigarayan Reading of the Book of Chronicles*, Bible World (London: Equinox, 2007). And Peter J. Sabo and I have drawn on Irigaray to describe figurations of the female body in relation to biblical stories of caves: Rhiannon Graybill and Peter Sabo, "Caves of the Hebrew Bible: A Speleology," *Biblical Interpretation* 26 (2018): 1–22.

29. Rhiannon Graybill, "Yahweh as Maternal Vampire in Second Isaiah: Reading from Violence to Fluid Possibility with Luce Irigaray," *Journal of Feminist Studies in Religion* 33 (2017): 9–25.

(56–66), Isaiah 40–55 contains maternal and other positive feminine imagery at a higher density than anywhere else in the prophetic literature. This is especially notable given the extreme misogyny and violence of the so-called "Marriage Metaphor" passages (e.g. Hos. 1–3; Jer. 3; Ezek. 16; 23) as well as the violence directed at female sexuality in books such as Nahum and Lamentations. Given the alternative that Isaiah 40–55 seems to pose, some scholars have argued for reading these chapters as a redemptive counterbalance to the violence or a form of "repair" to the misogyny of the marriage metaphor. Drawing on Irigaray's work to read the images of maternity and the womb, I have pushed back strenuously against this argument. I suggest, instead, that Second Isaiah is predicated on the appropriation and erasure of the female body. This appropriation and erasure occurs, moreover, *by the deity himself*, who assumes a vampiric relation to the female body.[30] Here, I continue my project of thinking about the maternal body in the prophets with Irigaray, but with a different textual focus, on Isaiah 56–66.

On Irigaray's Style, Stridency, and Scope

As this brief introduction to her work should already suggest, Irigaray does not do things by half measures. Her critiques are sweeping, her style outrageous, her targets nothing less than gender, language, and representation itself. Trained in psychoanalysis under Lacan, Irigaray rebelled against the phallocentrism of analytic theory and practice—not to mention the history of Western philosophy. Her body of work is a concerted response to these discourses. As Elizabeth Grosz summarizes, "Irigaray attempts a feminist deconstruction of psychoanalysis. Her project is both to undo the phallocentric constriction of women as men's others and to create a means by which women's specificity may figure in discourse in autonomous terms."[31] The work this method produces is, by necessity, formally and intellectually experimental: "Irigaray's texts are thus simultaneously 'serious' philosophical critiques of phallocentric

---

30. Ibid., 11–18. Central to framing this argument about Isa. 40–55 is Irigaray's description of the vampire from *Speculum of the Other Woman*: "The master is a vampire who needs to stay in disguise and do his work at night. Otherwise he is reminded that he is dependent on death. And on birth. On the material, uterine foundations of his mastery. Only if these be repressed can he enjoy sole ownership." Irigaray, *Speculum of the Other Woman*, 126–7.

31. Elizabeth Grosz, *Sexual Subversions* (Sydney: Allen & Unwin, 1989), 109.

discourses; and experiments in new conceptual and representational practices, carried out within *and* beyond phallocentric constraints."[32] Or as Irigaray herself writes:

> Thus it was necessary to destroy, but, as Rene Char wrote, with nuptial tools. The tool is not a feminine attribute. But woman may re-utilize its marks on her, in her. To put it another way: the option left to me was to *have a fling with the philosophers*, which is easier said than done…[33]

The difference between Grosz's summary and Irigaray's own account of her project is telling. Irigaray's writing is at once evocative and provocative (for example, naming the methods of feminist philosophical and psychoanalytic critique "a fling with the philosophers," appending the simultaneously humorous and serious aside that this is "easier said than done"). Her claims are broad, often universal in scope, as are her representations of the masculine and the feminine. Thus, in *Speculum of the Other Woman*, we read: "Any theory of the subject has always been appropriated by the 'masculine'"—*any* theory, *always* appropriated.[34] There is no nuance, no modulation, no strategic concession. And indeed, there can be none: Irigaray's claims are universalizing and essentialist by design.

Before returning to Isaiah, I offer two further observations about Irigaray. First, the reach—even hyperbole—of her claims is inseparable from her work. Her claims represent, moreover, the point where style and argument converge: *the impossibility of representing woman*. As she writes in *Speculum*, "Theoretically there would be no such thing as woman. She would not exist. The best that can be said is that she does *not exist yet*."[35] Second, because style is so fundamental to Irigaray's argument, when engaging her work, there is a strong pull to think (and to represent) using her rhetorical strategies—sweeping claims, subversive mimesis, verbless sentence fragments, ellipses and elliptical modes of representation, suggestions, subversions—as much as to apply specific concepts from her work. Because the masculine economy of representation *cannot represent* women, we must seek other ways to speak and write and deploy language. After all, "The tool [language] is not a feminine attribute. But woman may re-utilize its marks on her, in her."[36] So while

---

32. Ibid., 102.
33. Irigaray, *This Sex Which Is Not One*, 150 (ellipsis and emphasis in the original).
34. Irigaray, *Speculum of the Other Woman*, 133.
35. Ibid., 166 (emphasis in the original).
36. Irigaray, *This Sex Which Is Not One*, 150.

I construct this argument in the language and form familiar to biblical studies, I have also felt the pull of Irigaray's own distinctive style. Moreover, I have welcomed this pull. In tracing Clytemnestra, in exposing the working of the masculine economy of representation, I write beyond what Irigaray terms "the protective veil of a language that has already changed even its evasions into fetishes."[37] Third Isaiah has long awaited a reading without such a veil.

In Relation to the Mother in Isaiah 56–66

In this section, I use Irigaray's work to draw out some of the key themes in the representation of the maternal in Isaiah 56–66, building on the brief overview I have offered above. While there is significant feminine and maternal imagery in this collection of texts, these images do not provide a move beyond, or an alternative to, the highly negative and constraining images of the female body that are found elsewhere in the prophetic texts. Instead, they foreclose the horizons of possibility for the female subject in Third Isaiah.

First, while there is definite maternal imagery in the text, actual, embodied human mothers are hard to come by. The children of evil mothers are derided (57:3-4); the mothers themselves, however, are largely neglected in the scene of condemnation. The vividly imagined adulteress in 57:7-10 is not given children. Children are gathered, carried by nurses and brought on ships (60:4, 9), but without their mothers; Yahweh likewise oversees a scene of nursing 60:15-16 that is remarkably motherless (the breasts in question are attributed to kings, who possess them in one way if not another). Mothers do nurse and comfort children in 66:10, 16. However, the most frequent images of the maternal body are of childbirth itself, particularly miraculous labor (65:23; 66:7-9).

Thus, when the mother does appear, it is through particular body parts—sometimes as arms that carry children, sometimes as breasts, but most frequently as a womb. This is a common structure of patriarchal representation and a matter of significant discussion in Irigaray's work. Through a false-but-patriarchally-persuasive synecdoche, the womb is taken to stand in for the woman; as Irigaray puts it, "The womb is mistaken for all the female sexual organs since no valid representations of female sexuality exist."[38] In *Speculum of the Other Woman*, she writes:

---

37. Irigaray, *Speculum of the Other Woman*, 229.
38. Irigaray, *Sexes and Genealogies*, 16.

man is the procreator, that sexual *production-reproduction* is referable to his "activity" alone, to his "project" alone. Woman is nothing but the receptacle that passively receives his product, even if sometimes, by the display of her passively aimed instincts, she has pleaded, facilitated, even demanded that it be placed within her. Matrix—womb, earth, factor, bank.[39]

Such is the fate of the feminine in Third Isaiah.

The female body as a passive object to be acted upon by Yahweh also appears in descriptions of birth and the womb. Consider again this passage from the final chapter, where Yahweh abruptly switches from the threat of retribution to the topic of birth:

> [7] Before she labored, she gave birth,
> before her contractions came upon her, she gave birth to a son.
> [8] Who has heard of such a thing? Who has seen such things?
> Will a land be brought forth in a day? Can a nation be born in one moment?
> for as soon as Zion was in labor she brought forth her children.
> [9] Shall I burst open and not deliver? says Yahweh.
> Shall I, the one who delivers, close up [the womb]?, says your God.
> (66:7-9)

Though the image is in many ways lovely, it is also ominous. The woman in labor in v. 7 has disappeared by v. 9, her place filled by the deity who opens and closes her womb. The mother as *subject* (giving birth) becomes acted-upon *object* (being opened and closed up). Furthermore, as the emphasis of the passage shifts to Yahweh, both the woman and the children are elided. The sequence demonstrates the reproductive capacity of women in service of the reproduction of the nation. To quote again from Irigaray, "sexual *production-reproduction* is referable to his 'activity' alone, to his 'project' alone."[40] What Irigaray says about the man in general—"'his' activity," "'his' project"—here provides a fitting description of Yahweh. A few verses later, another passage, this time describing the comfort of the child, displays a similar shift:

> [12] For thus says Yahweh, Behold, I will extend peace to her like a river,
> and the glory of nations like an overflowing stream
> You shall nurse and be carried on the hip, and be dandled on the knees
> [13] Like one a mother comforts, so will I comfort you,
> and you will be comforted in Jerusalem. (Isa. 66:12-13)

---

39. Irigaray, *Speculum of the Other Woman*, 18 (emphasis in the original).
40. Ibid.

The images of infancy and maternity in fact are not about mothers and children at all. Instead, the metaphor is in praise of Yahweh. In the movement from vehicle to tenor, the maternal is elided and replaced by the male deity. This, in turn, reveals the instrumental use of the female body—especially the maternal body divided into parts (breasts, hips, knees; along with womb in the prior passage) and functions (nursing, carrying, comforting). The instrumentalization of the woman in service of the metaphorical child (also the text's "you") points to the larger instrumentalization of the woman in metaphor, in the service of the glorification of Yahweh and the masculine economy of representation more broadly.

The constraining of the feminine is also reflected in the limited representation of female sexuality in the text. In *This Sex Which Is Not One*, Irigaray writes, "Female sexuality has always been conceptualized on the basis of masculine parameters."[41] In Third Isaiah, this occurs in two major ways. First, the maternal body is fragmented and reduced to its parts: breasts, arms, womb. Furthermore, Yahweh asserts his own power over and through each of these parts: Yahweh nurses the infant nation; Yahweh gathers the people with arms; Yahweh controls not just the opening and closing of the womb, but all aspects of labor. As in Isaiah 40–55, the deity figures himself as a superior mother to all other female mothers, while also appropriating the power of the female body.

When the female body appears in terms other than those of maternity and birth, it is still configured according to male sexual desires. The beauty of the bride is a point of attention in the metaphor of rejoicing in 61:10.[42] In 62:4-5, Third Isaiah's version of the marriage metaphor, the physical beauty of the woman is a major point of attention, as well as the adornments that Yahweh provides. Yahweh is also particularly interested in how that beauty is viewed by others: "The nations shall see your vindication, and all the kings your glory" (62:2). There is a similar emphasis on the woman's appearance and her effect on other (presumably male) spectators in the description of the adulterous/idolatrous woman in 57:7-10. The female body, including the female experience, is represented and described entirely in terms of its relation to men. The male economy of representation extends to the gaze; woman remains the "blind spot in an old dream of symmetry."[43]

41. Irigaray, *This Sex Which Is Not One*, 23.
42. The bride is adorned for the gaze of the bridegroom (cf. Gen. 24:53; Ezek. 16:17). As Irigaray writes, "women have rarely used their beauty as a weapon for themselves, even more rarely as a spiritual weapon" (Irigaray, *Sexes and Genealogies*, 64).
43. On the masculinity of the gaze, see e.g. Irigaray, *Speculum of the Other Woman*, 144–6, 340; *Marine Lover of Friedrich Nietzsche*, 143–53.

Reading with Irigaray also clarifies an essential textual difficulty in Isa. 62:5. The first half of the verset reads "as a young man marries a young woman, so בניך will marry you." While the Hebrew text is pointed by the Masoretes as בָּנָיִךְ, "your sons" (also υἱοί σου, "your sons" in the LXX), the word is commonly emended and read "your builder." This emendation avoids what Niskanen terms "a bizarre and unseemly metaphor, with sons marrying their mother."[44] And yet it is precisely this blurring of the maternal, the marital, and the sexual that Irigaray describes as central to the patriarchal representation of the feminine. In *Speculum*, Irigaray writes, "If woman wishes to attract man, she must identify herself with his mother."[45] Furthermore, the context of the marriage metaphor in 62:4-5 reinforces the blurring of the roles of wife and mother vis-à-vis the masculine subject. As Niskanen notes, the passage in 62:1-6 alludes repeatedly to Isa. 49:14-19.[46] But while the passage in Isaiah 49 is rich with mother–child imagery, in ch. 62 this imagery is reconfigured to refer to marriage. The mother thus becomes the bride (whom, of course, she was already). Third Isaiah does not confuse, mistake, or pervert the metaphor, so much as disclose the understanding of woman as mother/ bride/use value that underlies the passages as a whole.

The masculine control over the female body, and female sexuality, is matched by a control over language and representation.[47] In Third Isaiah's marriage metaphor, the woman is not just decorated for the male gaze: she is also given a new name: "You shall be called by a new name that the mouth of Yahweh will establish" (62:2). Lest the point not be communicated clearly enough, Yahweh adds, two verses later, "You will no longer be called Forsaken, and your land will not be called Desolate, because you will be called My Delight is In Her and your land, Married, because Yahweh delights in you, and your land will be married (62:4). What is missing from such a scene is the possibility of female desire, or female language, other than that preordained by the masculine:

> Here again no economy would be possible whereby sexual reality can be represented by/for women. She remains forsaken and abandoned in her lack, default, absence, envy, etc. and is led to submit, to follow the dictates issued univocally by the sexual desire, discourse, and law of man. Of the father, in the first instance.[48]

---

44. Niskanen, *Isaiah 56–66*, 59.
45. Irigaray, *Speculum of the Other Woman*, 109; cf. Irigaray, *This Sex Which Is Not One*, 151–2.
46. Niskanen, *Isaiah 56–66*, 57.
47. Irigaray, *This Sex which Is Not One*, 100.
48. Irigaray, *Speculum of the Other Woman*, 49.

Also erased in this system is the possibility of relations between women, either as equals or as mother–daughter pairs. In *Sexes and Genealogies*, Irigaray comments on the disappearance of mother–daughter pairs, which forecloses the relationship to the mother.[49] Third Isaiah introduces the figure of the daughter, only to separate her from the mother. Isaiah 60:4 reads, "Lift your eyes and look around, all of them gather and come to you; your sons come from far away, and your daughters [are brought] on the hips of their nurses." Here we find daughters, daughters who are favored enough to be brought to the father/deity/Yahweh (Yahweh figures himself as father in 63:16). However, the daughters are separated from the *mother* who bore them. In *This Sex Which Is Not One*, Irigaray explains, "When I speak of the *relation to the mother*, I mean that in our patriarchal culture the daughter is absolutely unable to control her relation to her mother. Nor can the woman control her relation to maternity, unless she reduces herself to that role alone."[50] This is what we find in Third Isaiah.

Erasure and Alterity

This Irigarayan reading of Third Isaiah reveals at least three key dynamics in the text. First and most clearly, the text of Third Isaiah demonstrates the masculine appropriation of the female body. While the text includes images of the female body, including in both its sexual and reproductive functions, these images are—like "any theory of the Subject"—in the service of the masculine. The female body appears so that Yahweh may use it, display it, and demonstrate his superiority to it. Continuing a pattern found in Second Isaiah (40–55), Yahweh repeatedly positions himself as a "better mother" (Gerlinde Bauman's phrase), even as he sustains himself by vampirizing the reproductive fecundity of the female.[51] While the male deity's exploitation of the female body is hardly unique to Isaiah 56–66 or 40–55, what reading these texts with Irigaray demonstrates is that even in texts where the female body is not subjected to *explicit violence* (as, for example, in Hos. 2, Ezek. 16, and Ezek. 23), it is still exploited and erased. There is no female subject, only female bodies—or female body *parts*.

Second, reading with Irigaray indicates the impossibility of representing women or the feminine under a masculine economy of representation. This assumes most dramatic form in the scenes of renaming: the woman-as-bride must be called according to Yahweh's new names for her. This

---

49. Irigaray, *Sexes and Genealogies*, 189.
50. Irigaray, *This Sex Which Is Not One*, 143 (emphasis in the original).
51. Baumann, "Prophetic Objections to YHWH as the Violent Husband of Israel." See also Graybill, "Yahweh as Maternal Vampire in Second Isaiah."

recalls a more violent iteration of a similar scene of remarriage in Hosea 2, where Yahweh commands how the woman is to speak (Hos. 2:18-19 [2:16-17 Eng.]). In that passage, as in an earlier passage in Third Isaiah, the deity also asserts physical and linguistic control over the woman's *mouth*.

Third, reading with Irigaray, and with Irigaray's work on Clytemnestra in particular, makes clear the text's erasure of relations between women. While there are multiple female figures, and portions of multiple female bodies, in the text, there are no relations *between women*. Relationships *between* women are rendered impossible and even unthinkable in this system. Furthermore, the range of possibilities available to female subjects is limited to a single role, the mother. Irigaray argues that Clytemnestra is killed, in part, because she refuses the limits of the maternal role: "Clytemnestra certainly does not obey the image of the virgin-mother that has been held up to us for centuries. She is still a passionate lover. Moreover, she will go as far as a *crime passionel*: she will kill her husband."[52] In Third Isaiah, we find similar limits placed on the female body, and the female role. There is no passion allowed to women, or even any agency. Yahweh is the one who acts, and acts upon the feminine, while preventing any relationships between women. In addition to the erasure of the mother–daughter relationship, and the absenting of the mother from any lines of genealogy, the text thus also forecloses any relationships between women as equals.

This erasure of relations between women reduces the woman (singular) to a role supporting the masculine economy of representation. Furthermore, it sustains specific masculine fantasy. Julie Kelso makes a similar argument with respect to Chronicles, arguing that "the disavowal and repression of corporeal origins, the disavowal and repression of originary maternal space…enables the construction of the socio-political vision of Chronicles."[53] She terms the repressed and silenced maternal body "the unsayable of Chronicles."[54] In Third Isaiah, the feminine is similarly unsayable and unspeakable. The text's insistent emphasis on the singularity of Yahweh (e.g. 63:3) forecloses the possibility of negotiation across otherness, including the otherness of sexual difference. This emphasis also erases the possibility of forms of otherness—and of otherness as a mode of relationality—between women. In another Irigarayan reading, this time of the story of Dinah (Gen. 34), Kelso notes that the real threat of the

52. Irigaray, "The Bodily Encounter with the Mother," 36.
53. Kelso, *O Mother Where Art Thou?*, 3.
54. Ibid., 114.

story is "the possibility of women-amongst-themselves: 'And Dinah, the daughter of Leah whom she bore for Jacob, went out to see the daughters of the land.'"[55] The text, of course, violently curtails this possibility, via Dinah's rape and the violence that follows. Relations among women are curtailed, and the possibilities of "women-amongst-themselves" are erased. Third Isaiah, I suggest, effects a similar erasure, though without the explicit violence of Genesis 34.

Irigaray writes in "The Bodily Encounter of the Mother," "It is also necessary, if we are not to be accomplices in the murder of the mother, for us to assert that there is a genealogy of women."[56] Third Isaiah not only denies such a genealogy; it encourages us as readers to do the same.

An/other Reading: What if Clytemnestra and Yahweh Were Not So Different, After All?

Before concluding, I explore one not-yet-addressed peculiarity that emerges when the representation of Yahweh in Third Isaiah is read with and against Aeschylus's representation of Clytemnestra. I began with Bal's question *Where is Clytemnestra?*, using this framing of the text to draw out the absence of the maternal and the exploitation of the feminine in the text. Now I, tentatively, suggest a second way of answering the question, which moves beyond absence and complicates the representation of both Yahweh and Clytemnestra. Taking as my starting points Bal and Irigaray, I have endeavored to read these two figures as diametrically opposed to each other (representing two possible worlds, building on Irigaray's opposition of the primal murder of the mother to Freud's primal murder of the father). And yet in reading the texts together, I cannot help but notice a motif that unites them. This motif is blood.

Both Clytemnestra and Yahweh have a preternatural fondness for blood, and appear literally dripping with it at crucial moments in their respective texts. At the end of Aeschylus's play, after Agamemnon and Cassandra have been murdered, Clytemnestra emerges from the house, splattered in blood. She recounts to the horrified chorus the scene of the murder:

---

55. Julie Kelso, "Reading the Silence of Women in Genesis 34," in *Redirected Travel: Alternative Journeys and Places in Biblical Studies*, ed. Roland Boer and Edgar W. Conrad, JSOTSup 382 (New York: Bloomsbury T&T Clark, 2003), 85–109 (108–9).

56. Irigaray, "The Bodily Encounter with the Mother," 44.

and spouting out a sharp jet of blood
he struck me with a dark shower of gory dew
while I rejoiced no less than the crop rejoices
in the Zeus-given moisture at the birth of the bud.

(*Agamemnon* 1389–1392, trans. Hugh Lloyd-Jones)[57]

This image of a triumphant murderer, covered in blood, is a familiar one to readers of Third Isaiah. Isaiah 63, like the scene with Clytemnestra outside the house, opens with a dialogue:

> [1] Who is this coming from Edom, from Bozrah in crimson-stained garments?
> Who is this with honored robes, marching with great might?
> It is I, announcing justice, mighty to save.
> [2] Why are your clothes red, and your garments like those who tread the wine press?
> [3] I have trodden the winepress alone, and from the peoples, no one was with me
> I have tread them in my anger and I have trampled them in my wrath
> Their juice splattered on my garments and stained all of my clothes.
> (Isa. 63:1-3)

And a few verses later, he reiterates:

> I trampled the peoples in my anger, I crushed[58] them in my wrath,
> I poured out their juice on the earth (63:6).

As Yahweh enters, dripping blood, his garments splattered and stained, he resembles no one more than Clytemnestra, still wet with her late husband's blood.

Perhaps we should not be surprised that blood unites the two figures; Gil Anidjar suggests, riffing on the political theorist Carl Schmitt, "*All significant concepts of the history of the modern world are liquidated theological concepts*"—that is, *blood*.[59] In Irigaray's analysis, blood is associated with the female body and the feminine. Blood is part of a larger economy of fluids that challenges masculine claims to power and dominance. "Woman is the guardian of blood," Irigaray writes in *Speculum*:

---

57. Hugh Lloyd-Jones, *Agamemnon: A Translation with Commentary* (Upper Saddle River, NJ: Prentice-Hall, 1970), 91–2.

58. ואשכרם read ואשברם.

59. Gil Anidjar, *Blood: A Critique of Christianity*, Religion, Culture, and Public Life (New York: Columbia University Press, 2016), viii (emphasis in the original).

"Woman, virgin and mother, represents the blood reserves."[60] And yet blood also represents the (violent) silencing of the feminine, in that "the master is a vampire," drawing his sustenance from the "repressed" "maternal, uterine foundations of his mastery."[61] Blood presents as a sign of violence, including the violence of the murder of the mother. But it simultaneously represents fluidity, the body, the blood ties of the family, the blood of menstruation.[62] In *Speculum*, Irigaray expands on this idea: "Blood is not easily repressed. Its empire will be even greater as a result of the forgeries of maternal power that are to be turned out."[63] Even as the maternal and marital imagery indicates a repression and denial of the representation of the feminine, so too does the bloodiness of the text—bloodiness, in particular, associated with Yahweh—mark its unexpected and largely unheralded return.[64]

In particular, the association of Yahweh with blood suggests a gender instability in the text. Blood marks his body not just with violence, but with the larger economy of fluids. The bloody avenger of Isaiah 63 is linked to other moments of bloodiness (in warfare, in childbirth) and fluidity (often though not always associated with the female body). Thus this hypermasculine scene—the deity dripping the blood of his enemies—also threatens to feminize the deity—it is women's bodies that drip and leak, as the regulations placed upon these leaky bodies in the legal texts make clear. Yahweh not only dabbles in a fluid, bloody body; he also exerts his control over maternity and is associated with the feminine processes of birth and childrearing. As in Second Isaiah, these passages have the effect of representing the deity as a sort of "better mother." They also suggest a (not unproblematic) feminization of Yahweh, which depends upon the exploitation and use of the female body.[65]

We find another parallel to Clytemnestra in the gender transgression implied by the deity's dripping, bloody form. The Argive queen, like the Hebrew deity, transgresses gender boundaries, especially in moments of blood. Classicists have long noted the gender ambiguity and ambivalence of Aeschylus's Clytemnestra, in both her words and her actions. Walter Duvall Penrose Jr. summarizes:

60. Irigaray, *Speculum of the Other Woman*, 225, 125.
61. Ibid., 127.
62. On menstrual blood, see further Irigaray's essay "Belief Itself," found in *Sexes and Genealogies*, 23–54.
63. Irigaray, *Speculum of the Other Woman*, 126.
64. On this argument, see further Graybill, "Yahweh as Maternal Vampire in Second Isaiah."
65. Ibid.

Clytemnestra's masculinity is iterated and reiterated performatively through a series of acts: she is outspoken (Ag. 11-12), speaks reasonably like a man (331), and rules in the place of a man (whether it is Agamemnon or Aegisthus). Through her controlling, regal, speech and deeds, she usurps a position reserved for men in Athenian culture. Seizing male privileges, she kills in revenge and polices her own body (rather than allowing her husband, Agamemnon, to do so).[66]

In addition to her actions, Clytemnestra's masculinity comes across on the level of language. In the opening speech, the watchman describes her as "a woman who thinks like a man" (ἀνδρόβουλον, 11).[67] She is more than once charged with speaking in a masculine manner; the chorus praises her for speaking "like a sensible man" (κατ'ἄνδρα σώφρον). Noting the "gender ambiguity" that attends Aeschylus's representation of the queen, Laura McClure observes Clytemnestra's own gendered "code-switching," while Froma I. Zeitlin describes her representation as "masculinized female."[68] Thus Clytemnestra is masculinized, even as Yahweh vacillates between masculine and feminine representation, even (especially?) in the representation of extreme violence. Furthermore, both figures stand proud and bloody in moments that jar the dominant economy of gendered representation.

This comparison is unsettling to a straightforward feminist reading because it suggests that far from opposites, Clytemnestra and Yahweh resemble each other. What does it mean to find the traces of Clytemnestra not just in the silenced feminine, but in the central figure that speaks and exerts control throughout the passage? I am not interested in arguing that the traces of the murdered/murderous mother make Yahweh a more "maternal" figure. I am interested, instead, in the way that they challenge simple binary oppositions and suggest another moment in which alterity breaks down or finds a moment of recognition even in otherness. Of Chronicles, Kelso writes, "It is the disavowal and repression of corporeal origins, the disavowal and repression of originary maternal space, which *enables* the construction of the socio-political vision" of the text.[69] This

---

66. Walter Duvall Penrose Jr., *Postcolonial Amazons: Female Masculinity and Courage in Ancient Greek and Sanskrit Literature* (New York: Oxford University Press, 2016), 28–9.

67. As translated by Laura McClure in *Spoken Like a Woman: Speech and Gender in Athenian Drama* (Princeton, NJ: Princeton University Press, 2009), 73.

68. Ibid., 74, 75; Froma I. Zeitlin, *Playing the Other: Gender and Society in Classical Greek Literature* (Chicago: University of Chicago Press, 1996), 344.

69. Kelso, *O Mother, Where Art Thou?*, 3 (emphasis in the original).

reading, which finds a trace of Clytemnestra and what she represents even in the figure of Yahweh, suggests one possible crack in the structure of disavowal and repression.

Conclusion: Chasing Clytemnestra

This essay uses both the figure of Clytemnestra and the theory of Luce Irigaray to explore gender difference and violence in Third Isaiah. Taking as a starting point Irigaray's writing on the female body and the masculine economy of representation—including her description of the primal murder of the mother, a description that relies heavily on the Clytemnestra myth—I trace the female body in Third Isaiah. The final eleven chapters of Isaiah present both an extension and a subversion of the representations of femininity, female sexuality, and maternity that proceed them in Second Isaiah. Yahweh is still represented as masculine, and continues to assert his power over the female body. There is little explicit *gender violence* here, though violence certainly figures in the text (mostly against foreign enemies and unfaithful followers, presumed to be male). The Yahweh who stands triumphant, dripping the blood of those he has killed, is also the Yahweh who summons babies, oversees childbirth, and promises to remarry the female Israel.

Reading with Irigaray makes clear the mutual dependence of these parts of the text, as well as the ways in which the seemingly neutral or even positive representations of female bodies erase relations between women and female genealogies, while reducing the woman to a singular figure in service of the masculine economy of representation. Comparing the biblical texts to the myth of Clytemnestra, particularly as recounted in Aeschylus's *Oresteia*, makes this clear. However, this is not the only function of Clytemnestra, the passionate murderous mother. While it is tempting to construct a binary in which Clytemnestra and Yahweh represent two opposing organizations of gender, power, and violence, a close literary analysis reveals striking similarities between the two. Furthermore, just as Clytemnestra, one of Irigaray's central figures of the mother in the mother–daughter dyad, is frequently *masculinized* in the text, so too do we find Yahweh, associated with blood and interested in wombs, *feminized*. While there is not a complete crossing over, there is a certain degree of gender instability that challenges strict binarizations and opens, perhaps, a possibility for reading gender subversion even in the harshly oppositional representations of femininity (women as brides and mothers) and masculinity (Yahweh as warrior) in Third Isaiah.

Elsewhere, I have argued for reading Yahweh in Second Isaiah (40–55) as "maternal vampire," sustained by and taking advantage of the female body. I stand by that reading and am open to the possibility of a similar vampirism in the interest in the womb and childbirth that Yahweh expresses in Third Isaiah, though I think the evidence is somewhat less clear. Here, I add only that vampires, even misogynistic vampires, are not infrequently also queer figures. The exploitation and silencing of women in Third Isaiah does not erase the possibility of gender instability, just as the parallels between Yahweh and the feminist (anti)heroine Clytemnestra do not suggest that Yahweh himself acts in a feminist way. This is gender instability without feminist framing or implications, as is common in certain forms of drag and in certain branches of queer biblical interpretation (I am thinking, in particular, of Roland Boer's reading of Yahweh's masculinity in his "Yahweh as Top: A Lost Targum").[70] But if vampires teach us one thing, it is that blood is appealing, and even the murdered do not always stay dead—even, perhaps especially, when they are mothers.

Yahweh, bloody, begins to resemble Clytemnestra. Blood both marks violence and documents return. This blood does not heal. What it does do, perhaps, is speak. And as we as biblical readers know, when blood speaks, it is always a wise idea to listen.

---

70. Roland Boer, "Yahweh as Top: A Lost Targum," in *Queer Commentary and the Hebrew Bible*, ed. Ken Stone, JSOTSup 334 (Sheffield: Sheffield Academic, 2001), 75–105.

Chapter 5

LANGUAGE AND SILENCE IN ISAIAH'S
ORACLES AGAINST THE NATIONS

Francis Landy

"The Dream follows the Interpretation" – *Talmud Bavli, Berakhot* 58b.

Metaphor and Alterity

"Metaphor is the dreamwork of language", Donald Davidson writes.[1] It is dreamwork in that ordinary language and things, with their enormous symbolic freight, jostle together in ever more elaborate combinations, at least in large poetic books, and require imaginative effort, by the reader as well as the poet, to make sense, and like dreams, they always risk senselessness. Davidson polemicizes against regarding metaphor as a special use of language, and thus accords with the cognitive school, which holds that metaphor is the result of ordinary operations of the mind; we work through analogy and difference.[2] But what happens when language is intentionally, fundamentally, strange, when, as in the book of Isaiah, nothing means what it appears to mean, when every word, even the

---

1. Donald Davidson, "What Metaphors Mean," *Critical Inquiry* 5 (1978): 31–47 (31).
2. George Lakoff, *Metaphors We Live By* (Chicago: Chicago University Press, 1980); *Women, Fire, and Dangerous Things: What Categories Reveal about the Mind* (Chicago: Chicago University Press, 1982). For a recent update, see George Lakoff and Elisabeth Wehling, *Your Brain's Politics: How the Science of Mind Explains the Political Divide* (Exeter: Imprint, 2016).

simplest, signifies a new age and a new reality, when, as Isaiah is told in his call vision, every word is designed to block understanding? Perhaps, with Karsten Harries, we might say that "metaphor...gestures towards what transcends language,"[3] that it is the sign of a lack, an absence. The *tertium quid* may be something unknown, always open to more interpretation; it may join up with other metaphors, which point to things equally unknown. Ultimately what is being communicated in language is vision, with its promise of transparency that can never be fulfilled, a vision that comes from beyond the poet, a dreamwork of which the poet himself is an emissary and a participant. Metaphors, moreover, may cross the boundary between sense and meaning; what is communicated, seen as alike or different, may be sound, sensation, emotion; it evokes the complex human world in which the visible shades into the invisible and unknowable. Harries distinguishes between philosophical and poetic metaphor precisely on this point: poetic metaphor is untranslatable, cannot be paraphrased. This is perhaps what Davidson means when he says that the understanding of a metaphor depends on the collaboration of interpreter and maker, that there are no special metaphorical meanings, that we depend on intuitive, intersubjective sympathy.[4] Except that I have no idea what he means by literal or ordinary meaning.[5]

Jacques Derrida, in his essay "Literature in Secret"[6] (and everywhere), reflects on the tension between meaning and non-meaning, the wish and necessity to write and the impossibility of doing so, so as to be adequate to thought and meaning, so as not to venture into alternative worlds.[7] Every poetic enterprise, not least the book of Isaiah, tries to create a unified literary and political work, in which all the disparate phenomena

---

3. Karsten Harries, "Metaphor and Transcendence," *Critical Inquiry* 5 (1978): 74–90 (84).

4. Davidson, "What Metaphors Mean," 31.

5. For a strong critique of Davidson, see Max Black, "How Metaphors Work: A Reply to Donald Davidson," in *Perplexities* (Ithaca, NY: Cornell University Press, 1990), 77–91.

6. Jacques Derrida, *The Gift of Death and Literature in Secret*, trans. David Wills, 2nd ed. (Chicago: University of Chicago Press, 2007), 119–58.

7. The leitmotif of "Literature in Secret" is 'Pardon de ne pas vouloir dire" which means both "Pardon for not wanting to say" and "Pardon for not meaning..." The motif goes back at least to his early collection of interviews, "Positions" in which he says, in a piece originally published in 1967, "I try to write (in) the space where is posed the question of speech and meaning. I try to write the question: (what is) meaning to say" (Jacques Derrida, *Positions* [Paris: de Minuit, 1971], 23; English trans., *Positions*, trans. Alan Bass [Chicago: Chicago University Press, 1981], 14).

and nations of the world will finally be united. The statement, "*Tout autre est tout autre*," in the mind of God or the poet, is a dazzling tautology.[8] At the same time, "every other" (*tout autre*) is completely different, and incomparable with the self or anyone/thing else. Derrida coins the term "heterotautology" for this paradox, exemplified by Hegel.[9] Metaphor crosses gaps, but also opens differences, for instance between the familiar and the unfamiliar, as when the dead metaphor of "Assyria is a rod" is transformed by the addition of "of my anger."

Oracles Against/For the Nations

Oracles against the Nations sections occur in all the major prophets (Isa. 13–23; Jer. 46–51; Ezek. 25–32) and two of the minor ones (Amos 1–2; Zeph. 2).[10] They have several functions: (i) to establish YHWH's dominion over the whole earth and the prophet's worldwide mission; (ii) to differentiate Israel's destiny from that of the nations, especially if, as in the LXX version of Jeremiah,[11] Ezekiel, and Zephaniah, they mediate between the condemnation of Israel and its salvation; (iii) to point to parallels with or even intensification of the guilt of Israel. The prime instance is Amos 1–2, in which Israel is the climax of the sequence.

Isaiah 13–23 is the longest set of Oracles against the Nations (henceforth OAN).[12] Presumably deriving from different periods, it is unified by the generic superscription משא, "burden," which introduces them,[13] and by thematic and geographical trajectories, for instance from the terrestrial empire of Babylon in the east (chs 13–14) to the maritime power of Tyre in the west (ch. 23). Moreover, it includes a "burden" against Jerusalem,

---

8. "Tout autre est tout autre" is the title of the last chapter of *The Gift of Death*, 82–116.

9. *The Gift of Death*, 83.

10. In addition, two short prophetic books, Obadiah and Nahum, entirely concern foreign nations.

11. In the LXX, the OAN are situated in the middle of the book (chs 25–31) rather than at the end.

12. Many scholars include chs 24–27 (the so-called Little Isaiah Apocalypse) in the OAN (e.g. Joseph Blenkinsopp, *Isaiah 1–39: A New Translation with Introduction and Commentary*, AB 19 [New York: Doubleday, 2000], 271–2). In my view, that chs 24–27 are not directed against particular foreign nations and lack the superscription משא serves to differentiate them.

13. The one exception is the oracle concerning the land beyond the rivers of Kush in ch. 18, which is introduced by הוי, corresponding to imprecation against the nations in 17:12-14, also prefaced by הוי.

under the rubric of "the valley of vision" (22:1-14), as well as miscellaneous materials, such as an oracle concerning two officials (22:15-25) and a prophetic narrative (ch. 20). A "burden" over Damascus rapidly turns into one against northern Israel (17:1-11). Thus, the boundary between self and other, Israel and the nations, is blurred; likewise, the prophet becomes a marginal, liminal figure, mediating between God and humanity, and Israel and the nations.

The sequence of OAN in Isaiah contrasts with the preceding tightly organized set of oracles concerning Israel and Judah during the Assyrian crisis in the late eighth century BCE, as well as the succeeding set of oracles, unified by the superscription הוי, in chs 28–33. Superficially, they have little in common.[14] One wonders then what the OAN are doing at this point in the book of Isaiah. It could be that they are a standard prophetic genre; any prophet worth his salt inveighs against foreign nations. Nonetheless, there must be some poetic, structural reason for their inclusion in a book that has been highly edited. In other words, even if they are conventional (which they are not), one must still ask what is their poetic function, how do they contribute to the total discourse of the book.

My thesis is that the OAN constitute a Freudian displacement of the anxiety, grief, and hope expressed in the first twelve chapters. Chapters 1–12 are a statement of the themes and preoccupations of the book; chs 13–23 are a counter-statement. The nations are Israel writ large, and differently. The relation between Israel and the nations is thus metaphorical. It precisely comprises Derridean "heterotautology." The nations are exotic, other, yet linked to Israel through a common humanity. This is transcultural and translinguistic. A feature of the oracles on which I especially focus is the metaphorical import of alliterations, rhythms, vocalic patterns. On the sonic plane, this is equivalent to the vision which, I suggested earlier, is the goal of poetic metaphor.

One interesting feature of the OAN in Isaiah is the sympathy the prophet evinces for the other nations, and the prediction of an ultimate restitution. Hence the familiar label, "Oracles Against the Nations," is not wholly accurate. I convey this ambiguity by the title of this subsection, "Oracles Against/For the Nations."

---

14. There is, however, a structural link between ch. 13, the Oracle against Babylon, and ch. 34, addressed to Edom. See Burkhard M. Zapff, *Schriftgelehrte Prophetie— Jes 13 und die Komposition des Jesajabuches: Ein Beitrag zur Erförschung der Redaktionsgeschichte des Jesajabuches* (Würzburg: Echter, 1995).

Alliterations, Puns, and other Vocalic Figures

Alliterations, puns, anaphoras, rhymes, pervade these chapters, to a degree unparalleled in the rest of the book. These features communicate the non-signifying, emotive burden of the prophecy, for instance through repeated sounds of weeping. The alliterations and wordplays connect different oracles and the body of the prophet with the geographical landscape. Beyond that, however, the alliterations, puns etc., convey the mystique of poetry, by which I mean the technique for imparting mystery, for rendering language "rich and strange." On the one hand, there is pleasure in virtuosity, on the other the dissolution of meaning and the self under the impact of a vision which cannot be linguistically contained. In general, it is a vision of horror, of a malign *mysterium tremendum*. It is thus death which disrupts language and provides grounds for the dizzying verbal artifice, which transfers somatic experience onto imaginary edifices, the construction and deconstruction of worlds.

For instance, the envoys (צירים) sent by the "land of the susurration of wings" in 18:2 are echoed in the prophet's visionary travail (צירים) in 21:3:

> Which sends envoys (צירים) on the sea, in reed boats upon the waters, "Go, swift messengers…" (18:2)

> Therefore my thighs are filled with torment, pangs (צירים) have seized me like the pangs of childbirth… (21:3)[15]

The metaphorical interpretation of the homonym is less important than the collision of different worlds: Kush and Babylon, remote diplomatic voyages, and bodily eruptions. What is born, in this parody of childbirth, is death. The prophet travails and gives birth to the poem, which is full only of torment (חלחלה), a word associated both with childbirth

---

15. The verse is similar to 13:8, in which the same noun, צירים, is used to describe the travail of the Babylonians. Katherine Pfisterer Darr, *Isaiah's Vision and the Family of God* (Louisville, KY: Westminster John Knox, 1994), 103, points to the parallel and holds that the image here is ironic and conventional. John J. Schmitt, "The City as Woman in Isaiah 1–39," in *Writing and Reading the Scroll of Isaiah: Studies in an Interpretive Tradition*, ed. Craig C. Broyles and Craig A. Evans (Leiden: Brill, 1997), 95–120 (107), thinks that the speaker is Babylon, since it does not have the "reportorial" quality of vv. 2 and 6. There seems to be no reason to posit a change in the identity of the first person here.

and emptiness.[16] The vision is contracted into a failure of hearing and an incapacity to see: "A harsh vision is told to me…I am too contorted to hear, too appalled to see" (21:2-3).[17] The prophet is in the position of the mother who harbours death in her womb, who is both the one who grieves and the one whom the child mourns. He is then mother of himself, but only as the one who internalizes and enacts destruction. The liminality of the prophet is evident in the following verse: "the twilight of my desire is posed for me as a shivering" (21:4).[18] The twilight of desire implies cessation, and the transition from light to darkness, vitality to morbidity; the shivering may be the effect of excitement, or fear, or a paroxysm leading to death.

Moab and the Valley of Vision (Chapters 15–16)

The Oracle against/for Moab in chs 15–16 is characterized by intricate wordplays linking it to the fate of Zion, to other oracles in the sequence, and to the body of the prophet. It is an accumulation of sounds as much

---

16. חלחלה derives from חיל, "travail"; the duplicated "ל," however, associates it with חלל II, "empty." It may perhaps also be correlated with חלל I, "profane" i.e. be a profanation of the prophet/God.

17. E. Bosshard-Nepustil, *Rezeptionen von Jesaja 1–39 im Zwölfenprophetenbuch* (Freiburg: Universitätsverlag, 1997), 29, thinks that the preposition in משמע/מראות (lit. "from hearing, from seeing") is causative and not privative: the contortion and horror result from the vision and report, but do not lead to a loss of sight and hearing. See also John D. W. Watts, *Isaiah 1–33*, rev. ed., WBC 24 (Waco, TX: Word, 2005), 326, and Hans Wildberger, *Isaiah 13–27*, trans. Thomas Trapp, A Continental Commentary (Minneapolis, MN: Fortress, 1997), 304. The privative meaning, however, accords with the extremity of the imagery in the passage, as well as the general motif of seeing/not-seeing throughout the book.

18. The metaphor has caused difficulties for commentators. Most take it as referring to the cool of the evening e.g. Andrew A. Macintosh, *Isaiah XXI: A Palimpsest* (Cambridge: Cambridge University Press, 1980), 22. Ronald Clements, *Isaiah 1–39*, NCB (London: Marshall, Morgan & Scott, 1980), 178, thinks it conveys the duration of the anguish. Bernard Gosse, *Isaïe 13,1–14,23 dans la Tradition Littéraire du Livre d'Isaïe et dans la Tradition des Oracles Contre les Nations*, OBO 78 (Freiburg: Universitätsverlag; Göttingen Vandenhoeck & Ruprecht, 1988), 56, suggests a connection with traditions that Babylon fell on a festive night, and a linkage with 22:13. Watts, *Isaiah 1–33*, 329, proposes that the context is the failure of Merodach-Baladan in 703 BCE, which resulted in the collapse of hope for long term independence from Assyria. See also Jesper Høgenhaven, *Gott und Volk bei Jesaja: Eine Untersuchung zur Biblischen Theologie* (Leiden: Brill, 1988), 145–7 and Seth Erlandsson, *The Burden of Babylon: A Study of Isaiah 13:2–14.23*, ConBOT 4 (Lund: CWK Gleerup, 1970), 86–92.

as of images; Alonso-Schökel[19] aptly describes it as a litany. It begins: כי בליל שדד ער מואב נדמה כי בליל שדד קיר מואב נדמה: "For by night Ar/city of Moab is despoiled, destroyed/silenced, for by night Kir/wall/city of Moab is despoiled, destroyed/silenced." נדמה, "destroyed/silenced," echoes the Oracle of Silence (Dumah), in 21:11, likewise associated with ליל, "night."[20] As there, the repetition amplifies the resonance of the disaster and the succeeding silence. From the silence of the night arises weeping. This is confirmed through alliteration. The word for night, ליל, is echoed onomatopoeically in vv. 2 and 3 by יילל, "wails," and by the place name אלעלה in v. 4. Throughout the Burdens, indeed, ל's signify grief; one notes, for instance, the constellation of קמלו, דללו, and אמללו—all synonyms for "languish"—in 19:6 and 8. The intensity of the sound patterns and the evocation of weeping take us below the level of language as the domain of weeping, to a universal plangency.

In 15:1, *Qir* may juxtapose the Moabite word for city with the Hebrew word for "city," עיר; it may be a sign of heteroglossia, one of several in the sequence of Oracles.[21] But it is echoed intimately in the prophet's body: קרבי לקיר חרש, "my core is for Kir Hares," in 16:11. The inside of the poet is evoked metaphorically, through the ingenuity of the wordplay, as the outside, as the broken wall in a foreign country, since קיר also means "wall," and הרש "potsherd." The alliterative pattern connects self to other, across a fragile, dissolving boundary. It has a metaphorical function suggestive of the bond between קרבי, "my core," and קיר הרש, "Kir Hares." At the same time, it draws attention to the surplus of speech over signification. To see it simply as productive of metaphors, for example, between self and wall, or self and other, is to neglect its non-referential aspect. Play with words opens up the complex transactions between sound and meaning, self and word, body and society. It is difficult to mistake the poetic achievement of קרבי לקיר הרש, at the end of the burden of Moab, and the effect of convergence of the lyric voice and its subject. The poem began with the difference between Hebrew and Moabite, between עיר and קיר, and ends with its emotive and phonemic erasure.

---

19. Luis Alonso-Schökel, *Estudios de poética hébreo* (Barcelona: Flor, 1963), 417.

20. Macintosh, *Isaiah XXI*, 98–9, 135, argues that the two oracles share the same background.

21. Brian C. Jones, *Howling over Moab: Irony and Rhetoric in Isaiah 15–16*, SBL Dissertation Series 157 (Atlanta, GA: Scholars Press, 1996), 174, proposes that 15:1 parallels Hebrew (עיר) and Moabite (קיר) words for "city." See also Wildberger, *Isaiah 13–27*, 126–31; Clements *Isaiah 1–39*, 152. Similarly, according to Macintosh, *Isaiah XXI*, 79, 137, the oracle concerning Dumah evokes Edomite or international Aramaic.

How and why did these poets write? We do not know, of course, but perhaps the wordplays can give us a clue. In the verse previous (v. 10) to the conjunction of קרבי and קיר הרש, we have that of כרמל, "fertile land," and כרמים, "vineyards." The alliteration (כרם, כרם) is conventional, but it is also the stuff of poetry. קרבי and קיר fit together, like a key into a lock; so do כרמל and כרמים. Poetry consists of innumerable local triumphs. The satisfaction of joining one thing to another, like a jigsaw puzzle, is elementary poesis, making the world whole and breaking it up again.

In 22:5-6, the same paronomastic chain recurs in the oracle of the valley of vision, namely Jerusalem:

> For there is a day of uproar, confusion, and bewilderment for my Lord, YHWH of Hosts in the valley of vision; dismantling of walls (מקרקר קר), and shouting (שוע) to the mountain. And Elam bears the dart, with chariots of men and cavalry, and Kir bares the shield.

מקרקר קר occurs nowhere else, and is interpreted variously as referring to the breaking down of walls and to the noise of battle.[22] In either case, it is linked to a geographical and political entity, Kir.[23] Then the wall is identified with the enemy which destroys it, or, alternatively, the cries of battle, represented onomatopoeically by the threefold alliteration of מקרקר קר, are the effect of the impact of Kir, which disrupts language as well as the military and civic apparatus, since the valley of vision has turned into a place of uproar and confusion. There is thus an affinity between Moab and Jerusalem, between the interiority of the prophet, the Moabite landscape, the remote enemy, and the fragmentation and regression of language.

At the beginning of the Burden of Moab in 15:1, the nocturnal city is "despoiled, destroyed/silenced" (שדד, נדמה). The same combination of שדד and נד recurs in the centre of the oracle, in 16:1-4, in which Mt. Zion is urged to provide shelter to the fugitives:

---

22. Full discussions may be found in Wildberger, *Isaiah 13–27*, 350, and Blenkinsopp, *Isaiah 1–39*, 332. Num. 24:17 may support the first interpretation, if one does not read there קדקד, "crown," for MT קרקר. Watts, *Isaiah 1–33*, 336, derives מקרקר from מקור, "spring," to suggest "digging a ditch," anticipating vv. 9-11, which describe Hezekiah's waterworks.

23. Kir is mentioned in Amos 1:5 and 9:7, but is otherwise unknown. The name appears in no Akkadian source. In Amos 9:7, Kir is the original homeland of Aram, and in 1:5 it is predicted to be the place of their exile. Elam causes similar problems, since at no time was it an enemy of Israel; most commentators assume that contingents from Elam and Kir were part of the Assyrian or Babylonian armies, which does not solve the problem.

(1) Send a gift, O ruler of the land, from the crag of the wilderness to the mountain of the daughter of Zion. (2) And it shall be like a wandering (נודד) bird, a nest sent forth, the daughters of Moab crossing the Arnon. (3) Take counsel, do justly, spread your shade like night at midday, hide the outcast (נדחים), do not reveal the fugitive (נדד). (4) May those displaced from Moab find shelter among you, be a concealment for them from the despoiler (שודד); for the oppression is over, the pillage has ceased, the predators have vanished from the land.[24]

נודד and שודד rhyme, as if spoliation and flight go together. Of course, they do not, in that the fugitive escapes from the spoiler. But in the fantasy that this passage expresses, there is a perfect balance between them. The concealment of the נודד corresponds to the vanishing of the שודד. The נודד, for once, stands up to the שודד, through the protective figure of the daughter of Zion.

To disentangle the metaphorical from the phonological is impossible. נודד is embedded in the sentence, נדד אל תגלי, "the fugitive do not reveal," as if concealment happens also syntactically. "From the despoiler," מפני שודד, is appended as a prepositional phrase to "be a concealment for them," in which the emphatic למו, "for them," stands out against the force of the despoiler. In v. 2 the rhyming word נודד appears as part of a simile, כעוף נודד, "like a wandering bird." The rhyme itself wanders from place to place, interwoven with other combinations, such as נדחים, "outcast/displaced," in v. 3, to form the sequence נדחים נדד.

In 16:9-10, the same duplication occurs in the word הידד, which describes joy in the vintage:

> Therefore I weep in the weeping of Jazer, the vine of Sibmah, Ariawek, my tear is Heshbon and Elaleh, for upon your harvest/end and your vendange הידד has fallen. Gladness and joy will be gathered up from the fruitful land, and in the vineyards one will not shout or make jubilation; wine in the press the treader will not tread; I have made הידד cease.

---

24. Many critics transpose 16:2 and 16:1, or propose various rearrangements of the text, e.g., Blenkinsopp, *Isaiah 1–39*, 299; Thomas G. Smothers, "Isaiah 15–16," in *Forming Prophetic Literature: Essays on Isaiah and the Twelve in Honor of John D. W. Watts*, ed. James W. Watts and Paul R. House, JSOTSup 235 (Sheffield: Sheffield Academic, 1996), 70–84 (75); Clements, *Isaiah 1–39*, 154; Alonso-Schökel, *Estudios*, 418. Others retain the order of the text, e.g., Jones, *Howling Over Moab*, 260, and Watts, *Isaiah 1–33*, 284, for whom the coupling of 16:1 and 2 contributes to the chiastic structure of the oracle. The proposed transposition spoils the sequence of rhymes I point out here, as well as the juxtaposition of the daughters of Moab with the daughter of Zion.

הידד here has two opposite connotations. In the first verse, הידד refers to the joy of the conquerors, the familiar metaphor of the harvest of death, which pervades, for instance, ch. 18, as we see below. In the second, it is the literal הידד that has ceased. The metaphorical הידד is superimposed upon and nullifies the literal הידד.

הידד is an onomatopoeia, in which the rhythmic chant of the treaders coincides with the stamping of feet. The sound thus interfuses with the onomatopoeic representation of weeping throughout the Burden of Moab, for instance through double לs. The two הידדs match the two שודדs, "despoiled," with which the oracle opened.

The sack, destruction, and silencing of the city, and the rupture of its wall, corresponds to the victory march evoked by the first הידד and the end of the agricultural celebrations it imposes. Framed by the two is the pairing of נדד and שודד in the centre in Zion, where violence is abolished.

The oracle against Moab is paired in intricate ways I cannot pursue in detail with that against Arabia, in 21:13-17. There too the word נדד appears, as an inversion of the tribe *Dedan*. There too we find the motive of succouring the fugitives. What pressure, at whatever compositional level, is conducive to the twinning of these oracles? In the Burden of Moab, Zion is urged to provide shelter; in that of Arabia it is the Dedanites or the inhabitants of Tema who do so. Zion fulfils its function as a haven for the world, as expressed paradigmatically in chs 2 and 11. The role of the Davidic king is evident in 16:5: "And a throne will be established in חסד, and one will sit on it in truth in the tent of David, a judge, seeking justice, eager for righteousness." At the centre of the Moab oracle, then, is Zion, just as it is the centre of the symbolic world.

The Land Beyond the Rivers of Kush (Chapter 18)

(18.1) Woe, O land of the sussuration of wings, beyond the rivers of Kush, (2) Which sends messengers by sea, in papyrus boats on the face of the waters, 'Go, O swift messengers, to a people drawn out and burnished, a race terrible from time and beyond, a people קו קו[25] and trampling, whose land rivers bisect.

---

25. Many commentators think that קו קו is an onomatopoeia for the people's incomprehensible language (e.g. Blenkinsopp, *Isaiah 1–39*, 309). Others suggest "very strong" or "sinewy" (Wildberger, *Isaiah 13–27*, 208; Csaba Balogh, *The Stele of YHWH in Egypt: The Prophecies of Isaiah 18–20 concerning Egypt and Kush* [Leiden: Brill, 2011], 153); "very tall" or "ship-going" (Meir Lubetski and Claire

In ch. 18, every detail augments metonymically the exotic remoteness of the people beyond the rivers of Kush, over the geographical and political horizon.[26] The people and its land are never named, but manifest themselves through their effects and their emissaries. The "land of the susurration (צלצל) of wings"[27] presents us with the sound, perhaps even before they become visible, of creatures in flight—insects or birds—an intimation of migrations, swarms or flocks; we are immersed onomatopoeically in sonorities. In v. 2, this people is displaced by another, stranger still, to whom they send messages,[28] a גוי קו קו ומבוסה, "a nation קו קו and trampling," whose remoteness is intensified by the emphasis on distance induced by such details as the lightness of the papyrus boats, the swiftness of the messengers, the evocation of large bodies of water.

Gottlieb, "Isaiah 18: The Egyptian Nexus," in *Boundaries of the Ancient World: A Tribute to Cyrus Gordon*, ed. Meir Lubetski, Claire Gottlieb and Sharon Keller [Sheffield: Sheffield Academic, 1996], 364–84 [374]); and "drawn up in rows" (Marta Høyland Lavik, *A People Tall and Smooth-Skinned: The Rhetoric of Isaiah 18*, VTSup 112 [Leiden: Brill, 2007], 56). I have left it untranslated because of its resistance to interpretation and so as to draw attention to its sound. The whole passage is replete with textual problems, and I try to convey its recondite atmosphere in my translation.

26. Most commentators explain the oracle historically in the context of the rise of the Ethiopian dynasty in Egypt, and provide reconstructions; Alviero Niccacci, "Isaiah XVIII–XX from an Egyptological Perspective," *VT* 48 (1998): 214–38, is exemplary. This, however, is to reduce the lack of specificity of the title and misses the rhetorical point, that even those beyond the horizon of the known world are affected by current political perturbations.

27. The meaning of צלצל is disputed. "Whirring" or "susurration" relates to צלצל in Deut. 28:42 and many Semitic cognates meaning "cricket." צל has a ringing sound among its many connotations (Blenkinsopp, *Isaiah 1–39*, 206). See also Lavik, *A People Tall and Smooth-Skinned*, 50–1, who translates "buzzing." Others, following the Targum, render "ships" or "boats" with "wings" as a metonymy for sails (Wildberger, *Isaiah 13–27*, 207; Watts, *Isaiah 1–33*, 301). Lubetski and Gottlieb, "Isaiah 18," 371, followed by Balogh, *The Stele of YHWH*, 145, 165, identify צלצל with the scarab beetle, as a symbol for Egypt, and hence of the Ethiopian dynasty. Alonso-Schökel, *Estudios*, 285, brilliantly writes "to begin with, an impressionistic auditory detail, with closed eyes a noise of pertinacious insects envelops us, and then, when our eyes open, we admire the rapid reed canoes…" (my translation).

28. Most commentators identify the destination of the emissaries as Jerusalem (John Goldingay, *Isaiah* [Peabody, MA: Hendrickson, 2001], 116), or, on the contrary, as Judean envoys to Ethiopia (Marvin A. Sweeney, *Isaiah 1–39, with an Introduction to Prophetic Literature*, FOTL 16 [Grand Rapids, MI: Eerdmans, 1996], 257; Blenkinsopp, *Isaiah 1–39*, 309–10). There is nothing to support either conjecture.

The repeated קו also appears in 28:10 and 13 as an expression for the nonsense language which YHWH, or the prophet, speaks to the people, in order that they should be destroyed:

(9) Whom will he teach knowledge? And who will understand that which is heard? Those weaned from milk, snatched from the breasts!
(10) For צו to צו, צו to צו, קו to קו, קו to קו, a little here, a little there,
(11) For with stammering lips and another tongue will he speak to this people.
(12) To whom it was said: This is the resting place, leave it for the weary, and this is the repose, and they did not wish to hear.
(13) And the word of YHWH shall be for them צו to צו, צו to צו, קו to קו, קו to קו, a little here, a little there, so that they should go, and stumble backwards, and be broken, and ensnared, and taken.

What the enigmatic sequence "צו to קו, צו to קו" means is uncertain, but essentially it exemplifies YHWH's miscommunication, the distortion of language and meaning.[29] As Exum puts it, referring to the alphabetic interpretation, "the basic significants of meaning...are meaningless."[30] It suggests putting things together, just as "a little bit here, a little bit there" conveys the gradual accumulation of the prophetic message. But it does not add up; in the fullest sense of the word, it is deconstructive, language that has turned against meaning.

There are other possibilities: קו קו may mean "very tall" or "very strong" and thus be aligned to ומבוסה "trampling," or to their sea-going craft, or to military formations (18:2). At any rate, it suggests ferocity as well as incomprehensibility, as already suggested by their description as

---

29. Both Baruch Halpern, "'The Excremental Vision': The Doomed Priests of Doom in Isaiah 28," *HAR* 10 (1986): 109–21 (115–16) and Vincent Tanghe, "Dichtung und Ekel in Jesaja XXVIII 7-13," *VT* 43 (1993): 235–60 (246–7), think that both words play on terms used for priestly Torah: צו echoes מצוה, "commandment," while קו, according to Halpern, is used for a line of judgment, as in v. 17, while Tanghe points out that in Qumran (1QS 10:9) it refers to a "religious-ethical norm," and that this sense might already be found in Isaiah. If this is the case, we have another example of the priestly Torah turning into its opposite. Jörg Barthel, *Prophetenwort und Geschichte: Die Jesajaüberlieferung in Jes 6–8 und 28–31*, FAT 19 (Tübingen: Mohr Siebeck), 299 n. 49, thinks צו refers to the priests, and קו to the prophets.

30. J. Cheryl Exum, "Whom Will He Teach Knowledge? A Literary Approach to Isaiah 28," in *Art and Meaning: Rhetoric in Biblical Literature*, ed. David J. A. Clines, David M. Gunn, and Alan J. Hauser, JSOTSup 19 (Sheffield: JSOT), 108–39 (122).

עם נורא מן הוא והלאה, "a people terrible from time and beyond" (18:2).³¹ If קו קו is an onomatopoeia, concurring with the צלצל כנפים, "the susurration of wings," of the beginning of the oracle, we hear the harsh sound of the language of these remote people (think of the cawing of crows) as we hear their trampling feet, from an immense distance. We do not know where they are marching, or what the emissaries say to them. Theirs is a land divided by rivers: "whose land rivers bisect";³² likewise the land of the susurration of wings is "beyond the rivers of Kush" (18:1). We have a sense of infinite regress; if Kush marks the limit of the biblical world, that which is beyond the rivers of Kush is further still, and, presumably, the fabulous people to whom they send messengers, whose land rivers traverse, is even more ultimate. Rivers demarcate territory; that which is beyond the river is a different world. The cosmological significance of the rivers of Kush is augmented by their possible identification with the Gihon, the river which surrounds Kush in Gen. 2:13, thus giving them a paradisal quality.³³

But then in the next verse we turn from these remote regions to the whole world: "All you who inhabit earth, and dwell on land, when the banner on the mountains is lifted up, see! When the shofar is sounded, hear!" (18:3).³⁴ If the sound of the wings and incomprehensible speech evokes universal glossolalia, the multiplicity of languages, here humanity listens to a sound which is non-linguistic, a raw sign of alarm, like the tumultuous river in which Kubla Khan heard "ancestral voices

---

31. מן הוא והלאה only occurs here and in the parallel in v. 7. Most translate "far and wide" or the like; I think it may be temporal as well as spatial (see also J. J. M. Roberts, *First Isaiah*, Hermeneia [Minneapolis, MN: Fortress, 2015], 248).

32. בזא, "divide," is another *hapax*, but its meaning is fairly clear. Roberts, *First Isaiah*, 248, however, proposes "sweep away."

33. The Gihon is also the spring in Jerusalem where Solomon was crowned. For a relationship between the Gihon in Jerusalem and the river of Eden, see my essay "Fluvial Fantasies," in *Thinking of Water in the Early Second Temple Period*, ed. Ehud Ben Zvi and Christoph Levin, BZAW 461 (Berlin: de Gruyter), 437–56 (444–9).

34. Ulrich F. Berges, *The Book of Isaiah: Its Composition and Final Form*, trans. Millard C. Lind (Sheffield: Sheffield Phoenix, 2012), 145–6, sees this verse, together with v. 7, as a supplement which puts a positive spin on the nations. Otto Kaiser, *Der Prophet Jesaja Kapitel 13–39*, ATD 18 (Göttingen: Vandenhoeck & Ruprecht, 1983), 77–8, attributes it possibly to a proto-apocalyptic strand, which presages the unification of the nations in Zion. See also Wildberger, *Isaiah 13–27*, 209–10. As Blenkinsopp, *Isaiah 1–39*, 310, comments, "such decisions are always problematic and often arbitrary."

prophesying war." The banner (נס) on the mountain may likewise be a military standard, a conventional signal for battle, but it also recalls, intratextually, the standard that is raised for the root of Jesse in 11:10: "And it shall be on that day that the root of Jesse shall stand as a standard for peoples; towards it shall nations inquire, and its repose shall be glory." There the Davidic scion, and Mt. Zion on which the standard is raised, are a fulcrum for the world; the people's inquiring (ידרשו) recollects that of the nations in 2:2-4, and the inauguration of the era of non-violence by the new Davidide in 11:1-9. War is then peace. Likewise, the shofar to which the denizens of earth listen is the prophetic message, and, behind it, the divine summons. It corresponds, in the text of Isaiah, to the great shofar that heralds the return of the exiles in 27:13.

There is a twist, however. Instead of the whole world listening, there is one person, the prophet himself: "For thus said YHWH to me" (18:4a). An inner speech dramatizes the prophet's audition, either as representative of the nations, or as the one person who can hear what YHWH has to say, at the centre of the vast vistas evoked in vv. 1-3. Not Judah, but the prophet himself in his solitude who stands at the centre of the discourse. But the prophet's subjectivity is a prelude to that of YHWH: אשקוטה ואביטה במכוני, "I will be silent and gaze from my dwelling" (18:4b). YHWH speaks, only to say that he will be silent. It is perhaps self-reflexive, so that YHWH reveals to the prophet this inner speech, or determination not to speak, just as the prophet's words may be recursive, a justification to himself why he should address the nations, or perhaps this is the content of what the nations are supposed to hear.

The shofar blast introduces a summons to listen to this divine silence. Silence may portend the cessation of prophecy, as in Amos 8:11-14, or a refusal to communicate, despite the summons to hear, or the retraction of the divine voice into itself. The silence is absorbed into the gaze; the effect of distantiation is magnified by the detail that YHWH looks out from his abode, and from the impersonality of the succeeding verse. But here it immediately slides over into the silence of death: "For before the harvest, when the blossom is finished, and there are clusters of flowers on the ripening grape-berries, one will cut off the tendrils with pruning shears, and the young shoots discard, pare away" (v. 5). As ever, the harvest is a figure for death; death is the reaper.[35] The images, however, are anticipated in the previous verse: כחם צח עלי אור כעב טל בחם קציר, "Like shimmering

---

35. In the immediate context, the metaphor is used twice in the preceding oracles against Damascus/Israel (17:4-6, 11), and Moab (16:9).

heat over light, like a cloud of dew in the heat of harvest" (18:4c-d). The silent gaze is blazing, evoking wrath and portending destruction; synaesthesia, the rare word צח, associated with intense brightness and clarity, and its appearance above the light, together with the sense of divine vision from his celestial abode, make it a theophany; the gaze is seen, and sears. It combines with its opposite: "like a cloud of dew in the heat of harvest." The cloud of dew may promise relief, but it is also a conventional figure for evanescence. The repetition of חם, "heat," amplifies it; the heat of harvest is that of the gaze, but it is rendered dazzling and pernicious. The cloud (or better, mist) of dew burns away, and with it whatever obtrudes between YHWH's gaze and the fate he foresees. If it is a figure for compassion, that protection is flimsy indeed.

The harvest recurs in the next verse, as we have seen, as a metaphor for death as well as a temporal reference. But it is also characterized by preemption: כי לפני קציר, "For before the harvest..." Death precedes the harvest, which, in its literal sense, will not happen; death, as it were, cannot wait for itself. The sequence, from the divine gaze to what it sees, from prediction to consequence, is reversed; the imaginary harvest gives place to an absence of harvest, anticipated, with all its ominous implications, only to be taken away.[36]

There is, however, a counter-movement. כחם צח, "like shimmering heat," rhymes with כתם פרח, "when the blossom is over." The rhyme matches the two images (e.g., the flowers fade when the heat of summer comes, with the familiar pathos that it induces). One may note also in the insistent monosyllables,[37] interchanged with bisyllables, חם צח...אור... עב טל...תם, a lightness of vocalic texture contrasted with the malignity of the message.[38]

Rhymes and other rhythmic devices such as parallelism suggest couplings, affinities, a play of sound and sense, alongside and despite the overall plangency. They link centre to periphery, remote and unintelligible peoples to prophetic listening and divine silence, a silence

---

36. Temporal regression is a frequent poetic device in Isaiah, for instance in 28:4, in which the early fig is eaten while it is still in the hand. More generally, deliverance often overlaps with destruction.

37. For the poetic effect of the accumulation of short words, see also Lavik, *A People Tall and Smooth-Skinned*, 132, and Patricia Tull, *Isaiah 1–39* (Macon, GA: Smyth & Helwys, 2010), 316.

38. One may note that על עב טל is echoed in עב קל, the "swift cloud" on which YHWH rides at the beginning of the next oracle, against Egypt, in 19:1.

that can only express itself in language. We find this, for instance, in the correspondence between זלזלים, "tendrils" (18:5) and the initial צלצל, "whirring,"[39] the multiple meanings that attach to both it and the succeeding נטישות, "shoots,"[40] and the duplication of sounds, with the intimation of nonsense language, as in קו קו.

In v. 6 we pass from the human to the animal realms: "and they will be left to the raptors of the mountains and the beasts of the earth; the raptors will summer upon it, and all the beasts of the earth will winter upon it." Animals represent an ultimate alterity, even greater than that of the exotic peoples in vv. 1-2. The motif of animals feasting off corpses is a familiar trope for ultimate degradation; the bodies are not buried, are not restored to their ancestors, and pass through animal entrails. Summer and winter succeed each other, animal and avian predation, mountains and plain. The seasons are significant, not in themselves, but as indices of time, alternation, and the inexhaustibility of the carrion. They are, moreover, puns. "Winter" (תחרף) may also mean "taunt;" 'summer' (קץ) may be correlated with קיץ ("wake") or קוץ (feel disgust). There is thus a double reversal of the hierarchy: animals feed off humans, and despise them. Elsewhere it is the Assyrian Emperor who taunts YHWH, particularly in the narratives of chs 36–39. Here the animal consumption is linked to speech, and perhaps to the birds hovering over the corpses. One imagines the barbarous language of the people who are קו קו in vv. 1-2 as echoing and being displaced by the sounds of the animals and birds, a primeval vocalization expressive of satisfaction and triumph over humanity.

Then there is a reversal. "At that time the people drawn out and burnished, the people terrible from now and beyond, the nation קו קו and trampling, whose land the rivers divide, will send a gift to YHWH of Hosts, to the place of the name of YHWH of Hosts, in Mt. Zion" (v. 7).[41] The chapter is neatly rounded off; the end matches the beginning,

---

39. Lavik, *A People Tall and Smooth-Skinned*, 170–1, comments on this alliteration, though she identifies the זלזלים with the Judeans, for reasons that are unclear to me. See also John A. Hayes and Stuart A. Irvine, *Isaiah: The Eighth Century Prophet: His Times and His Preaching* (Nashville, TN: Abingdon, 1987), 256.

40. זלזלים is a hapax; זלל may means "despise" or "quiver." Lavik, *A People Tall and Smooth-Skinned*, 151, neatly translates, "quivering tendrils." I think, however, that the connotation of being despised is equally prominent. נטישות, likewise, can mean "forsaken" or "abandoned" (ibid., 163–4).

41. Most scholars regard this as an addition (Tull, *Isaiah 1–39*, 317; Berges, *The Book of Isaiah*, 148). However, this ignores the circularity of the passage.

with its strange, exoticizing phrases; the terror of those remote peoples, submits to, is brought under the domain of, the name of YHWH of Hosts in Jerusalem. There is perhaps a name-theology here,[42] but what is really important is the linguistic effect; the language of those peoples, and by implication of the entire poem, is subsumed under the name, silent as it may be. The prophet/poet listens, and what he hears is not just the pruning of the זלזלים, quivering "tendrils"—themselves figures for duplicated, meaningless syllables—but the gift of their speech, the acknowledgement of YHWH of Hosts.

The Song of the Prostitute and the Pornographic Gaze (Chapters 20; 23.15-18)

A similar moment is found at the end of ch. 23:

> (15) And it shall be on that day, when Tyre has been forgotten for seventy years, like the days of one king, at the end of seventy years it shall be for Tyre like the song of a whore. (16) "Take up the lyre, go about the city, O forgotten whore; play the melody well, sing much, that you may be remembered." (17) And it shall be at the end of seventy years, that YHWH will visit Tyre, and she will return to her hire; and she will prostitute herself to all the kingdoms of the earth, on the face of the ground. (18) And her trade and her hire will be holy to YHWH; it will not be treasured nor stored up, for to those who sit before YHWH will be her trade, to eat in plenty, and to be finely clothed.

The prostitute sings, and what she sings is song itself: "Take up the lyre, go about the city, O forgotten whore; play the melody well, sing much, that you may be remembered." The song signifies, apart from any actual lyrics, the capacity to sing, music beyond any particular meaning. The song may express the woman's abandonment, and ultimately her dependence on YHWH for restoration; at the same time, it communicates another message, of sexual promise and pleasure. The prostitute is recollecting or re-enacting her own past, as the עליזה, "the joyful one" (23:7), corresponding to Jerusalem as the קריה עליזה, "the joyful city," in 22:2. Of course, the joy may be a role she plays, a projection of male fantasy. It promises another world; she represents the Sea and the transformation

---

42. Willem A. M. Beuken, *Jesaja 13–27*, trans. Ulrich Berges and Andrea Spans, HKAT (Freiburg: Herder, 2007), 171, sees this as a Deuteronomistic intrusion, which introduces the motif of the Torah into the discussion.

of death and despair into something rich and strange.⁴³ The strangeness may be incorporated in the Temple. One can imagine those who sit before YHWH listening to her voice, like the lover in the Song of Songs. Perhaps also YHWH himself. It is a curious metaphor for YHWH, not to speak of his devotees. But it does suggest a linkage between prostitution and holiness. "Those who sit before YHWH" may be a scribal elite, ensconced in the Temple, to which the prophet belongs or with which he sympathises. If it is identical to the *golah* community in the post-restoration period, it may express their own feelings of impotence as well as their dreams for world domination.

The other prostitute in Isaiah 1–39 is Jerusalem (1:21). Tyre, representative of Canaan, is a lateral displacement of Jerusalem, a figure for its past self. YHWH's remembrance of Tyre recollects the restoration of Jerusalem as the קריה נאמנה, "the faithful city" (1:26). That which is made holy to YHWH is not only a mercantile and cultic economy, but, as Canaan, the world in its sacred and sexual diversity.

In ch. 20, there is a strange and nugatory narrative in which the prophet walks naked and barefoot for three years, in token of the humiliation of Egypt and Ethiopia. It is central to the OAN and extraneous to them, for example as an appendage to the oracles concerning Ethiopia and Egypt in chs 18–19. Nakedness is a sign of abjection, of pure physicality, deprived of all the symbols of prestige and culture.⁴⁴ It is a sign of non-significance, of the degradation and dissolution of the body politic. We do not know how Isaiah feels and reacts. The narrative lacks resistance and self-reflection; God commands and Isaiah complies, like a cipher.⁴⁵ The command marginalizes him, renders him a figure of destitution, an object of shame and certainly strangeness, but also a pure vehicle for the divine word, a "sign and portent," just as he and his sons are in 8:18.

---

43. Throughout the oracle about Tyre, Tyre (and its sister city Sidon) is represented as the Queen of the Sea, and the Sea, emblematic of chaos, is the real subject, as for instance in 23:4.

44. Commentators attempt to mitigate the scandal of Isaiah's nudity in various ways e.g. by suggesting that three years need only be 14 months, that Isaiah only appeared naked from time to time, that it may have been partial (Wildberger, *Isaiah 13–27*, 289, 294–5; Blenkinsopp, *Isaiah 1–39*, 323), a tendency that can be traced back to medieval philosophical interpretations of the signs as visions (Ibn Ezra). The discomfort of commentators itself attests to the shock of the sign.

45. Hanna Liss, *Die Unerhörte Wort: Kommunikative Strukturen prophetische Rede im Buch Yesha'yahu* (Leipzig: Evangelische Verlagsanstalt, 2003), 196, notes that the interpretation in v. 3 is not directly addressed to Isaiah, and speaks of him in the third person, so that it is possible that he himself does not know the meaning of his actions.

Through the sign, the prophet drops out of language; he does not speak, and he himself is that which is spoken.[46] That which is spoken is silence, the nullity of the human condition on the border between life and death, enacting a living death. Egypt and Ethiopia are destroyed, and the captives are deracinated animated husks. Except that the sign can only be interpreted in language, it is surrounded by speech. Only thus can it be meaningful, and known as a sign of the destruction of Egypt and Ethiopia.[47] Otherwise the naked prophet would be just a naked prophet.

Isaiah's nakedness suggests participation in the suffering of Egypt and Ethiopia, aligned with the other manifestations of prophetic sympathy, the labour pangs of 21:3, the refusal of comfort in 22:4, the weeping over Moab. Here, however, it is mandated by God. Whether it expresses God's sympathy with the victim, or it is a sign, to whatever audience, for the sake of prophetic or divine authentication, God via his emissary, as that which speaks through him, is subject to humiliation.

The nakedness may suggest sexual humiliation too, perhaps displaced onto the buttocks. The captives may be subject to rape; the buttocks in any case expose them to anal desire, fantasy, and disgust.

> (20:3) And YHWH said, "Just as my servant Isaiah has gone naked and barefoot for three years, a sign and a portent against Egypt and Ethiopia, (4) so the king of Assyria will lead the captives of Egypt and the deportees of Ethiopia, young and old, stripped and barefoot, bare of buttocks, the nakedness of Egypt. (5) They will be panicked and ashamed, from Ethiopia their prospect, from Egypt their splendour.

The identification of the prophet, and God, with the victim makes them, in turn, the subject for the pornographic gaze. The gaze is manifest in the loss of beauty and the look, the literal meaning of מבטם, "prospect." Nakedness also results in a refusal to look at oneself, the deprivation of a point of view. Egypt is divested of its תפארת, its "splendour" or "beauty," a key word in Isaiah associated elsewhere with the pride of Assyria and

---

46. Wildberger, *Isaiah 13–27*, 295, objects that to go about naked for three years without being able to say what it means would make Isaiah into "a comical figure." Indeed!

47. Liss, *Die Unerhörte Wort*, 195–8, argues that it can only be a sign of misunderstanding between the prophet and his audience, because of the three-year interval between the beginning of the performance and its explication, the gap between the prediction and its fulfillment, and the uncertainty about the addressee of the interpretation in v. 3.

of the daughters of Jerusalem. The pornographic gaze, on the other or/as the self, is an exposure of the human being as vulnerable, without pretensions, abject.

Conclusion: The Gift to YHWH (18:7)

Let us go back to the end of ch. 18.

> At that time the people drawn out and burnished, the people awesome from back and beyond, the nation lofty and trampling, whose land the rivers dissect, will bring a gift to YHWH, to the place of the name of YHWH of Hosts, Mount Zion. (18:7)

These people are the survivors, since in the previous verse the birds and the beasts feed off the corpses of the slain. Their bringing a gift to YHWH is a sign of the post-destruction era, and hence exemplifies paradigmatically the journey of the nations to Jerusalem in 2:2-4.[48] The association is reinforced by the detail that the vine shoots (זלזלים) will be cut off by "pruning hooks" (מזמרות) in v. 5, since in 2:4 the recycling of spears as pruning hooks is indicative of the abolition of war. Here, however, the pruning hooks are metaphors for weapons.

The people bring a gift, but primarily they bring themselves, acknowledging the supremacy of YHWH.[49] The linkage between the far and the intimate, the languages of the world and the ineffable divine name, is nowhere clearer, and is a summation of the dialectic of the OAN.

There are many linkages between the OAN: phonemic ones, suggestive of violence and lamentation; repeated motifs, for instance the supplementary notes attached to the oracles of Moab and Arabia; common metaphors, like the harvest of death; and an overarching structure, culminating in the vision of Tyre/Sea dedicating the wealth of the nations to YHWH. The poems, moreover, thematise fragmentation, and attempt to impose structure on the violence and anarchy they depict. The trajectory from predictions of doom to anticipations of restoration corresponds to the disjunction between the prophet who predicts disaster and the one who heralds a new utopian age, and hence to the primary poetic problem of the book. The nations are Israel writ large. The OAN, with their focus on the nations, are both a distraction from the fate of Israel and Judah and put it in a larger perspective.

---

48. Berges, *The Book of Isaiah*, 148; Kaiser, *Jesaja 13–39*, 80.
49. Beuken, *Jesaja 13–27*, 148, notes that in the MT the particle -מנ, "from," is omitted in the first clause, suggesting that the people themselves are the gift.

In this chapter, I argue that the OAN have a metaphorical function in the book of Isaiah; through them, the promise and the threat against Jerusalem and Judah is universalized, and reciprocally, Jerusalem and Judah become the world centre, as in the metanarrative of the book. Metaphor is a technique for making the familiar strange, and the strange familiar, as is the case with the oracle against Jerusalem in ch. 22, which, through the cacophanous image of the ruptured walls (מקרקר קר) breaks down the boundary between Judah, Moab, and the prophet's heart. If I had time I would analyse the chapter at length, with its concluding and fascinating condemnation of the royal officials, Shebna and Eliakim.

As a second objective, I examine the metaphorical relationship between meaning and non-meaning. The oracles are characterized by intense alliterative play, rhythms, rhymes, in other words musicality. These cross over between individual oracles and erase their distinctions. Meanings arise from these linkages, to generate a plenitude of metaphorical implication, without reducing the aural, sensory quality of the language to its signification. The chapters amplify this through their evocation of sound, of foreign, incomprehensible languages, and of silence, for example in the Oracle/Burden of Dumah/Silence (21:11).

There is much to do. I do not discuss the Burden of Babylon in chs 13–14, nor that against Egypt in ch. 19, both of which are intricately related to the rest of the sequence. My subheadings artificially demarcate topics and subjects which inevitably flow into each other. The music of the world is unending. That is what I set out to intimate.

Chapter 6

A Dragon, a Reed Staff, and a Towering
Cedar in Eden: Egypt in Ezekiel 29–32

Brittany Kim

In the Hebrew Bible, Egypt functions both as the paradigmatic symbol of Israelite oppression, provoking YHWH's miraculous deliverance, and as an on-again-off-again political ally to Israel and Judah in the face of threats from superpowers to the east. Since the Israelite prophets view alliances with Egypt as a threat to the people's sole dependence on YHWH, they thus present a predominantly negative perspective on Egypt. Ezekiel is no exception, indicating that Egypt has played a significant role in Israel's rejection of YHWH (e.g., 16:26; 20:7-8) and pronouncing devastating judgments on both the land and its people (e.g., 30:1-19). Nevertheless, the oracles against Egypt in Ezekiel 29–32 reveal a surprisingly complex portrait of that nation and its Pharaoh, providing a window into ancient Israel's attempts to make sense of national and ethnic Otherness.

The process of Othering nations like Egypt is deeply connected to Israel's efforts to define its own self-understanding. After all, constructing and maintaining a national identity involves not only developing a strong core of shared beliefs and practices but also drawing contrasts with those perceived as Other.[1] As Jeremiah Cataldo puts it, "there is no recognition of self, no concept of I (or We) without difference...the self-aware subject necessitates the Other as a contrasting foil."[2] And this is particularly true

---

1. Lawrence M. Wills, *Not God's People: Insiders and Outsiders in the Biblical World* (Lanham, MD: Rowman & Littlefield, 2008), 7.
2. Jeremiah W. Cataldo, "The Other: Sociological Perspectives in a Postcolonial Age," in *Imagining the Other and Constructing Israelite Identity in the Early Second*

when one's communal identity is threatened, as it would have been for the Judeans in the years just before and after the destruction of Jerusalem. The oracles against Egypt (OAE) in Ezekiel 29–32 offer an intriguing case study on Israel's efforts to define the boundaries between itself and other nations during that tumultuous time period.

We are deeply indebted to critical theories, such as postcolonial interpretation, for opening our eyes to how identities of the Self and Other are constructed both within modern cultural narratives and biblical texts. While each critical method offers a unique and illuminating perspective on this issue, this essay demonstrates that the standard tools of exegesis can also reveal how biblical texts construct particular people groups as Other. Therefore, this essay makes quite limited use of critical theory. Instead, the essay draws primarily on Lawrence Wills's categories for how Otherness is constructed in biblical texts as outlined in his monograph *Not God's People*. In developing his categories, Wills uses insights from postcolonial theorists like Edward Said concerning the creation of external (ethnic) Others as well as from Louis Dumont's anthropological study of India's caste system with its focus on internal Others.[3] However, Wills's work primarily involves a close reading of particular biblical texts, showing how the biblical texts themselves reveal various approaches to Othering. Therefore, ultimately, this essay demonstrates another way into Otherness in prophetic literature—through a careful exegetical analysis of how prophetic texts describe national and ethnic Others, especially in relation to their portraits of Israel. Moreover, with attention to internal as well as external Others, Wills's categories resist flat readings of Israel as the ideal We and the nations as the demonized Other. This approach proves particularly important for examining how prophetic texts depict Israel and the nations, as the boundaries between them are sometimes surprisingly permeable.

The essay begins with an outline of Wills's categories and then analyzes the images of Pharaoh as a dragon (29:3; 32:2), a reed staff (29:6), and a towering cedar in Eden (31:2-9) against their backgrounds in the book of Ezekiel, the Hebrew Bible as a whole, and Egyptian literature and iconography, in order to determine how they depict Egypt as an Other, following Wills's categories. The essay also considers what these metaphors would convey about Egypt's identity and relationship to Israel both to an Egyptian and a Judean audience. Ultimately, it finds that the OAE use metaphorical portrayals of Pharaoh that have symbolic freight

Temple Period, ed. Ehud Ben Zvi and Diana V. Edelman, LHBOTS 456 (London: Bloomsbury, 2014), 5.

3. Wills, *Not God's People*, 12.

within Egyptian and/or Israelite culture in order both to overturn perceptions of Egypt's immense power and to emphasize differences between Israel and Egypt. However, by employing images for Pharaoh that are similar to those used elsewhere in Ezekiel for Judah and its kings, these oracles also reveal considerable ambiguity in the distinction between Self and Other.

1. Categories for Constructing Otherness

Given the complex social, historical, political, and religious dynamics that are at work in fashioning identities of Self and Other, that process does not always follow the same path in every case—it can move in different directions that sometimes converge but at other times lead to different ends. Lawrence Wills's nine "theorems" concerning how Otherness is constructed in the biblical texts highlight some of this complexity:[4]

1. *"The construction of the Other serves to construct the We."*
2. *"The construction of the We serves to construct the Other."*
3. *"The Other is often in reality very similar to the We,"* leading the We-group to amplify small differences between them.
4. *"The Other has the ability to corrupt or infect the We, and the We is vulnerable."*
5. *"The depiction of the Other is often unreal, distorted, monstrous, mythical, and taboo."*
6. *"There are internal as well as external Others, and they are often seen as linked."*
7. *"Ambiguous groups are often reassigned either as an Other or as a special case of an adopted We or internal Other."*
8. *"Ancient, native, or traditional practices may be redefined as new or foreign and associated with the Other, while an originally foreign practice may be redefined as ancient, native, and traditional, now associated with the We."*
9. *"The Other is viewed as having existed from time immemorial and continues to exist, and cannot be permanently extirpated."*

These categories provide a helpful framework for examining Ezekiel's Othering of Egypt. Outside of the OAE in Ezekiel 29–32, many of Ezekiel's descriptions of that nation exemplify Wills's fourth theorem that *"the Other has the ability to corrupt or infect the We"* as well as his

---

4. Ibid., 12–14 (emphasis in the original).

third theorem that *"the Other is often in reality very similar to the We."*[5] The book frequently testifies to the contaminating power of Egypt and the ways in which Israel has imitated Egypt. Indeed, according to Ezekiel, Israel's identity is in jeopardy now because it has never been able to dissociate itself from the perverse influence of the Egyptians present from Israel's inception as a nation. YHWH's people have committed adultery against their God both by persistently following the Egyptians in their idolatry (20:7-8) and by entering into illicit political alliances with Egypt (16:26; 23:3, 8, 19-21, 27). From an external perspective the two nations are quite distinct, with significant differences in language, culture, and religion. Nevertheless, Ezekiel claims that at heart, the people of Judah resemble the Egyptians. This perspective forms the background for the portraits of Pharaoh as a dragon (29:3; 32:2), a reed staff (29:6), and a towering cedar in Eden (31:2-9) in the OAE.

2. *Pharaoh as a Dragon (תנים)*

The series of seven OAE in Ezekiel 29–32 are not entirely chronological but show some evidence of intentional ordering. In particular, the image of Pharaoh as a dragon (תנים) forms an *inclusio* around the first six oracles:[6]

Ezekiel 29:3:[7]

דבר ואמרת	Speak and say,
כה־אמר אדני יהוה	"Thus says the Lord YHWH,
הנני עליך	'Behold I am against you,
פרעה מלך־מצרים	Pharaoh, King of Egypt,
התנים הגדול	the great *tannim*
הרבץ בתוך יאריו	that lies in the midst of his streams,
אשר אמר לי יארי	who says, "My Nile is my own,
ואני עשיתני	and I made [it] for myself."'"[8]

---

5. Ibid., 13 (emphasis in the original).
6. Corinne L. Carvalho, "A Serpent in the Nile: Egypt in the Book of Ezekiel," in *Concerning the Nations: Essays on the Oracles Against the Nations in Isaiah, Jeremiah, and Ezekiel*, ed. Andrew Mein, Else K. Holt, and Hyun Chul Paul Kim, LHBOTS 612 (London: Bloomsbury, 2015), 217.
7. All biblical translations are mine unless otherwise noted.
8. This translation assumes, along with most interpreters (e.g., Safwat Marzouk, *Egypt as a Monster in the Book of Ezekiel* [Tübingen: Mohr Siebeck, 2015], 162; Daniel I. Block, *The Book of Ezekiel: Chapters 25–48*, NICOT [Grand Rapids, MI: Eerdmans, 1998], 135), that the first person suffix on עשיתני is a "datival accusative," on which see *IBHS* 10.2.1i. It is possible that Pharaoh is here claiming to have created

Ezekiel 32:2:

בן־אדם	Son of man,
שׂא קינה	raise a lamentation
על־פרעה מלך־מצרים	against Pharaoh, King of Egypt,
ואמרת אליו	and say to him,
כפיר גוים נדמית	"you are like a young lion of the nations;
ואתה כתנים בימים	you are like a *tannim* in the seas.
ותגח בנהרותיך	You burst forth in your rivers
ותדלח־מים ברגליך	and muddy the waters with your feet
ותרפס נהרותם	and pollute their[9] rivers."

a. *The Meaning of* תנים

Although תנים looks like a plural form of תן, which means "jackal," here it is usually taken as an alternate (or mistaken) form of תנין.[10] Elsewhere in the HB תנין can refer to a serpent (Exod. 7:9-10, 12), a sea creature (Gen. 1:21), or a mythological chaos monster—that is, a dragon (Isa. 51:9).[11] Scholars are divided on whether the reference in this passage is to a literal animal, to a mythological creature, or to both. Those who argue for a literal interpretation generally suggest that the word designates a crocodile, in view of the creature's scales (קשׂקשׂתיך, 29:4), feet (רגליך, 32:2), and Nile habitat.[12] However, nowhere else in the HB does תנין designate a crocodile, and here it is said to dwell not only in the streams, but also in the "seas" (ימים, 32:2), which fits the image of a chaos monster better than a Nile crocodile.[13] Furthermore, the creature is of such

himself (so Joseph Blenkinsopp, *Ezekiel*, IBC [Louisville, KY: John Knox, 1990], 129), but the parallel statement in v. 9 (יאר לי ואני עשׂיתי) lacks the pronominal suffix, making the Nile the natural direct object.

9. The LXX has a second per. pron. ("you"), but this translation follows the MT as the *lectio difficilior*.

10. This reading is supported by the Tg., the LXX, and the Vg., as well as the fact that the word is modified by the sg. form of the adjective גדול (see further Marzouk, *Egypt as a Monster*, 158).

11. Outside of Ezek. 29 and 32 תנין appears 12 times. Aside from the references already mentioned, it is found in Deut. 32:33; Isa. 27:1; Jer. 51:34; Pss. 74:13; 91:13; 148:7; Job 7:12, many of which are discussed further below.

12. Nancy R. Bowen, *Ezekiel*, AOTC (Nashville, TN: Abingdon, 2010), 180; Daniel Bodi, "Ezekiel," in *Zondervan Illustrated Bible Background Commentary*, ed. John H. Walton (Grand Rapids, MI: Zondervan, 2009), 4:467.

13. Tyler R. Yoder, "Ezekiel 29:3 and Its Ancient Near Eastern Context," *VT* 63 (2013): 489; Philippe Guillaume, "Metamorphosis of a Ferocious Pharaoh," *Bib*

immense proportions that its refuse fills valleys, and the land—"even up to the mountains"—is drenched with its blood (32:5-6). And Yahweh's defeat of the תנים is accompanied by cosmological signs involving the darkening of the heavens (32:7-8).[14] Thus even if the description suggests the image of a crocodile, תנים does not refer to a literal animal but to a mythological creature. In order to capture the mythological nature of the beast, it is best to translate תנים as "dragon" here, bringing it in line with passages like Isa. 51:9.[15]

b. *The Background of the Image in Egypt and Mesopotamia*

Some scholars who understand the תנים as a "crocodile" view that image against the background of Egyptian mythology, noting that Sobek, a fertility god of the Nile, was represented by a crocodile.[16] Moreover, in Egyptian funerary pictures a creature with the head of a crocodile consumes the dead whose hearts are found wanting and who thus have not earned the right to be reborn in the afterlife.[17] The applicability of this image to a Pharaoh is evidenced by an Egyptian hymn in which Amun-Re says to Thutmose III, "I cause them to see thy majesty as a crocodile, The lord of fear in the water, who cannot be approached."[18]

While observing the mythological associations with crocodiles, Corinne Carvalho argues that תנים might also suggest a connection to the serpentine imagery prevalent in Egyptian literature and iconography. Most notably, the front of the Pharaoh's headdress depicted an uraeus serpent, which was a representation of the snake goddess Wadjet and

---

85 (2004): 233; John Day, *God's Conflict with the Dragon and the Sea: Echoes of a Canaanite Myth in the Old Testament* (Cambridge: Cambridge University Press, 1985), 95.

14. Compare with Isa. 50:2-3; Ps. 18:10 (Day, *God's Conflict*, 95).

15. Daniel Block and Moshe Greenberg both translate תנים as "monster," though they also argue for an association with the crocodile (Block, *Ezekiel 25–48*, 135–7; Moshe Greenberg, *Ezekiel 21–37: A New Translation with Introduction and Commentary*, AB 22A [New York: Doubleday, 1997], 601–2; cf. Iain M. Duguid, *Ezekiel*, NIVAC [Grand Rapids, MI: Zondervan, 1999], 355–6; James A. Durlesser, *The Metaphorical Narratives in the Book of Ezekiel* [Lewiston, NY: Edwin Mellen, 2006], 209–11).

16. Bowen, *Ezekiel*, 180; Greenberg, *Ezekiel 21–37*, 612.

17. See Carvalho, "Serpent in the Nile," 212; Robert K. Ritner, "The Cult of the Dead," in *Ancient Egypt*, ed. David P. Silverman (Oxford: Oxford University Press, 1997), 137.

18. "Hymn of Victory of Thutmose III" (*ANET*, 374).

a symbol of protection over the Pharaoh. However, a snake could also symbolize chaos, since the serpent Apophis represented a continual threat to the order of the world and had to be defeated daily by the sun god.[19] Carvalho thus contends that the reference to Pharaoh as a תנים could have a dual function, "to represent both the Pharaoh in his boastful glory, and Pharaoh as the evil creature that God defeats."[20] This understanding fits with the clear reference to תנין as a serpent in Exod. 7:9-12, which also appears in an Egyptian context.[21]

While these connections may have suggested themselves to an Egyptian audience confronted with Ezekiel 29–32, given Ezekiel's location in Babylonian exile, it is also worthwhile to consider a possible Mesopotamian background for the image. As Tyler Yoder observes, Ezekiel's description of Pharaoh as a "great dragon" in 29:3 (התנים הגדול) parallels the Akkadian epithet *ušumgallu* (derived from Sumerian UŠUMGAL), which is often used of kings and gods. The title appears from Old Babylonian to Neo-Assyrian times and suggests the power, ferocity, and deadliness of those to whom it is ascribed.[22] For example, a royal inscription styles Shalmaneser as "vice-regent of Ashur, strong king, king of all people,...*great dragon* of conflict, curser of enemies, the weapon which destroys the insubmissive."[23] Thus Ezekiel may have ironically applied a standard royal epithet used of the dominant Mesopotamian kings to the weaker Pharaoh.[24]

This parallel may also shed light on the juxtaposition of the images of Pharaoh as a lion and a dragon in Ezek. 32:2. The use of the lion as a royal image is well-attested throughout the ancient world. For example, the Egyptian Pharaoh Ramses II calls himself, "the living lion...slayer

---

19. Carvalho, "Serpent in the Nile," 213–14; see further Nicole B. Hansen, "Snakes," in *Oxford Encyclopedia of Ancient Egypt*, ed. D. B. Redford, 3 vols (Oxford: Oxford University Press, 2001), 3:297–8; Maya Müller, "Re and Re-Horakhty," in Redford (ed.), *Oxford Encyclopedia of Ancient Egypt*, 3:125.

20. Carvalho, "Serpent in the Nile," 214.

21. For an argument that Exod. 7 also has mythological significance in dependence on Ezek. 29 and 32, see Guillaume, "Metamorphosis." The description of the creature as having feet (Ezek. 32:2) does not cohere with the portrait of a serpent, but Carvalho suggests that תנים could have flexibly evoked the images of both crocodile and snake ("Serpent in the Nile," 214).

22. Yoder, "Ezekiel 29:3," 487–92.

23. Ashur Inscription 556 (Albert Kirk Grayson, *Assyrian Royal Inscriptions, vol. 1: From the Beginning to Ashur-resha-isha I*, Records of the Ancient Near East [Wiesbaden: Otto Harrassowitz, 1972], 87), italics mine.

24. Yoder, "Ezekiel 29:3," 489–94.

of his enemies,"[25] and Sargon King of Assyria declares, "I set in motion the mighty armies of Aššur, and, raging like a lion, set out to conquer those lands."[26] So it is not surprising that Pharaoh would be described as a lion in Ezek. 32:2. However, most interpreters see a tension between the two disparate metaphors of lion and dragon,[27] which is often resolved by assuming a disjunction between how Pharaoh sees himself and how YHWH views him. The ESV is representative, reading, "You *consider yourself* a lion of the nations, but you are like a dragon in the seas."[28]

As Theodore Lewis points out, however, ancient Near Eastern literature and iconography sometimes combine images of lions and dragons, so these metaphors are not necessarily inconsistent.[29] For example, in Tishpak's battle with the dragon in *CT* 13.33-34, the dragon is called a *labbu* (an Akkadian word for "lion"),[30] and Lewis presents several iconographic depictions of a hybrid creature exhibiting both serpentine and leonine characteristics.[31] Moreover, the epithet *ušumgallu*, which Yoder takes as a "great dragon," is sometimes translated "lion-dragon" and depicted with the front legs and head of a lion, the tongue of a serpent, and

---

25. Cited by Lawrence Boadt, *Ezekiel's Oracles against Egypt: A Literary and Philological Study of Ezekiel 29–32* (Rome: Biblical Institute, 1980), 130; Marzouk, *Egypt as a Monster*, 169.

26. *CAD* L.23. For further parallels from both Egypt and Mesopotamia, see Brent A. Strawn, *What Is Stronger than a Lion? Leonine Image and Metaphor in the Hebrew Bible and the Ancient Near East*, OBO 212 (Göttingen: Vandenhoeck & Ruprecht, 2005), 174–80.

27. E.g., Boadt contends that "the mythopoeic image of the lion stands opposed to that of *tannîn*" (*Ezekiel's Oracles*, 130).

28. Italics mine; see also the NASB, NRSV, NET, NLT; Block, *Ezekiel 25–48*, 200–201. Duguid argues for a reflexive reading of the *nip'al* form of דמה ("to be like") here (*Ezekiel*, 374 n. 8). But since the *nip'al* appears nowhere else, it is not clear whether it carries that sense. And Marzouk contends that ואתה, which links the two clauses, is adversative when introducing a verbless clause, citing Ezek. 28:9 and 1 Sam. 28:12 (*Egypt as a Monster*, 169), but further evidence is required to demonstrate that it always functions that way. The parallelism between the two cola in Ezek. 32:2 suggests instead a conjunctive relationship. If Ezekiel wanted to highlight a contrast between Pharaoh's self-understanding and YHWH's perspective of him, he could have made that explicit by quoting Pharaoh as in 29:3 (see also 28:9 concerning the king of Tyre).

29. See the NIV, NKJV.

30. Lines 17, 20, 24 (obverse) and 4, 7, 9 (reverse; Theodore J. Lewis, "*CT* 13.33-34 and Ezekiel 32: Lion-Dragon Myths," *JAOS* 116 [1996]: 33–4).

31. Ibid., 34–7.

clawed hind legs and wings like a bird of prey.³² Therefore, I contend that it is best to interpret Ezek. 32:2 against this background and understand it as affirming that Pharaoh is like a lion as well as a dragon, both symbolizing royalty and might.³³

c. *The Background of the Image in the HB*

Other references to תנין in the HB also form an illuminating background for Ezekiel's use of the image. Like Ezek. 32:2, Isa. 27:1 refers to a תנין who is "in the sea" (בים), there paralleling "Leviathan, the twisting serpent" (נחש). The context is YHWH's eschatological day of judgment when he will "punish" Leviathan with the sword and "slay the dragon." Psalm 74:13-14 speaks of YHWH's defeat of these creatures in the past, declaring:

> You divided the sea by your might,
> and you broke the heads of the dragons (תנינים) on the waters.
> You crushed the heads of Leviathan;
> you would give him as food for a company of wild animals.

In light of the references to God's kingship and deliverance in v. 12, these verses seem at first glance to refer to YHWH's deliverance of his people at the Reed Sea, and John Goldingay suggests identifying the dragons with the Egyptian army, a reading supported by the Targum.³⁴ However,

---

32. See *CAD* U/W.330–1; Alberto R. W. Green, *The Storm-God in the Ancient Near East*, Biblical and Judaic Studies 8 (Winona Lake, IN: Eisenbrauns, 2003), 29–33, 46–7; Aage Westenholz, *Old Sumerian and Old Akkadian Texts in Philadelphia, vol. 2: The 'Akkadian' Texts, the Enlilemaba Texts, and the Onion Archive*, CNI Publications 3 (Copenhagen: Museum Tusculanum, 1987), 42; Othmar Keel, *The Symbolism of the Biblical World: Ancient Near Eastern Iconography and the Book of Psalms*, trans. Timothy J. Hallett (New York: Seabury, 1978; repr., Winona Lake, IN: Eisenbrauns, 1997), 50 (Fig. 44). A hymn to Ninurta describes the god as a "dragon with the 'hands' of a lion, the *claws* of an eagle" (*The Ancient Near East: An Anthology of Texts and Pictures*, ed. James B. Pritchard [Princeton, NJ: Princeton University Press, 2011], 331).

33. Lewis, "*CT* 13.33-34," 40–1.

34. John Goldingay, *Psalms vol. 2: Psalms 42–89*, Baker Commentary on the Old Testament Wisdom and Psalms (Grand Rapids, MI: Baker Academic, 2007), 431. The Targum of Ps. 74:13-14 reads, "You by your might cut off *the waters of* the sea; you broke the heads of the sea monsters; *and you drowned the Egyptians* upon the *sea*. Your [sic] shattered the heads of *the mighty ones of Pharaoh*; you gave them *for destruction to the people of the house of Israel, and their bodies to the yarods*" (David M. Stec, *The Targum of Psalms*, ArBib 16 [New York: T&T Clark, 2004]).

vv. 16-17 contain clear allusions to Genesis, prompting a re-reading of vv. 13-14 as also describing YHWH's defeat of the waters of chaos at creation, using imagery reminiscent of Baal's victory over Yam in the Baal Cycle and Marduk's slaying of Tiamat in *Enuma Elish*. YHWH's division of the waters at creation has merged in Israel's religious consciousness with the parting of the Reed Sea, and both the sea and the Egyptian army may be aptly represented as chaos monsters.

Isaiah 51:9 also refers to YHWH's mighty deliverance of Israel in the exodus, here pairing תנין not with Leviathan but with the chaos creature Rahab:

> Awake, awake, put on strength, O arm of YHWH,
> awake as in the days of old, the generations of long ago,
> was it not you who cut Rahab in pieces, who pierced the dragon (תנין)?

These references to תנין as a chaos creature all emphasize YHWH's victory over the dragon and place תנין in the same realm as Leviathan and Rahab. Given the connections made between the latter creatures and Egypt,[35] it is fitting that Ezekiel's OAE describe Pharaoh as a תנין.

As Yoder observes, however, the collocation תנין גדול ("great dragon"), which describes Pharaoh in Ezek. 29:3, appears elsewhere in the HB only in Gen. 1:21, where it is demythologized, designating God's creation of "the great sea creatures."[36] Whereas elsewhere creation can be depicted in terms of YHWH's victory over the forces of chaos (e.g., Ps. 74:13-17, as noted above), in Genesis 1 there is no battle and "the great sea creatures" (התנינם הגדלים) are simply part of God's created order, included with the rest of the sea-dwelling animals created on day five.

Another relevant parallel is found in Jer. 51:34, in which Jerusalem laments how Nebuchadnezzar "swallowed" (בלע) her like a תנין. Here the emphasis is on the voracious appetite and ferocity of the dragon as a great beast that devours whole cities. The passage does not elaborate on the dragon image except to say that YHWH will "take out of his mouth what he swallowed (בלעו)" (v. 44), now referring to the Babylonian god Bel rather than Nebuchadnezzar. Like Ezek. 32:2, Jeremiah 51 also draws together the images of dragon and lion, declaring that though the Babylonians will "roar together like young lions" (כפרים) seeking their prey, the feast they enjoy will induce a sleep from which they will never

---

35. See also Isa. 30:7, which calls Egypt, "Rahab, the one who sits still," and Ps. 87:4, which includes "Rahab" in a list of nations, clearly designating Egypt.

36. Yoder, "Ezekiel 29:3," 493.

wake (vv. 38-39).³⁷ While these fierce creatures succeed in capturing and consuming their prey, YHWH will ultimately intervene to bring judgment against them and restore his people.³⁸

Although תנין is lacking in Ezekiel 19, that chapter shares other important connections with the portrait of Pharaoh in Ezekiel 29 and 32. Ezekiel 19 describes a king of Judah as a "young lion" (כפיר), who "learned to catch prey [and] devour men" (v. 3). As a result of his rapaciousness, the nations "brought him with hooks (חחים) to the land of Egypt" (v. 4).³⁹ So another כפיר arose who was even more destructive (vv. 5-7). But the nations subdued him as well. They "spread their net over him" (ויפרשו עליו רשתם), caged him with "hooks" (חחים), and "brought him to the king of Babylon," ending his dominion over Judah (vv. 8-9).⁴⁰ Although these Judean kings are mighty beasts of prey, they are not as indomitable as they may think but are ensnared and held in captivity by other nations.

d. *Ezekiel's Development of the Image*

Ezekiel's portrait of the "great dragon" Pharaoh in 29:3 highlights his self-aggrandizement. The dragon declares, "My Nile is my own; *I* made [it] for myself" (see also v. 9), using the unnecessary first person pronoun in the second clause (ואני עשיתני). Elsewhere in Ezekiel's OAE אני appears only in YHWH's repeated refrain "then they will know that *I* am YHWH" (9×; or in the abbreviated formula "*I* am YHWH").⁴¹ Thus the use of the first person pronoun emphasizes the arrogant pretensions of Pharaoh and defies the sovereignty of YHWH.⁴² However, the HB consistently affirms YHWH's victory over every chaos creature. Moreover, with the use of creation language (עשה) and the collocation תנים גדול, Ezekiel may be

---

37. See further F. B. Huey, Jr., *Jeremiah, Lamentations*, NAC 16 (Nashville, TN: Broadman & Holman, 1993), 426–7.

38. תנין and כפיר also appear together in Ps. 91:13, which highlights YHWH's fierce protection of those who trust in him, enabling them to "trample the young lion and the serpent."

39. This king should presumably be identified as Jehoahaz (see 2 Kgs 23:34; Daniel I. Block, *The Book of Ezekiel: Chapters 1–24*, NICOT [Grand Rapids, MI: Eerdmans, 1997], 604).

40. This likely refers to Jehoiakim, but could be Jehoiachin or Zedekiah (Block, *Ezekiel 1–24*, 604–6).

41. וידעו כי־אני יהוה: Ezek. 29:6, 9, 16 [here with אדני יהוה], 21; 30:8, 19, 25-26; 32:15; אני יהוה: 30:12.

42. C. L. Crouch, "Ezekiel's Oracles against the Nations in Light of a Royal Ideology of Warfare," *JBL* 130 (2011): 480.

drawing an intentional connection with Genesis 1 to convey the idea that Pharaoh, who boasts of his creative powers, is himself just one of YHWH's created beings, thereby deconstructing the impression of his matchless power and might.[43]

Ezekiel's innovative development of the image further highlights YHWH's sovereignty over the dragon. In 29:4-5 YHWH declares:

ונתתי חחים בלחייך	4	But I will put hooks in your jaws,
והדבקתי דגת־יאריך		and I will make the fish of your streams stick
בקשקשתיך		to your scales,
והעליתיך		and I will draw you up
מתוך יאריך		from the midst of your streams
ואת כל־דגת יאריך		along with all the fish of your streams
בקשקשתיך תדבק		that stick to your scales.
ונטשתיך המדברה	5	And I will cast you into the wilderness,
אותך ואת כל־דגת יאריך		you and all the fish of your streams.
על־פני השדה תפול		On the open field you will fall;
לא תאסף ולא תקבץ		you will not be brought together or gathered.
לחית הארץ ולעוף השמים		To the beasts of the earth and the birds of the sky
נתתיך לאכל		I give you for food.

For all its strength, the great dragon is no match for YHWH. The mighty predator will become the prey when YHWH fishes the dragon out of the water and throws it into the wilderness as a feast of carrion for the wild beasts. Given the importance of proper burial and funerary rites in ancient Egypt to prepare the dead for the afterlife, such an end would be a fate far worse than death.[44]

The use of "hooks" (חחים) to subdue the animal recalls the nations' capture of Judah's lion-king in Ezek. 19:4, but the image of putting "hooks" in "jaws" (לחי) evokes Job 40:26 [Eng. 41:2], where YHWH asks Job whether he can "pierce [Leviathan's] jaw (לחי) with a hook (חוח)."[45] The rhetorical question is clearly intended to evoke a negative answer—only YHWH has the ability to overpower such a dangerous creature (see 40:32–41:2 [41:8-10]). Since the creature's jaws are its most dangerous and deadly feature, YHWH defeats the dragon by piercing its jaws.

---

43. Yoder, "Ezekiel 29:3," 493–6.
44. See further Carvalho, "Serpent in the Nile," 217.
45. Marzouk, *Egypt as a Monster*, 183. See also YHWH's promise to "put hooks in [Gog's] jaws" in Ezek. 38:4, though without the dragon imagery, as well as his declaration to Sennacherib in Isa. 37:29, "I will put my hook (חחי) in your nose and my bit in your mouth."

Whereas in Ezek. 29:3 Pharaoh the dragon is lying comfortably and complacently in his streams, in 32:2 he is wreaking havoc on his environment, "muddy[ing] the waters with [his] feet and pollut[ing]" them.[46] The rare verb רפס ("to pollute") appears also in Ezek. 34:18 (there spelled רפש), which speaks of some of the stronger of YHWH's sheep "drink[ing] clear water and pollut[ing] the rest with [their] feet" so that the weaker members have no access to clean water.[47] Thus YHWH judges between them, rescuing the weaker sheep (vv. 20-22). Although דלח ("to muddy") occurs only in this passage in the HB (also in v. 13), the Akkadian cognate *dalāḫu* is often used of throwing countries into confusion,[48] suggesting the idea that Pharaoh is stirring up chaos in his kingdom. Moreover, like the chaotic waters of the sea in Job 38:8, which "burst forth (גיח) from the womb," the dragon "burst[s] forth (גיח) in [its] rivers" (Ezek. 32:2). So as YHWH contained the waters of the sea by "shut[ting them] in with doors" in Job,[49] he contains the chaos monster with a net in Ezek. 32:3:

כה אמר אדני יהוה	Thus says the Lord YHWH,
ופרשתי עליך את־רשתי	"I will spread out my net over you
בקהל עמים רבים	with an assembly of many peoples,
והעלוך בחרמי	and they will lift you up in my net."

This fate echoes the capture of Judah's lion-king in Ezek. 19:8.[50] The nations are involved in both passages, though here the ensnaring of the dragon is ultimately attributed to YHWH.[51] Once confined, the dragon's end is described in terms similar to those in ch. 29. The creature is cast into a field, and its body provides a lavish banquet for all the wild animals (v. 4). But now Ezekiel also declares that its flesh will cover mountains and its refuse "will fill valleys" (v. 5). Indeed, even the earth itself will participate in the feast, as YHWH makes it "drink [the dragon's] flowing blood, even to the mountains" (v. 6). Moreover, the slaying of this chaos

---

46. See further Marzouk, *Egypt as a Monster*, 170.

47. Elsewhere it appears only in Ps. 68:31 [30] and Prov. 6:3 in the Hithpael and in Prov. 25:26 in the Niphal. The two occurrences in Ezekiel are both in the Qal.

48. Block, *Ezekiel 25–48*, 200 n. 14; see *CAD* D.43–46.

49. It is worth noting that while the sea escapes its bounds before YHWH shuts it in ("burst[ing] forth *from* [מן] the womb"), the dragon remains within its confines ("burst[ing] forth *in* [ב] the Nile"; Marzouk, *Egypt as a Monster*, 170).

50. Cf. Ezek. 12:13; 17:20; as well as Marduk's defeat of Tiamat in *Enuma Elish* IV 95. On the Mesopotamian background of this image, see further Boadt, *Ezekiel's Oracles*, 133–5.

51. Ezekiel 19 and 32 are further connected by the parallel statements, "lift up a lamentation" (שא קינה, 19:1; 32:2) and "this is a lamentation" (קינה היא, 19:14; 32:16), which frame both oracles.

creature will be accompanied by cosmic upheaval as the sky is darkened, demonstrating YHWH's victory over Egypt's highest god, Re (vv. 7-8) as in the plague of darkness in Exod. 10:21-29. And YHWH will destroy both human and beast, using the sword of Babylon to turn Egypt into a desolation so that no one will "muddy the waters" anymore (vv. 11-13). Then YHWH will "settle their waters," removing the chaos stirred up by the dragon and restoring order (v. 14).[52]

As Yoder observes, "given Egypt's weakness, Pharaoh may have been flattered when ascribed [the] royal Mesopotamian" title of "great dragon," but Ezekiel overturns the image, demonstrating YHWH's sovereignty over the beast.[53] This fierce chaos monster is merely one of the great sea creatures made by YHWH, so he will fish it out of its watery home and give it as food for the rest of his created works. Moreover, foremost among the "many peoples" who will "lift [the dragon] up in [YHWH's] net" (32:3) is the king of Babylon. Pharaoh should recognize the king of Babylon as the true *ušumgallu*, who will devastate Egypt with the sword (vv. 11-12).

For the people of Judah, the image of Pharaoh as a dragon offers a response to the crisis posed by Egypt's corrosive influence. In order to draw a clear line of distinction between Israel and Egypt, the passage depicts Pharaoh as a beastly Other. Corresponding to Wills's fifth theorem—that *"the depiction of the Other is often unreal, distorted, monstrous, mythical, and taboo"*[54]—here Pharaoh is painted in hyperbolic terms reflecting what the "We-group" most fears and abhors. Portraying the Egyptian ruler as a monster pushes Egypt to the periphery of the ordered world, firmly outside the boundaries of Israel's self-identity. Moreover, Marzouk observes that in Ezekiel's description of the creature's demise its "dismembered body… becomes a corporeally-inscribed 'text' of horror and terror to those who dare to oppose YHWH's plans."[55]

The date formula in the first OAE (29:1-16) positions it in January 587 BCE, placing it during the Babylonian siege of Jerusalem,[56] while the sixth oracle (32:1-16) is dated over two years later, after the city had been destroyed. Thus the portrait of Pharaoh as a dragon may initially have been intended to warn Judah against allying with Egypt in a fruitless attempt to fend off Babylon. When the dragon is pulled out of the water, so are "all the fish of [its] streams that stick to [its] scales" (29:4). While

---

52. See further Marzouk, *Egypt as a Monster*, 198. By contrast, in 30:12 YHWH declares that he will "dry up the Nile," which is the source of life in Egypt.
53. Yoder, "Ezekiel 29:3," 496 n. 51.
54. Wills, *Not God's People*, 13 (emphasis in the original).
55. Marzouk, *Egypt as a Monster*, 200.
56. Ibid., 162.

it may be most natural to take the fish of the Nile's streams as designating the people of Egypt,⁵⁷ the image is sufficiently ambiguous that it could also suggest the nations who seek Pharaoh's help.⁵⁸ If such a reference is intended, then the oracle conveys the idea that those who turn to Egypt will share the dragon's grim fate. In any case, although Pharaoh may seem like a fearsome monster, powerful enough to take on the mighty Babylonian army, he is no match for YHWH, who has decreed judgment against him. So all hope in Egypt is vain.

In the later oracle with its heightened mythological tone, the portrait of Pharaoh as a dragon may be intended to represent any nation that challenges YHWH's sovereignty. Indeed, the conclusion to the OAE (and the oracles against the nations as a whole) emphasizes that Egypt's fate will be just like all the nations who "put terror in the land of the living" (32:17-32). Thus, the image may encourage the Judean exiles neither to fear nor devote themselves to any worldly power.⁵⁹

3. *Pharaoh as a Reed Staff*

After YHWH describes how he will slay the dragon in the first OAE (29:4-5), he explains the reason for this judgment, now portraying Pharaoh as a "reed staff":

וידעו כל־ישבי מצרים	6	And all the inhabitants of Egypt will know
כי אני יהוה		that I am YHWH
יען היותם משענת קנה		because you have been⁶⁰ a reed staff
לבית ישראל		to the house of Israel.
בתפשם בך בכפך	7	When they grasped you by the hand,
תרוץ ובקעת להם כל־כתף		you broke and tore all their shoulder.
ובהשענם עליך		And when they leaned on you,
תשבר והעמדת להם כל־מתנים		you shattered and made all their loins shake.⁶¹

---

57. So Block, *Ezekiel 25–48*, 138; Marzouk, *Egypt as a Monster*, 183.

58. See Nancy R. Bowen, *Ezekiel*, AOTC (Nashville, TN: Abingdon, 2010), 181; Katheryn Pfisterer Darr, "The Book of Ezekiel," in *NIB*, ed. Leander E. Keck, 12 vols (Nashville, TN: Abingdon, 2001), 6:1405.

59. See further Carvalho, "Serpent in the Nile," 219.

60. The MT has "they have been," but this reading, following the LXX, Syr., and Vg., fits better with the second person singular forms in the next verse (Boadt, *Ezekiel's Oracles*, 36; Block, *Ezekiel 25–48*, 136).

61. This translation follows the majority of commentators in reading עמד as the result of metathesis from the root מעד ("to shake"; see Boadt, *Ezekiel's Oracles*, 39; Walther Zimmerli, *Ezekiel 2: A Commentary on the Book of the Prophet Ezekiel Chapters 25–48*, trans. James D. Martin [Minneapolis, MN: Fortress, 1983], 107).

The reed was widely recognized as an image for weakness in the ancient world. For example, a Hittite treaty curse states, "May the oaths sworn in the presence of these gods break you like reeds,"[62] and Ashurnasirpal II claimed to have "cut down...his enemies, like the reeds of a marsh."[63] Moreover, the prevalence of reeds along the Nile makes it a fitting image for the Egyptian Pharaoh.

Although the term for "staff" used in 29:6 (משענת) is found nowhere else in the book, Ezekiel 19 uses synonyms to describe Judah as a vine that had "strong staffs/branches (מטות עז), becoming scepters (שבטי) of rulers" (v. 11). However, fire came and consumed the vine, leaving it without "a strong staff/branch (מטה־עז), a scepter (שבט) for ruling" (v. 14). The image of Pharaoh as a "reed staff" forms a striking contrast with the "strong staffs" once produced by Judah, thus emphasizing Pharaoh's impotence.

The only other reference to a משענת קנה ("reed staff") in the HB also metaphorically depicts the Egyptian Pharaoh. In Isa. 36:6 (// 2 Kgs 18:21) the commander of Sennacherib's army declares to Hezekiah, "Look, you are trusting in this broken reed staff (משענת הקנה הרצוץ הזה), in Egypt, which goes into the hand (בכפו) of anyone who leans (יסמך) on it and pierces it. Thus is Pharaoh, king of Egypt, to all who trust in him." The fact that this description is placed in the mouth of the Assyrian commander may suggest the intention to portray this as a widespread image of Pharaoh,[64] or Ezekiel may be using it in dependence on the Isaianic/Kings account.[65] Either way, it has a similar import in Ezekiel in describing Pharaoh as a flimsy support that not only fails to hold weight, but also injures those who lean on it. However, the injury here is more significant—rather than merely piercing their hand, it wrenches their shoulder out of joint and completely destabilizes them.[66] As a result, YHWH is "bringing a sword against" Egypt and "will cut off...man and beast" (v. 8).

In light of Ezekiel's portrait of Judah's earlier kings as staffs (19:11), the image of Pharaoh as a reed staff reveals the striking similarity between

---

62. "God List, Blessings and Curses of the Treaty between Sippiluliumas and Kurtiwaza," trans. Albrecht Goetze (*ANET*, 206); cited by Block, *Ezekiel 25–48*, 139 n. 52.

63. E. A. Wallis Budge and L. W. King, *Annals of the Kings of Assyria* (London, 1902), 261–2; cited by Boadt, *Ezekiel's Oracles*, 38. On the metaphorical use of reeds, see further *CAD* Q.87–88.

64. Block, *Ezekiel 25–48*, 139.
65. Boadt, *Ezekiel's Oracles*, 38.
66. See Greenberg, *Ezekiel 21–37*, 604–5.

the We-group and the Other, corresponding to Wills's third theorem. Yet as Wills observes, such similarities often prompt the We-group to exaggerate minor differences between themselves and the Other.[67] Ezekiel amplifies these differences by highlighting Pharaoh's weakness as a reed staff that breaks when used as a support, in contrast to the "strong staffs" representing the Judean kings.

Like the preceding portrait of Pharaoh as a dragon, deployment of this image may have served to caution the people of Judah against any continued hopes that Egypt might rescue them from the Babylonian siege. The placement of the oracle within the ongoing Babylonian siege recalls the earlier march of the Egyptian army toward Jerusalem, causing the Babylonians to withdraw temporarily. Although Jeremiah prophesied on that occasion that the Egyptians would return home and the Babylonians would conquer the city (Jer. 37:3-8), the people of Judah may still have pinned their hopes on Egypt coming again.[68] Moreover, since according to Ezekiel, Israel's relationship with Egypt has led them into idolatry and apostasy against YHWH from the beginning (see 20:7-8; 23:3, 8, 19-21), alliance with Egypt is not only politically imprudent but also spiritually disastrous.[69]

4. *Pharaoh as a Towering Cedar*

Whereas the image of a reed staff underscores Pharaoh's weakness as a support, the fifth OAE uses another botanical image to emphasize his strength. The oracle is addressed not only to Pharaoh but also to המונו (31:2a), which is usually translated "his hordes" (NIV, NASB, NRSV)[70] and understood as designating Pharaoh's armies. However, Daniel Bodi argues that it instead denotes his "pomp."[71] In any case, the second person singular forms in v. 2b indicate that Pharaoh is the primary referent, though the comparison with Assyria in v. 3 also suggests that he represents Egypt as a whole. Like Assyria previously, Pharaoh is a famed "cedar in Lebanon," a symbol of beauty and majesty:

---

67. Wills, *Not God's People*, 13.
68. Blenkinsopp, *Ezekiel*, 128.
69. Marzouk, *Egypt as a Monster*, 42.
70. Or "his multitude" (ESV, NKJB).
71. Daniel Bodi, *The Book of Ezekiel and the Poem of Erra*, OBO 104 (Göttingen: Vandenhoeck & Ruprecht, 1991), 158, also 122–5; see also Zimmerli, *Ezekiel 2*, 148.

	אֶל־מִי דָמִיתָ בְגָדְלֶךָ	2b Whom are you like in your greatness?
3	הִנֵּה אַשּׁוּר אֶרֶז בַּלְּבָנוֹן	Look, Assyria[72] was a cedar in Lebanon,
	יְפֵה עָנָף וְחֹרֶשׁ מֵצַל וּגְבַהּ קוֹמָה	[with] beautiful branches and forest shading and towering height,
	וּבֵין עֲבֹתִים הָיְתָה צַמַּרְתּוֹ	and its top was among the clouds.
4	מַיִם גִּדְּלוּהוּ תְּהוֹם רֹמְמָתְהוּ	Waters made it grow, the deep made it tall,
	אֶת־נַהֲרֹתֶיהָ הֹלֵךְ סְבִיבוֹת מַטָּעָהּ	making its rivers flow[73] around its planting
	וְאֶת־תְּעָלֹתֶיהָ שִׁלְחָה	and sending out its streams
	אֶל כָּל־עֲצֵי הַשָּׂדֶה	to all the trees of the field.
	…	…
8	אֲרָזִים לֹא־עֲמָמֻהוּ בְּגַן־אֱלֹהִים	The cedars in the garden of God could not compare with it.
	בְּרוֹשִׁים לֹא דָמוּ אֶל־סְעַפֹּתָיו	Fir trees were not like its boughs,
	וְעַרְמֹנִים לֹא־הָיוּ כְּפֹארֹתָיו	nor were the plane trees like its branches.
	כָּל־עֵץ בְּגַן־אֱלֹהִים	No tree in the garden of God
	לֹא־דָמָה אֵלָיו בְּיָפְיוֹ	was like it in its beauty.
9	יָפֶה עֲשִׂיתִיו בְּרֹב דָּלִיּוֹתָיו	I made it beautiful in its many branches,
	וַיְקַנְאֻהוּ כָּל־עֲצֵי־עֵדֶן	and all the trees of Eden envied it,
	אֲשֶׁר בְּגַן הָאֱלֹהִים	those that were in the garden of God.

a. *The Background of the Image in Egypt and Mesopotamia*

Although cedar trees are not found naturally in Egypt, the Egyptians did make use of the motif of a sacred tree, which was often associated with a goddess and sometimes served as a symbol of protection. Moreover, the Book of the Dead uses the image of a cosmic sycamore tree with roots reaching down to the subterranean waters and its top in the sky to represent a goddess who provides food for the dead.[74] Similarly, the Babylonian

---

72. Many commentators follow the *BHS* in reading אשור as a variant or mistaken form of תאשור, which means "cypress" or "box tree" (e.g., Duguid, *Ezekiel*, 372 n. 3; Boadt, *Ezekiel's Oracles*, 96–9). However, the versions support the MT, and Assyria appears again in Ezekiel's final OAE as the first of the nations brought down to Sheol (32:21-22; cf. the fate of the cedar in 31:15-17; see Block, *Ezekiel 25–48*, 184; Paul M. Joyce, *Ezekiel: A Commentary*, LHBOTS 482 [New York: T&T Clark, 2007], 185).

73. This reading follows the LXX, understanding the MT as a Hiphil inf. abs. (see Block, *Ezekiel 25–48*, 182; J. B. Curtis, "On the *Hiphil* Infinitive Absolute of *Hālak*," *ZAH* 1 [1988]: 22–31). The Qal, as an intransitive verb, would not explain the direct object marker on את־נהרתיה.

74. Carvalho, "Serpent in the Nile," 214–15; see further E. O. James, *The Tree of Life: An Archaeological Study* (Leiden: Brill, 1966), 41; Marie-Louise Buhl, "The Goddesses of the Egyptian Tree Cult," *JNES* 6 (1947): 80–97, esp. pp. 91–2.

Story of Erra and Ishum speaks of a *mēsu* tree as "the proper insignia of the King of the World… / Whose roots reach down into the vast ocean through a hundred miles of water to the base of Arallu, / Whose topknot above rests on the heaven of Anu."[75] And in Assyrian iconography, a sacred tree can function as a royal symbol, perhaps to portray the king as upholding the world order,[76] though the image's significance is debated.[77]

b. *The Background of the Image in the Hebrew Bible*

The most important background for Ezekiel's use of this imagery, however, is found within the HB. Drawing on Israel's creation traditions, the passage describes the cedar as the most magnificent of all the trees in Eden, "the garden of God" (31:8-9). Genesis 2 describes Eden as full of all kinds of trees, but the two that stand out from the rest are the tree of life and the tree of the knowledge of good and evil (v. 9). These, along with the rest of the garden's plant life, are nourished by "a river (נהר)…going out from Eden to water the garden," which then splits into four rivers that flow through the surrounding country (vv. 10-14).

While creation as a theme appears in several places in the HB, references to Eden are rare outside of Genesis. However, Ezekiel employs the tradition elsewhere as an image of Judah's restoration (36:35; cf. Isa. 51:3),[78] as well as in the preceding oracle against Tyre (28:13). The latter passage, which shares several parallels with Ezekiel 31, describes the king of Tyre as "the seal of perfection, full of wisdom and perfect in beauty" (28:12). He was "placed" by God on his "holy mountain"—that is, "in Eden"—as (or perhaps "with")[79] "an anointed guardian cherub"

---

75. Stephanie Dalley (ed. and trans.), "Erra and Ishum," in *Myths from Mesopotamia: Creation, the Flood, Gilgamesh, and Others*, rev. ed. (Oxford: Oxford University Press, 2000), 291; cited by Bodi, "Ezekiel," 4:472.

76. Simo Parpola, "The Assyrian Tree of Life: Tracing the Origins of Jewish Monotheism and Greek Philosophy," *JNES* 52 (1993): 167–8; Carol A. Newsom and Brennan W. Breed, *Daniel*, OTL (Louisville, KY: Westminster John Knox, 2014), 137–8.

77. See Barbara Nevling Porter, "Sacred Trees, Date Palms, and the Royal Persona of Ashurnasirpal II," *JNES* 52 (1993): 129–39; Mariana Giovino, *The Assyrian Sacred Tree: A History of Interpretations*, OBO 230 (Fribourg: Academic, 2007). On the use of a tree to represent kings in Sumerian literature, see also Geo Widengren, *King and Savior, vol. 4: The King and the Tree of Life in Ancient Near Eastern Religion* (Uppsala: Lundequistska, 1951), 43–5.

78. In Joel 2:3 Judah is compared to Eden in order to heighten the contrast between its current state and its coming devastation.

79. See the LXX; also Carol Newsom, "A Maker of Metaphors—Ezekiel's Oracles Against Tyre," *Int* 38 (1984): 162 n. 28.

(vv. 13-14). Whether the king is here presented as the cherub itself or as an Adam figure,[80] he was "created" (ברא) by YHWH as a symbol of perfection and beauty (v. 13). Although he does not belong to YHWH's chosen people but is an ethnic Other, he is highly treasured and is installed in Eden as a guardian of YHWH's sacred space.[81] But the king "sinned" in his trade, and his "heart was proud in [his] beauty" (גבה לבך ביפיך, vv. 16-17). So YHWH "threw [him] down to the ground" and consumed him by fire in front of the watching nations.

The image of a cedar tree appears elsewhere in Ezekiel in the enigmatic fable in ch. 17, where it is applied to Judah.[82] The fable describes how a "great eagle" (presumably Nebuchadnezzar) "came to Lebanon and took the top (צמרת) of the cedar (הארז)" (i.e., Jehoiachin) and brought it into exile (vv. 3-4).[83] Then "he took from the seed of the land" (i.e., Zedekiah) and "put it in a fertile field...beside abundant waters" (על־מים רבים, v. 5; cf. v. 8), where "it sprouted and became a low spreading vine" (v. 6). But the vine "bent its roots toward" another eagle (i.e., Pharaoh), which will lead to its destruction, both by the first eagle and by the "east wind" (i.e., YHWH), since the king of Judah has violated covenants with both (vv. 9-21).[84] But later YHWH promises to "take from the lofty top (מצמרת) of the cedar (הארז)" and replant it so that it will "bear branches and produce fruit and become a noble cedar (ארז)" and "all birds of every kind will dwell under it" (vv. 22-23). As a result, "all the trees of the field" will recognize YHWH, who "makes the high tree low and exalts the low tree" (v. 24).

Ezekiel 19 does not refer to a cedar tree, but it describes the mother of Judah's lion-king (Jerusalem?)[85] as a vine that is "fruitful and full of branches (וענפה) because of abundant waters (ממים רבים)" (v. 10). Indeed, surprisingly, though just a vine, it "towered high (ותגבה קומתו) among the clouds (על־בין עבתים), and it was seen in its height with its many branches (ברב דליתיו)" (v. 11) like the cedar in Ezekiel 31.[86]

---

80. On the former, see Block, *Ezekiel 25–48*, 112–13; on the latter, see Newsom, "Maker of Metaphors," 160–1.

81. See further Newsom, "Maker of Metaphors," 161.

82. Aside from Ezek. 17 and 31, ארז ("cedar") is found in Ezekiel only in 27:5 as the source of a mast for a Tyrian ship.

83. צמרת ("top") appears in Ezekiel only in chs 17 and 31.

84. See further Moshe Greenberg, "Ezekiel 17: A Holistic Interpretation," *JAOS* 103 (1983): 149–54.

85. So Daniel I. Block, "The Tender Cedar Sprig: Ezekiel on Jehoiachin," *Hebrew Bible and Ancient Israel* 1 (2012): 186.

86. קומה, גבה, and עבות appear together only in Ezek. 19:11; 31:3, 10, and 14 in the HB. The NIV translates עבתים here as "thick foliage" (cf. the ESV, NRSV, NKJV),

Ultimately, however, "it was uprooted in anger, thrown down to the ground" and ravaged by fire (v. 12). Although it has now been replanted in the wilderness, its strong branches have been destroyed (vv. 13-14).

Independently of Ezekiel 31, Daniel 4 also uses the cedar tree to symbolize a foreign monarch.[87] The Daniel text recounts Nebuchadnezzar's dream of a cedar tree whose "top reached to the heavens" and who provided food and shelter for the birds and beasts (vv. 11-12). In the dream, however, a heavenly being commands an unnamed audience to cut the tree down, leaving behind only a stump (vv. 13-15). Daniel interprets the dream, explaining that Nebuchadnezzar is the cedar tree, who has exalted himself in pride. Like the downed tree, he will be removed from his throne, losing his sanity and living among the wild animals for seven years. In the end, he will recognize YHWH's sovereignty and his kingdom will be reestablished like the stump of the tree that remains standing (vv. 23-26). In each of these texts, the tree (or vine) faces destruction, at least in part due to its pride, though the passages display varying degrees of restoration.

c. *Ezekiel's Development of the Image*

Ezekiel 31 shares many points of correspondence with Ezekiel 17 and 19. Like the vines in those chapters, the roots of this cedar are beside "abundant waters" (מים רבים, 31:7; cf. 17:5, 8; 19:10). Moreover, both the Judah-vine in ch. 19 and the cedar representing Assyria (and by analogy Egypt) grow to legendary proportions with their tops reaching up to the heavens. However, the differences between these chapters highlight the greater splendor and magnificence of Pharaoh. While the restored Judah-cedar in ch. 17 becomes a habitation for birds (v. 23), the Pharaoh-cedar[88] is portrayed as a refuge for "all the birds of the heavens," "all the beasts of the field," and "all great nations" (31:6). Indeed, it is the greatest and most beautiful of all the cedars in Eden, provoking the other trees (including Judah?) to envy. And the reason it holds this place of distinction is because

---

which is a possible rendering and fits better with the image of a vine. However, in ch. 31 the word seems to indicate "clouds," emphasizing the remarkable stature of the cedar tree, so it should probably be understood in the same way here (Duguid, *Ezekiel*, 249 n. 13).

87. See further Newsom and Breed, *Daniel*, 138.

88. This image though does not represent Egypt's self-image. There's nothing I see in the passage to indicate that, as for example, in 29:3, which puts words in Pharaoh's mouth to indicate his self-aggrandizement. And the statement "I made it beautiful" seems to affirm the perspective of Assyria/Pharaoh's greatness found throughout the passage and attribute it to YHWH.

YHWH "made it beautiful" (v. 9). Thus, as in the oracle against Tyre, the Eden tradition is used to portray Egypt (like Assyria before it) as a magnificent creation of YHWH.

The "waters" (מים) and "deep" (תהום) that nourish the tree (v. 4a) echo Gen. 1:2, which speaks of God's Spirit hovering over the "waters" (המים), preparing to make life emerge from the primordial "deep" (תהום).[89] And as the primeval waters flow around the cedar, they divide into streams that nourish the other trees of the field (v. 4). Moreover, the cedar's abundant foliage provides shade and protection for the nations (v. 6). The preeminence of the cedar and its connection with the health and growth of the other trees evokes the image of the tree of life.[90]

The passage implies that the cedar owes its lofty stature to YHWH. who made its "height tower" (גבהא קמתו, v. 5) and placed "its top among the clouds" (ובין עבתים...צמרתו, v. 3). However, becoming arrogant in its splendor, the tree usurped YHWH's role—it "towered in its [own] height (גבהת בקומה) and set its [own] top among the clouds (ויתן צמרתו אל־בין עבותים)" (v. 10a). And like the king of Tyre, who gloried in his own beauty, the tree's "heart was lifted up in its height" (ורם לבבו בגבהו, v. 10b). Whereas in vv. 3-5 רום and גבה are used to indicate the imposing size of the tree, now they appear in an idiom that conveys its pride.[91] As a result, YHWH brought the judgment of Adam upon the Pharaoh-cedar, driving it out of the garden (גרש, v. 11; cf. Gen. 3:24).

Resuming the arboreal imagery, the passage explains that YHWH gave the tree over to foreigners, who "cut it down" and "cast it away" (נטש, v. 12a), as YHWH "cast (נטש) [the great dragon] out into the wilderness" (29:5; cf. 32:4).[92] Moreover, the cedar's fallen branches cover "mountains," "valleys," and "ravines" (v. 12b), like the refuse of the slain dragon (32:5-6). Now "all the peoples of the earth" have left its protective shade. And "all the birds of the heavens" and "all the beasts of the field," who once took refuge in the mighty tree (31:8), now perch on the fallen

---

89. Rather than seeing an allusion to the generative power of creation here, Marzouk focuses on the connotation of chaos associated with תהום and understands the description of the cedar being fed by these waters as an indication of the tree's monstrosity (*Egypt as a Monster*, 178).

90. See also Bodi, "Ezekiel," 4:473; Boadt, *Ezekiel's Oracles*, 99–100. Block rejects a comparison to the tree of life since Ezekiel's tree is not described as a source of food (*Ezekiel 25–48*, 188). While the differences between the Pharaoh-cedar and tree of life warrant caution in making a complete identification, there are nevertheless significant points of connection.

91. Block, *Ezekiel 25–48*, 191.

92. נטש appears only in these three verses in Ezekiel (Zimmerli, *Ezekiel 2*, 151).

log (v. 13), like the birds and beasts feasting on the dragon's carcass (29:5; 32:4). But the portrait of the cedar's great fall does not end there—it even "descended to Sheol" (v. 15a). Furthermore, YHWH "withheld the rivers [of the deep] and restrained abundant waters" (v. 15b), so "all the trees of Eden"—that is, those "who dwelt in its shade among the nations"— "descended to Sheol along with it" (vv. 16-17). Like the fish of the dragon's streams, who are captured along with the monster (29:4), so the trees that depend on the cedar will share in its fate.

Rhetorically, the comparison of Pharaoh with Assyria at the beginning of the oracle drives home the certainty of Egypt's coming demise. If even mighty Assyria met its downfall, what hope is there for Egypt? For an Egyptian audience, the great cedar in Sheol bears some similarity to the sycamore in the Book of the Dead, and its presence there brings a measure of comfort to other deceased nations (v. 16). However, unlike the cosmic sycamore with its top in the heavens, this tree has been cut down and completely disconnected from life in this world.

For the original Judean audience, whether receiving this oracle toward the end of the Babylonian siege of Jerusalem[93] or later in their troubled history, Egypt or any other earthly power may seem like their last hope—a tree of life in the face of the dire threat of death. However, this passage throws doubt on that perspective. Moreover, following Wills's ninth theorem—that *"the Other has ancient origins"*[94]—Pharaoh is portrayed as an Edenic tree, which has roots going down to the beginning of time. This image also suggests a military threat that is not easily eliminated and that will last forever. However, in Ezekiel 31 we see a transformation of Wills's ninth theorem, where the text assures its Judean audience that Pharaoh's continued existence will be confined to the underworld and warns that he will become a tree of death for those who turn to him for protection. If the people of Judah seek refuge in the cedar's shade, they will go down with it to Sheol (v. 17).

Nevertheless, this passage also suggests a special relationship between YHWH and Egypt and testifies to its preeminence among the nations, not merely in political terms but also in terms of its beauty and splendor before YHWH (v. 8). While a comparable depiction of the king of Tyre may be found in Ezekiel 28, nowhere does the book use such exalted language in describing Israel. Perhaps then this passage turns Wills's fifth theorem—that *"the depiction of the Other is often unreal, distorted, monstrous, mythical, and taboo"*[95]—on its head. Egypt is depicted in a

---

93. This oracle is dated to May or June of 587 BCE (Blenkinsopp, *Ezekiel*, 127).
94. Wills, *Not God's People*, 14 (emphasis in the original).
95. Ibid., 13 (emphasis in the original).

way that is *"unreal"* and *"mythical*," but is not presented as *"monstrous"* or *"taboo."* Instead, the portrait demonstrates Egypt's inherent value as YHWH's special creation.

Here Israel's particularistic tendency is directed not inward toward themselves as YHWH's "treasured possession" (Exod. 19:5), but outward toward Egypt as the most magnificent of all the trees (i.e., nations) in Eden. Thus Egypt's Otherness is found in its matchless splendor, which draws the envy of the other nations (presumably including Judah). Despite the assurance that judgment will soon fall upon Egypt, Ezek. 31:2-9 offers a retrospective view on that nation's origins that parallels the forward-looking perspective of Isa. 19:23-25, which declares that Israel will be counted third after Egypt, YHWH's "people," and "Assyria, the work of [his] hands."[96]

5. Conclusion

Ezekiel's OAE depict a complex portrait of Egypt and Pharaoh as national and ethnic Others, offering a reflection on Israel's struggle to make sense of Otherness in relation to its own self-identity. The metaphor of Pharaoh as a dragon exhibits a tendency to mythologize Egypt as monstrous (corresponding to Wills's fifth theorem), which is unsurprising in a judgment oracle against a foreign nation. However, an interesting feature of Ezekiel's OAE is that in many ways their portraits of Egypt mirror depictions of Judah found elsewhere in the book. A clear example may be found in the parallel images of Pharaoh and Judah's kings as staffs, though Ezekiel 29 magnifies the differences between them by emphasizing Pharaoh's weakness as a *reed* staff (reflecting Wills's third theorem).

In other cases, Ezekiel draws an even closer correspondence between the two nations. For instance, in Ezekiel's first OAE YHWH condemns Egypt to exile for forty years (29:11), the same length of time assigned for Judah's punishment in 4:6. YHWH also declares that he will "scatter" (פוץ) and "disperse" (זרה) the Egyptians "among the nations" (29:12; also 30:23, 26) but then will "gather" (קבץ) them again (29:13), using terms elsewhere associated with Judah's exile and return (see, e.g., 20:23, 34; 36:19, 24) and not applied to any other nations.[97] These similarities between the fates of Egypt and Judah come close to Wills's seventh

---

96. Intriguingly, both passages draw a connection between Egypt and Assyria.

97. Their shared punishment may be due to their shared history of idolatry (see Marzouk, *Egypt as a Monster*, 123). Crouch sees the punishment as involving the principle of *lex talionis* due to the implication of Egypt both in Israel's forty years of wandering in the wilderness and forty years of exile ("Ezekiel's Oracles," 491).

theorem, which states that *"ambiguous groups"* are sometimes adopted into the We-group. Here, however, Egypt is viewed as running on a parallel track of judgment and restoration rather than being assimilated into Judah. This suggests that YHWH may have dealings with Egypt that are analogous to but separate from his special relationship with Israel.[98]

Moreover, the metaphor of a cedar tree is applied to both Judah (Ezek. 17) and Pharaoh (on analogy with Assyria in Ezek. 31),[99] and comparing those two descriptions highlights the greater strength and splendor of Pharaoh. Even more astonishing is the use of Israel's sacred Eden traditions to describe Pharaoh's glory. Whereas the image of Pharaoh as a dragon emphasizes his apparent power and ferocity in order to underscore YHWH's sovereignty in destroying him,[100] the depiction of Pharaoh as a cedar tree in 31:2-9 declares that, like Assyria before him, his greatness derives from YHWH (see v. 9). Therefore, the mythical portrait of Pharaoh as an Edenic tree conveys his extraordinary worth (overturning Wills's fifth theorem).

As Wills observes, the great superpowers *"are not consistently mythologized as evil"* within the HB but only when they threaten or harm YHWH's people.[101] So at various points in Israel's history, the HB reflects differing attitudes toward Egypt. What is striking, however, is that these portraits of one foreign nation found in a single prophetic collection of judgment oracles purportedly given over a relatively short period of time (just over two years; see 29:1; 32:1) reveal a remarkable diversity of approaches to Israel's process of ethnic Othering. Although the OAE serve primarily to warn Israel against allying itself too closely with Egypt, they present widely divergent views on Egypt's strength, its value, and its relationships both to Israel and to YHWH. Despite the clear lines of distinction drawn between Israel and Egypt, these depictions reveal that in many ways, Egypt turns out to be not so Other after all.

---

98. Cf. the perspective on the Ethiopians, Philistines, and Arameans represented by Amos 9:7.

99. See also the metaphor of the mother of Judah's king (Jerusalem?) as a vine in Ezek. 19.

100. See Crouch, "Ezekiel's Oracles," 492.

101. Wills, *Not God's People*, 39 (emphasis in the original).

Chapter 7

UNSTABLE CONSTRUCTIONS OF IDENTITY:
OTHERNESS AND AMBIVALENT SUBJECTIVITIES
IN EZEKIEL 23

Diandra Chretain Erickson

1. *Introduction: Violence and Vulnerabilities in Ezekiel 23*

The book of Ezekiel portrays a complex process of rebuilding Judean group identity within the context of the Babylonian exile. The forced migration to a foreign territory, the loss of friends and family, and the destruction of Jerusalem and its temple were crucial and devastating experiences that created the urgency for the exiles to reassess and reformulate standard traditions and beliefs. As a result, the book presents the theological and ideological responses of a defeated and minoritized group with little military and political influence under the shadow of Babylon. Concerning the Judeans in the Babylonian exile, Joyce states:

> within just a few years Judah was robbed of all main elements in her theological system: land, chosen people status, city, temple and monarchy. The event of defeat and exile at the hands of the Babylonians and the theological questions that they posed are the essential key to understanding Ezekiel and his tradition.[1]

Joyce emphasizes that the devastating consequences of Babylonian oppression indubitably affects Ezekiel's theological notions. The Judean communities' loss of their homeland, their city, and the temple and monarchy illustrate loss of identity and social disempowerment.

---

1. Paul Joyce, *Ezekiel: A Commentary*, LHBOTS 482 (New York: T&T Clark, 2009), 4.

As a text written to capture the throes of chaos, disarray, and discontinuity, the book's literary dimension portrays fluctuating degrees of power and powerlessness that reflect the Judean exiles' malleable positions as subject and object. As subject, the Judeans male elites once occupied space within the upper echelons of society, where lower class men and women were subordinate. However, the imperial presence of Babylonia severely distorts the Judean elites' status as subject and causes them to become the victimized and disempowered objects. Undergoing colonization within a foreign space inevitably causes markers of group identity to become questioned, compromised, and ultimately transformed. The Judean exiles do not embody a fixed identity, but as seen in the book of Ezekiel, they exemplify aspects of both *power/powerlessness, self/other* and *subject/object*.

The exiles' ambivalent positioning as both subject and object is heavily depicted in Ezekiel 23. This text is notorious for its explicit sexual imagery that represents Yahweh as a husband who physically abuses his daughters/wives, Samaria and Jerusalem, and forces them to undergo extreme abuse by others.[2] Within this imagery, Ezekiel 23 produces contradictory renderings of power and powerlessness that provocatively describe the vulnerability of the exiles as a subjugated community. The metaphor is a discursive account of a liminal "in-between space" where the exiles, as colonized subjects, reside. The purpose of this study is to provide a literary examination that illuminates two instances of ambivalent representations of power in Ezekiel 23: (1) conflicting illustrations of empowerment and disempowerment through patriarchal power and sociopolitical powerlessness and (2) contradictory representations of the colonized subject's envy of and repulsion towards the colonizer.

2. *Method: A Literary Study of Otherness and Ambivalence through a Postcolonial Lens*

This study is a synchronic analysis of Ezekiel 23 that utilizes a postcolonial lens[3] in order to demonstrate the ambivalent ways that power and

---

2. Ezekiel 16 and 23 are two of three re-creative histories in the book of Ezekiel, the third being Ezek. 20. Joyce, *Ezekiel: A Commentary*, 161. Ezekiel 20 represents a hopeful recreation of Israelite history that focuses specifically on the exilic community. On the contrary, Ezek. 16 and 23 present a negative reconstruction of history that targets Jerusalem through female personification.

3. Postcolonialism as an academic discipline emerged from Commonwealth Literature, which developed in the 1950s and generally referred to writings that were produced within countries with a history of colonialism in Africa, the Caribbean, and

powerlessness are portrayed in this chapter. Even though a diachronic study of Ezekiel 23 can provide a wealth of information regarding the Judeans' struggle with colonization under the Babylonian empire, this study does not examine this text as a historical document that portrays the state of the Judeans during the exile. Instead, this reading of Ezekiel 23 focuses on the text's literary dimension and how it offers a creative expression of the Judean exiles' vulnerability, defeat, and their dismantling of identity.

The use of a contemporary postcolonial lens[4] alongside a synchronic examination of Ezekiel 23 helps illuminate how the chapter's rhetoric contains fluctuating interplays between agency and subjugation.[5]

South Asia that were under British rule. See John McLeod, *Beginning Postcolonialism*, 2nd ed. (Manchester: Manchester University Press, 2012), 12 and also Pramod K. Nayar, *Postcolonial Literature: An Introduction* (New Delhi: Pearson, 2008), 12–17. My use of a postcolonial lens functions as a reading strategy more than a systematic method of approaching the text. For an outline of the methodological challenges of postcolonialism in biblical studies, see R. S. Sugirtharajah, "Charting the Aftermath: A Review of Postcolonial Criticism," in *The Postcolonial Biblical Reader*, ed. R. S. Sugirtharajah (New York: Blackwell, 2006), 7–32.

4. This postcolonial reading draws heavily from works by Franz Fanon and Homi Bhabha. Fanon was a Martinique psychologist and a prolific writer in the mid-twentieth century who examined the psychology of colonized and oppressed groups and served as a prominent voice in Algeria's struggles for independence. For helpful biographies of Fanon, see David Macey, *Frantz Fanon: A Biography*, 2nd ed. (New York: Verso, 2012), Alice Cherki, *Fanon: A Portrait*, trans. Nadia Benabid (New York: Cornell University Press, 2006), and Hussein Abdailahi Bulhan, *Fanon and the Psychology of Oppression* (New York: Plenum, 1985). Homi Bhabha, a more recent postcolonial theorist, is heavily influenced by and builds upon Fanon's writings on the colonized psyche. He is currently a key figure in contemporary postcolonial studies and well-known for his theories on colonial mimicry and hybridity. He is mostly known for his collection of essays in *Location of Culture*, which is the primary text by Bhabha that is used for this study. Homi K. Bhabha, *The Location of Culture* (New York: Routledge, 1994). For a helpful introduction to the theories proposed by Bhabha, see David Huddart, *Homi K. Bhabha* (New York: Routledge, 2006).

5. There are a variety of effective contemporary approaches alongside postcolonial studies that can help illuminate how power is discursively represented in Ezekiel's Babylonian exilic ideology, including feminist interpretation, migration/diaspora studies, and subaltern studies. I choose to examine the book of Ezekiel through a postcolonial optic because this approach stands out as an effective lens for critically probing how the book's rhetoric contains ambivalent interplays between power and powerlessness. This decision to pursue the postcolonial optic over other interdisciplinary approaches is partially guided by Smith-Christopher's methodological approach to using social science literature in Biblical Studies. He states, "My

According to Homi Bhabha, a leading contemporary postcolonial theorist, colonial writings rarely present a binary relationship between the colonizer and the colonized, where the colonizer is fully subject and the colonizer is wholly object. On the contrary, texts written in the context of colonization portray ambivalent representations of the colonized that disrupt clear-cut boundaries between insiders/outsiders, self/other, us/them, and center/periphery. He states that the representation of cultures and identities in colonial texts are never represented as "unitary in themselves, nor simply dualistic in the relation of self to other."[6] In other words, colonized subjects do not reside in fixed social and cultural spaces but instead dwell in unstable borderlands on the periphery, where they constantly maneuver between various spatial and temporal realms.[7] This ambivalence creates a slippage that compromises the binaries between dominant and oppressed groups. Residing in the borderland and negotiating between various aspects of identity distort and obscure the boundaries between *self* and *other*.

Ambivalence in texts that purport to represent colonial power "disrupts the clear-cut authority of colonial domination because it disturbs the simple relationship between colonizer and colonized."[8] Building on this notion, McLeod states, "At the border, past and present, inside and outside no longer remain separated as binary opposites but instead commingle and conflict. From this emerge new, shifting complex forms of representation that deny binary patterning."[9] Within colonized contexts, identities of the colonizer and colonized are not based on binary oppositions but on fluctuating modes of domination and subjugation.

A postcolonial reading strategy that focuses on ambivalence serves as a beneficial tool for illuminating instances of instability in the literary dimension of Ezekiel 23. This essay identifies two ways in which the subtle and implicit ways that the exiles' hybrid identities as empowered

---

approach begins with the study of a particular text or historical issue in my work on the Bible, and is then followed by a consideration of the social-science literature that seems, *prima facie*, to be discussing similar circumstances." Daniel Smith-Christopher, "Reading Exile Then: Reconsidering the Methodological Debates for Biblical Analysis in Dialogue with Sociological and Literary Analysis," in *By the Irrigation Canals of Babylon: Approaches to the Study of Exile*, ed. John J. Ahn and Jill Middlemas, LHBOTS 526 (New York: T&T Clark, 2012), 146.

6. Bhabha, *The Location of Culture*, 35.
7. Ibid., 35–9.
8. Bill Ashcroft, Garret Griffiths, and Hellen Tiffin (eds), *Key Concepts in Postcolonial Studies* (London: Routledge, 1998), 10.
9. McLeod, *Beginning Postcolonialism*, 252.

and disempowered manifest within the chapter: First, ambivalence is presented through contradictory expressions of the exiles' empowerment and disempowerment through the images of Yahweh and the sisters. Both Yahweh and the sisters symbolize the Judean exiles' agency (*self*) and oppression (*other*) respectively. Second, ambivalence emerges through contradictory representations of desire. The sisters' desire for the colonizers oscillates between attraction and repulsion, which demonstrates how the colonized subject's envious fixation of the colonizer is not static but deeply ambivalent.

3. *Patriarchal Power and Sociopolitical Powerlessness in Ezekiel 23*

a. *Yahweh and the Sisters, Separated yet Combined Entities*

Ezekiel 23:1-49 is a single literary unit that begins with the standard prophetic word formula "The word of the Lord came to me," and consists of two speeches spoken by Yahweh (vv. 2-35 and 36-42). The first speech focuses on the two sisters' acts of infidelity and subsequent consequences, beginning with Oholah's desire for the Assyrians and her punishment of public stripping (23:5-10). Oholibah's narrative then continues when Oholah's story ends (23:11-35). Similarly to Oholah's story, Oholibah's portion of the chapter describes her lust towards imperial powers through an expanded format[10] that emphasizes her desire not only for the Assyrians but the Chaldeans and the Egyptians. Yahweh's second speech (23:36-49) continues to emphasize both Oholah's and Oholibah's charges and punishments, yet it departs from the frequent political language that describes the international relations between the sisters and the foreign imperial powers in the first speech. Instead, Yahweh's second speech portrays more cultic rhetoric that emphasizes the defilement of the sanctuary.

This chapter seemingly presents a dichotomous portrait of power and powerlessness through the characterizations of Yahweh and Oholah/Oholibah. Yahweh, the angered husband, illustrates the ability to control the foreign imperial powers' violent actions against Oholah and Oholibah, and possesses the power to subject the two sisters to sexual abuse and physical mutilation. The sisters demonstrate extensive levels of disempowerment and victimization in the metaphor that firmly contrasts with Yahweh's image of authority and potency. Through the hands of the

---

10. As Daniel Block states, Oholah's charges and punishment span six verses, while Oholibah's narrative spans 35 verses. Daniel Block, *The Book of Ezekiel*, NICOT (Grand Rapids, MI: Eerdmans, 1997), 731.

imperial rulers (set in motion by Yahweh), Oholah and Oholibah are violently stripped, left naked and bare (vv. 10, 26, 29), devoured by fire (v. 25), and grotesquely mutilated (vv. 25, 34) with no ability to defend themselves against their attackers.

Ultimately, a radical disparity of power exists between Yahweh and Oholah/Oholibah.[11] As a result of this deeply contrasting portrait of the deity and the sisters, many interpreters claim that the Judean exilic audience's experience should resonate with either Yahweh, the dominating husband, *or* Oholah/Oholibah, the powerless sisters. Regarding the former, Weems claims that the marriage metaphor helps the audience identify with Yahweh. She asserts that Ezekiel's Judean audience should primarily relate to the anger and betrayal that Yahweh embodies as a passionate husband who devastatingly witnesses his wife's infidelities. Weems states:

> Only an audience that had never been raped or had never perceived rape or sexual abuse as a real threat could be expected to hear the kinds of ribald descriptions of abused women, sexual humiliation, assault, gang rape, violation, and torture that the prophets described and not recoil in fear. Only an audience that could relate to and identify with the metaphorical husband's outrage and horror could possibly perceive his reactions as plausible and legitimate.[12]

According to Weems, the marriage metaphor helps the Judean audience further comprehend the emotional rage that fueled Yahweh's violent actions against Samaria and Jerusalem. Kamionkowski states a similar claim: "In Ezekiel 23, the writer identifies with YHWH, the jilted lover... Ezekiel's primary identification in this chapter is with YHWH."[13] For both Weems and Kamionkowski, the metaphor contains significant

---

11. Some feminist interpreters argue that Oholah and Oholibah (along with the figure of Jerusalem in Ezek. 16) do exhibit power over Yahweh. These scholars use deconstructionist readings of the texts that show how Yahweh essentially reacts to the actions of the women, thus exhibiting a level of powerlessness. Yahweh's authority and potency are ultimately threatened by the sisters' sexual desires and behaviors towards the foreign powers. See in particular Mary E. Shields, "An Abusive God? Identity and Power, Gender and Violence in Ezekiel 23," in *Postmodern Interpretations of the Bible: A Reader*, ed. A. K. M. Adam (St. Louis, MO: Chalice, 2001), 129–51.

12. Renita Weems, *Battered Love: Marriage, Sex, and Violence in the Hebrew Prophets*, OBT (Minneapolis, MN: Fortress, 1995), 14.

13. S. Tamar Kamionkowski, *Gender Reversal and Cosmic Chaos: A Study on the Book of Ezekiel*, JSOTSup 368 (Sheffield: Sheffield Academic, 2003), 148.

emotive worth for the audience in regards to traditional male and female roles within marital relationships. The expectation is that the male is the authority of the relationship while the woman is submissive. If these dynamics are subverted and the male in the relationship becomes the "jilted lover" instead of the respected patriarch, the emotional response from the audience could be immense. In other words, "the prophets chose an image that had enormous sentimental value in Hebrew society."[14] The metaphor is effective because the Judean male elites understood the extreme humiliation and shame that husbands undergo through the actions of an unfaithful wife.

However, other scholars claim the opposite perspective and assert that the Judean exiles' experience aligns more accurately with Oholah's and Oholibah's weakness and subjugation instead of Yahweh's patriarchal dominance. Patton points out that the metaphor is persuasive because the violent victimization experienced by the sisters reflect the Judeans' lived experiences of humiliation and emasculation. As Patton states: "Ezekiel knew what it meant to be sexually humiliated. He presumed his audience, the elders gathered around him, had experienced the same sexual humiliation."[15] Along similar lines, Smith-Christopher posits that the exilic community's own oppressive treatment by the Babylonians aligns them with "female Jerusalem, rather than the male God."[16] Patton and Smith-Christopher, along with others holding this position, argue that the sisters were not merely objects of the exiles' "male gaze." On the contrary, they posit that when the exiles "gazed" upon the sisters' violent interactions with Assyria, the Chaldeans, and Egyptians in the metaphor they would have seen a reflection of themselves and their own experiences as victims of warfare.[17]

The question concerning whether the Judean exiles should identify with Yahweh or the sisters is typically addressed dichotomously: should they resonate with Yahweh's patriarchal power *or* the sisters' sociopolitical

---

14. Weems, *Battered Love*, 14.

15. Corrine L. Patton, "Should Our Sister be Treated Like a Whore?," in *The Book of Ezekiel: Theological and Anthropological Perspectives*, ed. Margaret S. Odell and John T. Strong (Atlanta, GA: SBL, 2000), 224.

16. Daniel Smith-Christopher, "Ezekiel in Abu Ghraib: Rereading Ezekiel 16:37-39 in the Context of Imperial Conquest," in *Ezekiel's Hierarchical World: Wrestling with a Tiered Reality*, ed. Stephen L. Cook and Corrine L. Patton (Atlanta, GA: Society of Biblical Literature, 2004), 155.

17. Patton, "Should Our Sister be Treated Like a Whore?" 224 and Smith-Christopher, "Ezekiel in Abu Ghraib," 155.

disempowerment? Another way of framing this question is: who represents the *self* and who depicts the *other*? Is the irate Yahweh a symbolic representation of the Judean males' patriarchal authority while the sisters are the object of their male gaze? Or, are the submissive and abused sisters a reflection of the colonized Judean body while Yahweh, the domineering figure, is the distant *other*? Even though these questions are significant, what has not been discussed as readily is the possibility of the Judean exiles concurrently aligning with Yahweh's patriarchal dominance and Jerusalem's victimization. Since the levels of power embodied by Yahweh and the sisters are starkly dissimilar, it is uncommon for scholars to argue that the Judean exiles resonate with *both* Yahweh and the sisters.

Regarding the exiles' potential alignment with *both* Yahweh's dominance and the sisters' subjugation, Mein attempts to articulate the possibility of a simultaneous relationship between the Judean exiles, Yahweh, and the sisters that emphasizes the exiles' liminal states of power and powerlessness. He states:

> The brutal images quite possibly draw upon the humiliating and emasculating trauma of defeat and deportation, which Ezekiel's own community has experienced. This in turn may force the audience of Ezekiel 23 to see that the "theological 'answer' to the scandal of defeat comes only through embracing their identification with Oholah and Oholibah… But it is equally possible that the oracle expects its readers to identify primarily with the male character Yahweh, the humiliated husband who must act to restore his lost honor."[18]

Mein claims that the possibility to primarily identify with Yahweh or the two sisters represents the duality of the exilic experience and the struggle between two "moral worlds": the world in Judah and the world in exile.[19] I agree with Mein that Yahweh and the sisters symbolize two contrasting spaces consisting of their previous lifestyle in Judah and their current reality on the periphery in Babylon. However, while Mein acknowledges these two contrasting positions, he continues to uphold a binary between the sisters and Yahweh by stating that one of the challenges of interpreting the metaphor derives from the difficulties in deciphering whether the audience should primarily resonate with Yahweh *or* Jerusalem.

---

18. Andrew Mein, "Ezekiel: Structure, Themes, and Contested Issues," in *The Oxford Handbook of the Prophets*, ed. Carolyn J. Sharp (Oxford: Oxford University Press, 2016), 199, quoting Patton, "Should Our Sister be Treated Like a Whore?" 237–8.

19. Ibid.

Ultimately for Mein the fact that both responses are plausible presents a "conundrum."[20]

The extreme disparity of power between Yahweh and the sisters is not necessarily a conundrum, but exhibits the Judean exiles' two-pronged association with both dominance and subjugation. Examining their identification with Yahweh or Jerusalem in dichotomous terms obscures and underestimates how the exiles' liminal positionalities as colonized figures manifests within the metaphor. Since binaries tend to produce stability while the conflations of binaries are often believed to obscure meaning, it is reasonable that many interpreters indicate that the Judean exiles are meant to gravitate towards either Yahweh or the sisters. As commonly understood, binaries through their assumed modes of certainty help clarify meaning, while the indefinite nature of ambiguities conceal understanding. However, ambiguities can help accentuate a metaphor's "open-endedness," thus illuminating meaning. Radman in his work on metaphors challenges the notion that precision and clarity is produced through "straightforwardness," "closure," and "unambiguous denotation."[21] He states:

> The semantic dispersion we find in metaphors, even though rooted in vagueness and polysemic uncertainty, can and does lead to the specification of a new meaning if creatively employed…specification of meaning occurs not in spite of vagueness and ambiguity, but actually because of them.[22]

Kamionkowski, drawing from Radman, emphasizes a similar point, claiming that metaphors thrive on ambiguity. She states, "the flexibility of metaphors which deal with abstract, often conflicting subjects, actually increase our range of options for making meaning. Ezekiel's use of the marital metaphor allows for ambiguity and flexibility in a positive meaning-making fashion."[23] Through this perspective, one can argue that the metaphor in Ezekiel 23 is effective precisely due to the multiple possibilities regarding the Judean exiles' associations with both Yahweh and

---

20. Ibid., 198.
21. Zdravko Radman, "How to Make Our Ideas Clear with Metaphors," in *From a Metaphorical Point of View: A Multidisciplinary Approach to the Cognitive Content of Metaphor*, ed. Zdravko Radman, PWTS 7 (Berlin: de Gruyter, 1995), 224. See also Zdravko Radman, *Metaphors: Figures of the Mind*, Library of Rhetoric 4 (Berlin: Springer Science & Business Media, 1997).
22. Radman, "How to Make Our Ideas," 233.
23. Kamionkowski, *Gender Reversal and Cosmic Chaos*, 48.

Jerusalem. This open-endedness accentuates the ambivalent subjectivities of the conquered exiles as dissonantly placed in between spaces of power and powerlessness.

When examining the intricacies of this metaphor, it is productive to employ language that is more multivalent in order to express the metaphor's open-endedness. Returning to the previously stated question concerning how to determine which figures (Yahweh or Oholah/Oholibah) represent the *self* and *other*, it is more fruitful to inquire how liminal spaces created within the context of colonization challenge dichotomous understandings of *self* and *other*. Bhabha emphasizes how diasporic communities in colonized contexts do not reside in fixed social and cultural spaces but instead reside in unstable borderlands on the periphery, where they constantly maneuver between various spatial and temporal realms.[24] Residing in the borderland and negotiating between various aspects of identity distort and obscure the boundaries between *self* and *other*.[25] Within colonized contexts in the borderland, liminality reflects a state that is not based on binaries but polyvalence and malleability. Living in the diaspora within the periphery of Babylonian, the former Judean elite most likely had to cope with the uneasy co-existence between their newly found state of powerlessness and their memories of authority and prosperity, hence the ambiguous representations seen in Ezekiel 23.

The marriage metaphor in Ezekiel 23 skillfully depicts an ambivalent representation of the Judean exiles as both subject and object. In the metaphor, Yahweh and the two sisters illuminate the Judean exiles' "contradictory double positioning"[26] as simultaneous subject and object. The depiction of Yahweh's violence towards Jerusalem as fueled by the anger, devastation, and betrayal caused by the actions of an adulterous wife, possibly communicated to exiles Yahweh's fury and the subsequent brutality that the deity bestows on Jerusalem. In this regard, the representation aims at the exiles' alignment with Yahweh, the husband, in order to create distance between the audience and female Jerusalem, where Jerusalem becomes the object of the male audience's gaze. However, portraying the sisters' punishment through images of dismemberment and stripping that were perpetuated against victims in warfare reflects the

---

24. Bhabha, *The Location of Culture*, 35–9.

25. Ibid., 1–13. See also Gloria Anzaldúa, *Borderlands—La Fronteria: The New Mestiza* (San Francisco, CA: Aunt Lute Foundation Books, 1987), for a Chicana perspective concerning malleable movements within the borderland.

26. Gale A. Yee, *Poor Banished Children of Eve: Woman as Evil in the Hebrew Bible* (Minneapolis, MN: Fortress, 2003), 120.

raw violence of colonization. Identity within a colonized context cannot be uniformly characterized or explained through one-dimensional experiences. Instead, this conflict between patriarchal power and sociopolitical powerlessness demonstrates "an excess of identity positions" that liminal subjects tend to exemplify.[27]

The abused female body is a contested site that symbolizes both patriarchal power and its imperial victimization.[28] The literary representation of both Yahweh and the sisters exemplifies the Judeans' struggle with at least two contrasting yet interconnecting hierarchies: a *patriarchal hierarchy* that privileges the Judean male audience and adamantly promotes asymmetrical relationships between male and female, and an *imperial* hierarchy between the colonizer and colonized that emphasizes their oppression.[29] The severe subjugation of the female body represents the exiles' attempt to both control and cope with their emasculation. Within the metaphor, the intense depiction of violent and hypersexualized language on the female body allows images of empowerment and fragility to coalesce, which in turn produces a nuanced representation of the exile's liminality. The contrasting portrayals of Yahweh and the sisters is not necessarily a binary opposition that poses a "conundrum"

---

27. Hans Leander, *Discourses of Empire: The Gospel of Mark from a Postcolonial Perspective* (Atlanta, GA: SBL, 2013), 46.

28. In regards to patriarchal power, hierarchal relations between men and women are often used as a model for colonial domination. Rape and sexualized violence towards women is a frequent trope within colonial discourses. Ann Laura Stoler, *Carnal Knowledge and Imperial Power: Race and the Intimate in Colonial Rule* (Berkeley, CA: University of California Press), 44. The explicit hierarchy within sexualized violence illuminates oppressive power dynamics between the colonizer and the colonized. As Stoler states, within colonial contexts "sexual domination has been more often considered as a discursive symbol…a graphic substantiation of who was on the bottom and who was on the top" (ibid.). Colonial dominance is inextricably linked with patriarchal representations that associate men with agency, potency, and prestige and women with domesticated, feminine, and subjugated traits. Ania Loomba claims that even though there is a colonial divide between male colonizers and colonized men, "they also often collaborated when it comes to the domination of women." Ania Loomba, *Colonialism/Postcolonialism*, 3rd ed. (New York: Routledge, 2015), 168. As a symbol for submission within colonized contexts, the female body can transcend some boundaries between colonizing and colonized males. For both, the female figure is a symbol of marginality, and women's bodies signify unequal distributions of power.

29. Smith-Christopher alludes to this idea of multiple hierarchies at the conclusion of *Ezekiel in Abu Ghraib*, 157.

for interpretation. Instead, the distinct representations of power in the metaphor conflate and provide a meaningful symbolization of the Judean exiles' fluid maneuverings as colonized subjects residing on the borderland.

4. *Ambivalent Perceptions of the Colonizer: Attraction and Repulsion*

The previous section demonstrated that the images of Yahweh's power and the sisters' subjugation and abuse is a representation of the exiles' contentious positions within patriarchal power and sociopolitical powerlessness in Ezekiel 23. This next section illustrates that liminal positionalities not only manifest through conflicting representations of patriarchal power and imperial powerlessness but also through the sisters' ambivalent perceptions of the dominant power, here Yahweh as a stand in for colonized power. Colonized groups can become simultaneously attracted to and repulsed by the colonizer in the way that the metaphor demonstrates the sisters' desire and resistance of Yahweh. Albert Memmi helpfully emphasizes this disorienting stance of colonial desire quite succinctly when he asks, "how could [the colonized] hate the colonizers yet admire them so passionately?"[30] Ezekiel 23 conveys this negotiation between desire and repulsion towards the imperial authorities.

Before describing how desire and repulsion is portrayed in Ezekiel 23 it is first helpful to evaluate how longing and admiration functions in Ezekiel 16. The comparison with Ezekiel 16 helps to emphasize the distinctive and intricate ways that desire is depicted in Ezekiel 23. The concept of desirability is a major thematic element in both Ezekiel 16 and 23. However, the ways in which longing is portrayed in these two chapters serves as a crucial distinguishing factor. In Ezekiel 16, Jerusalem is the object of desire; she is a beautiful and wealthy woman that captures the attention of both Yahweh and the imperial figures. However, in Ezekiel 23 the opposite scenario appears; the object of desire is not Oholah or Oholibah but the Assyrians, Egyptians, and Babylonians.

In regards to Jerusalem's beauty in Ezekiel 16, Yahweh emphasizes on several occasions that Jerusalem wore embroidered clothing (רקמה) (16:10, 13, 18).[31] Jerusalem is also given leather sandals (נעל), fine linen

30. Albert Memmi, *The Colonizer and the Colonized*, trans. Howard Greenfeld (Boston, MA: Beacon, 1965), x.

31. The term also appears in Judg. 5:30, 1 Chron. 29:2, and Ps. 45:15. In addition, the verb form of רקם, "to embroider," is used more frequently and appears multiple times in Exodus in order to describe the process of creating the tabernacle

(שש), and expensive fabric (משי). She is also embellished with various ornaments (עדי), including bracelets (צמידים) on her wrists, chains (רביד) around her neck, and a beautiful crown upon her head (vv. 11-12).[32] In addition, lady Jerusalem is adorned in high-quality materials that are typically used for the tabernacle and the priests' clothing. She wears fine linen (שש) that covers the tabernacle (Exod. 26:1, 31) and provides garments for the Aaron and the priesthood (Exod. 28:5, 6, 8). As Galambush states, "the woman who is 'fit to be queen' (v. 13) is adorned with the same materials that adorn Yahweh's holy place."[33] Overall, Jerusalem is described as exceedingly beautiful and prosperous. Hals claims that Yahweh has "heaped upon his bride every kind of beautiful ornament so that her beauty was royal, resplendent, and internally acclaimed."[34] After Jerusalem is perfected by Yahweh, her role as an object of Yahweh's male gaze extends to the nations (v. 14). Through the eyes of many, Jerusalem becomes an object of admiration and desire.[35]

a. *The Sisters' Desire for the Assyrian Colonizers*

In Ezekiel 23, Jerusalem is not an extraordinary object of desire; instead, Jerusalem represented through the character of the sisters reflects desire for colonizers. There is no mention of the sisters' exceptional beauty, royal status, and excessive wealth. They are not the objects of the male gaze, but instead the colonizers are the exceedingly attractive figures who serve as the focal point of the sisters' longing. In Ezekiel 16, Jerusalem is gazed upon by imperial figures, while in ch. 23 Jerusalem and Samaria are the figures who fixate their gaze towards the colonizer. Throughout Ezekiel 23, the descriptions of Oholah's and Oholibah's desire are framed by two specific aspects: elaborate descriptions of the imperial authority's attractiveness and repetitive explanations of the sisters' stark fixation towards its alluring nature.

---

linens and the priestly garments (Exod. 27:16; 28:39; 35:35; 36:37; 38:18, 23; 39:29). See Julie Galambush, *Jerusalem in the Book of Ezekiel: The City as Yahweh's Wife*, SBL Dissertation Series 130 (Atlanta, GA: Scholars Press, 1992), 95. Embroidered clothing is also emphasized in the description of Tyre's self-proclamation of their beauty (27:7, 16, 24). רקמה is used in Ps. 45:15 to describe the clothing of a regal bride that enters the groom's home.

32. In addition to the physical descriptions of lady Jerusalem, she also eats fine flour, oil, and honey, which symbolizes her wealth and luxury.

33. Galambush, *Jerusalem in the Book of Ezekiel*, 95.

34. Ronald M. Hals, *Ezekiel*, FOTL 19 (Grand Rapids, MI: Eerdmans, 1989), 106.

35. Galambush, *Jerusalem in the Book of Ezekiel*, 94.

Regarding the first aspect, the Babylonians, Egyptians, and Assyrians are explicitly described as the apex of desirability: authoritative, potent, and generally masculine. Within the span of a few verses, their military prowess, wealth, social status, and physical attractiveness are explicitly emphasized. In vv. 5-10, the Assyrians are described as warriors and mounted horseman, men of high military status. They are clothed in blue, which is one of the more expensive dyes in the ancient Near East, thus symbolizing their wealth.[36] They are also governors, commanders, and men of high rank who are all described as handsome young men. In vv. 12-15, the Assyrians' potency is again described through an emphasis on their wealth, military status, and social rank. The immense masculine prowess that the foreign nations epitomize is a physical representation of what the sisters massively desire and crave, which is a type of political and socioeconomic power that the colonized Judean exiles no longer embody. In other words, this longing for the Assyrians, Egyptians, and Babylonians symbolically represents the colonized subject's desire of the hegemonic masculinity and prowess of the imperial powers.

Secondly, the sisters present a strong sexual fixation with the imperial powers' alluring nature. Their sexual infidelities with the foreign nations are frequently described by the term זנה, which often appears in ch. 23 and typically describes a woman's act of freely engaging in sexual activity outside the control of men such as a husband, father, or older male relative.[37] In addition to זנה, a term that is not examined as much in the metaphor is "passion/desire" (עגב). Even though this term receives less scholarly attention, it is a significant word that is employed repeatedly in Ezekiel 23 to describe Jerusalem's and Samaria's longing for the colonizer. The term עגב appears seven times within the metaphor and conveys a sensuous and/or passionate desire; the Arabic cognate *ajiba* means to be amazed and admire.[38] It is infrequently used in the Hebrew Bible and only appears in Ezekiel 23 and Jer. 4:30. In these two chapters,

---

36. Yee, *Poor Banished Children of Eve*, 125.

37. The term appears even more frequently in Ezek. 16. See 16:15, 16, 17, 26, 28, 30, 31, 33, 34, 35, 41. For a helpful explanation on זנה as prostitute, see Galambush, *Jerusalem in the Book of Ezekiel*, 27–31. However, I agree with Alice O'Keefe that prostitution is not an adequate translation because זנה contains a negative connotation that portrays illicit and sinful behavior. According to O'Keefe, the profession of prostitution "is not condemned, but is rather sanctioned within a patriarchal social system that has need of available 'other woman' with whom extramarital sexual relations are permitted." Alice O'Keefe, *Woman's Body and the Social Body in Hosea*, JSOTSup 338, GCT 10 (Sheffield: Sheffield Academic, 2001), 20 n. 10.

38. *HALOT* 2:783.

עגב indicates admiration of impressive fine garments.³⁹ Within Ezekiel 23, the term conveys both Oholah's and Oholibah's desire for the extravagant physicality of the foreign nations. In Jer. 4:30, there is a similar emphasis on external elegance.⁴⁰ However, it is not the imperial figures who are dressed in expensive attire in Jeremiah, but Jerusalem is the figure who is well-adorned through scarlet ornaments of gold in order to impress and attract her foreign lovers. Despite this difference, the type of desire expressed through עגב in both Ezekiel 23 and Jer. 4:30 is inextricably connected to beautification through expensive clothing and excessive embellishment. Arguably, in Ezekiel 23 עגב indicates attraction to wealth and ultimately the power that this type of adornment symbolizes. The term conveys a longing, or as Block states, a "craving," for resources that the foreign nations possess.⁴¹

Ezekiel 23 frequently pairs the terms זנה with עגב in order to describe the sisters' lust for the imperial figures. Similarly to זנה, the term עגב connotes sexual desire. However, a crucial difference is that זנה typically indicates a specific type of sexual behavior, while the use of עגב in Ezekiel 23 and Jeremiah 4 depicts more of an internalized emotion: a type of admiration or desire.⁴² Typically, studies of Ezekiel 23 that focus on the hypersexualized language emphasize the physical nature of the sisters' sexual activities. However, it is not only sexual acts of lust written upon Oholibah's body but also envy and attraction towards the imperial figures. In regards to the sexual infidelities committed by Jerusalem, Ezekiel 23 not only highlights Oholah's and Oholibah's lustful actions (זנה) but goes a step further to emphasize the internal and emotional elements that influence their physical acts of infidelity.

Oholibah's desire towards the imperial powers is further stressed by her act of "seeing." Her attraction towards the Assyrians and the Babylonians is frequently described by her ability to "see" (ראה) with her own eyes the physical potencies of the imperial conquerors. In addition, there is frequent vocabulary that accentuates the visual nature of her desire. First, she sees (ראה) the consequences of Oholah's behavior, which propels her to exhibit an even stronger desire for the Assyrians, Babylonians, and Egyptians (v. 13). In addition,

---

39. See Block, *Ezekiel*, 738.
40. Jack R. Lundbom, *Jeremiah 1–20: A New Translation with Introduction and Commentary*, AB 21 (New York: Doubleday, 1999), 364, 368. In addition, the substantive plural form is used (עגבים) rather than the verb, which is typically translated as "lovers" or "admirers."
41. Block, *Ezekiel*, 2:739.
42. See Kamionkowski, *Gender Reversal and Cosmic Chaos*, 136.

> She *saw* (ראה) male figures *carved* (חקה) upon the wall, *images* (צלם) of the Chaldeans *portrayed* (חקק) in vermilion with belts on their waists, with flowing turbans on their heads, all of them having the *appearance* (מראה) of officers—a *likeness* (דמות) of the Babylonians whose native land was Chaldea. When she *saw* (ראה) them she lusted after them and sent messengers to them in Chaldea. (vv. 14-17)

Within the metaphor, Oholibah's desire (עגב) that is expressed through her intense acts of *seeing* provides the reader with a view of her projected desire for the colonizer. Her fixation presents a "reverse gaze" that focuses not on the male perceptions of female Jerusalem, as in Ezekiel 16, but on the colonized subjects' admiration for the colonizer.

Ezekiel 23 explicitly illustrates the sister's admiration for and gravitation towards the imperial powers. However, the sisters' intense level of desire is not consistent throughout the chapter. On the contrary, ambivalence abounds within the representation of the sisters' perception of the imperial powers. The next section of this essay demonstrates how the sisters' desire for the colonizer is coupled with intense repulsion of the imperial powers.

b. *The Sisters' Repulsion of the Colonizers*

Oholibah's attraction towards the imperial powers turns out to be short-lived. After her sexual interactions with the Babylonians, her desire suddenly transforms: "she turns from them in disgust" (מהם נפשה ותקע, v. 17). The deep craving that Oholibah possessed for the Chaldeans quickly turns into repulsion. In v. 17, the expression נפשה ותקע literally translates as "dislocating her being/self," or in more colloquial terms, "she turned herself away."[43] The majority of lexicons and commentaries translate the verb יקע in conjunction with נפשה as "disgust." However, Lapsley asserts that one cannot merely assume that יקע should be specifically understood as disgust. She states, "Nowhere does the verb יקע denote 'disgust.' Rather it literally means 'to dislocate, tear away' and more should not be read into it."[44] I agree with Lapsley's assertion that the literal translation of יקע is to dislocate. However, her claim that the term in this context should not be interpreted as disgust or repulsion needs more attention.

---

43. The term יקע ("to dislocate") is another term that appears infrequently in the Hebrew Bible. See Gen. 32:26; Num. 25:4; 2 Sam. 21:6, 9, 13; Jer. 6:8; Ezek. 23:17, 18. A similar term נקע appears in Ezek. 23:18, 22, 28.

44. Jacqueline E. Lapsley, "Shame and Self-Knowledge: The Positive Role of Shame in Ezekiel's View of the Moral Self," in Odell and Strong (eds), *The Book of Ezekiel*, 170.

As Lapsley claims, the term יקע typically represents a physical type of dislocation. In Gen. 32:26, the term is used to indicate the dislocation of Jacob's hip. In Numbers and 2 Samuel, the term is employed in military contexts to describe the impalement of enemies.[45] However, the use of יקע in several passages, including Ezek. 23:17, 18 and Jer. 6:8, differs from this physical expression of disconnection and serve as the only instances where יקע is an emotional or internal type of disruption. In Jer. 6:8, יקע conveys Yahweh's threat to alienate himself from Jerusalem and ultimately lose affection for her.[46] According to Lundbom, יקע in this verse does not merely indicate Yahweh's separation from Jerusalem. On the contrary, the term in conjunction with נפשה is "very personal"[47] and represents a "strong sense of revulsion."[48] Within Ezekiel 23, the term not only describes Oholibah's perception of the colonizers but also Yahweh's negative perception of Oholah and Oholibah because of their actions of infidelity (vv. 22, 28). Similarly to Yahweh's distasteful feelings towards Jerusalem in Jer. 6:8, Yahweh's negative feelings towards the sisters is deeply personal in Ezekiel 23. The term indicates a subversion of the original state of positive emotions, which can indicate some form of repulsion, whether it is anger, loathing, or disgust. Regarding Oholibah's emotions, יקע represents a deep contrast from the initial feeling of עגב that she once harbored for the imperial figures.

In conclusion, the internal emotions that Oholibah harbors for the imperial authorities is presented through a contentious combination of desire and repulsion. The sisters' simultaneous attraction and repulsion toward imperial powers is a reflection of the colonized subject's ambivalent perceptions of the colonizer. Colonized individuals typically do not wholly despise or admire the colonizer, but they usually possess an uneasy coexistence of both emotions.

c. *Attraction and Repulsion Integrate: Ambivalent Perceptions of the Imperial Male Body*

A postcolonial lens can help to give further meaning to the sister's simultaneous desire and hatred towards the colonizer, particularly theories of attraction and repulsion provided by Frantz Fanon. Fanon emphasizes that the colonized, who are placed in inferior positions and confined to

---

45. Num. 25:4; 2 Sam. 21:6, 9, 13.
46. Lundbom, *Jeremiah 1–20*, 424.
47. Ibid.
48. Robert P. Carroll, *Jeremiah: A Commentary* (Louisville, KY: Westminster, 1986), 193.

powerless spaces on the periphery, fixate on the power of the colonizer and ultimately long for the wealth and prosperity, security, and freedom that the colonizer possesses. He claims that "the gaze that the colonized subject cast at the colonist's sector is a look of lust, a look of envy…the colonized man is an envious man."[49] However, alongside this envy, strong feelings of repulsion are present. Fanon additionally states:

> Confronted with the colonial order the colonized subject is in a permanent state of tension. The colonist's world is a hostile world, a world which excludes yet at the same time incites envy… The hostile, oppressive and aggressive world, bulldozing the colonized masses, represents not only the hell they would like to escape as quickly as possible but a paradise within arm's reach.[50]

According to Fanon, conflicting internal emotions, including desire, envy, disgust, and anger, are frequent within the internal state of the colonized. This ambivalence arises from the reality that colonized societies typically cannot unequivocally resist or reject the colonizers. On the contrary, colonized groups express simultaneous attraction and repulsion toward particular attributes portrayed by the colonizers.[51] As Moore states, the colonized condition can consist of an "unequal measure of loathing and admiration, resentment and envy, rejection and imitation, resistance and cooperation, separation and surrender."[52] The colonized subject experiences constant dehumanization by the colonizer but also realizes that the colonizer's lifestyle reflects the degree of humanity that was abolished for the colonized individual.[53] This tension between colonized subject's subjugated reality and an eagerness to transcend this state of oppression produces an ambivalent state of mind.

This simultaneous desire and repulsion that the sisters express towards the colonizer is further demonstrated through the representation of the Egyptians's sexual potencies. In addition to the description of the elaborate clothing and social rank (see above), Egypt is described in a highly sexualized manner as those "whose flesh was that of donkeys and whose emissions was that of stallions" (v. 20). The typical understanding of this

---

49. Fanon, *Wretched of the Earth*, 5.
50. Ibid., 16.
51. Ashcroft, Griffiths, and Tiffin, *Key Concepts in Postcolonial Studies*, 10.
52. Stephen D. Moore, *Empire and Apocalypse: Postcolonialism and the New Testament*, BMW 12 (Sheffield: Sheffield Phoenix, 2006), x.
53. Jean Marie Vivaldi, *Fanon: Collective Ethics and Humanism* (New York: Peter Lang, 2007), 24.

verse is that the sexual and animalizing language is a negative representation of the Egyptians that emphasizes their constructed lewdness and overall bestial nature.⁵⁴ For many interpreters, Egypt's sexualized comparison to donkeys and horses is meant to malign and disgrace.⁵⁵ This description is meant to counter the nations' attractive qualities of military and political affluence by emphasizing their undesirable attributes including lust, lewdness, and sinfulness. The hypersexualized language is used as a means to disempower and "other" the Egyptians as a nation consisting of highly licentious males who are morally corrupt.⁵⁶

However, Lemos offers an alternative reading that questions the disparaging nature of this sexualized representation of Egypt. She argues that wider ancient Near Eastern texts depict animalized images in sexual situations in order to positively depict authoritative figures.⁵⁷ Lemos claims that Mesopotamian potency incantations describe the desirable sexual prowess of kings and other authoritative figures through images of donkeys and stallions.⁵⁸ She states:

> These incantations present large genital size and equine-like prowess as desirable, a fact which should lead one to call into question whether or not Ezekiel's comparison of foreign men to animals in chapter 23 is meant to convey repulsiveness and a bestial character, or rather something else, something more complex and less denigrating.⁵⁹

With regards to the Egyptians in Ezekiel 23, the use of animalizing language to describe the size of the Egyptians's genitalia may not be negative but a representation of their potency and masculinity.

---

54. This licentious representation of Egypt is further buttressed by the portrayal of Egypt as "lustful" in Ezek. 16:26. See Joyce, *Ezekiel: A Commentary*, 162, and Moshe Greenberg, *Ezekiel: A New Translation with Introduction and Commentary*, AB 22 (New York: Doubleday, 1997), 480.

55. See Walther Zimmerli, *Ezekiel 2: A Commentary on the Book of the Prophet Ezekiel Chapters 25–48*, trans. James D. Martin, Hermeneia (Minneapolis, MN: Fortress, 1983), 487; Joyce, *Ezekiel: A Commentary*, 162; and Block, *Ezekiel*, 2:495.

56. T. M. Lemos, "The Emasculation of Exile: Hypermasculinity and Feminization in the Book of Ezekiel," in *Interpreting Exile: Displacement and Deportation in Biblical and Modern Contexts*, ed. Brad Kelle, Frank Ritchel Ames, and Jacob L. Wright (Atlanta, GA: SBL, 2011), 377–81.

57. Ibid., 380.

58. Ibid., 381. Mesopotamian potency incantations are meant to address sexual dysfunction; see ibid., 380.

59. Ibid., 383.

Initially it may seem as if Lemos's reading of v. 20 presents a perspective that is incompatible with the standard interpretation concerning Egypt's distasteful sexuality. However, as argued throughout this chapter, binaries become destabilized within colonial contexts, and contradictory points of view can coexist. Conflicting representations of agency and control thrive within liminal spaces (see above), and the literary construction of the Egyptians's sexual characteristics can embody a dissonant combination of desire and repulsion. Lemos alludes to this ambivalence by asserting that the graphic sexual nature of the Egyptians's representation can potentially be read as both a "powerful sense of disgust" and "an acknowledgement of the superior claim to masculinity held by the Egyptians, the Assyrians, and the Babylonians, the handsome foreigners that Jerusalem found so irresistible."[60] The representation of Egypt's sexual potency in v. 20 can convey a rhetoric of desirability, along with lewdness and disgust.

Frantz Fanon discusses this uneasy co-existence between sexual attraction and repulsion within colonized contexts in his discussion of how the Black male is perceived by the white man. According to Fanon, the white male is simultaneously infatuated and repulsed by Black male genitalia. He states: "The white man is convinced that the Negro is a beast; if it is not the length of this penis, then it is the sexual potency that impresses him."[61] He also states, "For the majority of white men, the Negro represents the sexual instinct (in its raw state). The negro is the incarnation of a genital potency beyond all moralities and prohibitions."[62] Fanon emphasizes that the white male fixates on his "perception"[63] of the Black man's hypersexualized potency. However, the white male's fascination is also accompanied by a strong feeling of anxiety and aggression, due to the fear that "the Other is more sexually potent than the white 'master.'"[64] For Fanon, the white male perceives Black male sexuality as

---

60. Ibid., 390.

61. Frantz Fanon, *Black Skin White Masks*, trans. Charles Lam Markmann (New York: Grove, 1967), 170.

62. Ibid., 177.

63. The term "perceived" is used because the white male's interpretation of the Black male's unnatural, unseemly, and robust sexuality is not necessarily based on truth but on belief. This issue relates to Bhabha's notion of the "stereotype" and how degenerate depictions of the colonized are meant to present a fixed image that is not necessarily a real depiction but constructed in order to cast the colonized as inferior. See Bhabha, *The Location of Culture*, 94–120.

64. Lori Merish, *Sentimental Materialism: Gender, Commodity Culture, and Nineteenth Century African American Literature* (Durham, NC: Duke University Press, 2000), 273.

an attribute that he can never achieve, and as a result, he fears that this lack of sexual prowess is a representation of his insufficiency and failed masculinity in relation to the colonized Black male "other."⁶⁵ Essentially the white man executes a precarious "gaze" onto the Black male body that is split between infatuation and anxiety; the white male is intrigued yet emasculated by Black male genitalia. Fanon additionally discusses how white women illustrate this ambivalent fixation on Black male sexuality. White women are fearful of the Black male's perceived sexual potency but this fear also serves as masked infatuation. The Black male's bestial sexuality is "hallucinating" for the white woman and invites a socially taboo yet desirable sexual experience that cannot be fulfilled by the white male.⁶⁶ For Fanon, both the white male and female understand Black male sexuality as bestial and unnatural, and the Black male's barbarous sexuality is not viewed as solely grotesque but also as desirable.

Although Fanon's writings were clearly produced in a different time period and context than Ezekiel 23, both texts speak to the ambivalence that the colonized subject embodies. Fanon's reading of the colonized condition can help provide a fresh look at the sisters' ambivalent perception of the colonizer in the literary dimension of Ezekiel 23. Fanon's understanding of the ambivalent perceptions of the Black male body helps to illuminate a nuanced reading of the sexualized description of the Egyptian in Ezekiel 23 not as solely grotesque or purely admirable but as dissonant and liminal.⁶⁷ Through this perspective, the explicit illustration

---

65. Clare Counihan, "Reading the Figure of Woman in African Literature: Psychoanalysis, Difference, and Desire," *Research in African Literatures* 30, no. 2 (2007): 161–80. See also Jana Evans Braziel, "Trans-American Constructions of Black Masculinity: Dany Laferrière, le negrè, and the Late Capitalist American Racial machine-desirante," *Callaloo* 26, no. 3 (2003): 867–900, particularly 884–90.

66. Fanon states, "The women among the whites, by a genuine process of induction, invariably view the Negro as the keeper of the impalpable gate that opens into the realm of orgies, of bacchanals, of delirious sexual sensations." Fanon, *Black Skin*, 177. Fanon has been highly criticized for his representation of female sexual desire and accused of sexist interpretations of both white and Black women. For feminist critiques of Fanon, see Gwen Bergner, "Who Is That Marked Woman? Or The Role of Gender in Fanon's *Black Skin White Masks*," *PMLA* 110, no 1. (1995): 75–88; bell hooks, "Feminism as a Persistent Critique of History: What's Love Got to Do with It?," in *The Fact of Blackness: Franz Fanon and Representation*, ed. Alan Read (London: ICA, 1996), 76–85; and in the same volume, Lola Young, "Missing Persons: Fantasizing Black Women in *Black Skin, White Masks*," 102–13, and Kobena Mercer, "Decolonisation and Disappointment: Reading Fanon's Sexual Politics," 114–26.

67. A significant difference between Fanon's theory of the Black male sexualized body and the Egyptians's hypersexualized representation is the direction of the

of the Egyptians's sexual potency can serve as a literary construction of the contradictory nature of desire within a colonized setting. Ezekiel 23:30 indicates that the imperial figures' sexual potency is admirable, but the colonizer is still "othered" as a distant entity that generates disgust for the colonized. The liminal space where the exiles reside as former elites who were emasculated by imperial authorities is rhetorically presented through ambivalent images of masculinity. The Egyptians's sexual potency is a representation of both the exiles' defeat, humiliation, and emasculation and their desire to embody a "laudable, esteem-worthy image of masculinity."[68]

5. Conclusion and Questions for Further Study:

This essay argues that the metaphor in Ezekiel 23 illuminates the vulnerable positions of the exiles as colonized subjects in Babylon. The extreme range of empowerment and disempowerment between Yahweh and Oholah/Oholibah somewhat prevents interpreters from claiming that the Judean audience identifies with both the dominating husband and the subjugated sisters. However, the hierarchal power dynamic between Yahweh and the sisters discursively presents liminality through conflicting illustrations of patriarchal agency and sociopolitical oppression. In addition, the relationship between Oholah/Oholibah and the imperial authorities in Ezekiel 23 reflects the sisters' desire and repulsion for the colonizer. Contrary to Ezekiel 16, which focuses on the figure of Jerusalem as the object of desire, Ezekiel 23 emphasizes the subjugated sisters as the ones who uphold the gaze towards the more affluent foreign nations. This ambivalent presentation of the sisters' affections is a literary construction of the Judeans' precarious position as colonized entities. Even though the oppressed group develops anger and animosity towards the colonizer as a result of their subjugation, the colonized group can also envy the privilege and authority that the dominant group possesses.

"gaze." Fanon's description of the white male's simultaneous attraction to and fear of the Black male genitalia unmasks the anxiety of the *colonizer* towards the colonized other. However, within Ezek. 23, the "gaze" is reversed, and it is the *colonized subject* (Oholibah) that ambivalently directs her fixation towards the imperial powers.

68. Lemos, "The Emasculation of Exile," 389.

Chapter 8

THE CONSTRUCTION AND DECONSTRUCTION OF
ETHNIC/NATIONAL OTHERING IN
THE BOOK OF THE TWELVE*

Daniel C. Timmer

The Hebrew Bible's Minor Prophets consistently present non-Israelite nations as such, that is, as culturally, religiously, and politically other vis-à-vis Israel in the historical present.[1] However, these books also occasionally predict that some of these nations will be reconciled with restored Israel or share in its utopian destiny at some future time.[2] Such future scenarios are made possible by the de-othering of non-Israelites in various ways and to various degrees. This essay analyzes several examples of de-othering of non-Israelites in the Book of the Twelve with the help of recent theories of social identity and othering. Its primary foci are the use of criteria of identity that are shared by Israelite and

---

* I am happy to express my gratitude for the generous support provided by the Priscilla and Stanford Reid Trust for the research activities that underlie this essay.

1. Their distinct ethnicity seems both presumed and inconsequential. Cf. Anselm C. Hagedorn, "Looking at Foreigners in Biblical and Greek Prophecy," *VT* 57 (2007): 432–48 (436).

2. This point is noted only in passing by Lawrence M. Wills, *Not God's People: Insiders and Outsiders in the Biblical World*, Religion in the Modern World (Lanham, MD: Rowman & Littlefield, 2008), 38–9. For surveys of othering and de-othering elsewhere in the HB/OT, cf. Sadler, *Can a Cushite Change His Skin?*; Ehud Ben Zvi and Diana. V. Edelman (eds), *Imagining the Other and Constructing Israelite Identity in the Early Second Temple Period*, LHBOTS 591 (London: T&T Clark, 2014).

non-Israelite groups, the use of non-binary or incremental othering, and the relationship between othering and power.[3] After examining several of these varied relativizations of otherness in the Book of the Twelve, the chapter compares and contrasts these Hebraic phenomena with theoretical understandings and empirical descriptions of othering and de-othering in order to appreciate their distinctive features and significance for theoretical and theological reflection.

1. *Definitions and Method*

I begin by sketching the methodological and theoretical orientation of the present study. First, we employ a heuristic approach to othering and de-othering to avoid the dangers associated with fitting the data into a preconceived grid. Among other things, because this corpus describes the most important forms of de-othering in religious terms, we can avoid entering the larger discussion of ethnicity, in which "the one crucial factor…is a myth of common ancestry."[4] Despite the inductive and heuristic nature of this study, however, it remains in close conversation with current theorizing and reflection on otherness and social identity. The following points in particular become important as the study unfolds:

---

3. Cf. the overview provided by Lajos L. Brons, "Othering, an Analysis," *Transcience* 6 (2015): 69–90.

4. James C. Miller, "Ethnicity and the Hebrew Bible: Problems and Prospects, *CBR* 6 (2008): 170–213 (175). For further theoretical reflection, see Sadler, *Can a Cushite Change His Skin?*, and Jeremy McInerney, "Ethnicity: An Introduction," in *A Companion to Ethnicity in the Ancient Mediterranean*, ed. J. McInerney, Blackwell Companions to the Ancient World (Oxford: Wiley-Blackwell, 2014), 1–16. Some define ethnicity as a constructed social relation that distinguishes between one group and others on the basis of name, ancestry, shared memory, common culture, common homeland, or perceived solidarity; see John Hutchinson and Anthony D. Smith, "Introduction," in *Ethnicity*, ed. John Hutchinson and Anthony D. Smith (Oxford: Oxford University Press, 1996), 3–15, esp. 6–7, citing R. A. Schermerhorn, *Comparative Ethnic Relations: A Framework for Theory and Research*, 2nd ed. (Chicago: University of Chicago Press, 1978), 12. Compare Sadler, Jr., for whom "ethnic group" denotes "a human population distinguished by delineated boundary markers that are recognized by members of the group and by Others as distinct, that generally share certain social and cultural features that change over time, and that are generally viewed as deriving from common biological origins"; Sadler, *Can a Cushite Change His Skin?*, 11. It is important that some Israelite eschatology ignores ethnicity as a grounds for ultimate weal or woe.

1. While some argue that othering is invariably a binary, either–or process, that view is drawn into question by non-binary phenomena like the "proximate Other" and by the processes of segmentation and encompassment noted by the social anthropologists Sir Edward E. Evans-Pritchard and Louis Dumont, respectively.[5] The "proximate Other" category designates a degree of alterity that is not absolute, such that the Other is not completely different from the Self. This non-absolute othering is often the result of *multiple, competing* processes of othering and identification (or, de-othering) that operate simultaneously.[6] While some difference between Self and Other remains, that difference may be less or more significant than the features shared by the Self and the Other. In short, otherness should be conceived of as a spectrum bounded by complete identity on the one hand and complete difference on the other. In the following analyses, modifiers such as most significant, fundamental, and superlative highlight the relative importance of othering or unifying features.
2. Some binary otherings are overcome or relativized by processes of de-othering without themselves disappearing or being completely undone. The result is a multidimensional other/not-other reality that could be described as hierarchialized or hybrid. For example, the process of segmentation proposed by Evans-Pritchard recognized in the Nuer people of Southern Sudan "a logic of fission or enmity at a lower level of segmentation" (e.g., between families of the same clan) which is "overcome by a logic of fusion or neutralization of conflict at higher levels of segmentation" (e.g., when rival clans unite against a common threat).[7] These identifying and othering processes operate simultaneously, as does the encompassment model of the Indian caste system proposed by Dumont. Encompassment, "an act of selfing by appropriating...selected kinds of otherness," also involves a qualified degree of difference that is subsumed by "that which is universal."[8]

---

5. For a convenient overview, see Gerd Baumann, "Grammars of Identity/Alterity: A Structural Approach," in *Grammars of Identity/Alterity*, ed. G. Baumann and A. Gingrich, EASA 3 (New York: Berghahn, 2004), 16–48.

6. Ibid., 22, 25.

7. Ibid., 22. Evans-Pritchard presented his interpretation of the Nuer society in *The Nuer* (Oxford: Clarendon, 1940).

8. Baumann, "Grammars of Identity/Alterity," 25. Dumont presented his system in *Homo Hierarchicus*, 2nd ed. (Chicago: University of Chicago Press, 1980).

3. While on many accounts othering is inseparable from the exercise of power,[9] some Israelite prophetic literature de-others members of more powerful states while othering groups *within* Israel. In some cases it is also evident that the Israelite Self occupies a lower social status than the Israelite group that it others. These phenomena invite a closer examination of othering and de-othering processes in which power does not play its usual role.[10]

Second, apart from recognizing a diachronic element in the insistence by almost all authors of the Book of the Twelve that this undoing of otherness will take place in the distant future, I give little attention to reconstructing precise historical settings for the initial articulation of these phenomena in prophetic discourse. Although Amos, Nahum, and Malachi arguably coincide with or represent the beginning, middle, and end of Israelite prophecy, I do not think that we possess enough data to formulate convincing arguments for a precise chronological progression in Israelite, Judahite, and Yehudite attitudes toward outsiders in the Twelve.[11] The varied depictions of and responses to the Other in Yehudite literature of the Achaemenid period, for example, caution us against attempting a broad-brush presentation of these attitudes in connection with neatly demarcated historical periods or supposedly homogeneous and hermetic social groups.[12] Accordingly, the historical development

---

9. Sune Q. Jensen, "Othering, Identity Formation and Agency," *Qualitative Studies* 2, no. 2 (2011): 63–78 (65), who refers to the Other as "subordinate" in the estimation of the ingroup.

10. Given the limited scope of this study, we cannot distinguish between the varied definitions of power and their theoretical foundations, e.g., Hobbes's understanding of power as involving the imposition of one's will through the threat of violence and Foucault's institution-based and individual-based understandings of power. Given the diversity of the prophetic books involved and their varied historical and social settings, this should not reduce the utility of our conclusions. See James H. Read, "Thomas Hobbes: Power in the State of Nature, Power in Civil Society," *Polity* 23 (1991): 505–25; Michel Foucault, *The Foucault Reader*, ed. P. Rainbow (New York: Pantheon, 1984), 12–23.

11. See, contrariwise, Anselm C. Hagedorn, *Die Anderen im Spiegel: Israels Auseinandersetzung mit den Völkern in den Büchern Nahum, Zefanja, Obadja und Joel*, BZAW 414 (Berlin: de Gruyter, 2011).

12. Contrast, for example, the reticence to integrate non-Israelites in Ezra–Nehemiah versus the openness to the same in Malachi, and see Philip F. Esler, "Ezra–Nehemiah as a Narrative of (Re-Invented) Israelite Identity," *BibInt* 11 (2003): 413–26; Peter Lau, "Gentile Incorporation into Israel in Ezra–Nehemiah," *Bib* 90

of the texts in question, however complex it may have been, does not bear on our findings. In what follows, therefore, I avoid correlating the study's conclusions with a particular reconstruction of Israelite history and religion, or formulating a developmental history of othering in ancient Israelite literature.[13]

2. The Othering of Non-Israelites and its Relativization in Amos

Our starting point in Amos is the nations (גוים, consistently non-Israelite throughout the book) as states that are geopolitically, religiously, and culturally distinct from Israel. Despite the strong moral tone of the oracles against the nations in 1:3–2:3 that condemn them for past misdeeds and threaten future punishment for the same reason, this ethical evaluation does not go beyond the geopolitical othering just mentioned because the book goes on to condemn Judah and especially Israel for similar offenses and to threaten them with similarly grave punishments.[14] Indeed, later in the book Ashdod and Egypt are invited to witness Israel's "unrest" and "oppression" (3:9), and 5:27 contemplates the "house of Israel" being exiled to a nation "beyond Damascus" (i.e., Assyria),[15] an action that definitively ends its existence as a nation.[16] Notably, in neither of these passages is the sin or punishment of these non-Israelite groups mentioned, nor is any new aspect of alterity added. These passages' emphasis on the

---

(2009): 356–73. On the difficulty of correlating a text with a specific historical situation, note especially Benjamin D. Sommer, "Dating Pentateuchal Texts and the Perils of Pseudo-Historicism," in *The Pentateuch: International Perspectives on Current Research*, ed. T. B. Dozeman, K. Schmid, and B. W. Schwartz, FAT 78 (Tübingen: Mohr Siebeck, 2011), 85–108.

13. For representative examples of such an approach, see Ann E. Killebrew, *Biblical Peoples and Ethnicity*, ABS 9 (Atlanta, GA: SBL, 2005); Kenton Sparks, *Ethnicity and Identity in Ancient Israel* (Winona Lake, IN: Eisenbrauns, 1998); and Hagedorn, *Anderen*.

14. The fact that Israel is condemned for moral and social sins while the nations are punished for other offenses is of no consequence for their othering here; cf. Baruch A. Levine, "Some Indices of Israelite Ethnicity," in *Ethnicity in Ancient Mesopotamia: Papers Read at the 48th Rencontre Assyriologique Internationale, Leiden, 1–4 July 2002*, ed. W. H. van Soldt (Leiden: Nederlands Instituut voor het Nabije Oosten, 2005), 189–97 (196).

15. Jorg Jeremias, *The Book of Amos*, trans. D. W. Stott, OTL (Louisville, KY: Westminster John Knox, 1998), 106.

16. Daniel L. Smith-Christopher, *A Biblical Theology of Exile*, OBT (Minneapolis, MN: Fortress, 2002), 22.

similarity of Israel and the nations in moral and juridical terms attenuates the geopolitical otherness of the non-Israelite groups with which the book began, and together these aspects outline a relationship between the two that involves roughly equal proportions of identity and otherness.

The historical reflection in 9:7, however, clearly departs from this roughly balanced othering/de-othering by emphatically de-othering several non-Israelite groups in the present. The verse denies that Israel's exodus from Egypt was unique, arguing that YHWH was also responsible for similar movements of the Philistines from Caphtor and the Arameans from Kir. In YHWH's estimation, furthermore, Israel is like Kush (i.e., currently without a special relationship to YHWH), since Israel's exodus from Egypt did not confer upon it a permanent, absolute difference with respect to all other nations.[17] Israel, in other words, is not as different from other nations as some Israelites at the time may have thought.

This deconstruction of a fundamental aspect of exclusively Israelite identity (its deliverance from Egypt and the covenant establishment that followed) leads directly into a group of strongly eschatological passages that other *within* Israel and the nations rather than *between* them. First, YHWH announces that he will destroy the "sinful kingdom," which apparently overlaps substantially with Israel, without entirely destroying the "house of Jacob" (9:8). In 9:9 this process is compared to sifting Israel with a sieve, and is an othering process that destroys "all the sinners" in Israel (9:9-10). This division of Israel on moral-spiritual grounds radically changes the identity of "Israel." As such, it continues the movement away from an inherently distinct, geopolitically defined and unified Israel begun in 9:7.

Following "blood and iron" with "roses and lavender," 9:11 goes on to predict the revival of the Davidic monarchy, followed in 9:12 by its "possession" of the remnant of Edom and "all the nations that are called by [YHWH's] name."[18] The elements of political leadership (a Davidic

---

17. M. Zehnder, *Umgang mit Fremden in Israel und Assyrien: Ein Beitrag zur Anthropologie des 'Fremden' im Licht antiker Quellen*, BWANT 168 (Stuttgart: W. Kohlhammer, 2005), 299–301. The fact that the exoduses mentioned in Amos 9:7 include all three of the lines descended from Noah (Israel from Shem, the Philistines from Japheth, and Cush from Ham, cf. Gen. 10:1-22) strengthens this de-othering, as suggested by Brent A. Strawn, "What is Cush Doing in Amos 9:7? The Poetics of Exodus in the Plural," *VT* 63 (2003): 99–123.

18. This passage is explored briefly in Daniel C. Timmer, "The Use and Abuse of Power in Amos: Identity and Ideology," *JSOT* 39 (2014): 101–18, and I draw on some of those arguments here.

king), additional citizens (9:12), and the recovery of land (9:13-15) complete the re-definition of YHWH's people with a radically new identity.

While this extension of Davidic power and control might appear to revert to a binary othering of non-Israelites, the fact that these non-Israelites have YHWH's name called over them makes that conclusion unlikely.[19] The phrase אשר נקרא שמי עליהם ("over whom my name is called") is used of a people group only five other times in the Hebrew Bible and refers in every case to YHWH's beneficent election of, ownership of, and relationship with Israel (Deut. 28:10; 2 Chron. 7:14; Dan. 9:19; Isa. 63:19; Jer. 14:9; note also the semantically equivalent statement in Isa. 43:7, בשמי נקרא and similar language in Isa. 63:19).[20] In these passages, Israel is sometimes obedient and other times disobedient, yet YHWH's relationship with her is too strong to be completely broken by her sin. Instead, the fact that YHWH has laid claim to Israel becomes the basis for requests for YHWH to restore her (Dan. 9:19), to forgive her sins (2 Chron. 7:14; Dan. 9:19), and to maintain his relationship with her (Jer. 14:9; Isa. 63:19). This relationship is rooted in the covenant made with Israel at Sinai (cf. Deut. 28:9-10 and context with Exod. 19:5-6) and ultimately in YHWH's covenant with Abraham (Gen. 15; 17), and the book of Amos makes indirect reference to this covenantal matrix at several prior points (3:1, 2; 9:7).

The consistently positive sense of YHWH calling his name over Israel prompts us to consider the applicability of the same characteristic to non-Israelite groups in Amos 9:12 as a criterion of identity it shares with (renewed) Israel.[21] While some exegetes assign a non-relational sense to the phrase based on analogues in which human beings take control

---

19. In this and the following paragraph I draw on Daniel C. Timmer, *The Non-Israelite Nations in the Book of the Twelve: Thematic Coherence and the Diachronic-Synchronic Relationship in the Minor Prophets*, BINS 135 (Leiden: Brill, 2015), 51–61.

20. Adam S. van der Woude, "שם," *TLOT* 1363; C. J. Labuschagne, "קרא," *TLOT* 1162; F. L. Hossfeld and H. Lamberty-Zielinski, "קרא," *TDOT* 13:132 (their article does not mention Amos 9:12); Sandra Richter, *The Deuteronomic History and Name Theology: lᵉšakkēn šᵉmō šām in the Bible and the Ancient Near East*, BZAW 318 (Berlin: de Gruyter, 2002), 84–5.

21. Arthur Gibson, *Biblical Semantic Logic: A Preliminary Analysis*, 2nd ed., BibSem 75 (Sheffield: Sheffield Academic, 2001), 140, defines a criterion of identity as "that which x must be to be y."

of cities (2 Sam. 12:28) or territory (Ps. 49:12),[22] the phrases "remnant of Edom" and "the nations over which my name is called" both refer to people groups.[23] Together with the apparently fixed and positive sense conveyed by "over whom *YHWH's* name has been called" when used of a population rather than a defeated city or territory, these points favor the conclusion that the groups in Amos 9:12 will be drawn into a beneficial relationship with YHWH in a way analogous to Israel's acceptance of YHWH's covenant offer at Sinai, albeit now in a process that involves the restored Davidic line. Predictions of the nations' harmonious, beneficial relationship to Israel and to her God appear elsewhere in the prophetic books (Isa. 19:18-25; Zeph. 2:11; 3:9; Zech. 2:15 [Eng. 2:11]; 8:22-23; 9:5-7), and so a similar idea is not implausible here.[24]

Understood this way, Amos 9:11-12 is an inverted mirror image of the othering of some Israelites in the immediately preceding context (9:7-10). This exceptional denouement correlates well with the muted othering of non-Israelites elsewhere in the book, on the one hand, and is closely tied to the prominence of the Israelite remnant on the other (i.e., othering within Israel; cf. 3:12; 4:11; 5:3; 6:9). Most notably, if this understanding of the passage is correct, it announces a predominant de-othering of some non-Israelite groups that identifies them with some of national Israel by means of a criterion of identity according to which they belong to YHWH in essentially the same way that Israel does.[25] We can thus conclude that

---

22. E.g., Shalom Paul, *Amos: A Commentary on the Book of Amos*, Hermeneia (Minneapolis, MN: Augsburg Fortress, 1991), 292. For Jerusalem, see Jer. 25:29; Dan. 9:18, 19. For the temple, see 1 Kgs 8:43 // 2 Chron. 6:33; Jer. 7:10, 11, 14, 30; 32:34; 34:15. In 2 Sam. 12:28, Joab, fighting on David's behalf, says that unless David comes to Rabbah himself and takes the city, Joab will do so, and will "call his name over it." Several aspects of this scenario distinguish it from that of Amos 9:12, most notably the fact that the remnant of Edom and the other nations have YHWH's name called over them and so belong to him. As for the 2 Samuel passage, the difference between human fame in connection with possession of a conquered city and its population and divine possession of a people group must be appreciated. Cf. Arnold A. Anderson, *2 Samuel*, WBC 11 (Dallas, TX: Word, 1989), 168.

23. A syntagm composed of שארית in construct with a proper noun always refers to territory or to a state inclusive of its populations, but never to territory alone; cf. Hans Wildberger, "שאר," *TLOT* 1284–92 (1286); Ronald E. Clements, "שאר," *TDOT* 14:277, 283.

24. As Joel Kaminsky notes, such passages continue to affirm Israel's election even as they speak of Gentile inclusion; *Yet I Loved Jacob: Reclaiming the Biblical Concept of Election* (Nashville, TN: Abingdon, 2007), 152.

25. The fact that ירש often means "dispossess" is not an insurmountable argument against this view given the semantics of 9:12b and analogues like Ps. 72, where

Amos 9:11-12 constitutes a social and spiritual intervention that creates "a sense of common identity" and so reduces "intergroup bias."[26] This passage's focus on YHWH as the only agent for these changes makes him the one whose power others and de-others parts of the nations and of Israel alike.

3. *The Othering of Non-Israelites and its Relativization in Nahum*

To say that Nahum others non-Israelites is an understatement. At the same time, it is not a *comprehensive* statement of Nahum's perspective on the nations. Although the other nations in Judah's orbit exist as geopolitically, religiously, and culturally distinct entities just like Assyria, in Nahum they are anonymously lumped together with Judah as Assyria's victims (3:4, 19) in an othering that employs several varieties of the victim/ victimizer polarity (2:12-14 [Eng. 11-13]; 3:7, 19, etc.). The social and gender ramifications of Assyria's presentation as an abusive but now disempowered and shamed prostitute other her still more with respect to the various nations that she has abused (3:4-7).

Nahum's main concern, however, is the Judah/YHWH vs. Assyria opposition, and this relationship bristles with alterity.[27] To begin with the Judah–Assyria pair, which involves selective, stereotypical representations of both states,

- Assyria is the suzerain and Judah is its vassal;
- Assyria is polytheistic while Judah is assumed to be monotheistic;
- Assyria is involved in iconic worship of her deities, while (divinely authorized) Judean religion is assumed to be aniconic (1:14);

---

subdued non-Israelites (72:8-11) clearly reside in their own homelands while being under Davidic rule and respond to that rule with submission and even enthusiasm in light of the Davidide's exceptional justice and mercy (72:12-14). See further Timmer, "The Use and Abuse of Power in Amos," 112–13, and note Georg Braulik's argument that Deuteronomy's description of exiled Israel's return to the land in Deut. 30:4-5 has omitted the military tone and features of Deut. 7:1, which lays out guidelines for the initial conquest of Canaan. Braulik, "Die Völkervernichtung und die Rückkehr Israels ins Verheissungsland: Hermeneutische Bemerkungen zum Buch Deuteronomium," in *Deuteronomy and Deuteronomic Literature*, ed. M. Vervenne and J. Lust, BETL 133 (Leuven: Leuven University Press, 1997), 3–38, esp. 33–7.

26. Richard J. Crisp and Miles Hewstone, *Multiple Social Categorization: Processes, Models and Applications* (New York: Taylor & Francis, 2013), 65–89 (83).

27. These are explored in more detail in Daniel C. Timmer, "Boundaries without Judah, Boundaries within Judah: Hybridity and Identity in Nahum," *HBT* 34 (2012): 173–89, and I draw on that discussion here.

- Assyria is radically more violent than Judah (2:12-14[11-13]); and
- Assyria is exceptionally unjust and rapacious in its international and economic relationships, while Judah has only suffered its ravages.

While some of these points (e.g., Judah's vassal status) are historically attested in addition to being affirmed by the text, others (while presumably reflecting historical realities, albeit selectively) give evidence of an approach to othering that stereotypes Judah positively and Assyria negatively.[28] As a result, Judah lacks Assyria's negative features (e.g., worship of other gods), and negative characteristics not attributed to Judah are characteristic of Assyria (e.g., exploitative economic practices).

Assyria's alterity with respect to Judah is amplified by YHWH's adversarial relationship with Assyria and her king.[29] This othering involves the following features:

- Assyria is repeatedly described as YHWH's adversary and opponent (cf. YHWH's edict against the king that involves first-person divine actions, 1:14; the *Herausforderungsformel* הנני אליך נאם יהוה, "Beware, I am against you! Utterance of YHWH" in 2:14[13]; 3:5) while Judah is his covenant partner, formerly under discipline but now awaiting his deliverance (1:12) and restoration (2:3[2]);
- Assyria has consciously plotted evil against YHWH (חשב אל\על־יהוה, 1:9, 11);
- As a result, YHWH commits to destroying Assyria/Nineveh, in particular by ending the Assyrian monarch's reputation and dynasty, by destroying the images of the gods who authorize and support him (1:14; cf. 3:18-19), and by bringing about the destruction of the empire (2:12-14[11-13]; 3:5-7, 12-19) and its leading city (2:4-11[3-10]; 3:8-11).

This theological and religious othering, with YHWH as Assyria's adversary and Judah as his covenant partner, is significant enough to account for the diametrically opposed fates of Judah and Assyria in the book (contrast 2:1[1:15]; 2:3[2] for Judah with 1:14; 3:18-19 for Assyria).

28. Cf. Hagedorn, *Anderen*, 82–6.
29. Detailed interpretation of these passages can be found in Daniel C. Timmer, *Nahum: A Discourse Analysis of the Hebrew Bible*, ZECOT (Grand Rapids, MI: Zondervan Academic, 2020).

A different othering appears in the opening hymn of 1:2-8, this time between two anonymous groups that are identified only in terms of their relationship with YHWH. This section's description of YHWH's definitive and final intervention in human affairs exhibits several notable differences with respect to the rest of the book.

1. There is no cultural or geopolitical identification of the human beings involved in these superlative acts of divine judgment and deliverance. In other words, the Self is not Judah as an oppressed nation among other oppressed nations, but rather an amorphous and anonymous group who believes that seeking refuge in YHWH is the only way to survive the coming global judgment (1:6-8). Likewise, the Other is not the Neo-Assyrian empire but an amorphous collective identified only as YHWH's enemies. The operative polarity in the passage is thus between YHWH's "enemies" and "those who take refuge in him," a binary othering cast in terms of individuals' relation to YHWH.
2. The allusion to Exod. 34:7 (and/or Exod. 20:7) in Nah. 1:3b makes a link to a passage that others guilty Israelites (Exod. 34:7, or Israelites who take YHWH's name in vain in 20:7) from the point of view of an ideal Israelite Self that *does not* transgress YHWH's commands.[30] The inner-Israel othering on spiritual and moral grounds in Exodus is of a piece with the spiritual and moral othering that predominates in Nah. 1:2-8, and shows that othering within Judah and outside it are equally plausible in Israelite thought.

On these grounds we can suggest that Nahum's opening hymn affirms the applicability, regardless of geopolitical or cultural otherness, of a definitive or superlative othering in which trusting YHWH for deliverance from his retribution against his enemies is the only avenue to permanent well-being. Against what many scholars have seen as radically different theological or ideological outlooks in 1:2-8 over against the rest of the book, however, the Assyria-focused othering that dominates most of the

---

30. Heinz-Josef Fabry, *Nahum*, HTKAT (Herder: Freiburg im Breisgau, 2006), 134; Gerlinde Baumann, *Gottes Gewalt im Wandel: Traditionsgeschichtliche und intertextuelle Studien zu Nahum 1,2-8*, WMANT 108 (Neukirchen-Vluyn: Neukirchener Verlag, 2005), 82–102; cf. Michael Widmer, *Moses, God, and the Dynamics of Intercessory Prayer: A Study of Exodus 32–34 and Numbers 13–14*, FAT 2/8 (Tübingen: Mohr Siebeck, 2004), 183–203.

book complements the global application of a similar othering in 1:2-8. As our examination of YHWH's adversarial relationship with Assyria shows, both parts of the book (thanks largely to the idealized stereotype of Judah in 1:12; 2:1[1:15], 2[3]) represent other human beings primarily in terms of their opposition to, or submission to and trust in, YHWH. The difference between the book's two parts is one of scope and specificity, involving stereotypical presentations of Assyria and Judah as collectives outside the opening hymn, and absolute representations of individuals in 1:2-8. The exercise of divine power against Assyria in 1:9–3:19 undoes the empire and simultaneously frees and restores to full statehood its former vassals who are, at least in practical and political terms, powerless. The same power wielded directly against all those in a binary opposition to YHWH destroys them (rather than their corresponding political units) in a final theophanic judgment that can be seen as the establishment of YHWH's kingdom to the exclusion of all others.

4. *The Othering of Non-Israelites and its Relativization in Malachi*

The book of Malachi presents us with two modes of othering non-Israelites, one regarding Edom and the other vis-à-vis "all the nations." In the first disputation, Edom is othered from "Jacob" by the diachronic criteria of its past non-election, its nearly total destruction in the present, and YHWH's future opposition to and unending anger against it.[31] The climactic undoing of a state that repeatedly attempts to re-establish itself underlines Edom's static character as YHWH's opponent.

Against the backdrop of this total divine rejection of Edom, it is somewhat surprising that Malachi presents the other non-Israelite nations positively. As usual in the XII, their present otherness in geopolitical and cultural terms is presupposed, but as was the case in Amos and Nahum, this feature is of limited significance. Their religious otherness is also presupposed, but unlike Edom, it is not static and it plays a significant role.

Malachi gives close attention to the future de-othering of these nations, and this emphasis is strengthened by its juxtaposition with the othering of some Israelites in Yehud. In ch. 1 at least some of the Israelites living in Yehud, as represented by their priests, are accused of undervaluing

---

31. Elie Assis suggests, quite plausibly, that Edom's "ideological and theological significance" as the non-elect but apparently ascendant counterpart of Israel lies behind Malachi's emphasis here; "Why Edom? On the Hostility towards Jacob's Brother in Prophetic Sources," *VT* 56 (2006): 1–20 (15).

the cult, offering flawed animals as sacrifices, and finding temple service wearisome (1:7-8, 12-13). This sharp critique of the Yehudite priests leads YHWH to express the wish that their cult would end and to predict—surprisingly—that incense and a pure offering will be offered to his name "among the nations" (1:11). In this future setting these nations are still geopolitically and culturally distinct from Israelites in Yehud, yet this otherness is apparently consistent and contemporaneous with their offering YHWH acceptable worship far from his temple (1:11).

This transformation of the nations presupposes a distinction between the nations in Malachi's day, which per the available historical evidence were not YHWHistic nor seen as indirectly worshipping YHWH through non-YHWHistic cults,[32] and the nations at some future time, who will worship YHWH acceptably.[33] The following points support this diachronic schema: (1) the wish that Yehud would put an end to its flawed cult is prospective, and it is in the same future context that the nations will revere YHWH's name. (2) There is no evidence of YHWH-worship among non-Israelite groups in the post-exilic period. References to the "God of heaven" (e.g., Ezra 1:2), if in fact Persian in origin, would more likely exemplify the Achaemenid practice of using indigenous titles for deities than a reference to YHWH as known by Israelites.[34] In any case, this possibility can be dismissed since Israelites beyond the reach of Persian influence (e.g., at Elephantine) used the same divine title in their correspondence.[35] (3) The idea of acceptable non-YHWHistic worship is incompatible with Malachi's emphasis on YHWH's *name* and thus on his historically specific identity. Markus Zehnder adds to this the twin consideration of Malachi's condemnation of marriages with non-YHWHistic wives (Mal. 2:11).[36] This point is further strengthened by the use of "reverence for YHWH's name" (Mal. 2:11), a *terminus technicus*

---

32. Lester Grabbe, "'Many Nations will be Joined to YHWH in That Day': The Question of YHWH outside Judah," in *Religious Diversity in Ancient Israel and Judah*, ed. F. Stavrakopoulou and J. Barton (London: T&T Clark, 2010), 175–87.

33. See in more detail Timmer, *The Non-Israelite Nations*, 211–14, on which I draw here.

34. H. G. M. Williamson, *Ezra, Nehemiah*, WBC 16 (Waco, TX: Word, 1985), 11–12; see further Amélie Kuhrt, "The Problem of Achaemenid 'Religious Policy'," in *Die Welt der Götterbilder*, ed. B. Groneberg and H. Spieckermann, BZAW 376 (Berlin: de Gruyter, 2007), 117–42.

35. Herbert Niehr, "God of Heaven," *DDD* 371.

36. Zehnder, *Umgang mit Fremden*, 308; S. D. (Fanie) Snyman, *Malachi*, HCOT (Leuven: Peeters, 2015), 107.

for authentic, legitimate religious relationship to YHWH, to describe non-Israelites (1:14).[37]

We can now return to our reflection on the significance of the two-fold shift which consists of the present disqualification of the Yehudite priests (and perhaps some lay Yehudites, 1:13-14) and the contrasting future offering of acceptable worship by non-Israelites outside the boundaries of the temple cult. The admission of non-Israelites to such roles and the statement that they will "revere YHWH's name" (1:14) bring those with no genealogical tie to the Aaronic line into the closest possible proximity to YHWH, whose intolerance of unsuitable cult personnel can hardly be doubted. By pairing this de-othering of non-Israelites with the othering of ordained Yehudite priests, Malachi juxtaposes othering and de-othering processes and reinforces that contrastive movement by explicitly identifying both the othered (some Yehudites) and the de-othered (some non-Israelites) groups.[38]

Before moving on, two points should be noted. First, the operative difference between the two groups is expressed in terms of internal ("reverence") and external (priestly functions) religious criteria, and not in terms of ethnic or geopolitical factors.[39] Second, it is improbable that the idealized Israelite Self that others the Yehudite priests would benefit directly from the future changes it anticipates. Not only does the ideal Israelite Self lack the social and religious status of the priests, but YHWH is solely responsible for these changes (2:14). The result of the othering here is thus without any clear link to easily recognized forms of power. It can only create and clarify a religious-spiritual description of a purified "Israel" (cf. 3:3, 17) that will come fully into view in the Day of YHWH (3:19[4:1]) and is defined by reverence for him (3:16, 20[4:2]). Significantly, this criterion of identity is shared with some non-Israelites (1:14).

We return to our consideration of the processes of othering that Malachi predicts will operate within Yehud. The prominence of the priests in Malachi 1 suggests that not all Yehudites are in view in the critique there,

---

37. See Roland Murphy, *The Tree of Life: An Exploration of Biblical Wisdom Literature*, 3rd ed. (Grand Rapids, MI: Eerdmans, 2002), 16, and Deryck Sheriffs, *The Friendship of the LORD* (Carlisle: Paternoster, 1996), 162–4.

38. In contrast to the frequent othering through description of only what the Self is not, or what the Other is, this example involves the othering of some of the Self's social-political and religious group as well as the de-othering of some outside that group.

39. A similar othering of Yehudites is evident in the "elimination" (Hiphil כרת) of those who intermarry with non-YHWHists (2:11).

and Mal. 3:16-18 makes explicit a bipartite view of Yehud by othering those Yehudites who *do not* serve or revere YHWH with respect to those who *do*, another moral-spiritual criterion. The final verses of Malachi 3 return to the paradigm of the Sinai covenant by applying language from Exodus 19 to the faithful Yehudite *remnant* (Mal. 3:17), and employ the righteous/wicked polarity to make a binary moral–religious distinction *within Yehud* (3:18, between the righteous, צדיק, and the wicked, רשע). Strikingly, the uses of עשי רשעה in 3:15 and of רשע in 3:18 to refer to some Yehudites associate them with Edomites, since רשע-language appears previously in Malachi only in the phrase גבול רשעה in 1:4, referring to Edom (see, subsequently, 3:19[4:1], 21[4:3]).[40]

Interestingly, Malachi is less clear about a similar distinction among non-Israelites (apart from Edom, of course). At least some non-Israelites who are not Edomites share "reverence for YHWH" (1:14, a verbal form of ירא with YHWH or a pronoun for the divine name as its object) with Levi (2:5), Israelites who follow Torah (3:5), Israelites who refuse to call the proud "blessed" and who "esteem" YHWH's name (3:16), and those whom the "sun of righteousness" will deliver from YHWH's coming judgment (3:20[4:2]). This criterion of identity superlatively de-others these non-Israelites by identifying them with the faithful Yehudite Self on the basis of an essentially identical relationship with YHWH (reverence for his name) and shared status (צדיק and/or not רשע).

The statement in 3:12 that *all* non-Israelites except Edom will pronounce restored Yehud happy (Piel of אשר) goes further still. This statement, the only time that כל־הגוים appears in Malachi, distinguishes "all the nations" from two groups: the "wicked" Edom (רשע, 1:4), whose antipathy for Israelites is taken for granted in ch. 1, and the Israelites who pronounce happy the arrogant doers of wickedness among their kin (עשי רשעה, 3:15, again with the Piel of אשר). The nations' interest in restored Israel's well-being shows that they identify or sympathize with her, and intimates that they will share the blessing that Abraham's line transmits to all the peoples of the earth (Gen. 12:3), since God promises to bless those who bless Abraham.

While their geopolitical otherness remains, the prospect of these nations recognizing Israel's future blessing (possibly enjoying it with them) and sharing with ideal Israel an authentic relationship with YHWH and the status of being "just" (3:18) as criteria of identity brings "all the

---

40. Rainer Kessler pointed out to me in a personal communication that Mal. 1:3-5 and 3:15-18 also share the root בנה in their description of the othered group, where what is built (and will be destroyed) represents the accomplishments of the Other. See further his *Maleachi*, HTKAT (Freiburg: Herder, 2011), 272.

nations" as close as possible to an outright identification with the ideal, faithful Yehudite Self that the author of Malachi creates, and thus to the limits of de-othering, namely, Self–Other identification. Interestingly, even as identities are radically changed (with the de-formation and re-formation dynamics evident elsewhere), the political affiliation of those who constitute them remains unchanged.

5. Conclusions

We can summarize the findings of our brief and partial survey of selected sections of the Book of the Twelve as follows:[41]

1. Cultural, religious, and geopolitical otherness in the present is predicated or presupposed of all non-Israelite states and groups;
2. Future religious *otherness* and *non-otherness* are occasionally predicated of some Israelites *and* of some non-Israelites;
3. Cultural and geopolitical dimensions of otherness can coexist alongside, but are subordinate to, religious non-otherness that involves survival of YHWH's definitive judgment, relationship with, and/or enjoyment of the blessings promised in Israel's national covenant.

Each of the three Israelite prophetic books examined above anticipate, in various ways and to varying degrees, the future undoing of the religious otherness that characterized some non-Israelite groups in their present. While on one level this is simply to recognize that ancient Israel's religion contained a strong universalist facet, it is worth reflecting on how othering and de-othering contribute to this aspect of ancient Israelite thought.

1. Some social identity mechanisms produce or preserve otherings that are not absolutely binary and which can therefore accommodate a "proximate Other," who while remaining *other* in some ways is simultaneously *identified with* the Self (in this case, Israel's religiously pure core or remnant).[42] This demonstrates

---

41. For a full survey of the Book of the Twelve that reaches similar conclusions for the collection as a whole, see Timmer, *Non-Israelite Nations*, and, for Joel, Obadiah, Nahum, and Habakkuk, Hagedorn, *Anderen*. Note also Antonio Finitsis, "The Other in Haggai and Zechariah 1–8," in *The "Other" in Second Temple Judaism*, ed. Daniel C. Harlow et al. (Grand Rapids, MI: Eerdmans, 2011), 116–31.

42. See the discussion of Baumann, "Grammars of Identity/Alterity," and note Wills's concept of the "stranger," who is "not necessarily Other" but simply "distant and different" (Wills, *Not God's People*, 12).

that othering and de-othering can operate simultaneously, and that some non-absolute otherings can be relativized by others, as Evans-Pritchard and Dumont suggested.[43]

2. The most significant expressions of identity or otherness between Israelites and non-Israelites are expressed in religious terms, specifically in terms of a relationship to YHWH.[44]

3. The othering and de-othering of non-Israelites surveyed here offer no easy correlation of these processes with Israelite, Judahite, or Yehudite power.[45] In the three books we studied, the Israelite authors other *and* de-other those more powerful than themselves, whether Israelite or not.[46] In Amos 9, the exercise of power by the restored Davidic line extends only to non-Israelites who belong to YHWH and so would gladly submit to his rule or ruler (cf. Exod. 19; Ps. 72). The political context Amos presupposes means that the more powerful Northern Kingdom is othered (cf. Amos 7:10-17) while those in the Southern Kingdom of Judah are assumed to share the author's religious and political identity. In parts of Nahum and all of Malachi, the link between othering and power is even less evident, since Nah. 1:2-8 employs no social or political categories and the author of Malachi frankly states that the socially powerful Yehudite priesthood *is* the Other. These cases suggest that othering in ancient Israelite literature was sometimes the purview of the socially weak or of the religious minority and not exclusively a

---

43. See Baumann, "Grammars of Identity/Alterity," 19–22.

44. Cf. Peter Machinist's assertion that "the core of Israel's claim to distinctiveness is her special relationship to her God." "Distinctiveness in Ancient Israel," in *Ah, Assyria! Studies in Assyrian History and Ancient Near Eastern Historiography Presented to Hayim Tadmor*, ed. M. Cogan and I. Eph'al, ScrHier 33 (Jerusalem: Magnes, 1991), 196–212 (205). This is difficult to deny, and supports the conclusions that the de-othering in the passages studied above relativizes all remaining forms of otherness.

45. Contrast Jensen's (colonial) understanding of othering as "discursive processes by which powerful groups, who may or may not make up a numerical majority, define subordinate groups into existence in a reductionistic way which ascribe [*sic*] problematic and/or inferior characteristics to these subordinate groups. Such discursive processes affirm the legitimacy and superiority of the powerful and condition identity formation among the subordinate." Jensen, "Othering, Identity Formation and Agency," 65.

46. Contrast McInerney, "Ethnicity: An Introduction," 3: "Ethnicity makes no sense outside a continuous dynamic of inclusion and exclusion. It is always inflected by power."

tool of the powerful. While this othering could itself be seen as an exercise of power, it is one whose realization is deferred to a future time and whose only agent is YHWH.

4. Last, the absence of consistent links between othering and power in these books confirms and informs our understanding of the predominantly religious nature of the othering and de-othering processes by which some of the Twelve connect Israelites and non-Israelites to a shared, permanent, beneficial relationship with YHWH.[47] While the othering of Israelites confers woe on the Israelite Other and the de-othering of non-Israelites confers good upon them, good and woe come (at least ultimately) from YHWH, not from the ideal Israelite Self.[48] By making a particular sort of relationship with YHWH the predominant criterion of identity, and by disconnecting that relationship from ethnic, cultural, or geopolitical factors (some aspects of Amos 9:11-12 excepted), this dual movement of othering and de-othering involves neither the exercise nor the accumulation of power by the idealized Israelite Self, while it anticipates the experience of the greatest possible good by the non-Israelite "proximate Other."

While othering typically results in the invisibility, essentializing, or stigmatization of the Other,[49] the Book of the Twelve presents several cases in which simultaneous othering and de-othering processes relativize and, in some cases, almost undo otherness. The salutary effects of this de-othering are reminiscent of the relational ethos of othering as Lévinas understood it: the "other is a neighbor, and the Self is constituted in its relation to that other-as-neighbor."[50] As elsewhere in the HB/OT, this

47. As opposed to a hybrid othering involving political, social, and other factors in roughly equal parts. "Inclusive or exclusive religious identity in the Old Testament is usually linked to the identity of Yahweh." Jan P. Bosman, *Social Identity in Nahum: A Theological-ethical Enquiry*, Biblical Intersections 1 (Piscataway, NJ: Gorgias, 2008), 62.

48. Cf. Andrew J. Critchfield, "Other, the," in *Encyclopedia of Identity*, ed. R. L. Jackson II, 2 vols. (London: Sage, 2010), 1:520–6 (520, emphasis in the original): "Othering is rooted in the concepts of ingroup favoritism and outgroup bias. Ingroup favoritism suggests that a person deemed similar…to the self will be treated well or better than a dissimilar person and will receive some favoritism in interactions or behaviors *by the self*… Conversely, when someone is deemed a member of an outgroup, or unlike the self, that person will be Othered, or treated poorly or worse than someone in the ingroup."

49. Critchfield, "Other," 520–1.

50. Brons, "Othering, an Analysis," 74.

neighborly relationship makes the idealized Israelite Self responsible for the well-being of the Other and vice-versa. The relationships presented in the passages surveyed above involve or even integrate the Other in the greatest good known to the ideal Israelite Self.[51] This phenomenon merits continued reflection as much for its peaceable, relational, and inclusive trajectory as for its relevance to theoretical, historical, and theological analyses of othering and of social and religious identity.

---

51. Ibid., 85, makes reference to Hegel's insight that "the transcendence of othering both releases the other from her otherness, thus rehumanizing her, and brings back the self."

Chapter 9

GEOGRAPHIES OF OTHERNESS: OTHERNESS IN TERRITORIAL ORGANIZATION IN THE ORACLES AGAINST THE NATIONS

Steed Vernyl Davidson

Introduction

"No one, wise Kublai, knows better than you that the city must never be confused with the words that describe it. And yet between the one and the other there is a connection."[1] Geography pervades the Bible. Yet in the study of the Bible geography receives minimal attention. No reader of the Bible, no matter how casual, can escape geography as an important feature of the text and as a result conjure up the physical setting against which much of the narrative or other literary forms take shape. In this essay, I show how geography shapes interpretation of biblical narratives and the assessment of characters in those narratives. The way the biblical texts represent geographical space has a lot to do with who occupies those spaces as well as where those spaces are located.

The easy acceptance of geography—landscape, terrain, settlements, and so on—as givens that remain immutable enables the seamless integration of the physical setting into and by the literary text or its erasure from it. To the extent that geography captures the imagination of the biblical reader, the relationship between the imaginary and the materiality of the texts remains hidden to most readers. The modern Bible reader remains

---

1. From Italo Calvino's *Invisible Cities* where Marco Polo speaks to Kublai Khan. Cited in Russell West-Pavlov, *Spaces of Fiction/Fictions of Space: Postcolonial Place and Literary DeiXis* (Hampshire, UK: Palgrave Macmillan, 2010), 2.

unconscious of his reality not because the text lacks the appropriate photographs to bring the geography to life or even an attached video that offers scanned scenes of the terrain but because we do not always see how social practices shape physical space and the way texts describe those social spaces. While accepting that the foreignness of the geography of the biblical world contributes significantly to this knowledge gap, the biblical text nonetheless provides the appropriate descriptive, visual, and spatial information about its setting to orient readers to its geography. Cultural geography, as described by Johnson, Schein, and Winders, "problematizes the ideas of culture, landscape, and nature"[2] in ways that can indicate that geography in biblical texts is more than a decorative appendage but can cue readers to the values the texts hold about particular characters.

The oracles against the nations in the biblical prophetic books provide one of the best opportunities to focus on geography in an intentional way.[3] These oracles consist of lists of several place names covering a vast geography of the ancient Near East. The oracles provide readers/listeners with a view of the world along with oracular details about the fate of these places. The oracles represent one of the most deliberate collections of place names in the Bible. Yohanon Aharoni estimates that over four hundred and seventy-five different place names occur in the Hebrew Bible.[4] From my approximation, of this total over one hundred different geographic locales are mentioned in the oracles against the nations. This extensive attention to geography in the oracles does not occur by chance but rather forms part of the textual representation of physical space. Naturally, since the oracles are concerned with foreign nations, almost ninety-eight percent of these references involve locations outside of Israel/Judah. The result of this focus on foreign places is the construction of a visual representation of the geography of what lays outside "us," establishing a sharp divide that calls attention to "them." The attention to place names in the oracles goes beyond the headlines that introduce the respective oracle to include, as far as possible, multiple instances of place names in the local geography of the respective nation.[5] Within the flow

---

2. Nuala C. Johnson, Richard H. Schein, and Jamie Winders, "Introduction," in *Wiley-Blackwell Companion to Cultural Geography*, edited by Nuala C. Johnson, Richard H. Schein, and Jamie Winders (Malden, MA: Wiley-Blackwell, 2013), 2.

3. I consider the oracles against the nations to be Amos 1–2; Isa. 13–23; Jer. 46–51; Ezek. 25–32; Joel 3:1-21; Nahum; Obadiah; Zeph. 2:4-15; and Zech. 9:1-8.

4. Yohanan Aharoni, *The Land of the Bible: A Historical Geography* (Philadelphia: Westminster, 1979), 81.

5. No consistent term introduces each collection of oracles in the different books. Only the books of Isaiah and Nahum employ the expected term "oracle" (משא).

of the prophetic books, therefore, the oracles mark a perceptible shift in gaze as the focus moves away from the sins and settings of Judah to the failings of foreign nations.[6]

My concern in this essay lies not so much in trying to reconstruct the geography that lies underneath the oracles. Rather, I am more concerned to draw attention to the fact that geography plays a role in the construction and presentation of the oracles. Past attempts to discern a coherent logic in the geographical lists of these oracles, particularly the ones in the book of Amos, have focused on the order of the main nations listed in part to reconstruct some sort of a ritualized travel across the physical terrain in a systematic fashion.[7] This notion presumes the oracles to function in a way similar to Egyptian execration texts where curses were recorded against nations on pottery that was subsequently smashed in order to ritualize the destruction of the named nations.[8] While a sequential order can be established in the Egyptian texts, application of this concept to the oracles, particularly the Amos collection, proves that it does not always fit with the biblical lists. My purpose in this essay is less ambitious than reconstructing original intentionality in the respective lists. Rather, in my reading I bring geography to the foreground to show how it supports the rhetoric of destruction—rhetoric built upon the notion that these nations are not "us" and therefore should be justly punished. Even further, the rhetoric of otherness pushes past the issue of punishment to some form of transformation either in the nations themselves or in the "world" at large that is created by these collections. That transformation is as much about the people as about place.

I draw upon the postcolonial turn in the field of human geography for my theoretical ground in this essay. Following the work of Edward Said, postcolonial geography pays attention to the material aspects of textual representation rather than simply the abstract or idealized terrains.[9] Said maintains that "everything about human history is rooted in the earth" and

---

Jeremiah simply uses either the preposition ל (Jer. 46:2) or אל (Jer. 47:1) as does Obadiah (1:1), while Ezekiel employs the more elaborate phrasings "set your face against x and prophesy against y" (e.g. Ezek. 25:2).

6. The location of the collections of oracles varies in each book. They appear at the start of Amos (chs 1–2) but close at the end of Jeremiah (chs 46–51). They fall somewhere in the middle of Isaiah (13–23) and Ezekiel (25–32).

7. John H. Hayes, "Amos's Oracles Against the Nations," *RevExp* 92 (1995): 163.

8. M. Weiss, "The Pattern of the 'Execration Texts' in the Prophetic Literature," *IEJ* 19 (1969): 150–7.

9. Alison Blunt and Cheryl McEwan, "Introduction," in *Postcolonial Geographies*, ed. Alison Blunt and Cheryl McEwan (London: Continuum, 2002), 6.

that no one is "outside or beyond geography, none of us is completely free from the struggle over geography."[10] The resistant mode that Said takes suggests the need to question and challenge geographical representation. Postcolonial geography interrogates the knowledge of the world presented in various forms and whether that dominant form of knowledge includes all cultures. Since the oracles demonstrate more than a cursory interest in the geography of these foreign nations, I am alert to the production of knowledge about these nations as a form of power. That the presentation in the oracles hardly makes mention of the relationship between Israel/Judah and these nations but exclusively focuses on them in the context of divinely sanctioned violence also suggests the deploying of alterity in the text. In this essay, I highlight the geographical construction of otherness and offer some insights as to how this challenges our reading and understanding of the function of these oracles.

Oracles Against the Nations as Maps

The descriptive geographies in the oracles perform a role similar to maps in our visual culture. Maps attempt to make the world known through a set of signs and symbols.[11] They aim to fulfill the need to express spatial knowledge in a coherent and accessible way. They in effect compress space in a manageable form that can be communicated. Obviously such spatial representations already fall within narrow ideological and cultural categories. Yet maps present themselves as universally and objectively factual. The skill of cartography as we know it derives from Western mapping traditions that pay attention to scale, geometry, and so on, taking on a clearly culture-specific means of communicating spatial knowledge.[12] As ideologies of power feature prominently in knowledge, ideologies also determine spatial knowledge. Traditions of mapmaking reflect Western forms of knowledge as James Sidaway indicates: "geography, its norms, definitions, inclusions, exclusions and structure cannot be disassociated from certain European philosophical concepts of presence, order and intelligibility."[13] While the oracles are not maps in the modern sense, my point here is that systems of spatial knowledge are ideological products.

10. Edward Said, *Culture and Imperialism* (New York: Alfred Knopf, 1993), 7.
11. Denis Cosgrove, "Mapping/Cartography," in *Cultural Geography: A Critical Dictionary of Key Ideas*, ed. David Sibley, David Atkinson, and Peter Jackson (London: I. B. Tauris, 2005), 28.
12. Ibid., 29.
13. James D. Sidaway, "Postcolonial Geographies: Survey-Explore-Review," in Blunt and McEwan (eds), *Postcolonial Geographies*, 11.

Of course, maps as we know them today do not exist in the Bible. Cartographic representations, to the extent they exist in the Bible, are embedded in texts. These textual precursors perform some of the functions of the modern map. Geographical texts such as the Table of Nations in Genesis 10 purport to give textual descriptions of populations, borders, and boundaries of territories, as well as the cultural activities that take place in these locations. Geographical texts in the Bible largely come from administrative and governmental sources, for example the list of Solomon's district commissioners in 1 Kgs 4:7-19 or the conquests of territory in Israel by Tiglath-pileser III in 2 Kgs 15:29. Yohanan Aharoni divides the various geographical texts in the Hebrew Bible into three main categories of historical-geographical descriptions, administrative lists, and expeditions and conquests.[14] He places the oracles against the nations into the category of expeditions and conquests.[15] Aharoni's interests, however, lie more with the geographical data that he can glean from the oracles regarding the place names that populate these texts. Therefore, he does not make an explicit claim that they function like proto-maps.

Maps, in providing data of geographical space that cannot be imagined by a single human eye, function as ordered statements of reality. This ordering function has traditionally been part of modern empire's mechanisms of control. Maps supply the data for control. As 246Daniel Clayton offers, maps "draw geographical order out of chaos—to travel, collect, map, represent, govern, survive, and draw material and imaginative lines on the ground."[16] The oracles perform a similar role of providing knowledge about various places around the "world." Even more, they purport to provide a sense of how the "world" should be ordered. The order offered by the oracles sets out to make the world a better place through the elimination of the practices of the people who occupy the different nations, and to establish the worldview of Israel/Judah in their place. In this regard, the oracles reflect an imperial outlook that views everything else, others, as less than best and in need of amelioration. Andrew Sluyter shows how colonization operates as Westernization with the corresponding view that the landscape was being improved.[17]

14. Aharoni, *Land of the Bible*, 83.
15. Ibid., 92.
16. Daniel Clayton, "Imperial Geographies," in *A Companion to Cultural Geography*, ed. James S. Duncan, Nuala C. Johnson, and Richard H. Schein (Malden, MA: Blackwell, 2004), 455.
17. Andrew Sluyter, *Colonialism and Landscape: Postcolonial Theory and Applications* (Lanham, MD: Rowman & Littlefield, 2002), 3.

Rhetorically, the oracles present themselves as mechanisms of control that are in essence largely about the conquest of the land of other people. The form of the oracles as texts means that their descriptions of specific geographic locations call attention to spaces in an abstract or metaphorical manner but they are in effect concerned with physical space. In so doing the oracles offer representations of space in a compressed form that communicate a clear ideological position. The oracles are not unlike other forms of geographical representations in other ancient Near Eastern cultures that feature extensive lists and descriptions, for example Egyptian expedition journals that narrate military conquests in the Syria-Palestine region, the hymn of Merneptah that mentions several place names in Egypt and other parts of North Africa, or the walls of Medinet Habu that depict Ramses III battles against Libya and the Sea Peoples.[18] Egyptians also used topographical lists of geographical locations represented through images of rings symbolizing fortified cities under the name of the location. Within these rings a partial figure of the leader of that city is shown with his arms tied behind his back, his neck bound with a rope that is held by a deity who is handing him over as a prisoner to Pharaoh. This visualizing of conquest first appears with Thutmose III and consists of a list of one hundred and nineteen places conquered in Syria-Palestine.[19] These representations approximate what we may call a map today and resemble the evocation in the oracles of broad geographical spaces under the sway of a divine regime that places them in their proper place in the world.

In the practice of imperialism, maps serve as one of the empire's technological tools along with what John Morrissey views as "military capability, and legal registers to underwrite colonial violence and (bio) political governmentality."[20] Maps offer to the empire a ready visual representation of conquests either completed or in process.[21] In this way, maps confirm the success of the imperial project and provide insights and resources for the application of further political, economic, and cultural regimes of power needed to advance the imperium. Similarly, the oracles provide a systematic overview of territory that has been subdued and brought under divine influence, much like the digest of information in

---

18. Aharoni, *Land of the Bible*, 93.
19. Ibid., 94.
20. John Morrissey, "The Imperial Present: Geography, Imperialism, and Its Continued Effects," in Johnson, Schein, and Winders (eds), *Wiley-Blackwell Companion to Cultural Geography*, 496.
21. Clayton, "Imperial Geographies," 454.

imperial military planning. Consequently, the geographic descriptions available in the oracles serve as an exercise of power with a view to legitimizing the divine conquest and control of these spaces.

Maps are snapshots in time that present themselves as timeless. The relationship between time and space, therefore, is not always immediately clear in a map. The oracles describe, not so much the reality on the ground, but an anticipated future where the described vision will be realized. The oracles hide the relationship between time and space. By blurring the relationship between time and space, the oracles, *cum* maps, present a distorted reality in which divine activity occurs, and consequently present a revision of history. At the same time, the oracles also enable readers to participate in the divine gaze over an expanding realm of influence in the way that maps enabled the imperial project to advance.[22] Unlike the specialization in modern imperialism that divides the skills of the cartographer and the historian, though not their objectives, the oracles attempt to offer to readers both geographic and historical details, albeit fictive details since the capacity to know all the details of foreign nations and the future is in doubt.[23] The details here constitute what Blunt and Rose see as the perceiving of "an external reality to be mimetically represented."[24] The representation in the oracles begins with geographic spaces and keeps geography present through the provision of various locales and place names in the named "nations." Geographic spaces are further filled in at times with bodies, that is those who are native to those spaces, with cultural and religious practices, with histories, and consistently with divine interventions that reconfigure that geographic space into conformity with the divine will. This collective description of geographic space along with their native inhabitants together with their practices forms the basis of the construction of otherness in the oracles.

Jeremiah's oracle against Babylon opens with the declaration that its interest is decidedly about "the land of the Chaldeans" (50:1).[25] Having established itself in this geographic space the oracle immediately sets

---

22. Alison Blunt and Gillian Rose, "Introduction," in *Writing Women and Space: Colonial and Postcolonial Geographies*, ed. Alison Blunt and Gillian Rose (New York: Guilford, 1994), 9.

23. Jonathan Stökl raises questions about Ezekiel's extensive knowledge of cuneiform and suggests that one source of his knowledge may be attendance at a cuneiform school. Jonathan Stökl, "Schoolboy Ezekiel: Remarks on the Transmission of Learning," *Die Welt des Orients* 45 (2015): 60. To the extent that this seems plausible, prophets as scribes or scribes as prophets would need to have an internationally broad learning curriculum.

24. Blunt and Rose, "Introduction," 10.

25. All biblical references are from the NRSV.

itself apart from the world of the readers. Spatially, this land is distant and foreign. The strangeness of the land is confirmed by the invocation of the names of the Babylonian gods, Bel and Marduk (50:2). No attribution appears in this verse for the desecration and humiliation of these deities and correspondingly the destruction of Babylon, but readers in the ancient world would immediately associate such a fate with the inability of the deities to forestall the defeat of the nation. The next verse quickly credits an unnamed force with the destruction. The peculiar use of geography in the common Jeremiah formulation, "out of the north a nation has come" (50:4), sets up the physical binary between this nation and that of Babylon. This antithesis appears in spatial terms as well as moral terms. The ability of the nation from the north to conquer Babylon implies its moral superiority over Babylon. The description of the desolation of Babylon indicates that Babylon is unfit for both humans and animals and points to an intolerance of moral otherness. Babylon is rhetorically linked with places from which people escape. Textual insertions of displaced or deported Judeans wandering and returning (50:4-7) preface the call to leave Babylon. The mention in the preface of disobedience, straying, and sin as practices occurring in foreign spaces sets up those foreign spaces as dangerous (e.g., the possibility of being devoured, v. 7). Further, this description is conflated with Babylon as the site of otherness that must be both avoided and destroyed (50:9-10).

The oracles use geography, and attention to landscape and spaces to provide a vision for a future that is ordered according to the divine will. The oracles represent space through several place names to provide knowledge of what the world looks like. By showing the world in its chaotic state, the oracles draw the line between in/out, good/bad, and us/them. Constructing otherness through space sets up the need for the type of reform and improvement of space as relentlessly offered in the oracles. The nature of the violence needed to order these spaces—the universal destruction of the war club (Jer. 51:22), the unremitting use of fire to destroy cities in Amos (1:4, 7, 10, 12, 14; 2:2, 5) or the wanton slaughter of innocents (Isa. 13:18)—demonstrates the level of intolerance of otherness in the prophetic texts.

Point of View

The oracles offer an unsettled perspective on the location of the speaker and subsequently on the site of enunciation.[26] The fluidity between third and first person speech, the messenger form of the third party

26. West-Pavlov, *Spaces of Fiction*, 2.

communication used in most of the oracles,[27] as well as the lack of a clear physical location for the source of knowledge about the geography and events may suggest the unimportance of geographical location. Yet this myth of detached observation forms part of the persuasive appeal of the geographical constructions noted here. The descriptions play upon what Nedra Reynolds regards as "visualism," an emphasis upon the visual that radically offers the view from the best seat in the house, the "God's eye view."[28] This God's eye view enables the reader to participate in omniscience that makes the sight of destroyed foreign nations unproblematic. Though a non-physical position, the seeing position of God occupies a moral ground that automatically labels everything viewed as other and therefore not always sharing in the ontological and consequently ethical values of divine space. However, even God's sight in the texts is fixed in a geographical setting in that it is communicated via the place of enunciation from which either the historical prophet or literary tradents anchor these utterances. A book like Ezekiel pivots around the binary between Jerusalem and the foreign nations (punishment of Jerusalem [chs 1–24], punishment of foreign nations [chs 25–32], restoration of Jerusalem[29]) that can arguably be seen in other prophetic books. In any event, prophetic literature provides the view of the world from the viewing position of Judah's deity. The divine vision in these oracles represents a view and ethical evaluation of the world from an insider position: seeing the world from inside out. As the one looking out on the rest of the world, this view provides the geographical evidence of the otherness of these spaces.

Each oracle takes a geographic space and provides a description of that space as markedly different from the national space. The national space of these oracles in the prophetic literature, with perhaps the exception of Amos, is the chastened and redeemed land of Judah. The national Self surveys the unreached spaces of disarray in these nations and produces knowledge about these spaces of otherness. This production of otherness, Homi Bhabha indicates, poses the curious case of "pleasure and unpleasure" as well as distanciation from the other that is at the same time "entirely knowable and visible."[30] The nations' obdurate degeneracy

---

27. All the oracular collections except the isolated occurrences in Zephaniah and Zechariah use the messenger formula, indicating that the prophet participates in viewing these events from a fixed location.

28. Nedra Reynolds, *Geographies of Writing: Inhabiting Places and Encountering Difference* (Carbondale, IL: Southern Illinois University Press, 2007), 63.

29. Tyler Mayfield, *Literary Structure and Setting in Ezekiel* (Tübingen: Mohr Siebeck, 2010), 24–5.

30. Homi K. Bhabha, *The Location of Culture* (London: Routledge, 1994), 70–1.

requires outside intervention in these geographic spaces, and this dynamic forms the dominant discourse in the oracles.

Let me illustrate with an example from Jeremiah's oracle against/ concerning Egypt. Although the oracle starts by invoking a location outside of Egypt in Carchemish on the Euphrates, the descriptive but distorted history that implicates Nebuchadnezzar in the defeat of Pharaoh Necho during the early reign of King Jehoiakim positions Egypt as a place that harbors militaristic ambitions. Here, at the outset of this oracle, a swift Babylonian response could contain their military adventurism (Jer. 46:2). Yet Egypt's thirst for war seems as intrinsic to its character as the Nile. This rising and uncontained threat poses a greater menace to the nations of the earth than does the localized floods of the Nile: *"Who is this, rising like the Nile (the river), like rivers whose waters surge? Egypt rises like the Nile, like rivers whose waters surge. It said, Let me rise, let me cover the earth, let me destroy cities and their inhabitants"* (Jer. 46:7-8). At first, Babylon proves inadequate to deal with this unique threat, for while this may be Egypt's nature, this disorder proves incurable for even the cure-all balm of Gilead (46:11), much to the discomfort of the nations (46:12). In the decisive attack led by Nebuchadnezzar but really prosecuted by the LORD (46:18), much of the major geography of Egypt appears under the sway of the lethal sword (46:14, 19).[31] The ultimate fall of the nation takes place at the all-important site of Thebes (46:25), a center of administration, monarchy, religion, and culture, as described in the phrase where punishment falls upon "Pharaoh, and Egypt and her gods and her kings, upon Pharaoh and those who trust in him." The departure of the Apis bull confirms the degeneracy of the space that even Egyptians and Egyptian gods appear to disavow as their homeland (46:15-16). As in other oracles, Egypt's otherness can be cured with an application of divine violence that rids the space of its people, culture, religion, and way of life. In this oracle the combination of self-exile (46:16), forced exile (46:19, 26), and annihilation (46:14) wipes the space clean of its otherness to enable its rehabilitation (46:26).

The details in each oracle may vary, but for the most part they follow the same plot. The simple outline consists of naming the nation, laying out or implying some form of description of the use of their space mostly in

---

31. Apart from Egypt as a whole, three possible geographic locations appear—Migdol, Memphis, and Tahpanhes. I could discern no clear geographic value in this combination to suggest coverage of all the major cardinal points. Migdol when referring to the north is normally paired with Syene, a southern locale not mentioned here. Tahpanhes is the site that the book of Jeremiah records for his place of "exile" in Jer. 43:7. Memphis served as a major administrative and royal center.

generic and non-specific ways, and then unleashing divine power to reconstitute a more acceptable space. This outline contains obvious colonialist discourse, a discourse that indicates a preoccupation in the oracles with foreign nations not only at the level of their moral disorders but also from a geographic point view. Though not present in every prophetic book, the presence of the oracles in the major prophets and even the exclusive use of this form by Nahum and Obadiah suggests the worry that geographic separateness does not serve as a sufficient buffer to isolate redeemed Israel/Judah from the taint/lure of otherness. While past imperialist actions may lead us to think of territorial possession for acquisitive and profit purposes, Said notes that the loftier goal of aiding inferior people in a geographic space on the "outside" helps to support imperialism.[32] In this century the civilizing mission continues in the form of the Euro-American military and cultural alliance's maintenance of the "West/rest" binaries to promote what Priyamvada Gopal calls "liberal imperialism"[33] intended to make the world more safe, more democratic, more inclusive, and more of everything seen as better. Similarly, these oracles rise above the low bar of territorial conquest driven by greed or gold. Instead, these oracles see territory for the purposes of the other "G" that usually mark the imperial impulse. God's purposes over territory animate these oracles, but not simply from a narrow sectarian position. These spaces of difference explored in the oracles must come into conformity with the divine will.

Overcoming Otherness

Despite the embrace of imperial rhetoric, the oracles do not share the aim of occupying the world. Rather, the remnant of Judah reconstituting itself in geographic space as a political entity revives or develops this vision in the prophetic corpus to guide its future. Part of that future lies in remaking the world to ensure its stability. Given that the community involved in the transmission of prophetic texts would have transcended a more parochial existence, the view of the future should be more cosmopolitan. Instead, the oracles embrace fears of otherness with the aim of erasing the other to make a better world. The global outlook of the oracles may not reflect

---

32. Said, *Culture and Imperialism*, 10.
33. Liberal imperialism can be defined as the belief that liberal ideals need to be the path of all people in the world. It further holds that liberal values should be spread gently but by force of arms when necessary. Priyamvada Gopal, "Renegade Prophets and Native Acolytes: Liberalism and Imperialism Today," in *The Oxford Handbook of Postcolonial Studies* ed. Graham Huggan (Oxford: Oxford University Press, 2013), 198.

cosmopolitan ideals but what Jamil Khader sees as "cosmopolitics," a notion that rests upon Kant's idea of world citizenship. Cosmopolitics trades upon the erasure of borders, multilingual competence, and the end of nations.[34] In this postnational world narratives of the civilizing mission still issue forth, perhaps in stronger cadences because the once foreign dominant culture faces an even larger population in need of conversion away from otherness, except this time they willingly convert.

Should the oracles provide a "one-world vision," they do so by showing how otherness can be removed in place and geography can be reshaped. The oracles communicate the possibilities of overcoming geographic otherness at two levels: geographic and literary. In the oracles the divine hand wipes otherness off the face of geographic space through the destruction of nations: Isaiah imagines Babylon obliterated like Sodom and Gomorrah (13:19), Jeremiah anticipates a similar fate for Edom (49:18), Ezekiel blandly states that Ammon will be destroyed (25:7). In the literary text traces of otherness are removed in the happy ending form of the story: the world converts to God. By following what Svend Erik Larsen calls a "relay story" in which one element of a plot is handed over to another in a smooth transition that lends coherence to the story structure,[35] we can see how the oracles follow the simple form that leaves no room for ambiguity about the culmination of the fate of a particular nation and its absorption into the divine will. The case of Nineveh in response to Jonah's oracle against that city serves as a clear case. The Ninevites pray to God with the hope of being saved.[36] Contrary to Jonah's expectations they are saved. Each oracle resolves in gruesome but successful containment of the monster with no possibilities of revival either in physical space or a forthcoming sequel.[37]

If overcoming otherness is the goal of the oracles, as Hegel's parable of the master/slave suggests, the elimination of otherness leads to the death of the Self. In Hegel's parable, the master discovers that the slave's consciousness of its place as slave has the potential for the slave to kill

---

34. Jamil Khader, *Cartographies of Transnationalism in Postcolonial Feminisms: Geography, Culture, Identity, Politics* (Lanham, MD: Lexington, 2013), 2.

35. Svend Erik Larsen, "How to Narrate the Other," in *Otherness: A Multilateral Perspective*, ed. Susan Yi Sencindiver, Maria Beville, and Marie Lauritzen (Frankfurt: Peter Lang, 2011), 207.

36. Notably, the text does not indicate veneration of YHWH, but the use of the definitive article before "God" (אלהים, Jon. 3:9) implies a preliminary searching by this foreign king for the proper name of the deity.

37. The ending of Nahum offers some ambiguity regarding the Assyrian leadership's sleep that could be read as death or a future revival.

himself, therefore imperiling the dominance of the master. In this dialectic, the master discovers his precarity and his dependence upon the slave for the maintenance of the antithetical and asymmetrical relationship. Perhaps rather than the otherness of others, the oracles provide insight into Judah's dealings with its own othered Self. Carolyn Sharp offers an initial foray in this direction through her essay on Jeremiah's oracle concerning Moab. She draws attention to how fears of foreignness reflected in this oracle may well be Judah's own fear of its foreignness as it deals with its fractured social body.[38] I make a similar claim that ties the social body to the geographic space. By embracing both the rhetoric and techniques of imperial conquest that come with mapmaking, the oracles provide an opportunity to imagine the world not as it is but as it can be. A new map written on a clean sheet, reterritorializing by delimiting and defining new territories, adding new meanings to old names, steps towards revising history, and (re)placing the nation on the map not as a dot but as the focal point from which the map is conceived are some of the potential appropriations of the imperialist techniques that address the othered Self. As David Punter notes, geography is actually the soft underbelly of the empire, since cartography quite often reveals a reality that does not exist on the ground. He offers that "geography…would be the key to resistance, even though geography itself is immovable."[39] The geographic otherness in the oracles serves as the ground upon which Judah rewrites itself.

In the oracles, geography offers the ground upon which the binaries between the Self and otherness can thrive. Geography provides sufficient distance between the two so that they do not exist in a contact zone. National borders provide what Luce Irigaray refers to as the "threshold [or]…spatial architecture…between oneself and the beyond."[40] Yet as we read these oracles the sense of *déjà vu* occurs, for the descriptions of the degeneracy of the foreign nations resemble the ones leveled at Judah, revealing the descriptive geography of the oracles to be as much of a myth as colonialist maps. Rannfrid Thelle explores the similarities between the oracles and judgment speeches against Judah using the notion

---

38. Carolyn J. Sharp, "Embodying Moab: The Figuring of Moab in Jeremiah 48 as Reinscription of the Judean Body," in *Concerning the Nations: Essays on the Oracles Against the Nations in Isaiah, Jeremiah and Ezekiel*, ed. Else K. Holt, Hyun Chul Paul Kim and Andrew Mein (London: Bloomsbury, 2015), 106.

39. David Punter, *Postcolonial Imaginings: Fictions of a New World Order* (Edinburgh: Edinburgh University Press, 2000), 33.

40. Luce Irigaray, "How Can We Meet the Other?," in Sencindiver, Beville, and Lauritzen (eds), *Otherness*, 108.

of the *Doppelgänger* in relation to Jeremiah's Babylon oracle, where the discourse against Judah is simply reapplied to Babylon.[41] Thelle shows that though made to look the same, the sameness cannot hold together and the relationship ultimately breaks down.[42] In the conception of the *Doppelgänger* that Thelle proposes, sameness is not salvation but disaster[43] requiring a disavowal of intimacy in order, as Irigaray puts it, to make that which is most intimate visible.[44] Geography makes it possible to produce otherness in the form of Lacan's notion of extimacy, which is not a resolution or recovery of subjectivity but merely an ambiguity between inside and outside. As reflections at the crossroads of Judah's search for a relationship with the world—the collapse of the nation, the diasporic context, new imperialism, old wounds—the interrelations of the outside and inside surface in the oracles. The physical distance of geography in the oracles perhaps affords an exploration of the viability of life in the diaspora—can redeemed Israel exist in new geographies that have been similarly reconstituted by the restorative power of divine violence? Or does the extimacy of oracles seek to recover home, the land of birth, not only as geographic space but also as initial subjectivity?

Critiquing *Doppelgänger* literature for its masculinist notions, Susan Yi Sencindiver explores the *Doppelgänger* from the perspective of the pregnant woman[45] rather than the dominant Oedipal contours. In this way, she sees the crises of subjectivity as the need to reclaim the mother missing in the mirror.[46] The production in the oracles of geographic spaces that reflect the otherness of Judah reveals a search for umbilical reattachment in foreign spaces that achieves spectral results of the sort that subscribe to the myth of mapmaking. Apart from the gendered representations of these nations, in keeping with the ancient practice, the oracles deploy images of childbirth to undercut the masculinity of the muscular strength of these nations. The taunt of feminized warriors (Jer. 48:41; 49:22; 50:24; Nah. 3:13) indicates a preoccupation with the ambiguities of women in labor, which on first reading seems a mark of weakness but on further reflection

---

41. Ranfrid Thelle, "Babylon as Judah's *Doppelgänger*: The Identity of Opposites in the Book of Jeremiah (MT)," in Holt, Kim, and Mein (eds), *Concerning the Nations*, 82.

42. Ibid., 92.

43. Ibid., 93.

44. Irigaray, "How Can We Meet the Other?," 109.

45. Susan Yi Sencindiver, "Pregnant Doppelgängers: Lived and Literary," in Sencindiver, Beville, and Lauritzen (eds), *Otherness*, 61.

46. Ibid., 66.

demonstrates fearful appreciation for the strength to withstand this pain. Evidently, in rejecting foreign spaces, the oracles convey a preoccupation with the fear that these spaces may be suitable sites for reconnecting with the missing mother.

If we read the oracles as products of the Persian period, whether previously constructed or simply codified as part of prophetic books of the period, we read them from a site of enunciation best described as marginal placelessness. Obviously, the oracles attempt to mask the provisionality of its geographic space by mimicking sites of power. The oracles afford no vision of resistance either from the nations overcome by divine violence or from the site of observation. The fantasy of the oracles provides a recalibrated geography, a refusal to accept reality, in the words of Katherine McKittrick, as what "just is."[47] McKittrick notes the lure of merely giving in to space as "just is," inscribing one's powerlessness over space. She pays attention to this from the perspective of race, sex, and economic hierarchies where geography can be presented as secure and therefore comfortable for certain subjects, rendering them easily invisible. The oracles disturb the security of geographic space in major power centers, challenging their construction of the order of the world.[48] And at the same time, by refusing to spatialize the Judean identity, the oracles provide no space in which its own othered Self can be normalized by geography that "just is." The violent discourse of the oracles does not provide suitable similitude for the sort of refusal to accept reality that McKittrick details. Rather, the oracles reveal through their grotesquery the limits of geographical domination.

Conclusion

The oracles come from a time before the invention of maps. Yet they reflect an ageless practice of "the codification and interpretation of the world."[49] These practices are not neutral since the producers of knowledge always hold some form of power. Whether through texts or images, representations of space convey the views of their creators about the world. Thinking through space and with space reveals the limits and possibilities for control of space as well as the differences in space. More than simply space as naturally constituted, as it "just is," spatial thinking and spatial

47. Katherine McKittrick, *Demonic Grounds: Black Women and the Cartographies of Struggle* (Minneapolis, MN: University of Minnesota Press, 2006), xi.

48. Ibid., xv.

49. Scott Fitzgerald Johnson, *Literary Territories: Cartographical Thinking in Late Antiquity* (New York: Oxford University Press), 1.

knowledge creates possibilities for the demarcation of various layers of difference. Through spatial thinking, the oracles construct a world of difference that they seek to eliminate. In the oracles otherness is removed by violent destruction or assimilation. The quest to make the world the same reveals it to be already almost the same.

The oracles also show how geographic space uncannily resembles Judah. The other remains too close to the Self. Modern scholarship may approach these oracles against the nations as if they were really about foreign places. However, the oracles may purport to be about the nations when in fact their concern is about the nation of Judah, its fate not in the past but in the future.

As textual descriptions, the oracles rely upon visualism to appeal to readers. This vantage point of power draws readers into the seduction of both the omniscience of sight and the distortions that come with the certainties of sight. The oracles provide an encyclopedic list of place names, landscape features, the names of deities, vegetation, and other details of different places around the "world." This broad vista builds out the readers' imagined geography and in the process confirms the difference between those places and the Self/home. In a time when lines drawn on maps as borders do not exist, the visuality of the oracles places lines in physical spaces for the reader and confirms even further sharp separations of "us" and "them." The invitation to participate in such constructions alongside the deity encourages the use of the tools of imperial power. The oracles reflect several aspects of the imperial register, such as control over territory, ordering of space, and the demarcation of limits, among other things. The certainty that otherness can be seen, controlled, and made discernable ultimately breaks down. Systems to delineate "us" from "them" reach their limits as the particular threatens to eliminate the universal. The quest to assert the lordship of the Self exposes the dependence upon the other. The certainties of sight no longer contain the force or produce the meaning that it once did.

The Hebrew terminology in some of the prophetic books leaves some uncertainty for translators as to whether the oracles should be seen as "against" or "concerning" a particular nation. This hesitation stems from whether the oracles are meant to signal salvation for Israel/Judah through the destruction of a foreign nation or whether the destruction of the foreign nations hints at a similar fate for Israel/Judah. The discourse of the oracles seems to settle that debate quite easily, since they are decidedly antagonistic against every single nation named. As the exploration here reveals, the case may not be that easily settled, since geography raises new interpretive possibilities.

Bibliography

Adams, Rebecca, and René Girard. "Violence, Difference, Sacrifice: A Conversation with René Girard." *Religion and Literature* 25 (1993): 9–33.
Aeschylus, and Hugh Lloyd-Jones. *Agamemnon. A Translation with Commentary by Hugh Lloyd-Jones*. Translated by Hugh Lloyd-Jones. Upper Saddle River, NJ: Prentice–Hall, 1970.
Aeschylus, and Alan H. Sommerstein. *Aeschylus: Agamemnon; Libation Bearers; Eumenides*. Translated by Alan H. Sommerstein. Cambridge, MA: Harvard University Press, 2009.
Aharoni, Yohanan. *The Land of the Bible: A Historical Geography*. Philadelphia: Westminster, 1979.
Ahmed, Sara. *Strange Encounters: Embodied Others in Post-Coloniality*. London: Routledge, 2000.
Allport, Floyd H. *Social Psychology*. New York: Houghton Mifflin, 1924.
Alonso-Schökel, Luis. *Estudios de poética hébreo*. Barcelona: Flor, 1963.
Anderson, Arnold A. *2 Samuel*. WBC 11. Dallas, TX: Word, 1989.
Anderson, Bradford A. *Brotherhood and Inheritance: A Canonical Reading of the Esau and Edom Traditions*. LHBOTS 556. London: T&T Clark International, 2012.
Anidjar, Gil. *Blood: A Critique of Christianity*. New York: Columbia University Press, 2014.
Anzaldúa, Gloria. *Borderlands—La Fronteria: The New Mestiza*. San Francisco: Aunt Lute Foundation Books, 1987.
Ashcroft, Bill, Garret Griffiths, and Hellen Tiffin, eds. *Key Concepts in Postcolonial Studies*. London: Routledge, 1998.
Assis, Elie. *Identity in Conflict: The Struggle between Esau and Jacob, Edom and Israel*. Siphrut 19. Winona Lake, IN: Eisenbrauns, 2016.
Assis, Elie. "Why Edom? On the Hostility towards Jacob's Brother in Prophetic Sources." *VT* 56 (2006): 1–20.
Atay, Abmet. "Hybridity." In *Encyclopedia of Identity*, edited by Ed R. L. Jackson II, 1:338–9. 2 vols. Thousand Oaks, CA: SAGE, 2010.
Bailey, Randall C. "Beyond Identification: The Use of Africans in Old Testament Poetry and Narratives." In *Stony the Road We Trod: African American Biblical Interpretation*, edited by Cain Hope Felder, 165–84. Minneapolis, MN: Fortress, 1991.
Bal, Mieke. *Death and Dissymmetry: The Politics of Coherence in the Book of Judges*. Chicago: University of Chicago Press, 1988.
Balogh, Csaba. *The Stele of YHWH in Egypt: The Prophecies of Isaiah 18–20 concerning Egypt and Kush*. OtSt 60. Leiden: Brill, 2011.

Barstad, Hans M. "Isaiah 56–66 in Relation to Isaiah 40–55. Why a New Reading Is Necessary." In *Continuity and Discontinuity: Chronological and Thematic Development in Isaiah 40–66*, edited by Lena-Sofia Tiemeyer and Hans M. Barstad, 41–62. Göttingen: Vandenhoeck & Ruprecht, 2014.

Barthel, Jörg. *Prophetenwort und Geschichte: Die Jesajaüberlieferung in Jes 6–8 und 28–31*. FAT 19. Tübingen: Mohr Siebeck, 1997.

Bartlett, John R. *Edom and the Edomites*. JSOTSup 77. Sheffield: JSOT, 1989.

Baumann, Gerd. "Grammars of Identity/Alterity: A Structural Approach." In *Grammars of Identity/Alterity*, edited by G. Baumann and A. Gingrich, 16–48. EASA 3. New York: Berghahn, 2004.

Baumann, Gerlinde. *Gottes Gewalt im Wandel: Traditionsgeschichtliche und intertextuelle Studien zu Nahum 1,2–8*. WMANT 108. Neukirchen–Vluyn: Neukirchener, 2005.

Baumann, Gerlinde. "Prophetic Objections to YHWH as the Violent Husband of Israel: Reinterpretations of the Prophetic Marriage Metaphor in Second Isaiah (Isaiah 40–55)." In *A Feminist Companion to Prophets and Daniel*, edited by Athalya Brenner, 88–120. A Feminist Companion to the Bible (2nd Series) 8. London: Sheffield Academic, 2002.

Beal, Lissa Wray. *1 & 2 Kings*. ApOTC. Downers Grove, IL: InterVarsity, 2014.

Beauvoir, Simone de. *The Second Sex*. Translated by Constance Borde and Sheila Malovany-Chevallier. New York: Vintage, 2011.

Beit-Arieh, Itzhaq. "The Edomites in Cisjordan." In *You Shall Not Abhor an Edomite for He Is Your Brother: Edom and Seir in History and Tradition*, edited by D. V. Edelman, 33–40. ABS 3. Atlanta, GA: Scholars Press, 1995.

Beit-Arieh, Itzhaq. "New Data on the Relationship between Judah and Edom toward the End of the Iron Age." In *Recent Excavations in Israel: Studies in Iron Age Archaeology*, edited by Seymour Gitin and William G. Dever, 125–31. AASOR 49. Winona Lake, IN: Eisenbrauns, 1989.

Ben Zvi, Ehud, and Diana V. Edelman (eds). *Imagining the Other and Constructing Israelite Identity in the Early Second Temple Period*. LHBOTS 591. London: T&T Clark, 2014.

Berges, Ulrich. "Where Does Trito-Isaiah Start in the Book of Isaiah?" In *Continuity and Discontinuity: Chronological and Thematic Development in Isaiah 40–66*, edited by Lena-Sofia Tiemeyer and Hans M. Barstad, 63–76. Göttingen: Vandenhoeck & Ruprecht, 2014.

Berges, Ulrich F. *The Book of Isaiah: Its Composition and Final Form*. Translated by Millard C. Lind. HBM 46. Sheffield: Sheffield Phoenix, 2012.

Bergner, Gwen. "Who Is That Marked Woman? Or the Role of Gender in Fanon's *Black Skin White Masks*." PMLA 110 (1995): 75–88.

Berquist, Jon L. "Reading Difference in Isaiah 56–66: The Interplay of Literary and Sociological Strategies." *Method & Theory in the Study of Religion* 7 (1995): 23–42.

Beuken, Willem A. M. *Jesaja 13–27*. Translated by Ulrich Berges and Andrea Spans. HThKAT. Freiburg: Herder, 2007.

Bhabha, Homi K. *The Location of Culture*. London: Routledge, 1994.

Bhabha, Homi K. "Of Mimicry and Man: The Ambivalence of Colonial Discourse." In *The Location of Culture*, 121–31. 2nd ed. New York: Routledge, 2004.

Bimson, John. "Old Testament History and Sociology." In *Interpreting the Old Testament: A Guide for Exegesis*, edited by C. C. Broyles, 125–55. Grand Rapids, MI: Baker Academic, 2001.

Black, Max. "How Metaphors Work: A Reply to Donald Davidson." In *Perplexities*, 77–91. Ithaca, NY: Cornell University Press, 1990.

Blenkinsopp, Joseph. *Ezekiel*. IBC. Louisville, KY: John Knox, 1990.
Blenkinsopp, Joseph. *Isaiah 1–39: A New Translation with Introduction and Commentary*. AB 19A. New York: Doubleday, 2000.
Blenkinsopp, Joseph. *Isaiah 56–66: A New Translation with Introduction and Commentary*. AB 19B. New York: Doubleday, 2003.
Blenkinsopp, Joseph. *Judaism: The First Phase: The Place of Ezra–Nehemiah in the Origins of Judaism*. Grand Rapids, MI: Eerdmans, 2009.
Block, Daniel I. *The Book of Ezekiel: Chapters 1–24*. NICOT. Grand Rapids, MI: Eerdmans, 1997.
Block, Daniel I. *The Book of Ezekiel: Chapters 25–48*. NICOT. Grand Rapids, MI: Eerdmans, 1998.
Block, Daniel I. "The Tender Cedar Sprig: Ezekiel on Jehoiachin." *HBAI* 1 (2012): 173–202.
Blunt, Alison, and Cheryl McEwan. "Introduction." In *Postcolonial Geographies*, edited by Alison Blunt and Cheryl McEwan, 1–6. London: Continuum, 2002.
Blunt, Alison, and Gillian Rose. "Introduction: Women's Colonial and Postcolonial Geographies." In *Writing Women and Space: Colonial and Postcolonial Geographies*, edited by Alison Blunt and Gillian Rose, 1–27. New York: Guilford, 1994.
Boadt, Lawrence. *Ezekiel's Oracles against Egypt: A Literary and Philological Study of Ezekiel 29–32*. BibOr 37. Rome: Biblical Institute, 1980.
Bodéüs, Richard. "Aristotle." In *The Columbia History of Western Philosophy*, edited by Richard H. Popkin, 52–72. New York: Columbia University Press, 1999.
Bodi, Daniel. *The Book of Ezekiel and the Poem of Erra*. OBO 104. Göttingen: Vandenhoeck & Ruprecht, 1991.
Bodi, Daniel. "Ezekiel." In *Zondervan Illustrated Bible Background Commentary*, edited by John H. Walton, 4:400–517. Grand Rapids, MI: Zondervan, 2009.
Boer, Roland. "Yahweh as Top: A Lost Targum." In *Queer Commentary and the Hebrew Bible*, edited by Ken Stone, 75–105. JSOTSup 334. Sheffield: Sheffield Academic, 2001.
Bosman, Jan P. *Social Identity in Nahum: A Theological–Ethical Enquiry*. Biblical Intersections 1. Piscataway, NJ: Gorgias, 2008.
Bosshard-Nepustil, E. *Rezeptionen von Jesaja 1–39 im Zwölfenprophetenbuch*. OBO 154. Freiburg: Universitätsverlag, 1997.
Bowen, Nancy R. *Ezekiel*. AOTC. Nashville, TN: Abingdon, 2010.
Braulik, Georg. "Die Völkervernichtung und die Rückkehr Israels ins Verheissungsland: Hermeneutische Bemerkungen zum Buch Deuteronomium." In *Deuteronomy and Deuteronomic Literature*, edited by M. Vervenne and J. Lust, 3–38. BETL 133. Leuven: Leuven University Press, 1997.
Braziel, Jana Evans. "Trans-American Constructions of Black Masculinity: Dany Laferrière, le Negrè, and the Late Capitalist American Racial Machine Desirante." *Callaloo* 26 (2003): 867–900.
Brenner, Athalya. *The Intercourse of Knowledge: On Gendering Desire and Sexuality in the Hebrew Bible*. BibInt 26. Leiden: Brill, 1997.
Brett, Mark G. *Decolonizing God: The Bible in the Tides of Empire*. BMW 16. Sheffield: Sheffield Phoenix, 2009.
Brink, Laurie. "In Search of the Biblical Foundations of Prophetic Dialogue: Engaging a Hermeneutic of Otherness." *Missiology* 41 (2013): 9–21.
Brons, Lajos L. "Othering, an Analysis." *Transcience* 6 (2015): 69–90.

Brueggemann, Walter. *Isaiah 40–66*. Westminster Bible Companion. Louisville, KY: Westminster John Knox, 1998.
Buck-Morss, Susan. *Hegel, Haiti, and Universal History.* Pittsburgh, PA: University of Pittsburgh Press, 2009.
Budge, E. A. Wallis, and L. W. King. *Annals of the Kings of Assyria.* London, 1902.
Buhl, Marie-Louise. "The Goddesses of the Egyptian Tree Cult." *JNES* 6 (1947): 80–97.
Bulhan, Hussein Abdailahi. *Fanon and the Psychology of Oppression.* New York: Plenum, 1985.
Burdon, Christopher. "Jacob, Esau and the Strife of Meanings." In *Self, Same, Other: Re-Visioning the Subject in Literature and Theology*, edited by H. Walton and A. Hass, 160–74. Sheffield: Sheffield Academic, 2000.
Carroll, Robert. *Jeremiah: A Commentary*. OTL. Louisville, KY: Westminster, 1986.
Carter, Charles E. "A Discipline in Transition: The Contributions of the Social Sciences to the Study of the Hebrew Bible." In *Community and Ideology: Social Science Approaches to the Hebrew Bible*, 3–36. SBTS 6. Winona Lake, IN: Eisenbrauns, 1996.
Carvalho, Corinne L. "A Serpent in the Nile: Egypt in the Book of Ezekiel." In *Concerning the Nations: Essays on the Oracles Against the Nations in Isaiah, Jeremiah, and Ezekiel*, edited by Andrew Mein, Else K. Holt, and Hyun Chul Paul Kim, 195–220. LHBOTS 612. London: Bloomsbury, 2015.
Cataldo, Jeremiah W. "The Other: Sociological Perspectives in a Postcolonial Age." In *Imagining the Other and Constructing Israelite Identity in the Early Second Temple Period*, edited by Ehud Ben Zvi and Diana V. Edelman, 1–19. LHBOTS 456. London: Bloomsbury, 2014.
Chan, Michael J. "Isaiah 65–66 and the Genesis of Reorienting Speech." *CBQ* 72 (2010): 445–63.
Cherki, Alice. *Fanon: A Portrait.* Translated by Nadia Benabid. New York: Cornell University Press, 2006.
Chiesa, Lorenzo. *Subjectivity and Otherness: A Philosophical Reading of Lacan.* Cambridge, MA: MIT, 2007.
Childs, Brevard S. *Isaiah: A Commentary.* OTL. Louisville, KY: Westminster John Knox, 2001.
Chow, Rey. "Where have all the Natives Gone?" In *Feminist Postcolonial Theory: A Reader*, edited by Reina Lewis and Sara Mills, 324–49. New York: Routledge, 2003.
Clayton, Daniel. "Imperial Geographies." In *A Companion to Cultural Geography*, edited by James S. Duncan, Nuala C. Johnson, and Richard H. Schein, 449–68. Malden, MA: Blackwell, 2004.
Clements, Ronald E. *Isaiah 1–39.* NCB. London: Marshall, Morgan & Scott, 1980.
Coggins, R. J., and S. P. Re'emi. *Israel Among the Nations: A Commentary on the Books of Nahum, Obadiah, and Esther.* ITC. Grand Rapids, MI: Eerdmans, 1985.
Cordero, Nestor-Luis "Du non-être à l'autre: La découverte de l'altérité dans le Sophiste de Platon." *Revue Philosophique de la France et de l'Étranger* 130 (2005): 175–89.
Cosby, Alfred W. *The Columbian Exchange: Biological and Cultural Consequences of 1492.* 30th Anniversary ed. Westport, CT: Praeger, 2003.
Cosgrove, Denis. "Mapping/Cartography." In *Cultural Geography: A Critical Dictionary of Key Ideas*, edited by David Sibley, David Atkinson, and Peter Jackson, 27–33. London: I. B. Tauris, 2005.
Counihan, Clare. "Reading the Figure of Woman in African Literature: Psychoanalysis, Difference, and Desire." *Research in African Literatures* 30 (2007): 161–80.

Cresson, Bruce C. "The Condemnation of Edom in Post-Exilic Judaism." In *Use of the Old Testament in the New and Other Essays: Studies in Honor of William Franklin Stinespring*, edited by James M. Efird, 125–48. Durham, NC: Duke University Press, 1972.

Cresson, Bruce C. "Edom." In *Eerdmans Dictionary of the Bible*, edited by David N. Freedman. Grand Rapids, MI: Eerdmans, 2000.

Crisp, Richard J., and Miles Hewstone. *Multiple Social Categorization: Processes, Models and Applications*. New York: Taylor & Francis, 2013.

Critchfield, Andrew J. "Other, the." In *Encyclopedia of Identity*, edited by R. L. Jackson II. 1:520–6. 2 vols. London: Sage, 2010.

Crouch, C. L. "Ezekiel's Oracles against the Nations in Light of a Royal Ideology of Warfare." *JBL* 130 (2011): 473–92.

Crowell, Bradley L. "Postcolonial Studies and the Hebrew Bible." *CBR* 7, no. 2 (2009): 217–44.

Culbertson, Diana. "'Ain't Nobody Clean': The Liturgy of Violence in *Glory.*" *Religion and Literature* 25 (1993): 37–52.

Curtis, J. B. "On the *Hiphil* Infinitive Absolute of *Hālak*." *ZAH* 1 (1988): 22–31.

Dalley, Stephanie. *Myths from Mesopotamia: Creation, the Flood, Gilgamesh, and Others*. Rev. ed. Oxford: Oxford University Press, 2000.

Darr, Katheryn Pfisterer. "The Book of Ezekiel." In *The New Interpreter's Bible*, edited by Leander E. Keck et al., 6:1073–607. Nashville, TN: Abingdon, 2001.

Darr, Katheryn Pfisterer. *Isaiah's Vision and the Family of God*. Literary Currents in Biblical Interpretation. Louisville, KY: Westminster John Knox, 1994.

Davidson, Donald. "What Metaphors Mean." *Critical Inquiry* 5 (1978): 31–47. Reprinted in *The Essential Davidson*, 209–24. Introduction by E. Lepore and K. Ludwig. Oxford: Oxford University Press, 2006.

Davidson, Steed Vernyl. "'Every Green Tree and the Streets of Jerusalem': Counter Constructions of Gendered Sacred Space in the Book of Jeremiah." In *Constructions of Space IV: Further Developments in Examining Ancient Israel's Social Space*, edited by Mark K. George, 111–31. LHBOTS 569. New York: Bloomsbury, 2013.

Davidson, Steed Vernyl. "'Exoticizing the Otter': The Curious Case of the Rechabites in Jeremiah 35." In *Prophecy and Power: Jeremiah in Feminist and Postcolonial Perspective*, edited by Christl M. Maier and Carolyn J. Sharp, 189–207. LHBOTS 577. London: Bloomsbury T&T Clark, 2013.

Davies, Martin. "Philosophy of Language." In *The Blackwell Companion to Philosophy*, edited by N. Bunnin and E. P. Tsui-James, 90–146. Oxford: Blackwell, 2003.

Day, John. *God's Conflict with the Dragon and the Sea: Echoes of a Canaanite Myth in the Old Testament*. Cambridge: Cambridge University Press, 1985.

Derrida, Jacques. *The Gift of Death*. Translated by David Wills. Chicago: University of Chicago Press, 1995.

Derrida, Jacques. *The Gift of Death (2nd ed.) and Literature in Secret*. Translated by David Wills. Chicago: University of Chicago Press, 2007.

Derrida, Jacques. *Positions*. Translated by Alan Bass. Chicago: University of Chicago Press, 1981. French original, *Positions*. Paris: de Minuit, 1971.

Derrida, Jacques. *Writing and Difference*. Translated by Alan Bass. London: Routledge, 1978.

Deutsch, Nathaniel. "The Proximate Other: The Nation of Islam and Judaism." In *Black Zion: African American Religious Encounters with Judaism*, edited by Yvonne P. Chireau and Nathaniel Deutsch, 91–117. Religion in America Series. New York: Oxford University Press, 2000.

Dicou, Bert. *Edom, Israel's Brother and Antagonist: The Role of Edom in Biblical Prophecy and Story*. JSOTSup 169. Sheffield: JSOT, 1994.

Dille, Sarah J. "Honor Restored: Honor, Shame and God as Redeeming Kinsman in Second Isaiah." In *Relating to the Text: Interdisciplinary and Form-Critical Insights on the Bible*, edited by T. Sandoval and C. Mandolfo, 232–50. London: T&T Clark International, 2003.

Douglas, Mary. *In the Wilderness: The Doctrine of Defilement in the Book of Numbers*. Sheffield: Sheffield Academic, 1993.

Dozeman, Thomas B. *God at War: Power in the Exodus Tradition*. New York: Oxford University Press, 1996.

Drabinski, John E. *Levinas and the Postcolonial: Race, Nation, Other*. Edinburgh: Edinburgh University Press, 2013.

Duguid, Iain M. *Ezekiel*. NIV Application Commentary. Grand Rapids, MI: Zondervan, 1999.

Duhm, Bernhard. *Das Buch Jesaia*. Göttingen: Vandenhoeck & Ruprecht, 1902.

Dumont, Louis. *Homo Hierarchicus*. 2nd ed. Chicago: University of Chicago Press, 1980.

Durkheim, Emile. *The Elementary Forms of the Religious Life*. Translated by J. W. Swain. New York: The Free Press, 1915.

Durlesser, James A. *The Metaphorical Narratives in the Book of Ezekiel*. Lewiston, NY: Edwin Mellen, 2006.

Eidevall, Göran. *Prophecy and Propaganda: Images of Enemies in the Book of Isaiah*. ConBOT 56. Winona Lake, IN: Eisenbrauns, 2009.

Ellemers, Naomi, and S. Alexander Haslam. "Social Identity Theory." In *Handbook of Theories of Social Psychology*, edited by Paul A. M. Van Lange, Arie W. Kruglanski, and E. Tory Higgins, 379–98. 2 vols. Thousand Oaks, CA: SAGE, 2012.

Emmerson, Grace. *Isaiah 56–66*. T&T Clark Study Guides. New York: T&T Clark, 2004.

Erlandsson, Seth. *The Burden of Babylon: A Study of Isaiah 13:2–14:23*. ConBOT 4. Lund: CWK Gleerup, 1970.

Esler, Philip F. "Ezra–Nehemiah as a Narrative of (Re-Invented) Israelite Identity." *BibInt* 11 (2003): 413–26.

Evans-Pritchard, Sir Edward Evan. *The Nuer*. Oxford: Clarendon, 1940.

Exum, J. Cheryl. *Fragmented Women: Feminist (Sub)Versions of Biblical Narratives*. T&T Clark Cornerstones. Sheffield: JSOT, 1993.

Exum, J. Cheryl. "Whom Will He Teach Knowledge?" A Literary Approach to Isaiah 28." In *Art and Meaning: Rhetoric in Biblical Literature*, edited by David J. A. Clines, David M. Gunn, and Alan J. Hauser, 108–39. JSOTSup 19. Sheffield: JSOT, 1982.

Fabry, Heinz-Josef. *Nahum*. HThKAT. Herder: Freiburg im Breisgau, 2006.

Fanon, Frantz. *Black Skin, White Masks*. Translated by Richard Philcox. New York: Grove, 2008.

Fanon, Frantz. *The Wretched of the Earth*. Translated by Constance Farrington. New York: Grove, 1969.

Fantalkin, Alexander, and Oren Tal. "Redating Lachish Level I: Identifying Achaemenid Imperial Policy at the Southern Frontier of the Fifth Satrapy." In *Judah and the Judeans in the Persian Period*, edited by O. Lipschits and M. Oeming, 167–97. Winona Lake, IN: Eisenbrauns, 2006.
Finitsis, Antonio. "The Other in Haggai and Zechariah 1–8." In *The "Other" in Second Temple Judaism*, edited by Daniel C. Harlow et al., 116–31. Grand Rapids, MI: Eerdmans, 2011.
Finkelstein, Israel, and Amihay Mazar. *The Quest for the Historical Israel: Debating Archaeology and the History of Early Israel*. Edited by Brian B. Schmidt. ABS 17. Atlanta, GA: Society of Biblical Literature, 2007.
Foucault, Michel. *The Order of Things: An Archaeology of the Human Sciences*. London: Routledge, 1989.
Freud, Sigmund. "An Outline of Psycho-analysis." *International Journal of Psychoanalysis* 21 (1940): 27–84.
Freud, Sigmund. *The Ego and the Id*. Translated by Joan Riviere. Revised and edited by James Strachey. New York: Norton, 1960.
Gagne, A., A. Gignac, and G. Oegema (eds). *Constructing Religious Identities during the Second Temple Period/Construction des identités religieuses à l'époque du Second Temple*. Biblical Tools and Studies 24. Leuven: Peeters, 2016.
Galambush, Julie. *Jerusalem in the Book of Ezekiel: The City as Yahweh's Wife*. SBL Dissertation Series 130. Atlanta, GA: Scholar's Press, 1992.
Garrett, Don. "Introduction." In *The Cambridge Companion to Spinoza*, edited by Don Garrett, 1–12. Cambridge: Cambridge University Press, 1996.
Gelb, Ignace J., et al. 1956–2010. *The Assyrian Dictionary of the Oriental Institute of the University of Chicago*. 21 vols. Chicago: The Oriental Institute of the University of Chicago.
Genoni, Mia R. "Otherness, History of." In *Encyclopedia of Identity*, edited by Ronald L. Jackson II, 526–30. Thousand Oaks, CA: SAGE, 2010.
Gibson, Arthur. *Biblical Semantic Logic: A Preliminary Analysis*. 2nd ed. BibSem 75. Sheffield: Sheffield Academic, 2001.
Giovino, Mariana. *The Assyrian Sacred Tree: A History of Interpretations*. OBO 230. Fribourg: Academic, 2007.
Girard, René. *I See Satan Fall Like Lightning*. Translated by James G. Williams. Maryknoll, NY: Orbis, 2001.
Girard, René. *Mimesis and Theory: Essays on Literature and Criticism*. Edited by Robert Doran. Stanford, CA: Stanford University Press, 2008.
Girard, René. *Violence and the Sacred*. Translated by Patrick Gregory. London: Continuum, 2005.
Goldingay, John. *Isaiah*. NIBC. Peabody, MA: Hendrickson, 2001.
Goldingay, John. *Psalms 42–89*. Vol. 2 of *Psalms*. Baker Commentary on the Old Testament. Grand Rapids, MI: Baker Academic, 2007.
Gopal, Priyamvada. "Renegade Prophets and Native Acolytes: Liberalism and Imperialism Today." In *The Oxford Handbook of Postcolonial Studies*, edited by Graham Huggan, 197–216. Oxford: Oxford University Press, 2013.
Gossai, Hemchand (ed.). *Postcolonial Commentary and the Old Testament*. London: T&T Clark, 2019.
Gosse, Bernard. *Isaïe 13,1–14,23 dans la Tradition Littéraire du Livre d'Isaïe et dans la Tradition des Oracles Contre les Nations*. OBO 78. Freiburg: Universitätsverlag; Göttingen: Vandenhoeck & Ruprecht, 1988.

Grabbe, Lester. "'Many Nations will be Joined to YHWH in That Day': The Question of YHWH outside Judah." In *Religious Diversity in Ancient Israel and Judah*, edited by F. Stavrakopoulou and J. Barton, 175–87. London: T&T Clark, 2010.

Graybill, Rhiannon. *Are We Not Men? Unstable Masculinity in the Hebrew Prophets*. New York: Oxford University Press, 2016.

Graybill, Rhiannon. "Yahweh as Maternal Vampire in Second Isaiah: Reading from Violence to Fluid Possibility with Luce Irigaray." *Journal of Feminist Studies in Religion* 33 (2017): 9–25.

Graybill, Rhiannon, and Peter Sabo. "Caves of the Hebrew Bible: A Speleology." *BibInt* 26 (2018): 1–22.

Grayson, Albert Kirk. *Assyrian Royal Inscriptions, vol. 1: From the Beginning to Ashur-resha-isha I*. RANE. Wiesbaden: Otto Harrassowitz, 1972.

Green, Alberto R. W. *The Storm-God in the Ancient Near East*. Biblical and Judaic Studies 8. Winona Lake, IN: Eisenbrauns, 2003.

Greenberg, Moshe. "Ezekiel 17: A Holistic Interpretation." *JAOS* 103 (1983): 149–54.

Greenberg, Moshe. *Ezekiel 21–37: A New Translation with Introduction and Commentary*. AB 22A. New York: Doubleday, 1997.

Greenberg, Moshe. *Ezekiel: A New Translation with Introduction and Commentary*. AB 22. New York: Doubleday, 1997.

Grossman, Maxine L. "Is Ancient Jewish Studies (Still) Postmodern (Yet)?" *CBR* 13 (2015): 245–83.

Grosz, Elizabeth. *Sexual Subversions: Three French Feminists*. Sydney: Allen & Unwin, 1989.

Guillaume, Philippe. "Metamorphosis of a Ferocious Pharaoh." *Bib* 85 (2004): 232–6.

Hagedorn, Anselm C. *Die Anderen im Spiegel: Israels Auseinandersetzung mit den Völkern in den Büchern Nahum, Zefanja, Obadja und Joel*. BZAW 414. Berlin: de Gruyter, 2011.

Hagedorn, Anselm. "Institutions and Social Life in Ancient Israel: Sociological Aspects." In *Hebrew Bible/Old Testament: The History of Its Interpretation*, vol. 3.2. *The Twentieth Century: From Modernism to Post-Modernism*, edited by M. Sæbø, 58–95. Göttingen: Vandenhoeck & Ruprecht, 2015.

Hall, Stuart. "Introduction." In *Representation: Cultural Representations and Signifying Practices*, edited by Stuart Hall, 1–12. London: Sage, 2003.

Hall, Stuart. "The Spectacle of the 'Other.'" In *Representation: Cultural Representations and Signifying Practices*, edited by Stuart Hall, 223–90. London: Sage, 2003.

Hall, Stuart. "The Work of Representation." In *Representation: Cultural Representations and Signifying Practices*, edited by Stuart Hall, 13–74. London: Sage, 2003.

Halpern, Baruch. "'The Excremental Vision': The Doomed Priests of Doom in Isaiah 28." *HAR* 10 (1986): 109–21.

Hals, Ronald M. *Ezekiel*. FOTL 19. Grand Rapids, MI: Eerdmans, 1989.

Haney, Linda. "Yhwh, the God of Israel…and of Edom? The Relationships in the Oracle to Edom in Jeremiah 49:7–22." In *Uprooting and Planting: Essays on Jeremiah for Leslie Allen*, edited by John Goldingay, 78–115. LHBOTS 459. New York: T&T Clark, 2007.

Hansen, Nicole B. "Snakes." In *Oxford Encyclopedia of Ancient Egypt*, edited by D. B. Redford, 3:297–8. 3 vols. Oxford: Oxford University Press, 2001.

Hanson, Paul D. *The Dawn of Apocalyptic: The Historical and Sociological Roots of Jewish Apocalyptic Eschatology*. Philadelphia: Fortress, 1979.

Hanson, Paul D. *Isaiah 40–66*. Interpretation. A Biblical Commentary for Teaching and Preaching. Louisville, KY: Westminster John Knox, 1995.

Harding, James. "In the Name of Love: Resisting Reader and Abusive Redeemer in Deutero-Isaiah." *The Bible and Critical Theory* 2, no. 2 (2006): 14.1–14.15.

Harlow, D. C., K. M. Hogan, M. Goff and J. S. Kaminsky (eds). *The "Other" in Second Temple Judaism: Essays in Honor of John J. Collins*. Grand Rapids, MI: Eerdmans, 2011.

Harries, Karsten. "Metaphor and Transcendence" *Critical Inquiry* 5 (1978): 73–90.

Hayes, John H. "Amos's Oracles Against the Nations." *RevExp* 92 (1995): 153–67.

Hayes, John H., and Stuart A. Irvine. *Isaiah: The Eighth Century Prophet, His Times and His Preaching*. Nashville, TN: Abingdon, 1987.

Hegel, G. W. F. *The Phenomenology of Spirit*. Translated by Michael Inwood. Oxford: Oxford University Press, 2018.

Hill Collins, Patricia. "Learning from the Outside Within: The Sociological Significance of Black Feminist Thought." *Social Problems* 33 (1986): 14–32.

Høgenhaven, Jesper. *Gott und Volk bei Jesaja: Eine Untersuchung zur Biblischen Theologie*. Acta Theologica Danica. Leiden: Brill, 1988.

Hogg, Michael A. "Social Identity Theory." In *Encyclopedia of Identity*, edited by Ronald L. Jackson II, 749–52. Thousand Oaks, CA: SAGE, 2010.

Holladay, William L. "Was Trito-Isaiah Deutero-Isaiah After All?" In *Writing and Reading the Scroll of Isaiah: Studies of an Interpretive Tradition*, edited by Craig C. Broyles and Craig A. Evans, 1:193–217. FOTL 1. VTSup 70. Leiden: Brill, 1997.

hooks, bell. "Feminism as a Persistent Critique of History: What's Love Got to Do with It?" In *The Fact of Blackness: Franz Fanon and Representation*, edited by Alan Read, 76–86. London: ICA, 1996.

Horrell, David G. (ed.). *Social-Scientific Approaches to New Testament Interpretation*. Edinburgh: T. & T. Clark, 1999.

Howard-Brook, Wes. *"Come Out, My People!" God's Call out of Empire in the Bible and Beyond*. Maryknoll, NY: Orbis, 2010.

Huddart, David. *Homi K. Bhabha*. New York: Routledge, 2006.

Huey, F. B., Jr. *Jeremiah, Lamentations*. NAC 16. Nashville, TN: Broadman & Holman, 1993.

Hulster, Izaak J. de. *Iconographic Exegesis and Third Isaiah*. FAT 2/36. Tübingen: Mohr Siebeck, 2009.

Hutchinson, John, and Anthony D. Smith. "Introduction." In *Ethnicity*, edited by John Hutchinson and Anthony D. Smith, 3–15. Oxford: Oxford University Press, 1996.

Irigaray, Luce. "The Bodily Encounter with the Mother." In *The Irigaray Reader*, edited by Margaret Whitford, 34–46. Cambridge, MA: Blackwell, 1991.

Irigaray, Luce. "How Can We Meet the Other?" In *Otherness: A Multilateral Perspective*, edited by Susan Yi Sencindiver, Maria Beville, and Marie Lauritzen, 107–20. Frankfurt: Peter Lang, 2011.

Irigaray, Luce. *Marine Lover of Friedrich Nietzsche*. Translated by Gillian C. Gill. New York: Columbia University Press, 1991.

Irigaray, Luce. *Sexes and Genealogies*. Translated by Gillian C. Gill. New York: Columbia University Press, 1993.

Irigaray, Luce. *Speculum of the Other Woman*. Translated by Gillian C. Gill. Ithaca, NY: Cornell University Press, 1985.

Irigaray, Luce. *Thinking the Difference: For a Peaceful Revolution*. Translated by Karin Montin. London: Athlone, 2001.

Irigaray, Luce. *This Sex Which Is Not One*. Translated by Catherine Porter. Ithaca, NY: Cornell University Press, 1985.

Irudayaraj, Dominic S. "Edom, the Proximate 'Other': Persisting Category and Permeable Boundary. A Social Identity Reading of Isaiah 63:1-6." Paper presented at the SBL Annual Meeting, San Diego, CA, 2014.

Irudayaraj, Dominic S. *Violence, Otherness, and Identity in Isaiah 63:1–6: The Trampling One Coming from Edom*. LHBOTS 633. London/New York: Bloomsbury T&T Clark, 2017.

Isherwood, Lisa, and David Harris. *Radical Otherness: Sociological and Theological Approaches*. Durham, UK: Acumen, 2013.

Jackson, Ronald L. II. "Introduction." In *Encyclopedia of Identity*, edited by R. L. Jackson II, 1:xxv–xxvii. 2 vols. Thousand Oaks, CA: SAGE, 2010.

James, E. O. *The Tree of Life: An Archaeological Study*. Leiden: Brill, 1966.

JanMohamed, Abdul R. "The Economy of Manichean Allegory." In *The Postcolonial Studies Reader*, edited by Bill Ashcroft, Gareth Griffiths, and Helen Tiffin, 18–23. London: Routledge, 1995.

Jenkins, Richard. "Society and Social Identity." In *Encyclopedia of Identity*, edited by Ronald L. Jackson II, 766–72. Thousand Oaks, CA: SAGE, 2010.

Jensen, Sune Q. "Othering, Identity Formation and Agency." *Qualitative Studies* 2, no. 2 (2011): 63–78.

Jeremias, Jorg. *The Book of Amos*. Translated by D. W. Stott. OTL. Louisville, KY: Westminster John Knox, 1998.

Jervis, John. *Transgressing the Modern: Explorations in the Western Experience of Otherness*. Oxford: Blackwell, 1999.

Johnson, Nuala C., Richard H. Schein, and Jamie Winders. "Introduction." In *Wiley-Blackwell Companion to Cultural Geography*, edited by Nuala C. Johnson, Richard H. Schein, and Jamie Winders, 1–13. Malden, MA: Wiley-Blackwell, 2013.

Johnson, Scott Fitzgerald. *Literary Territories: Cartographical Thinking in Late Antiquity*. New York: Oxford University Press. 2016

Jokiranta, Jutta. "Sectarianism." In *The Eerdmans Dictionary of Early Judaism*, edited by J. J. Collins and D. C. Harlow, 1209–11. Grand Rapids, MI: Eerdmans, 2010.

Jokiranta, Jutta. *Social Identity and Sectarianism in the Qumran Movement*. STDJ 105. Leiden: Brill, 2013.

Jokiranta, Jutta. "Social Identity Approach: Identity-Construction Elements in the Psalms Pesher." In *Defining Identities: We, You, and the Other in the Dead Sea Scrolls: Proceedings of the Fifth Meeting of the IOQS in Gröningen*, edited by F. G. Martínez and M. Popović, 85–109. STDJ 70. Boston, MA: Brill, 2008.

Jokiranta, Jutta. "Social-Scientific Approaches to the Dead Sea Scrolls." In *Rediscovering the Dead Sea Scrolls: An Assessment of Old and New Approaches and Methods*, edited by Maxine L. Grossman, 246–63. Grand Rapids, MI: Eerdmans, 2010.

Jones, Brian C. *Howling over Moab: Irony and Rhetoric in Isaiah 15–16*. SBL Dissertation Series 157. Atlanta, GA: Scholars, 1996.

Joyce, Paul M. *Ezekiel: A Commentary*. LHBOTS 482. London: T&T Clark, 2007.

Kaiser, Otto. *Isaiah 13–39*. Translated by R. A. Wilson. OTL. London: SCM, 1980. German rev. ed.: *Der Prophet Jesaja Kapitel 13–39*. ATD 18. Göttingen: Vandenhoeck & Ruprecht, 1983.

Kalmanofsky, Amy. "'As She Did, Do to Her!': Jeremiah's OAN as Revenge Fantasies." In *Concerning the Nations: Essays on the Oracles Against the Nations in Isaiah, Jeremiah and Ezekiel*, edited by Else K. Holt, Hyun Chul Paul Kim, and Andrew Mein, 109–27. LHBOTS 612. London: Bloomsbury T&T Clark, 2015.

Kaminsky, Joel. *Yet I Loved Jacob: Reclaiming the Biblical Concept of Election*. Nashville, TN: Abingdon, 2007.

Kamionkowski, S. Tamar. *Gender Reversal and Cosmic Chaos: A Study on the Book of Ezekiel*. JSOTSup 368. Sheffield: Sheffield Academic, 2003.

Kearney, Richard. *Strangers, Gods and Monsters: Interpreting Otherness*. London: Routledge, 2003.

Keel, Othmar. *The Symbolism of the Biblical World: Ancient Near Eastern Iconography and the Book of Psalms*. Translated by Timothy J. Hallett. New York: Seabury, 1978. Repr. Winona Lake, IN: Eisenbrauns, 1997.

Kelm, George L. "Edom/Edomites/Idumaea." In *Mercer Dictionary of the Bible*, edited by W. E. Mills and R. A. Bullard, 232–3. Macon, GA: Mercer University Press, 1990.

Kelso, Julie. *O Mother, Where Art Thou? An Irigarayan Reading of the Book of Chronicles*. Oakville, CT: Equinox, 2007.

Kelso, Julie. "Reading the Silence of Women in Genesis 34." In *Redirected Travel: Alternative Journeys and Places in Biblical Studies*, edited by Roland Boer and Edgar W. Conrad, 85–109. JSOTSup 382. New York: T&T Clark, 2003.

Kessler, Rainer. *Maleachi*. HThKAT. Freiburg: Herder, 2011.

Khader, Jamil. *Cartographies of Transnationalism in Postcolonial Feminisms: Geography, Culture, Identity, Politics*. Lanham, MD: Lexington, 2013.

Killebrew, Ann E. *Biblical Peoples and Ethnicity*. ABS 9. Atlanta, GA: SBL, 2005.

Kim, Hyun Chul Paul. *Reading Isaiah: A Literary and Theological Commentary*. Reading the Old Testament. Macon, GA: Smyth & Helwys, 2016.

Koole, Jan L. *Isaiah, vol. 3*. HCOT. Leuven: Peeters, 2001.

Kuhrt, Amélie. "The Problem of Achaemenid 'Religious Policy'." In *Die Welt der Götterbilder*, edited by B. Groneberg and H. Spieckermann, 117–42. BZAW 376. Berlin: de Gruyter, 2007.

Lacan, Jacques. *Formations of the Unconscious: The Seminary of Jacques Lacan, Book V*. Edited by Jacques-Alain Miller. Translated by Russell Grigg. Cambridge: Polity, 1998.

Lacan, Jacques. *The Language of the Self: The Function of Language in Psychoanalysis*. Translated by Anthony Wilden. Baltimore, MD: The Johns Hopkins University Press, 1968.

Lacan, Jacques. *The Seminar of Jacques Lacan. Book XI The Four Fundamental Concepts of Psychoanalysis*. Edited by Jacques-Alain Miller. Translated by Alan Sheridan. New York: Norton, 1978.

Lakoff, George, and Elisabeth Wehling. *Your Brain's Politics: How the Science of Mind Explains the Political Divide*. Exeter: Imprint, 2016.

Lakoff, George. *Metaphors We Live By*. Chicago: Chicago University Press, 1980.

Lakoff, George. *Women, Fire, and Dangerous Things: What Categories Reveal about the Mind*. Chicago: University of Chicago Press. 1982.

Landy, Francis. "Fluvial Fantasies." In *Thinking of Water in the Early Second Temple Period*, edited by Ehud Ben Zvi and Christoph Levin, 437–56. BZAW 461. Berlin: de Gruyter, 2014.

Lapsley, Jacqueline E. "Shame and Self-Knowledge: The Positive Role of Shame in Ezekiel's View of the Moral Self." In *The Book of Ezekiel: Theological and Anthropological Perspectives*, edited by Margaret S. Odell and John T. Strong, 143–74. Atlanta, GA: SBL, 2000.

Larsen, Svend Erik. "How to Narrate the Other." In *Otherness: A Multilateral Perspective*, edited by Susan Yi Sencindiver, Maria Beville, and Marie Lauritzen, 201–20. Frankfurt: Peter Lang, 2011.
Lau, Peter. "Gentile Incorporation into Israel in Ezra–Nehemiah." *Bib* 90 (2009): 356–73.
Lavik, Marta Høyland. *A People Tall and Smooth-Skinned: The Rhetoric of Isaiah 18*. VTSup 112. Leiden: Brill, 2007.
Leander, Hans. *Discourses of Empire: The Gospel of Mark from a Postcolonial Perspective*. Atlanta, GA: SBL, 2013.
Lemos, T. M. "The Emasculation of Exile: Hypermasculinity and Feminization in the Book of Ezekiel." In *Interpreting Exile: Displacement and Deportation in Biblical and Modern Contexts*, edited by Brad Kelle, Frank Ritchel Ames, and Jacob L. Wright, 377–96. AIL 10. Atlanta, GA: SBL, 2011.
Levenson, Jon D. "The Universal Horizon of Biblical Particularism." In *Ethnicity and the Bible*, ed. M. Brett, 143–69. BibInt 19. Leiden: Brill, 1996.
Lévinas, Emmanuel. *Totality and Infinity: An Essay on Exteriority*. Translated by Alphonso Lingis. The Hague: Martinus Nijhoff, 1979.
Levine, Baruch A. "Some Indices of Israelite Ethnicity." In *Ethnicity in Ancient Mesopotamia: Papers Read at the 48th Rencontre Assyriologique Internationale, Leiden, 1–4 July 2002*, edited by W. H. van Soldt, 189–97. Leiden: Nederlands Instituut voor het Nabije Oosten, 2005.
Lewis, Theodore J. "*CT* 13.33-34 and Ezekiel 32: Lion-Dragon Myths." *JAOS* 116 (1996): 28–47.
Liss, Hanna. *Die Unerhörte Wort: Kommunikative Strukturen prophetische Rede im Buch Yesha'yahu*. ABG 14. Leipzig: Evangelische Verlagsanstalt, 2003.
Løland, Hanne. *Silent or Salient Gender? The Interpretation of Gendered God–Language in the Hebrew Bible, Exemplified in Isaiah 42, 46 and 49*. FAT 2/32. Tübingen: Mohr Siebeck, 2007.
Loomba, Ania. *Colonialism/Postcolonialism*. 3rd ed. New York: Routledge, 2015.
Lubetski, Meir, and Claire Gottlieb. "Isaiah 18: The Egyptian Nexus." In *Boundaries of the Ancient World: A Tribute to Cyrus Gordon*, edited by Meir Lubetski, Claire Gottlieb, and Sharon Keller, 364–84. JSOTSup 273. Sheffield: Sheffield Academic, 1986.
Lundbom, Jack M. *Jeremiah: A New Translation with Introduction and Commentary*. AB 21. New York: Doubleday, 2004.
Lynch, Matthew J. "Zion's Warrior and the Nations: Isaiah 59:15b–63:6 in Isaiah's Zion Traditions." *CBQ* 70 (2008): 244–63.
Lyons, C. W., and Thomas Deliduka. *The Catholic Bible Concordance: Revised Standard Version, Catholic Edition*. Steubenville, OH: Emmaus Road, 2009.
MacDonald, Burton. "Edom, Edomites." In *Dictionary of the Old Testament: Historical Books*, edited by B. T. Arnold and H. G. M. Williamson, 231–6. Downers Grove, IL: InterVarsity, 2011.
Macey, David. *Frantz Fanon: A Biography*. 2nd ed. New York: Verso, 2012.
Machinist, Peter. "Distinctiveness in Ancient Israel." In *Ah, Assyria! Studies in Assyrian History and Ancient Near Eastern Historiography Presented to Hayim Tadmor*, edited by M. Cogan and I. Eph'al, 196–212. ScrHier 33. Jerusalem: Magnes, 1991.
Macintosh, Andrew A. *Isaiah XXI: A Palimpsest*. Cambridge: Cambridge University Press, 1980.
Malina, Bruce J. *The New Testament World: Insights from Cultural Anthropology*. Rev. ed. Louisville, KY: Westminster John Knox, 1993.
Mann, Charles C. *1493: Uncovering the New World Columbus Invented*. New York: Knopf, 2011.

Marzouk, Safwat. *Egypt as a Monster in the Book of Ezekiel.* FAT 2/76. Tübingen: Mohr Siebeck, 2015.
Mayes, Andrew D. H. "Idealism and Materialism in Weber and Gottwald." *Proceedings of the Irish Biblical Association* 11 (1988): 44–8.
Mayes, Andrew D. H. "Sociology of the Old Testament." In *The World of Ancient Israel: Sociological, Anthropological and Political Perspectives*, edited by R. E. Clements, 39–63. Cambridge: Cambridge University Press, 1989.
Mayfield, Tyler. *Literary Structure and Setting in Ezekiel.* FAT 2/43. Tübingen: Mohr Siebeck, 2010.
McClure, Laura. *Spoken Like a Woman: Speech and Gender in Athenian Drama.* Princeton, NJ: Princeton University Press, 2009.
McInerney, Jeremy. "Ethnicity: An Introduction." In *A Companion to Ethnicity in the Ancient Mediterranean*, edited by J. McInerney, 1–16. BCAW. Oxford: Wiley-Blackwell, 2014.
McKittrick, Katherine. *Demonic Grounds: Black Women and the Cartographies of Struggle.* Minneapolis, MN: University of Minnesota Press, 2006.
McLeod, John. *Beginning Postcolonialism.* 2nd ed. Manchester: Manchester University Press, 2012.
Mein, Andrew. "Ezekiel: Structure, Themes, and Contested Issues." In *The Oxford Handbook of the Prophets*, edited by Carolyn J. Sharp, 190–206. Oxford: Oxford University Press, 2016.
Memmi, Albert. *The Colonizer and the Colonized.* Translated by Howard Greenfeld. Boston: Beacon, 1965.
Mendenhall, George. "The Hebrew Conquest of Palestine." *BibArch* 25 (1962): 66–87.
Mercer, Kobena. "Decolonisation and Disappointment: Reading Fanon's Sexual Politics." In *The Fact of Blackness: Franz Fanon and Representation*, edited by Alan Read, 114–26. London: ICA, 1996.
Merish, Lori, *Sentimental Materialism: Gender, Commodity Culture, and Nineteenth Century African American Literature.* Durham, NC: Duke University Press, 2000.
Miller, James C. "Ethnicity and the Hebrew Bible: Problems and Prospects." *CBR* 6 (2008): 170–213.
Mills, Mary E. *Alterity, Pain, and Suffering in Isaiah, Jeremiah, and Ezekiel.* LHBOTS 479. New York: T&T Clark, 2007.
Mmembe, Achille. "Necropolics." *Public Culture* 15 (2003): 11–40.
Moore, Stephen D. *Empire and Apocalypse: Postcolonialism and the New Testament.* BMW 12. Sheffield: Sheffield Phoenix, 2006.
Moore, Stephen D. *Gospel Jesuses and Other Nonhumans: Biblical Criticism Postpoststructuralism.* SemeiaSt 89. Atlanta, GA: SBL, 2017.
Moore, Stephen D., and Yvonne Sherwood. *The Invention of the Biblical Scholars: A Critical Manifesto.* Minneapolis, MN: Fortress, 2011.
Morrison, Toni. *The Origin of Others.* Cambridge, MA: Harvard University Press, 2017.
Morrissey, John. "The Imperial Present: Geography, Imperialism, and Its Continued Effects." In *Wiley-Blackwell Companion to Cultural Geography*, edited by Nuala C. Johnson, Richard H. Schein, and Jamie Winders, 494–507. Malden, MA: Wiley-Blackwell, 2013.
Mouffe, Chantal. "An Agonistic Approach to the Future of Europe." *New Literary History* 43 (2012): 629–40.
Müller, Maya. "Re and Re-Horakhty." In *Oxford Encyclopedia of Ancient Egypt*, edited by D. B. Redford, 3:125. 3 vols. Oxford: Oxford University Press, 2001.

Murphy, Roland. *The Tree of Life: An Exploration of Biblical Wisdom Literature*. 3rd ed. Grand Rapids, MI: Eerdmans, 2002.
Nayar, Pramod K. *Postcolonial Literature: An Introduction*. New Delhi: Pearson, 2008.
Newsom, Carol A., and Brennan W. Breed. *Daniel*. OTL. Louisville, KY: Westminster John Knox, 2014.
Newsom, Carol. "A Maker of Metaphors—Ezekiel's Oracles Against Tyre." *Int* 38 (1984): 151–64.
Niccacci, Alviero. "Isaiah XVIII–XX from an Egyptological Perspective" *VT* 48 (1998): 214–38.
Niehr, Herbert. "God of Heaven." *DDD* 370–2.
Nietzsche, Friedrich. *Beyond Good and Evil: Prelude to a Philosophy of the Future*. Edited by Rolf-Peter Horstmann. Translated by Judith Norman. Cambridge Texts in the History of Philosophy. New York: Cambridge University Press, 2002.
Nickelsburg, George W. E., and James C. VanderKam. *First Enoch*. Minneapolis, MN: Fortress, 2004.
Niskanen, Paul V. *Isaiah 56–66*. Berit Olam. Collegeville, MN: Liturgical, 2014.
O'Keefe, Alice. *Woman's Body and the Social Body in Hosea*. JSOTSup 338. Sheffield: Sheffield Academic, 2001.
Oswalt, John. *The Book of Isaiah: Chapters 1–39*. NICOT. Grand Rapids, MI: Eerdmans, 1986.
Parpola, Simo. "The Assyrian Tree of Life: Tracing the Origins of Jewish Monotheism and Greek Philosophy." *JNES* 52 (1993): 161–208.
Patton, Corrine L. "Should Our Sister be Treated Like a Whore?" In *The Book of Ezekiel: Theological and Anthropological Perspectives*, edited by Margaret S. Odell and John T. Strong, 221–38. Atlanta, GA: SBL, 2000.
Paul, Shalom. *Amos: A Commentary on the Book of Amos*. Hermeneia. Minneapolis, MN: Augsburg Fortress, 1991.
Paul, Shalom M. *Isaiah 40–66: Translation and Commentary*. ECC. Grand Rapids, MI: Eerdmans, 2012.
Penrose, Walter Duvall. *Postcolonial Amazons: Female Masculinity and Courage in Ancient Greek and Sanskrit Literature*. New York: Oxford University Press, 2016.
Perdue, Leo G. *Reconstructing Old Testament Theology: After the Collapse of History*. OBT. Minneapolis, MN: Fortress, 2005.
Pleins, David. *The Social Visions of the Hebrew Bible: A Theological Introduction*. Louisville, KY: Westminster John Knox, 2001.
Porter, Barbara Nevling. "Sacred Trees, Date Palms, and the Royal Persona of Ashurnasirpal II." *JNES* 52 (1993): 129–39.
Pritchard, James B. (ed.). *The Ancient Near East: An Anthology of Texts and Pictures*. Princeton, NJ: Princeton University Press, 2011.
Pritchard, James B. (ed.). *Ancient Near Eastern Texts Relating to the Old Testament*. 3rd ed. Princeton, NJ: Princeton University Press, 1969.
Punter, David. *Postcolonial Imaginings: Fictions of a New World Order*. Edinburgh: Edinburgh University Press, 2000.
Radman, Zdravko. "How to Make Our Ideas Clear with Metaphors." In *From a Metaphorical Point of View: A Multidisciplinary Approach to the Cognitive Content of Metaphor*, edited by Zdravko Radman, 225–58. PW 7. Brill: de Gruyter, 1995.
Radman, Zdravko. *Metaphors: Figures of the Mind*. Library of Rhetoric 4. Berlin: Springer Science & Business Media, 1997.
Ramírez Kidd, José E. *Alterity and Identity in Israel*. BZAW 283. Berlin: de Gruyter, 1999.

Ramsey, E. "Philosophical History of Identity." In *Encyclopedia of Identity*, edited by Ronald L. Jackson II, 556–60. Thousand Oaks, CA: SAGE, 2010.

Read, James H. "Thomas Hobbes: Power in the State of Nature, Power in Civil Society." *Polity* 23 (1991): 505–25.

Redford, Donald B., ed. *The Oxford Encyclopedia of Ancient Egypt*. 3 vols. Oxford: Oxford University Press, 2001.

Reynolds, Nedra. *Geographies of Writing: Inhabiting Places and Encountering Difference*. Carbondale, IL: Southern Illinois University Press, 2007.

Richter, Sandra. *The Deuteronomic History and Name Theology: lešakkēn šemō šām in the Bible and the Ancient Near East*. BZAW 318. Berlin: de Gruyter, 2002.

Ritner, Robert K. "The Cult of the Dead." In *Ancient Egypt*, edited by David P. Silverman, 132–47. Oxford: Oxford University Press, 1997.

Roberts, J. J. M. *First Isaiah*. Hermeneia. Minneapolis, MN: Fortress, 2015.

Runions, Erin. (2016) "Biobible: Biblical Provocations to Biocapital in the US Culture Wars." *The Bible and Critical Theory* 12 (2016): 1–23.

Runions, Erin. "Political Theologies of the Surveilled Womb?" *Political Theology* 16 (2015): 301–4.

Sadler, Rodney S., Jr. *Can a Cushite Change His Skin? An Examination of Race, Ethnicity, and Othering in the Hebrew Bible*. LHBOTS 425. London: T&T Clark, 2005.

Said, Edward. *Culture and Imperialism*. New York: Alfred Knopf, 1993.

Sawyer, John F. A. *Isaiah*. The Daily Study Bible Series. 2 vols. Louisville, KY: Westminster John Knox, 1984–1986.

Sawyer, John F. A. "Radical Images of Yahweh in Isaiah 63." In *Among the Prophets: Language, Image and Structure in the Prophetic Writings*, edited by P. R. Davies and D. J. A. Clines, 72–82. JSOTSup 144. Sheffield: JSOT, 1993.

Schermerhorn, R. A. *Comparative Ethnic Relations: A Framework for Theory and Research*. 2nd ed. Chicago: University of Chicago Press, 1978.

Schmitt, John J. "The City as Woman in Isaiah 1–39." In *Writing and Reading the Scroll of Isaiah: Studies in an Interpretive Tradition*, edited by Craig C. Broyles and Craig A. Evans, 1:95–120. VTSup 70. 2 vols. Leiden: Brill, 1997.

Schramm, Brooks. *The Opponents of Third Isaiah: Reconstructing the Cultic History of the Restoration*. JSOTSup 193. Sheffield: JSOT, 1995.

Segovia, Fernando F., and R. S. Sugirtharajah (eds). *A Postcolonial Commentary on the New Testament*. London: Bloomsbury/T&T Clark, 2007.

Sharp, Carolyn J. "Embodying Moab: The Figuring of Moab in Jeremiah 48 as Reinscription of the Judean Body." In *Concerning the Nations: Essays on the Oracles Against the Nations in Isaiah, Jeremiah and Ezekiel*, edited by Else K. Holt, Hyun Chul Paul Kim, and Andrew Mein, 95–108. LHBOTS 612. London: Bloomsbury, 2015.

Sharp, Carolyn J. "The Formation of Godly Community: Old Testament Hermeneutics in the Presence of the Other." *AThR* 86 (2004): 623–36.

Sheriffs, Deryck. *The Friendship of the LORD*. Carlisle: Paternoster, 1996.

Shields, Mary E. "An Abusive God? Identity and Power, Gender and Violence in Ezekiel 23." In *Postmodern Interpretations of the Bible: A Reader*, edited by A. K. M. Adam, 129–51. St. Louis, MO: Chalice, 2001.

Sidaway, James D. "Postcolonial Geographies: Survey-Explore-Review." In *Postcolonial Geographies*, edited by Alison Blunt and Cheryl McEwan, 11–28. New York: Continuum, 2002.

Sluyter, Andrew. *Colonialism and Landscape: Postcolonial Theory and Applications*. Lanham, MD: Rowman & Littlefield, 2002.

Smith, Antony. "Migrancy, Hybridity, and Postcolonial Literary Studies." In *The Cambridge Companion to Postcolonial Literary Studies*, edited by N. Lazarus, 241–61. Cambridge: Cambridge University Press, 2004.

Smith, Jonathan Z. *Relating Religion: Essays in the Study of Religion*. Chicago: University of Chicago Press, 2004.

Smith, Jonathan Z. "What a Difference a Difference Makes." In *"To See Ourselves as Others See Us": Christians, Jews, "Others" in Late Antiquity*, edited by Jacob Neusner, Ernest S. Frerichs, and Caroline McCracken-Flesher, 3–48. Chico, CA: Scholars Press, 1985.

Smith, Mark S. *God in Translation: Deities in Cross-Cultural Discourse in the Biblical World*. Grand Rapids, MI: Eerdmans, 2010.

Smith, Mark S. *The Origins of Biblical Monotheism: Israel's Polytheistic Background and the Ugaritic Texts*. New York: Oxford University Press, 2003.

Smith, Mark S. *The Rituals and Myths of the Feast of the Goodly Gods of KTU/CAT 1.23: Royal Constructions of Opposition, Intersection, Integration, and Domination*. Atlanta, GA: Society of Biblical Literature, 2006.

Smith, Paul Allan. *Rhetoric and Redaction in Trito-Isaiah: The Structure, Growth, and Authorship of Isaiah 56–66*. VTSup 62. Leiden: Brill, 1995.

Smith, Gary V. *Isaiah 40–66*. NAC 15B. Nashville, TN: Broadman & Holman, 2009.

Smith-Christopher, Daniel L. *A Biblical Theology of Exile*. OBT. Minneapolis, MN: Fortress, 2002. 342

Smith-Christopher, Daniel. "Ezekiel in Abu Ghraib: Rereading Ezekiel 16:37-39 in the Context of Imperial Conquest." In *Ezekiel's Hierarchical World: Wrestling with a Tiered Reality*, edited by Stephen L. Cook and Corrine L. Patton, 141–58. Atlanta, GA: Society of Biblical Literature, 2004.

Smith-Christopher, Daniel. "Reading Exile Then: Reconsidering the Methodological Debates for Biblical Analysis in Dialogue with Sociological and Literary Analysis." In *By the Irrigation Canals of Babylon: Approaches to the Study of Exile*, edited by John J. Ahn and Jill Middlemas, 135–57. LHBOTS 526. New York: T&T Clark, 2012.

Smothers, Thomas G. "Isaiah 15–16." In *Forming Prophetic Literature: Essays on Isaiah and the Twelve in Honor of John D. W. Watts*, edited by James W. Watts and Paul R. House, 70–84. JSOTSup 235. Sheffield: Sheffield Academic, 1996.

Snyman, S. D. (Fanie). *Malachi*. HCOT. Leuven: Peeters, 2015.

Sommer, Benjamin D. "Dating Pentateuchal Texts and the Perils of Pseudo-Historicism." In *The Pentateuch: International Perspectives on Current Research*, edited by T. B. Dozeman, K. Schmid, and B. W. Schwartz, 85–108. FAT 78. Tübingen: Mohr Siebeck, 2011.

Sparks, Kenton. *Ethnicity and Identity in Ancient Israel*. Winona Lake, IN: Eisenbrauns, 1998.

Spears, Russell. "Social Identity, Legitimacy, and Intergroup Conflict: The Rocky Road to Reconciliation." In *Social Psychology of Intergroup Reconciliation*, edited by Arie Nadler, Thomas E. Malloy, and Jeffrey D. Fisher, 319–45. New York: Oxford University Press, 2008.

Spickard, James V. "A Revised Functionalism in the Sociology of Religion: Mary Douglas's Recent Work." *Religion* 21 (1991): 141–64.

Spivak, Gayatri Chakravorty. *An Aesthetic Education in the Era of Globalization*. Cambridge, MA: Harvard University Press, 2012.

Stec, David M. *The Targum of Psalms*. ArBib 16. New York: T&T Clark, 2004.

Stets, Jan E., and Peter J. Burke. "A Sociological Approach to Self and Identity." In *Handbook of Self and Identity*, edited by Mark R. Leary and June P. Tangney, 128–52. New York: Guilford, 2003.

Stökl, Jonathan. "Schoolboy Ezekiel: Remarks on the Transmission of Learning." *De Welt des Orients* 45 (2015): 50–61.

Stoler, Ann Laura. *Carnal Knowledge and Imperial Power: Race and the Intimate in Colonial Rule*. 2nd ed. Berkeley, CA: University of California Press, 2010.

Strawn, Brent A. *What Is Stronger than a Lion? Leonine Image and Metaphor in the Hebrew Bible and the Ancient Near East*. OBO 212. Göttingen: Vandenhoeck & Ruprecht, 2005.

Strong, John T. Review of *The Opponents of Third Isaiah: Reconstructing the Cultic History of the Restoration*, by Brooks Schramm. *CBQ* 58 (1996): 333–4.

Sugirtharajah, R. S. "A Brief Memorandum on Postcolonialism and Biblical Studies." *JSNT* 73 (1999): 3–5.

Sugirtharajah, R. S. *Exploring Postcolonial Biblical Criticism: History, Method, Practice*. Chichester: Wiley-Blackwell, 2012.

Sweeney, Marvin A. *Isaiah 1–39, With an Introduction to Prophetic Literature*. FOTL 16. Grand Rapids, MI: Eerdmans, 1996.

Talmon, Shemaryahu. "The Emergence of Jewish Sectarianism in the Early Second Temple Period." In *Ancient Israelite Religion: Essays in Honor of Frank Moore Cross*, edited by P. D. Miller, P. D. Hanson, and S. D. McBride, 587–616. Minneapolis, MN: Fortress, 1987.

Tanghe, Vincent. "Dichtung und Ekel in Jesaja XXVIII 7-13." *VT* 43 (1993): 235–60.

Thelle, Ranfrid. "Babylon as Judah's *Doppelgänger*: The Identity of Opposites in the Book of Jeremiah (MT)." In *Concerning the Nations: Essays on the Oracles Against the Nations in Isaiah, Jeremiah and Ezekiel*, edited by Else K. Holt, Hyun Chul Paul Kim, and Andrew Mein, 77–94. LHBOTS 612. London: Bloomsbury, 2015.

Tiemeyer, Lena-Sofia. "Continuity and Discontinuity in Isaiah 40–66: History of Research." In *Continuity and Discontinuity: Chronological and Thematic Development in Isaiah 40–66*, edited by L.-S. Tiemeyer and H. M. Barstad, 13–40. FRLANT 225. Göttingen: Vandenhoeck & Ruprecht, 2014.

Tiller, Patrick A. *A Commentary on the Animal Apocalypse*. Atlanta, GA: Scholars Press, 1993.

Tiller, Patrick A. "The 'Eternal Planting' in the Dead Sea Scrolls." *DSD* 4 (1997): 312–35.

Timmer, Daniel C. "Boundaries without Judah, Boundaries within Judah: Hybridity and Identity in Nahum." *HBT* 34 (2012): 173–89.

Timmer, Daniel C. *Nahum: A Discourse Analysis of the Hebrew Bible*. ZECOT. Grand Rapids, MI: Zondervan Academic, 2020.

Timmer, Daniel C. *The Non-Israelite Nations in the Book of the Twelve: Thematic Coherence and the Diachronic–Synchronic Relationship in the Minor Prophets*. BibInt 135. Leiden: Brill, 2015.

Timmer, Daniel C. "Sectarianism and Soteriology: The Priestly Blessing (Numbers 6,24-26) in the Qumranite Community Rule (1QS)." *Bib* 89 (2008): 389–96.

Timmer, Daniel C. "The Use and Abuse of Power in Amos: Identity and Ideology." *JSOT* 39 (2014): 101–18.

Tull, Patricia K. *Isaiah 1–39*. SHBC. Macon, GA: Smyth & Helwys, 2010.

Turner, John C. "Henri Tajfel: An Introduction." In *Social Groups and Identities: Developing the Legacy of Henri Tajfel*, edited by W. P. Robinson, 1–23. International Series in Social Psychology. Oxford: Butterworth-Heinemann, 1996.

VanderKam, James C. "Sinai Revisited." In *Biblical Interpretation at Qumran*, edited by Matthias Henze, 44–60. SDSSRL. Grand Rapids, MI: Eerdmans, 2005.

Vivaldi, Jean-Marie. *Fanon: Collective Ethics and Humanism*. New York: Peter Lang 2007.

Waltke, Bruce K., and M. O'Connor. *An Introduction to Biblical Hebrew Syntax*. Winona Lake, IN: Eisenbrauns, 1990.

Watts, John D. W. *Isaiah 1–33*. WBC 24. Rev. ed. Waco, TX: Word, 2005.

Weems, Renita. *Battered Love: Marriage, Sex, and Violence in the Hebrew Prophets*. OBT. Minneapolis, MN: Fortress, 1995.

Weiss, Meir. "The Pattern of the 'Execration Texts' in the Prophetic Literature." *IEJ* 19 (1969): 150–7.

West-Pavlov, Russell. *Spaces of Fiction/Fictions of Space: Postcolonial Place and Literary DeiXis*. Hampshire, UK: Palgrave MacMillan, 2010.

Westenholz, Aage. *The 'Akkadian' Texts, the Enlilemaba Texts, and the Onion Archive*. Vol. 2 of *Old Sumerian and Old Akkadian Texts in Philadelphia*. CNI Publications 3. Copenhagen: Museum Tusculanum, 1987.

Whybray, R. N. *Isaiah 40–66*. NCBC. Grand Rapids, MI: Eerdmans, 1984.

Widengren, Geo. *King and Savior, Vol. 4. The King and the Tree of Life in Ancient Near Eastern Religion*. Uppsala: Lundequistska, 1951.

Widmer, Michael. *Moses, God, and the Dynamics of Intercessory Prayer: A Study of Exodus 32–34 and Numbers 13–14*. FAT 2/8. Tübingen: Mohr Siebeck, 2004.

Wildberger, Hans. *Isaiah 13–27*. Translated by Thomas Trapp. CC. Minneapolis, MN: Fortress, 1997.

Williamson, H. G. M. *Ezra, Nehemiah*. WBC 16. Waco, TX: Word, 1985.

Wills, Lawrence M. *Not God's People: Insiders and Outsiders in the Biblical World*. Religion in the Modern World. Lanham, MD: Rowman & Littlefield, 2008.

Wilson, Bryan. *The Social Dimensions of Sectarianism: Sects and New Religious Movements in Contemporary Society*. Oxford: Clarendon, 1990.

Wright, John W. "Remapping Yehud: The Borders of Yehud and the Genealogies of Chronicles." In *Judah and the Judeans in the Persian Period*, edited by O. Lipschitz and M. Oeming, 67–89. Winona Lake, IN: Eisenbrauns, 2006.

Yee, Gale A. *Poor Banished Children of Eve: Woman as Evil in the Hebrew Bible*. Minneapolis, MN: Augsburg Fortress, 2003.

Yi Sencindiver, Susan. "Pregnant Doppelgängers: Lived and Literary." In *Otherness: A Multilateral Perspective*, edited by Susan Yi Sencindiver, Maria Beville, and Marie Lauritzen, 61–88. Frankfurt: Peter Lang, 2011.

Yoder, Tyler R. "Ezekiel 29:3 and Its Ancient Near Eastern Context." *VT* 63 (2013): 486–96.

Young, Lola. "Missing Persons: Fantasizing Black Women in *Black Skin, White Masks*." In *The Fact of Blackness: Franz Fanon and Representation*, edited by Alan Read, 102–22. London: ICA, 1996.

Zapff, Burkhard M. *Schriftgelehrte Prophetie—Jes 13 und die Komposition des Jesajabuches: Ein Beitrag zur Erförschung der Redaktionsgeschichte des Jesajabuches*. FB 74. Würzburg: Echter, 1995.

Zehnder, Markus. *Umgang mit Fremden in Israel und Assyrien: Ein Beitrag zur Anthropologie des 'Fremden' im Licht antiker Quellen*. BWANT 168. Stuttgart: W. Kohlhammer, 2005.

Zeitlin, Froma I. *Playing the Other: Gender and Society in Classical Greek Literature*. Chicago: University of Chicago Press, 1996.

Zimmerli, Walther. *Ezekiel 2: A Commentary on the Book of the Prophet Ezekiel Chapters 25–48*. Translated by James D. Martin. Hermeneia. Minneapolis, MN: Fortress, 1983.

Zimmerli, Walther. "Zur Sprache Triojesaias." In *Gottes Offenbarung: Gesammelte Aufsätze zum Alten Testament*, 217–33. TB 19. Munich: Kaiser, 1963.

Index of References

Hebrew Bible/Old Testament

Genesis
1	89, 135, 137
1:21	130, 135
2	144
2:9	144
2:10-14	144
2:13	117
3:24	147
10	196
10:1-22	178
12:3	187
15	179
17	179
24:53	95
26	73
32:26	166, 167
33	79
33:3-4	79
34	98, 99
51:3	144

Exodus
7:9-12	132
7:9-10	130
7:12	130
10:21-29	139
15:16	71
19	187, 189
19:5-6	179
19:5	149
20:7	183
27:7	163
27:16	163
27:24	163
28:5	163
28:6	163
28:8	163
28:39	163
34:7	183
35:35	163
36:37	163
38:18	163
38:23	163
39:29	163

Leviticus
18:21	86
20:2-5	86

Numbers
6:24-26	11
24:17	112
25:4	166, 167

Deuteronomy
4:34	71
5:15	71
7:1	181
7:19	71
11:2	71
23	73
28:9-10	179
28:10	179
28:42	115
30:4-5	181
32:33	130
33:2	63, 73

Joshua
15:1	72
15:21	72

Judges
5:4	63, 73
5:5	63
5:30	162
11	82

1 Samuel
28:12	133

2 Samuel
8	76
12:28	180
21:6	166, 167
21:9	166, 167
21:13	166, 167

1 Kings
4:7-19	196
8:43	180

2 Kings
8	76
8:20-22	76
15:29	196
18:21	141
23:34	136

1 Chronicles
29:2	162

2 Chronicles
6:33	180
7:14	179
25:5-24	74
36:22-23	68

Ezra
1:2	185

Job
7:12	130
38:8	138

Job (cont.)		11:12	63	20:3	122, 123
40:26	137	11:14-21	76	21	17
40:32–41:2	137	11:14	17, 63	21:2-3	110
41:2 Eng.	137	13–23	107, 108,	21:2	109, 111
41:8-10 Eng.	137		193, 194	21:3	109, 111, 123
		13–14	125		
Psalms		13	108	21:4	110, 111
18:10	131	13:8	109	21:6	109
45:15	162, 163	13:18	199	21:11-12	74
49:12	180	13:19	203	21:11	111, 125
68:9	63	15–16	110	21:13-17	114
68:18	63	15:1	111, 112	22	18, 125
68:30 Eng.	138	16	18	22:1-14	108
68:31	138	16:1-4	112	22:2	121
72	180, 189	16:1	113	22:4	123
72:8-11	181	16:2	113	22:5-6	112
72:12-14	181	16:3	113	22:9-11	112
74:12	134	16:5	18, 114	22:13	110
74:13-17	135	16:9-10	113	22:15-25	108
74:13-14	134, 135	16:9	118	23	107, 121
74:13	130	16:10	112	23:4	122
74:16-17	135	16:11	111	23:7	121
87:4	135	17:4-6	118	23:15-18	121
91:13	130, 136	17:11	118	24–27	107
137:7	63	17:12-14	107	25–31	107
148:7	130	18–19	122	27:1	130, 134
		18	107, 114, 115, 124	27:13	118
Proverbs				28–33	108
6:3	138	18:1-3	118	28:10	116
25:26	138	18:1-2	120	28:13	116
		18:1	117	28:17	116
Isaiah		18:2	109, 115–17	30:7	135
1–39	80, 85, 122			33:23-29	76
		18:3	18, 117	34	17, 63, 71, 76, 108
1–12	108	18:4	118, 119		
1:21	122	18:5	118, 120	34:2	72
1:26	122	18:6	120	34:5	72
2	114	18:7	18, 117, 120, 124	34:6	71
2:1-4	57			34:11	76
2:2-4	118, 124	19	125	34:12	76
2:4	124	19:1	119	34:17	76
2:5	124	19:6	111	36:6	141
5	12	19:8	111	37:29	137
8:18	122	19:18-25	16, 180	40–55	80, 83–5, 90, 91, 95, 97, 104
11	63, 114	19:23-25	149		
11:1-9	118	20	108, 121, 122		
11:10	118			40:1	68

40:10	71	63	62, 63, 72,	7:14	180	
42:14	75		75, 77,	7:17-18	59	
43	68		101	7:30	180	
43:7	179	63:1-6	17, 64, 68,	14:9	179	
44:9-20	56		69, 74	21:5	71	
45:1	68	63:1-5	85	25:29	180	
48:14	71	63:1-3	100	32:34	180	
49	96	63:1	62, 63, 69,	34:15	180	
49:14-19	96		70, 72, 74,	37:3-8	142	
50:2-3	131		75, 78	38	28	
50:2	71	63:2	70	43:7	201	
51:9	130, 131,	63:3	62, 70, 71,	44	59	
	135		78, 98	44:20-22	59	
51:14	75	63:4-6	70	46–51	107, 193,	
54	77	63:4	78		194	
54:7-8	75	63:5	71, 77, 78	46	21	
56–66	17, 18, 62,	63:6	62, 100	46:2	194, 201	
	80, 81,	63:16	87, 97	46:7-8	201	
	83–5, 87,	63:19	179	46:11	201	
	88, 91, 93,	65–66	84	46:12	201	
	97	65:1-7	68	46:14	201	
56:4-5	84	65:11-15	68	46:15-16	201	
57:3-13	68	65:19	81	46:16	201	
57:3-4	81, 93	65:20-23	87	46:18	201	
57:3	17, 85	65:23	93	46:19	201	
57:7-10	17, 81, 86,	66:3-4	68	46:25	201	
	93, 95	66:7-9	17, 18, 81,	46:26	201	
57:7-8	86		87, 88, 93,	47:1	194	
57:8	86		94	48:41	205	
59	62	66:7	94	49:18	203	
59:16	71, 77	66:9	75, 94	49:22	205	
60–62	62	66:10	93	50:1	198	
60:4	93, 97	66:12-13	18, 94	50:2	199	
60:9	93	66:13	87, 88	50:4-7	199	
60:15-16	93	66:16	93	50:4	199	
60:16	87, 88	66:17	68	50:7	199	
61:10	70, 87, 95			50:9-10	199	
62	87, 96	*Jeremiah*		50:24	205	
62:1-6	96	2:2	56	51	135	
62:2-5	17, 87	3	86, 91	51:22	199	
62:2	70, 95, 96	3:1-3	58	51:34	130, 135	
62:4-5	81, 85, 95,	3:3	58	51:38-39	136	
	96	4	165	51:44	135	
62:4	96	4:30	164, 165			
62:5	96	6:8	166, 167	*Ezekiel*		
62:6-7	74	7:10	180	1–24	200	
62:8	71	7:11	180	4:6	149	

Ezekiel (cont.)		19:11	19, 141,	25:7	203
12:13	138		145	26:1–28:19	57
16	56, 58, 86,	19:12	146	27:5	145
	91, 97,	19:13-14	146	28	148
	152, 156,	19:14	138, 141	28:9	133
	162–4,	20	152	28:12	144
	166, 172	20:7-8	126, 129,	28:13-14	145
16:10	162		142	28:13	144, 145
16:11-12	163	20:23	149	28:16-17	145
16:13	162, 163	20:34	149	29–32	18, 57,
16:14	163	23	16, 19, 58,		126–9,
16:15	164		86, 91, 97,		132
16:16	164		151–6,	29	130, 132,
16:17	86, 95,		158–60,		138, 149
	164		162–7,	29:1-16	139
16:18	162		169, 171,	29:1	150
16:20	86		172	29:3	127, 129,
16:26	126, 129,	23:1-49	155		132, 133,
	164, 169	23:2-35	155		135, 136,
16:28	164	23:3	129, 142		138, 146
16:30	164	23:4	57	29:4-5	137, 140
16:31	164	23:5-10	155, 164	29:4	130, 139,
16:33	164	23:8	129, 142		148
16:34	164	23:10	156	29:5	147, 148
16:35	164	23:11-35	155	29:6	127, 129,
16:41	164	23:12-21	59		136, 140,
17	145, 146,	23:12-15	164		141
	150	23:13	165	29:7	140
17:3-4	145	23:14-17	166	29:8	141
17:5	145, 146	23:17	166, 167	29:9	130, 136
17:6	145	23:18	166, 167	29:11	149
17:8	145, 146	23:19-21	129, 142	29:12	149
17:9-21	145	23:20	168, 170	29:13	149
17:20	138	23:22	166, 167	29:16	136
17:22-23	145	23:25	156	29:21	136
17:23	146	23:26	156	30:1-19	126
17:24	145	23:27	129	30:8	136
19	136, 138,	23:28	166, 167	30:12	136
	141, 145,	23:29	156	30:19	136
	146, 150	23:30	172	30:23	149
19:1	138	23:34	156	30:25-26	136
19:3	136	23:36-49	155	30:26	149
19:4	136, 137	23:36-42	155	31	144-46,
19:5-7	136	25–32	107, 194,		148, 150
19:8-9	136		200	31:2-9	127, 129,
19:8	138	25:-32	193		143, 149,
19:10	145, 146	25:2	194		150

31:2	142	36:19	149	9:7-10	180
31:3-5	147	36:24	149	9:7	20, 112, 150, 178, 179
31:3	142, 145, 147	36:35	144		
		38:4	137		
31:4	147			9:8	178
31:5	147	*Daniel*		9:9-10	178
31:6	146, 147	4	146	9:9	178
31:7	146	4:11-12	146	9:11-12	20, 180, 181, 190
31:8-9	144	4:13-15	146		
31:8	147, 148	4:23-26	146	9:11	178
31:9	147	9:18	180	9:12	64, 178–80
31:10	145, 147	9:19	179, 180		
31:11	147			9:13-15	179
31:12	147	*Hosea*			
31:13	148	1–3	86, 91	*Obadiah*	
31:14	145	1:2-3	57	1:1	194
31:15-17	143	2	97, 98	8–15	63
31:15	148	2:16-17 Eng.	98	19–20	64
31:16-17	148	2:18-19	98		
31:16	148			*Jonah*	
31:17	148	*Joel*		3:9	203
32	19, 130, 132, 136, 138	2:3	144		
		3:1-21	193	*Micah*	
				4:1-5	57
32:1-16	139	*Amos*		4:4-5	57
32:1	150	1–2	107, 193, 194		
32:2	127, 129, 130, 132–5, 138			*Nahum*	
		1:3–2:3	20, 177	1:2-8	20, 183, 184, 189
		1:4	199		
32:3	19, 139	1:5	112	1:3	183
32:4	138, 147, 148	1:7	199	1:6-8	183
		1:10	199	1:7-8	20
32:5-6	131, 147	1:12	199	1:9–3:19	184
32:5	138	1:14	199	1:9	182
32:6	138	2:2	199	1:11	182
32:7-8	131, 139	2:5	199	1:12	182, 184
32:11-13	139	3:1	179	1:14	181, 182
32:11-12	139	3:2	179	1:15 Eng.	182, 184
32:14	139	3:9	177	2:1	182, 184
32:15	136	3:12	180	2:2	184
32:16	138	4:11	180	2:2 Eng.	182
32:17-32	140	5:3	180	2:3	182
32:21-22	143	5:27	177	2:3 Eng.	184
34:13 32:3	138	6:9	180	2:3-10 Eng.	182
34:18	138	7:10-17	189	2:4-11	182
34:20-22	138	8:11-14	118	2:11-13 Eng.	181, 182
35:10	64	9	189	2:12-14	181, 182

Nahum (cont.)
2:13 Eng.	182
2:14	182
3:4-7	181
3:4	181
3:5-7	182
3:5	58, 182
3:7	181
3:8-11	182
3:12-19	182
3:13	205
3:18-19	182
3:19	181

Habakkuk
3:3-4	63
3:3	63

Zephaniah
2	107
2:4-15	193
2:11	180
3:9	180

Zechariah
2:11 Eng.	180
2:15	180
8:22-23	180
9:1-8	193
9:5-7	180
14:16-19	57

Malachi
1	184, 187
1:2-5	20, 76
1:3-5	187
1:4	187
1:6–3:21	20
1:7-8	185
1:11	21, 185
1:12-13	185
1:13-14	186
1:14	21, 186, 187
2:5	187
2:11	185, 186
2:14	186
3	187
3:3	186
3:5	187
3:12	187
3:15-18	187
3:15	187
3:16-18	187
3:16	186, 187
3:17	186, 187
3:18	187
3:19	186, 187
3:20	186, 187
3:21	187
4:1 Eng.	186, 187
4:2 Eng.	186, 187
4:3 Eng.	20
4:3 Eng.	187

PSEUDEPIGRAPHA
1 Enoch
89:73	11
89:74	11
90:7	11
90:21	11
90:29	11

DEAD SEA SCROLLS
1QS
2:1b-7	11
10:9	116

CLASSICAL AND ANCIENT CHRISTIAN LITERATURE
Aeschylus
Agamemnon
11–12	102
11	102
331	102

ANCIENT NEAR EASTERN LITERATURE
CT 13.33-34	133
line 4	133
line 7	133
line 9	133
line 17	133
line 20	133
line 24	133

Enuma Elish
IV 95	138

Index of Authors

Adams, R. 38
Aharoni, Y. 193, 196, 197
Ahmed, S. 23, 24, 28–30, 46, 47, 49, 54, 55, 57, 58, 60
Albright, W. F. 63
Allport, F. H. 67
Alonso-Schökel, L. 111, 113, 115
Anderson, A. A. 180
Anderson, B. A. 76
Anidjar, G. 100
Anzaldúa, G, 160
Ashcroft, B. 154, 168
Assis, E. 64, 184
Atay, A. 15

Bailey, R. C. 60
Bal, M. 82
Balogh, C. 114, 115
Barstad, H. M. 80
Barthel, J. 116
Bartlett, J. R. 72–4
Baumann, G. 84, 85, 97, 175, 183, 188, 189
Beal, L. W. 76
Beauvoir, S. de 2
Beit-Arieh, I. 64, 72
Ben Zvi, E. 9, 28, 56, 57, 173
Berges, U. 81, 117, 120, 124
Bergner, G. 171
Berquist, J. L. 84
Beuken, W. A. M. 121, 124
Bhabha, H. K. 1, 4, 50, 52, 53, 60, 75, 153, 154, 160, 170, 200
Bimson, J. 9
Black, M. 106
Blenkinsopp, J. 10, 80, 107, 112–15, 117, 122, 130, 142, 148
Block, D. I. 129, 131, 133, 136, 138, 140, 141, 143, 145, 147, 155, 165, 169
Blunt, A. 194, 198
Boadt, L. 133, 138, 140, 141, 143, 147

Bodéüs, R. 1
Bodi, D. 130, 142, 144, 147
Boer, R. 104
Bosman, J. P. 190
Bosshard-Nepustil, E. 110
Bowen, N. R. 130, 131, 140
Braulik, G. 181
Braziel, J. E. 171
Breed, B. W. 144, 146
Brenner, A. 88
Brett, M. G. 7, 13
Brink, L. 10
Brons, L. L. 174, 190, 191
Brueggemann, W. 70
Buck-Morss, S. 5, 40–3
Budge, E. A. W. 141
Buhl, M.-L. 143
Bulhan, H. A. 153
Burdon, C. 79
Burke, P. J. 15

Carroll, R. 167
Carter, C. E. 7, 9
Carvalho, C. L. 129, 131, 132, 137, 140, 143
Cataldo, J. W. 10, 126, 127
Chan, M. J. 84
Cherki, A. 153
Chiesa, L. 34
Childs, B. S. 63, 64, 74
Chow, R. 49
Clayton, D. 196, 197
Clements, R. E. 110, 111, 113, 180
Coggins, R. J. 73
Cordero, N.-L. 22
Cosby, A. W. 4
Cosgrove, D. 195
Counihan, C. 171
Cresson, B. C. 63, 72
Crisp, R. 181
Critchfield, B. C. 190

Crouch, C. L. 136, 149, 150
Crowell, B. L. 12, 13
Culbertson, D. 36, 38
Curtis, J. B. 143

Dalley, S. 144
Darr, K. P. 109, 140
Davidson, D. 28, 105, 106
Davidson, S. V. 59
Davies, M. 1
Day, J. 131
Deliduka, T. 63
Derrida, J. 6, 47, 48, 106, 107
Deutsch, N. 65
Dicou, B. 64, 77
Dille, S. J. 70
Douglas, M. 9
Dozeman, T. B. 63
Drabinski, J. E. 44, 45
Duguid, I. M. 131, 133, 143, 146
Duhm, B. 80
Dumont, L. 175
Durkheim, E. 8
Durlesser, J. A. 131

Edelman, D. V. 9, 173
Eidevall, G. 76, 77
Ellemers, N. 67
Emmerson, G. 84
Erlandsson, S. 110
Esler, P. F. 176
Evans-Pritchard, E. E. 175
Exum, J. C. 88, 116

Fabry, H.-J. 183
Fanon, F. 2, 35, 50–2, 59, 168, 170, 171
Fantalkin, A. 64
Finitsis, A. 188
Finkelstein, I. 73
Foucault, M. 3, 176
Freud, S. 32, 33

Gagne, A. 12
Galambush, J. 163, 164
Garrett, D. 1
Genoni, M. R. 7
Gibson, A. 179
Gignac, A. 12
Giovino, M. 144
Girard, R. 36–9

Goff, M. 12
Goldingay, J. 115, 134
Gopal, P. 202
Gossai, H. 7
Gosse, B. 110
Gottlieb, C. 115
Grabbe, L. 185
Graybill, R. 58, 90, 91, 97, 101
Grayson, A. K. 132
Green, A. R. W. 134, 169
Greenberg, M. 131, 141, 145
Griffiths, G. 154, 168
Grossman, M. L. 13
Grosz, E. 91
Guillaume, P. 130, 131

Hagedorn, A. C. 7–9, 173, 176, 182, 188
Hall, S. 26–8, 30, 35, 49, 59
Halpern, B. 116
Hals, R. M. 163
Haney, L. 79
Hansen, N. B. 132
Hanson, P. D. 68, 84
Harding, J. 84
Harlow, D. C. 12
Harries, K. 106
Harris, D. 25
Haslam, S. A. 67
Hayes, J. H. 120, 194
Hegel, G. W. F. 4, 40–3
Hewstone, M. 181
Hill Collins, P. 24
Hogan, K. M. 12
Høgenhaven, J. 110
Hogg, M. A. 10
Holladay, W. L. 81
hooks, b. 171
Horrell, D. G. 7
Hossfeld, F. L. 179
Howard-Brook, W. 7
Huddart, D. 153
Huey, F. B., Jr. 136
Hulster, I. J. de 77
Hutchinson, J. 174

Irigaray, L. 82, 83, 89–99, 101, 204, 205
Irudayaraj, D. S. 55, 62, 71
Irvine, S. A. 120
Isaac, E. 11
Isherwood, L. 25

Jackson, R. L., II 7
James, E. O. 143
JanMohamed, A. R. 5
Jenkins, R. 9
Jensen, S. Q. 176, 189
Jeremias, J. 177
Jervis, J. 4
Johnson, N. C. 193
Johnson, S. F. 206
Jokiranta, J. 10, 11, 64, 78
Jones, B. C. 111, 113
Joyce, P. M. 143, 151, 152, 169
Kaiser, O. 117, 124

Kalmanofsky, A. 38
Kaminsky, J. 180
Kaminsky, J. S. 12
Kamionkowski, S. T. 156, 159, 165
Kearney, R. 23, 24
Keel, O. 134
Kelm, G. L. 73
Kelso, J. 90, 98, 99, 102
Kessler, R. 187
Khader, J. 203
Killebrew, A. E. 177
Kim, H.C.P. 75
King, L. W. 141
Koole, J. L. 62, 63, 74
Kuhrt, A. 185

Labuschagne, C. J. 179
Lacan, J. 32–4
Lakoff, G. 105
Lamberty-Zielinski, H. 179
Landy, F. 117
Lapsley, J. E. 166
Larsen, S. E. 203
Lau, P. 176, 177
Lavik, M. H. 115, 119, 120
Leander, H. 161
Lemos, T. M. 169, 170, 172
Levenson, J. D. 15
Lévi-Strauss, C. 66
Levinas, E. 2, 3, 6, 44–7
Levine, B. A. 177
Lewis, T. J. 133, 134
Liss, H. 122, 123
Lloyd-Jones, H. 100
Løland, H. 84
Loomba, A. 161

Lubetski, C. G. 114, 115
Lubetski, M. 114, 115
Lundbom, J. M. 165, 167
Lynch, M. J. 64
Lyons, C. W. 63

MacDonald, B. 72
Macey, D. 153
Machinist, P. 189
Macintosh, A. A. 110, 111
Malina, B. J. 70
Mann, C. C. 6
Marzouk, S. 129, 130, 133, 137–40, 142, 147, 149
Mayes, A. D. H. 8
Mayfield, T. 200
Mazar, A. 73
McClure, L. 102
McEwan, C. 194
McInerney, J. 174, 189
McKittrick, K. 206
McLeod, J. 153, 154
Mein, A. 158, 159
Memmi, A. 162
Mendenhall, G. 9
Mercer, K. 171
Merish, L. 170
Miller, J. C. 174
Mills, M. E. 56
Mmembe, A. 43
Moore, S. D. 55, 56
Morrison, T. 31, 39, 40
Morrissey, J. 197
Mouffe, C. 69
Müller, M. 132
Murphy, R. 186

Nayar, P. K. 153
Newsom, C. A. 144–6
Niccacci, A. 115
Nickelsburg, G. W. E. 11
Niehr, H. 185
Nietzsche, F. 79
Niskanen, P. V. 80, 84, 85, 96

O'Keefe, A. 164
Oegema, G. 12
Oswalt, J. 75

Parpola, S. 144
Patton, C. L. 157, 158
Paul, S. M. 63, 71, 74, 180
Penrose, W. D. 102
Perdue, L. G. 1, 9, 13
Pleins, D. 8, 9
Porter, B. N. 144
Pritchard, J. B. 134
Punter, D. 204

Radman, Z. 159
Ramírez Kidd, J. E. 55
Ramsey, R. E. 7, 13
Re'emi, S. P. 73
Read, J. H. 176
Reynolds, N. 200
Richter, S. 179
Ritner, R. K. 131
Roberts, J. J. M. 117
Rose, G. 198
Runions, E. 88

Sabo, P. 90
Sadler, R. S., Jr. 173, 174
Sadler, R., Jr. 10
Said, E. 195, 202
Sawyer, J. F. A. 74, 75
Schein, R. H. 193
Schermerhorn, R. A. 174
Schmitt, J. J. 109
Schramm, B. 68, 77
Segovia, F. F. 13
Sharp, C. J. 10, 204
Sheriffs, D. 186
Sherwood, Y. 55
Shields, M. E. 156
Sidaway, J. D. 195
Sluyter, A. 196
Smith, A. D. 12, 174
Smith, G. V. 64
Smith, J. Z. 65, 66
Smith, M. S. 73, 74, 86
Smith, P. A. 80
Smith-Christopher, D. L. 154, 157, 161, 177
Smothers, T. G. 113
Snyman, S. D. 185
Sommer, B. D. 177
Sparks, K. 177
Spears, R. 67

Spickard, J. V. 9
Spivak, G. C. 58
Stec, D. M. 134
Stets, J. E. 15
Stökl, J. 198
Stoler, A. L. 161
Strawn, B. A. 133, 178
Strong, J. T. 68
Sugirtharajah, R. S. 6, 13, 153
Sweeney, M. A. 115

Tal, O. 64
Talmon, S. 10
Tanghe, V. 116
Thelle, R. 205
Tiemeyer, L.-S. 71
Tiffin, H. 154, 168
Tiller, P. A. 11, 12
Timmer, D. C. 12, 178, 179, 181, 182, 185, 188
Tull, P. K. 63, 76, 119, 120
Turner, J. C. 67

VanderKam, J. C. 11, 12
Vivaldi, J.-M. 168

Watts, J. D. W. 110, 112, 113, 115
Weems, R. 156, 157
Wehling, E. 105
Weiss, M. 194
West-Pavlov, R. 192, 199
Westenholz, A. 134
Whybray, R. N. 63, 64
Widengren, G. 144
Widmer, M. 183
Wildberger, H. 110–12, 114, 115, 117, 122, 123, 180
Wilden, A. 34
Williamson, H. G. M. 185
Wills, L. M. 126–9, 139, 142, 148, 150, 173, 188
Wilson, B. 10
Winders, J. 193
Woude, A. S. van der 179
Wright, J. W. 64

Yee, G. A. 85, 160, 164
Yi Sencindiver, S. 205
Yoder, T. R. 130, 132, 135, 137, 139
Young, L. 1713

Zapff, B. M. 108
Zehnder, M. 178, 185
Zeitlin, F. I. 102
Zimmerli, W. 83, 140, 142, 147, 169

www.ingramcontent.com/pod-product-compliance
Lightning Source LLC
Chambersburg PA
CBHW062142300426
44115CB00012BA/2010